Message
Effects in
Communication
Science

SAGE ANNUAL REVIEWS OF
COMMUNICATION RESEARCH

SERIES EDITORS

Books in This Edited Series:

Editor
James J. Bradac

Message Effects in Communication Science

Sage Annual Reviews of Communication Research

Volume 17

SAGE PUBLICATIONS
The Publishers of Professional Social Science
Newbury Park   London   New Delhi

For information address:

SAGE Publications, Inc.
2111 West Hillcrest Drive
Newbury Park, California 91320

SAGE Publications Ltd.
28 Banner Street
London EC1Y 8QE
England

SAGE Publications India Pvt. Ltd.
M-32 Market
Greater Kailash I
New Delhi 110 048 India

Printed in the United States of America

Library of Congress Cataloging-in-Publication Data

Main entry under title:
Message effects in communication science / edited by James J. Bradac.
     p.   cm. — (Sage annual reviews of communication research ; v. 17)
   "Grew out of a program sponsored by the Research Board at the 1986 meeting of the Speech Communication Association"—Pref.
   Includes bibliographies.
   ISBN 0-8039-3224-3. — ISBN 0-8039-3225-1 (pbk.)
   1. Mass media—Psychological aspects. 2. Mass media—Social aspects. 3. Content analysis (Communication)   I. Bradac, James J.
II. Speech Communication Association. Research Board.   III. Series.
P96.P75M38   1989
302.2'34—dc19   89-5928
                                               CIP

FIRST PRINTING, 1989

CONTENTS

This volume is dedicated to E. person; P., S., F., Z., and H. kits; L. W. M./T. R. F. friends; the P. s; and S. W. H.

PREFACE

THIS VOLUME GREW OUT of a program sponsored by the Research Board at the 1986 meeting of the Speech Communication Association: "Message Variables Research: Past, Present, and Prospects." I proposed and ultimately convened this session because I believed (and continue to believe) that the study of messages is central to the communication research enterprise. The detailed examination of message content and form is the one activity that most distinguishes communication scientists from linguists, social psychologists, and others. Whereas social psychologists are primarily concerned with social knowledge and linguists with symbolic structures, communication scientists are concerned with the ways in which symbols affect social knowledge and vice versa, with the symbolic links between "mind," "society," and "behavior." I also believed that the study of messages had come a long way since midcentury and accordingly that it would be useful to consider these advances in a public forum. Of course, advances are not unproblematically linear, so there was a good deal of salutary criticism offered at the SCA session, as there is in this volume. Several persons who were not involved in the 1986 program have contributed chapters to this book, and several others not involved might have contributed chapters had I been rational enough to invite them. (These last-mentioned others are heavily cited throughout.)

Initially, I had hoped to examine in this work both the antecedents and the consequences of messages. But as the title indicates, I decided to focus upon message consequences exclusively. The length constraints of a single volume precluded the double focus. Most of my research has been on message consequences, so I was predisposed to select this half of the pair. But also this is arguably the bottom line: We would not pay much attention to messages were they inconsequential. Some other volume may well focus upon the social psychological factors that give rise to messages; there is an ample literature here. However, as the reader will see, despite the clear focus upon effects, questions of "encoding" are raised in several of the chapters. And some topics and issues discussed pertain equally to both influences upon message production and the consequences of messages.

The volume is organized in the following way: An initial section is introductory. This includes Bowers's opening statement in the first chapter, which serves as an orientation to the domain of message study. The chapters by Cappella and Street and by Mulac and Kunkel raise various conceptual, theoretical, and methodological issues that are germane to the study of message effects, regardless of one's particular focus.

The second section examines knowledge-generating messages. Some messages have as their primary function the creation of knowledge structures in audiences. Theoretical entities such as "beliefs," "plans," and "schemas" are relevant here. The chapters by Berger and by Keller-mann and Lim discuss knowledge generation from somewhat different standpoints. It is interesting and symptomatic (as Berger observes about the literature he examines) that many of the studies cited in these two chapters were conducted not by communication researchers but by persons identifying with the emerging discipline of cognitive science. This is not the case for the other chapters in the volume, although many of them draw heavily from the literature of cognitive social psychology.

The third part comprises three chapters that focus upon strategic or persuasive messages. Burgoon surveys a large body of research on messages designed to change attitudes or behavior. The material exam-ined in this chapter includes the kind of research that has historically constituted the core of message-effects study. Sanders departs radically from this core in the chapter that follows. He argues that some persua-sive messages do *not* change the cognitive worlds of message recipients thereby changing their behavior in turn; rather these sorts of messages induce behavior changes by virtue of their perceived relevance to prior messages. Questions of coherence are paramount here and a new direc-tion for research is suggested. In the third chapter of this section, Thorson narrows the focus to a particular kind of persuasive message: the ubiquitous television advertisement. Many studies are examined, including a surprisingly large number that a significant percentage of readers of this volume will probably not have encountered before. The particular results discussed have implications that go well beyond the realm of advertising.

Two chapters constitute the fourth section of the volume; these examine effects of messages that are designed primarily for on-the-spot consumption as opposed to subsequent knowledge gain or behavior change—messages designed to stimulate their audiences. Bryant sur-veys research on messages designed to entertain. Here the focus is upon messages that are in some sense enjoyed by message recipients, although such messages may produce secondary effects such as learning. This may represent something of a neglected area in the study of message effects (compared to messages and persuasion, for example). This neglect may reflect our culture's abiding distrust of the frivolous and pleasurable. By contrast, the research examined by Linz and Donnerstein represents a topic that has been examined with fervor for many years: the consequences of violent messages. This chapter attends primarily to the theories and models that have evolved in this area, examining along the way some of the most recent explanations that have been offered for the effects of messages depicting violence.

A final chapter (and fifth section) concludes the volume: Bradac, Hopper, and Wiemann summarize and discuss some of the issues that have emerged in the preceding chapters, and we consider prospects for future work in the area.

Although the second, third, and fourth sections are discrete in their primary emphases, there is overlap. Some theories are mentioned in several chapters, as are particular studies. This reflects the fact that messages are multifunctional. Also, some topics are pertinent to the whole domain of message-effects research. So, the organizational scheme is not very procrustean. Still, there is some potential usefulness in thinking about the primary questions pertaining to the relationship between messages and knowledge structures apart from those pertaining to messages and physical arousal, for example. One cannot think about everything at once. I hope that the chapter groupings are useful in this thought-directive way.

—James J. Bradac

Chapter 1

INTRODUCTION

John Waite Bowers

IN 1966, GERALD MILLER organized a program on "current research" for the Central States Speech Association. He assigned me the topic "message variables" (Bowers, 1966). (As I recall, the other two papers were called "source variables" and "receiver variables.") Operationalizing "current," I examined experimental studies abstracted in the *Psychological Abstracts*, 1965 volume (which included research reported in journals through 1963); research reported in *Journal of Abnormal and Social Psychology* in 1964; and research reported in *Speech* (now *Communication*) *Monographs* through 1965 and including the first *Speech Monographs* issue of 1966. This search isolated 46 studies experimentally conducted on message variables in communication, the oldest of which were published in 1959, and the newest in 1966.

By contrast, last year Stohl and Redding (1987) published a paper on message variables in organizational communication. Their definition of "message" was relatively conservative (Stohl & Redding, 1987, p. 452):

> An identifiable unit of oral or written discourse, emitted in a context leading one or more observers to believe that, in all probability, the utterance is related to some sort of conscious intent on the part of the message-sender.

Despite the study's conservative definition and despite the restriction to organizational communication, Stohl and Redding's (1987) bibliography comprises 192 items. I discovered no overlap between the Stohl and Redding (1987) reference list and the Bowers (1966) reference list.

Again by contrast, Bradac, Bowers, and Courtright (1979, 1980) wrote a paper synthesizing research on three "lexical variables" in communication research—language intensity, verbal immediacy, and lexical diversity. Again, the definition of "message" implied by this study is relatively conservative, for the study is restricted to verbal messages, consciously encoded. Nevertheless, the reference list for a study of those three variables alone consists of 89 items, about twice as many as the 46 items in my 1966 study of *all* message variables. I believe that only two or three items overlap in the two studies.

I now perceive the tone of my 1966 study to be mildly quaint and naive in its absolute restriction to studies carried out within the experimental paradigm and in its low level of generalization and systematization. I divided the 46 studies inductively into 12 categories: (a) delivery (paralanguage and kinesics) variables, seven studies— Hildebrandt and Stevens (1963), Cobin (1962), Addington (1965), Miller and Hewgill (1964), Bowers (1965), Voor and Miller (1965), and Vohs (1964); (b) language variables, four studies—Bowers (1963), Carmichael and Cronkhite (1965), Nichols (1965), and DeVito (1965); (c) message organization, six studies—Darnell (1963), Schultz (1963), Lana (1963a, 1963b), Lana and Rosnow (1963), and Anderson and Norman (1964); (d) satire, one study—Gruner (1965); (e) evidence, one study—Dresser (1963); (f) resistance to and persistence of opinion change (includes several different message variables), seven studies— Insko (1962), Papageorgis (1963), Kiesler and Kiesler (1964), Utterback (1964), McGuire (1961, 1962), and Crane (1962), (g) pro-attitudinality and counterattitudinality of messages (though we did not use those words in 1966), two studies—Aronson, Turner, and Carlsmith (1963) and Whittaker (1963); (h) programming and feedback, two studies—Tucker (1964) and Amato (1964); (i) fear appeals, seven studies—Lazarus and Alfert (1964), Kraus, El-Assal, and De Fleur (1966), Frandsen (1963), Hewgill and Miller (1965), Powell (1965), Janis and Terwilliger (1962), and Merrill (1962); (j) anxiety, three studies—McCormack, Elkin, and Westley (1959), McNulty and Walters (1962), and Weiss, Rawson, and Pasamanick (1963); (k) aggression, three studies—Walters, Thomas, and Acker (1962), Stricker (1963), and Berkowitz and Rawlings (1963); and (l) miscellaneous, four studies—Greenberg (1963), Leventhal and Perlow (1964), Festinger and Maccoby (1964), and Walster and Festinger (1962).

Most studies in my 1966 population of studies tested two levels of a single message variable on subjects assigned (more or less randomly) to treatment groups. But a healthy minority also manipulated (or took into account) other message variables, situational variables, contextual variables, and/or organismic variables. Bowers (1965) controlled for introverts and extroverts in his audiences and manipulated introverted and extroverted delivery styles in his messages (and found no effect for the controlled audience variable). Vohs (1964) manipulated distracting tasks (which might be thought of as competing messages) as well as "good" and "poor" delivery (and found that good delivery competed more successfully with the tasks). Festinger and Maccoby (1964) also distracted some of their subjects with the visual portion of a travelogue instead of with tasks. Carmichael and Cronkhite (1965) frustrated some of their subjects (and found that high-intensity messages boomeranged further with frustrated than with nonfrustrated subjects). Schultz (1963) manipulated time intervals between messages, awareness and unawareness of subjects about persuasive intent, and primacy and recency. He found that the recency effect was enhanced by a time interval between messages when subjects were unaware of persuasive intent. Lana (1963a, 1963b; Lana & Rosnow, 1963) controlled or manipulated maturation of subjects, medium of communication, and "hiddenness" of the pretest in his studies of primacy and recency. McGuire (1962) manipulated time lapse between messages as well as the refutational/supportive variable. Hewgill and Miller (1965) manipulated both credibility of communicator and various fear-appeal variables. Both McNulty and Walters (1962) and Weiss et al. (1963) studied anxiety of subjects in combination with argument conditions. Berkowitz and Rawlings (1963) studied aggression in films and levels of frustration in audiences. Leventhal and Perlow (1962) examined "optimistic" and "pessimistic" messages and controlled for levels of self-esteem in their audiences.

My 1966 predictions about the future of research on message variables might also strike a contemporary reader as quaint and naive. In general, I predicted more of the same: experimental studies in which independent variables would be more carefully defined and manipulated; more studies of the interactions of independent variables; and more studies of the effects of syntax in communication.

I have meandered down memory lane to demonstrate the need for unifying theories (and the need for this book). The volume of work done on message variables from a social science perspective in 1966 may have justified only low-level generalizations, inductively generated. The volume of work now is much greater, and the need for synthesis increases as the magnitude of the literature to be synthesized increases. We had the idea, in 1966, that message variables (including variations in media, or "channel" as we called it then) somehow combined with situational, contextual, and organismic variables in producing their effects, but our tendency was to test those relationships in an ad hoc manner one by one or, in a given study, not to test them at all. We seldom stood back and tried to synthesize the past of our research or to project its future coherently.

Things are improving in that respect. Stohl and Redding (1987, pp. 462-474), in their examination of message variables in organizational communication, identify 48 functions of messages, grouped under five headings: individual functions (from speech act theory), relational functions, instrumental functions, contextual functions, and structural functions. Bradac et al. (1979, 1980), in their analysis and synthesis of research on three lexical variables, devise a theory consisting of 21 axioms and 68 theorems. They group the variables treated in their synthesis into four types, the first three of which may be either independent or dependent variables: source characteristics, experimentally manipulated source variables, message variables, receiver variables, and message effects. The figure illustrating their theory (1980, p. 206) appears, at least, to represent a system, where "causes" can become "effects" and "effects" can become "causes," and equifinality prevails. This volume, *Message Effects in Communication Science*, represents a significant additional step in systematizing thought on message variables.

My contemplation of message variables did not stop in the spring of 1966. (See, for example, Bowers, 1974, 1982, 1985; Bowers & Bradac, 1982, 1984; Bowers, Elliott, & Desmond, 1977; Bowers, Metts, & Duncanson, 1985; Bowers & Osborn, 1966; Bradac et al., 1979, 1980; Harrell, Bowers, & Bacal, 1973; Houck & Bowers, 1969; Murdock, Bradac, & Bowers, 1984, 1986.) In the rest of this introduction, I will report the more or less tentative conclusions to which this thought has led, phrasing them as recommendations for communication theory.

SEVEN ADMONITIONS

(1) Communication theory will benefit from a liberal definition of "message." Watzlawick, Beavin, and Jackson (1967, p. 51) imply this liberal definition in their now famous (or infamous) axiom, "one cannot *not* communicate." Accepting this axiom requires that the definition of "message" include behavior other than traditional rhetorical behavior, other than intentionally encoded symbols, whether verbal or nonverbal, digital or analogic. Rather, the concept "message" would include any human behavior interpreted—assigned meaning—by another human being. Messages clearly generated intentionally, then, are rhetorical messages (and such messages are obviously worthy of the study they receive). But other human behavior, when interpreted, also has message value, and in fact an important part of that value may be the attribution or nonattribution of intention by the interpreter (see Darnell, 1971, and the impressive literature accumulated since on attribution theory and communication). The concept "message" must include the expressive as well as the instrumental. To deny that such phenomena as Freudian slips, undesired nonfluencies, restlessness in sleep, and thoughtlessly leaving a toilet seat raised in a mixed-sex household (or, for that matter, installing a thick cozy on the lid, disenabling the user from leaving the seat raised) are messages would be to restrict the scope of communication studies unnecessarily. Furthermore, to deny that intentional behavior can be made to appear, by a skilled actor, unintentional would be to exclude from theory a set of phenomena that manifestly exist in real life.

(2) Communication theory will benefit from continued and concentrated work to develop a theory of pragmatics. I have called such a theory (Bowers, 1985; Bowers & Bradac, 1984) "pragmemics" and have described it (Bowers, 1985, pp. 2-3) this way:

> To scholars acquainted with linguistics, the word [pragmemics] will reverberate. It will bring to mind "phonemics" and "morphemics," branches of linguistics concerned with meaning in the syntactic and semantic domains of semiotics. . . .
>
> Phonemics and morphemics have characteristics that should be very interesting to students of pragmatics. Phonemes and morphemes are not strongly or clearly ordered by their physical features. Physically . . . phonemes and morphemes sometimes have more variance *within* classes

than they have *among* classes. Hence, they are defined perceptually—by their *meanings*—rather than physically—by their characteristics as stimuli.

The point is that phonemics and morphemics work according to systems. And those systems are systems of *meaning*. Linguists . . . have gone a long way toward articulating those systems of meaning. We can say that phonemics and morphemics have powerful theories . . . .

Pragmatic behavior is systematic in the same sense that syntactic and semantic behavior are systematic. . . . [L]anguage develops *in the service of communication*, an opinion that may seem obvious to us but that has not always been obvious in the scholarly literature of psychology and linguistics. . . . [P]honemics and morphemics are subsystems that develop in the service of a suprasystem: pragmemics. In fact, it now seems likely that pragmatic needs generate each state of linguistic development, so that pragmatic development probably precedes and produces linguistic development.

This kind of theory of pragmatics might be developed most efficiently (from an empirical point of view) from studies of children or of the mentally retarded, where systems might be in their least subtle states. Such a theory would require taxonomies of situations, contexts, psychological states, and messages related in such a way that interpretations of the messages (meanings) would be predictable, at least within a range, to a theorist. In other words, it would answer such questions (Bowers, 1985, p. 3) as:

How is it that different utterances by different people in different social and linguistic situations have the same communicative force? How is it that the same utterance by different people in different social and linguistic situations have different communicative force? What sort of competence do human beings acquire so that they can use this system, both in production and in interpretation, more or less effectively?

Such a theory would necessarily cut across the subfields that have developed in the discipline, just as the concept "message" cuts across those subfields. In that respect, the development of a theory of pragmatics might fit the unifying, transcending spirit of the age, as manifested in volumes like this one and in the new journal projected by the International Communication Association, *Communication Theory*.

The recommendations to follow will place particular kinds of work into the projected theory of pragmatics.

(3) Communication theory will benefit from the recognition that a theory of pragmatics will be largely rhetorical. I once wrote a paper (Bowers, 1968) that has generated volumes of response in think-pieces by graduate students and that even now ignites some controversy (see Lucas, 1988, p. 255). In "The Pre-Scientific Function of Rhetorical Criticism," I expressed the hope that rhetorical criticism would contribute to rhetorical theory and that rhetorical theory, in turn, would contribute to communication theory. I dignified communication theory by calling it "scientific."

The hope has begun to be realized in a concentrated way, as scholars like P. K. Tompkins, G. Cheney, and E. V. B. Tompkins explore the relevance of rhetoric to communication theory, especially in organizational communication. (For recent works with many references, see Cheney & Tompkins, 1987; Tompkins, Tompkins, & Cheney, in press.) Such concepts as identification and alienation, for example, are likely to be important explanatory elements in a theory of pragmatics. Whether or not such a theory should be called "scientific" (as in my "pre-scientific function") has now become a trivial question, although I would still hold that, in the interest of establishing confidence, predictions from such a theory should be tested experimentally either with prediction or with postdiction whenever such tests are reasonably available.

(4) Communication theory will benefit from continued concentration on structural matters (though not to the exclusion of functional matters). Messages occur in the context of other messages, and they do not do so randomly. Since Cushman and Whiting's (1972) important theoretical contribution on the "rules" perspective, essentially a structural/functional perspective emphasizing the structural aspect, communication theorists have been struggling to explicate structural constraints on the acceptability or unacceptability (or well-formedness or ill-formedness) of utterances in context. This difficult work is essential to a theory of pragmatics. It includes studies of conversational coherence (e.g., Craig & Tracy, 1983; Jackson, Jacobs, & Rossi, 1987) and cohesiveness (e.g., Planalp, Graham, & Paulson, 1987). It also includes more highly theoretical work from a communication (rather than a linguistic or philosophical) point of view. The most prominent current exemplar of this point of view is Sanders (1987; this volume; Sanders & Cushman, 1984). And it includes work on the exploitation or subversion of structural rules (e.g., Bowers, Elliott, & Desmond, 1977; Goffman, 1974, and other works; Watzlawick, Beavin, & Jack-

son, 1967). Structural studies almost necessarily must consider both syntagmatic (what follows what) and paradigmatic (what fits with what conceptually) elements.

(5) Communication theory will benefit from continued attention to cognitive aspects of communication. Messages obviously are influenced in a primary and ultimate way by the psychological states of their senders and receivers. To the extent that the psychology of communication is a special problem, communication theorists may have to devise their own psychologies. Those psychologies will have to take into account strategic considerations including the assessment of values connected to outcomes and the calculation of the probability of those outcomes (e.g., Bowers & Bradac, 1984; Watkins, 1974). But they also will have to take into account problems of habit, memory, motivation, cognitive capacity, and cognitive functioning. The chapters in this volume by Berger and by Kellermann and Lim are relevant to these questions, as is Cronkhite (1984). The contemporary emphasis on cognition in psychology is a fortunate development for attempts to develop a theory of pragmatics.

(6) Communication theory will benefit from continued attention to established (and developing) social relationships and the ways in which they constrain and liberate messages. I have suggested elsewhere (Bowers, 1985) that the two most promising social variables generally might be relative power of the communicators (the degree to which each perceives that the other is capable of facilitating or impeding progress toward goals, the realization of positive values or avoidance of negative values) and compatibility (the degree to which each perceives that the other subscribes to the same or compatible values and goals). For both of these social variables, an important message variable to be considered might be relative transparency/opacity. Bradley (1978) has ingeniously studied the effects of the power relationship on certain characteristics of messages. In problem-solving discussions where confederates were assigned high-power or low-power roles, she discovered that more powerful personages received more messages, longer messages, more reasonable messages, and friendlier messages. Status (holding a prestigious position without instrumental power in the specific situation), however, had very little effect on messages received.

Although social variables such as power and compatibility can be investigated experimentally, the most important insights may come from case or field studies of particular relationships. Hence, the next recommendation:

(7) Communication theory will benefit from examination of particular relationships and classes of relationships and from participant observation of important communication events by theory-minded individuals. Some scholars study marriages, others study intimate relationships, still others study communication within and among particular organizations and particular kinds of organizations. Such studies, if executed with an eye toward systematic generalization, have the potential to contribute powerfully to a theory of pragmatics. Furthermore, theory devised with an eye toward particular relationships and classes of relationships has the potential to powerfully influence those who, in a practical way, try to affect the relationships. Cronkhite (1969) expressed this point of view relatively early, in his "Out of the Ivory Palaces: A Proposal for Useful Research in Communication and Decision." Among many other things, he perceived that theory-minded attention to practical affairs would have the effect of forcing researchers to discover dependent variables more useful than attitude scales and to apply methods of analysis more process-oriented than ANOVA. These things have come and are coming to pass.

Two dangers attend potential theorists who engage themselves in practical matters. The first is that they will be seduced by the situations they observe and will become therapists or consultants rather than theorists. The second is that, to the extent that they theorize, they will become proprietarial about the theories, letting the entrepreneurial motive dominate the scholarly one.

CONCLUSION

These few pages have provided something of a retrospect on message research as well as my perspective on the considerations that should govern its prospect. Each of the chapters that follows relates unambiguously to this prospect. I have not analyzed those relationships except in passing, leaving that task for the more ambitious final chapter.

I remember in 1961 presenting a dissertation proposal to the Ph.D. Seminar (a weekly gathering of faculty and doctoral students) of the then Department of Speech at the University of Iowa. The proposal was for a study of "language intensity, social introversion, and attitude change." Though I mentioned Aristotle, most of my sources were from the literature of social psychology. During the question period, the department chair, H. Clay Harshbarger, asked me, "Why do you propose to do this study in a Department of Speech?"

Looking back on the experience, I believe that Clay was asking the question to give me a chance to show off. The study I proposed, after all, used messages (and oral messages at that) to operationalize one of its two independent variables.

And I was prepared for the question. I had heard it many times before, asked of doctoral candidates who, in a Department of Speech, proposed experimental studies that did *not* take as important variables messages rather conservatively defined. Those doctoral students had inadequate disciplinary identification, and Clay believed that they should be forced to wriggle about it.

Almost all scholars identified with communication now understand that what we are as a discipline depends upon what we do about systematically understanding the operation of messages. And we have now accumulated a literature so that our graduate students are unlikely to somehow miss that lesson. One hopes that H. Clay Harshbarger's recurrent question has now become a largely unnecessary one.

Possibly this book will make the question completely unnecessary.

REFERENCES

Addington, D. W. (1965). The effect of mispronunciation on general speaking effectiveness. *Speech Monographs, 32,* 159-163.

Amato, P. P. (1964). A comparative study of programmed instruction and videotaped lectures as part of a course in public speaking. *Speech Monographs, 31,* 461-466.

Anderson, N. H., & Norman, A. (1964). Order effects in impression formation in four classes of stimuli. *Journal of Abnormal and Social Psychology, 69,* 467-471.

Aronson, E., Turner, J. A., & Carlsmith, J. M. (1963). Communicator credibility and communication discrepancy as determinants of opinion change. *Journal of Abnormal and Social Psychology, 67,* 31-36.

Berkowitz, L., & Rawlings, E. (1963). Effects of film violence on inhibitions against subsequent aggression. *Journal of Abnormal and Social Psychology, 66,* 405-412.

Bowers, J. W. (1963). Language intensity, social introversion, and attitude change. *Speech Monographs, 30,* 345-352.

Bowers, J. W. (1965). The influence of delivery on attitudes toward concepts and speakers. *Speech Monographs, 32,* 154-158.

Bowers, J. W. (1966, April). *Current research: Message variables.* Paper presented at the convention of the Central States Speech Association, Chicago.

Bowers, J. W. (1968). The pre-scientific function of rhetorical criticism. In T. Nilsen (Ed.), *Essays on rhetorical criticism* (pp. 126-145). New York: Random House.

Bowers, J. W. (1974). Guest editor's introduction: Beyond threats and promises. *Speech Monographs, 41,* ix-xi.

Bowers, J. W. (1982). Does a duck have antlers? Some pragmatics of "transparent questions." *Communication Monographs, 49,* 63-69.

Bowers, J. W. (1985, January). On the pragmeme. *Spectra* (Newsletter of the Speech Communication Association), pp. 2-3.

Bowers, J. W., & Bradac, J. J. (1982). Issues in communication theory. In M. Burgoon (Ed.), *Communication yearbook* (Vol. 5, pp. 1-27). New Brunswick, NJ: Transaction.

Bowers, J. W., & Bradac, J. J. (1984). Contemporary problems in human communication theory. In C. C. Arnold & J. W. Bowers (Eds.), *Handbook of rhetorical and communication theory* (pp. 871-893). Boston: Allyn & Bacon.

Bowers, J. W., Elliott, N., & Desmond, R. (1977). Exploiting pragmatic rules: Devious messages. *Human Communication Research, 3,* 235-242.

Bowers, J. W., Metts, S., & Duncanson, T. (1985). Emotion and interpersonal communication. In M. L. Knapp & G. R. Miller (Eds.), *Handbook of interpersonal communication* (pp. 500-550). Beverly Hills, CA: Sage.

Bowers, J. W., & Osborn, M. M. (1966). Effects of concluding metaphors in persuasion. *Speech Monographs, 33,* 147-155.

Bradac, J. J., Bowers, J. W., & Courtright, J. A. (1979). Three lexical variables in communication: Intensity, diversity and immediacy. *Human Communication Research, 25,* 257-269.

Bradac, J. J., Bowers, J. W., & Courtright, J. A. (1980). Lexical variations in intensity, immediacy, and diversity: An axiomatic theory and causal model. In R. N. St. Clair & H. Giles (Eds.), *The social and psychological contexts of language* (pp. 193-223). London: Lawrence Erlbaum.

Bradley, P. H. (1978). Power, status, and upward communication in small decision-making groups. *Communication Monographs, 45,* 33-43.

Carmichael, C. W., & Cronkhite, G. L. (1965). Frustration and language intensity. *Speech Monographs, 32,* 107-111.

Cheney, G., & Tompkins, P. K. (1987). Coming to terms with organizational identification and commitment. *Central States Speech Journal, 38,* 1-15.

Cobin, M. (1962). Response to eye-contact. *Quarterly Journal of Speech, 48,* 415-418.

Craig, R. T., & Tracy, K. (Eds.). (1983). *Conversational coherence: Form, structure, and strategy.* Beverly Hills, CA: Sage.

Crane, E. (1962). Immunization—with and without use of counter-arguments. *Journalism Quarterly, 39,* 445-450.

Cronkhite, G. (1969). Out of the ivory palaces: A proposal for useful research in communication and decision. In R. J. Kibler & L. L. Barker (Eds.), *Conceptual frontiers in speech-communication* (pp. 113-135). New York: Speech Association of America.

Cronkhite, G. (1984). Perception and meaning. In C. C. Arnold & J. W. Bowers (Eds.), *Handbook of rhetorical and communication theory.* Boston: Allyn & Bacon.

Cushman, D. P., & Whiting, G. C. (1972). An approach to communication theory: Toward consensus on rules. *Journal of Communication, 22,* 217-238.

Darnell, D. K. (1963). The relation between sentence order and comprehension. *Speech Monographs, 30,* 97-100.

Darnell, D. K. (1971). Toward a reconceptualization of communication. *Journal of Communication, 21*, 5-16.

DeVito, J. A. (1965). Comprehension factors in oral and written discourse of skilled communicators. *Speech Monographs, 32*, 124-128.

Dresser, W. R. (1963). Effects of "satisfactory" and "unsatisfactory" evidence in a speech of advocacy. *Speech Monographs, 30*, 302-306.

Festinger, L., & Maccoby, N. (1964). On resistance to persuasive communication. *Journal of Abnormal and Social Psychology, 68*, 359-366.

Frandsen, K. D. (1963). Effects of threat appeals and media of transmission. *Speech Monographs, 30*, 101-104.

Goffman, E. (1974). *Frame analysis: An essay on the organization of experience.* New York: Harper & Row.

Greenberg, B. S. (1963). Operation abolition and operation correction. *Audio Visual Communication Review, 11*, 40-46.

Gruner, C. R. (1965). An experimental study of satire as persuasion. *Speech Monographs, 32*, 149-153.

Harrell, M., Bowers, J. W., & Bacal, J. P. (1973). Another stab at "meaning": Concreteness, iconicity, and conventionality. *Speech Monographs, 40*, 199-207.

Hewgill, M. A., & Miller, G. R. (1965). Source credibility and response to fear-arousing communications. *Speech Monographs, 32*, 95-101.

Hildebrandt, H. W., & Stevens, W. W. (1963). Manuscript and extemporaneous delivery in communication of information. *Speech Monographs, 30*, 369-372.

Houck, C., & Bowers, J. W. (1969). Dialect and identification. *Language and Speech, 12*, 180-186.

Insko, C. A. (1962). One-sided versus two-sided communications and counter communications. *Journal of Abnormal and Social Psychology, 65*, 203-206.

Jackson, S., Jacobs, S., & Rossi, A. (1987). Conversational relevance: Three experiments on pragmatic connectedness in conversation. In M. McLaughlin (Ed.), *Communication yearbook* (Vol. 10, pp. 323-347). Beverly Hills, CA: Sage.

Janis, I. L., & Terwilliger, R. F. (1962). An experimental study of psychological resistance to fear arousing communications. *Journal of Abnormal and Social Psychology, 65*, 403-410.

Kiesler, C. A., & Kiesler, S. B. (1964). Role of forewarning in persuasive communications. *Journal of Abnormal and Social Psychology, 68*, 547-549.

Kraus, S., El-Assal, E., & De Fleur, M. L. (1966). Fear-threat appeals in mass communication: An apparent contradiction. *Speech Monographs, 33*, 23-29.

Lana, R. E. (1963a). Controversy of the topic and the order of presentation in persuasive communications. *Psychological Reports, 12*, 163-170.

Lana, R. E. (1963b). Interest, media, and order effects in persuasive communications. *Journal of Psychology, 41*, 9-13.

Lana, R. E., & Rosnow, R. L. (1963). Subject awareness and order effects in persuasive communications. *Psychological Reports, 12*, 523-529.

Lazarus, R. S., & Alfert, E. (1964). Short-circuiting of threat by experimentally altering cognitive appraisal. *Journal of Abnormal and Social Psychology, 69*, 192-205.

Leventhal, H., & Perlow, S. I. (1962). A relationship between self-esteem and persuasibility. *Journal of Abnormal and Social Psychology, 64*, 385-388.

Lucas, S. E. (1988). The renaissance of American public address. *Quarterly Journal of Speech, 74*, 241-260.

McCormack, T., Elkin, F., & Westley, W. A. (1959). Anxiety and persuasion. *Public Opinion Quarterly, 23*, 127-133.

McGuire, W. J. (1961). Resistance to persuasion conferred by active and passive prior refutation of the same and alternative counterarguments. *Journal of Abnormal and Social Psychology, 63*, 326-332.

McGuire, W. J. (1962). Persistence of the resistance to persuasion of prior belief defenses. *Journal of Abnormal and Social Psychology, 64*, 241-248.

McNulty, J. A., & Walters, R. H. (1962). Emotional arousal, conflict, and susceptibility to social influence. *Canadian Journal of Psychology, 16*, 211-220.

Merrill, I. R. (1962). Attitude films and attitude change. *Audio Visual Communication Review, 10*, 3-10.

Miller, G. R., & Hewgill, M. A. (1964). The effect of variations in nonfluency on audience ratings of source credibility. *Quarterly Journal of Speech, 50*, 36-44.

Murdock, J. I., Bradac, J. J., & Bowers, J. W. (1984). Effects of power on the perception of explicit threats, promises, and thromises: A rule-governed perspective. *Western Journal of Speech Communication, 48*, 344-361.

Murdock, J. I., Bradac, J. J., & Bowers, J. W. (1986). On the "equivalency assumption" and other tangential matters: A reply to Schenck-Hamlin and Georgacarakos. *Western Journal of Speech Communication, 50*, 208-213.

Nichols, A. C. (1965). Effects of three aspects of sentence structure on immediate recall. *Speech Monographs, 32*, 164-168.

Papageorgis, D. (1963). Bartlett effect and the persistence of induced opinion change. *Journal of Abnormal and Social Psychology, 67*, 61-67.

Planalp, S., Graham, M., & Paulson, L. (1987). Cohesive devices in conversations. *Communication Monographs, 54*, 325-343.

Powell, F. A. (1965). The effect of anxiety-arousing messages when related to personal, familial, and impersonal referents. *Speech Monographs, 32*, 102-106.

Sanders, R. E. (1987). *Cognitive foundations of calculated speech: Controlling understandings in conversation and persuasion.* Albany: SUNY Press.

Sanders, R. E., & Cushman, D. P. (1984). Rules, constraints, and strategies in human communication. In C. C. Arnold & J. W. Bowers (Eds.), *Handbook of rhetorical and communication theory* (pp. 230-269). Boston: Allyn & Bacon.

Schultz, D. P. (1963). Time, awareness, and order of presentation in opinion change. *Journal of Applied Psychology, 47*, 280-283.

Stohl, C., & Redding, W. C. (1987). Messages and message exchange processes. In F. M. Jablin, L. L. Putnam, K. H. Roberts, & L. W. Porter (Eds.), *Handbook of organizational communication: An interdisciplinary perspective* (pp. 451-502). Beverly Hills, CA: Sage.

Stricker, G. (1963). Scapegoating: An experimental investigation. *Journal of Abnormal and Social Psychology, 67*, 125-131.

Tompkins, E. V. B., Tompkins, P. K., & Cheney, G. (in press). Organizations, texts, arguments and premises: Critical textualism and the study of organizational communication. *Journal of Management Systems, 1*.

Tucker, C. O. (1964). An application of programmed learning to informative speech. *Speech Monographs, 31*, 142-152.

Utterback, W. E. (1964). Radio panel vs. group discussion. *Quarterly Journal of Speech, 50*, 374-377.

Vohs, J. L. (1964). An empirical approach to the concept of attention. *Speech Monographs, 31*, 355-360.

Voor, J. B., & Miller, J. M. (1965). The effect of practice upon the comprehension of time-compressed speech. *Speech Monographs, 32*, 452-454.

Walster, E., & Festinger, L. (1962). The effectiveness of "overheard" persuasive communications. *Journal of Abnormal and Social Psychology, 65*, 395-402.

Walters, R. H., Thomas, L. T., & Acker, C. W. (1962). Enhancement of punitive behavior by audio-visual display. *Science, 136*(3519), 872.

Watkins, C. E. (1974). An analytic model of conflict. *Speech Monographs, 41*, 1-5.

Watzlawick, P., Beavin, J. H., & Jackson, D. D. (1967). *Pragmatics of human communication*. New York: Norton.

Weiss, R. F., Rawson, H. E., & Pasamanick, B. (1963). Argument strength, delay of argument, and anxiety in the "conditioning" and "selective learning" of attitudes. *Journal of Abnormal and Social Psychology, 67*, 157-165.

Whittaker, J. O. (1963). Opinion change as a function of communication-attitude discrepancy. *Psychological Reports, 13*, 763-772.

Chapter 2

MESSAGE EFFECTS
Theory and Research on
Mental Models of Messages

Joseph N. Cappella and Richard L. Street, Jr.

THE PURPOSE OF THIS CHAPTER is to present a "theoretical analysis" of research within the "message variable" research domain. There are, of course, numerous avenues for accomplishing this task such as proposing new theoretical models, summarizing and synthesizing available theories, as well as other state-of-the-art reviews. We chose not to do a general summary because other scholars have fulfilled these needs (see Berger & Bradac, 1982; Bradac, Bowers, & Courtright, 1979; Giles, Mulac, Bradac, & Johnson, 1987; Ryan & Giles, 1982; Street & Giles, 1982). Rather, we will examine extant research and theory in terms of the *assumptions* scholars have made about messages and message-users, and the *conditions* in which they have studied messages, communicators, and receivers.

MENTAL MODELS

The thesis to be elaborated in this section is simply that the interesting questions about messages for students of communication are related to the mental representations of those messages rather than the representations of the text per se and, as a corollary, that mental models of

AUTHORS' NOTE: A version of this chapter was presented to the annual meeting of the Speech Communication Association, Chicago, November 1986.

messages are homomorphisms rather than isomorphisms of the text itself. This two-pronged thesis means that, although it is perfectly plausible for researchers in other disciplines to study messages themselves and, hence, to study how texts can be represented for analysis as texts, such an approach to message representations for communication researchers is not a viable option.

Communication focuses on the delivered message and the production of messages for delivery. Thus communication research must be centrally concerned with the message as represented by the audience or by the deliverer. The second, and more interesting, part of the thesis is that a mental model of the message and a textual model of the message are likely to be strikingly different in that the mental model will be more homomorphic, with many features of the message mapped into a few features in the mental model, while the textual model will be more isomorphic, with one feature of the message mapped into one feature of the textual model. Until recently, most of the work in cognition has been directed at textual models rather than mental models (van Dijk & Kintsch, 1983).

Our thesis is based upon certain assumptions that we believe are obvious. The first is that, because any definition of communication assumes a sender and a receiver, every definition of messages within a system of communication must be concerned with the message as received. It is not that messages cannot be treated apart from their reception; they most certainly can. Linguists and cognitivists do this all the time. However, the questions about the effectiveness of messages for persuasion, comprehension, recall, for manifesting concern, empathy, emotion, outrage, and so on are questions about the message as received. The claim is not that messages do not exist apart from their receipt but rather that the receipt of messages is more important to communication studies, and any domain interested in effects, than is the structure of the messages themselves, devoid of the audiences that receive them or are calculated to be their recipients. For communication scholars, then, the first task of a theory of messages is to study how messages are represented by audiences and represented by speakers and writers, not how messages are represented in themselves.

The second assumption is that messages, as text models or as mental models, are infinitely describable (O'Keefe, 1987). That is, the number of different conceptualizations, features, variables, categories, and so on that could be applied to messages is limited only by the insights and creativity of the research community. This assumption is based upon the further assumption that meaningful categories and variables for natural and social phenomena are supplied by the community of researchers and do not exist in some well- (or even ill-) defined set of natural categories. This assumption is, of course, unremarkable, lying behind all forms of inquiry save an unsophisticated and bald empiricism. There is no salvation from the study of mental models of messages by appealing to some apparently obvious structure of messages such as phrase structure constituents, cases from Case Grammar, language intensity variables, and so on.

The third assumption is that messages are information-dense in an objective sense. That is, the stimulation of the visual, auditory, and other senses per unit time is very high even in ordinary social encounters where the verbal and nonverbal messages are not engineered for maximum effect. The concern here is with raw sensory stimulation, not with its perception, interpretation, or categorization. Another way of describing the information density of messages is in terms of the number of bits of information required per time unit to provide a high fidelity re-creation of the sound and visual tracks of a delivered message. The amount of information required is very high as would be expected from our naive impressions.

We present these assumptions not because they are controversial or because they represent new insights about the nature of messages but because of the implications they carry. Let us turn to these implications.

The first implication is that, in the abstract, the representation of messages whether as mental models or as text models is an insoluble problem. Rather, representations will be more or less useful to solve more or less specific problems. However, certain problems are central to the study of human communication and, hence, are at least a set of the specific problems that mental models of messages must help solve. These include the problems of comprehensibility, recallability, and the effects of messages on attitudes, beliefs, and opinions including as a nontrivial subset the affective and social control character implied by messages in interpersonal settings. The former pair are necessary conditions to all sorts of subsequent effects and the latter set concerns the set of message effects and central interpersonal judgments that characterize face-to-face encounters.

The third assumption in combination with the first assumption above implies that people cannot process the full complexity of information present in messages and, hence, must use some heuristic devices to handle the density of information. These heuristics may operate at the sensory, attentional, perceptual, or memorial levels and may be very complex or very simple (Kahneman, Slovic, & Tversky, 1982). In any case, the heuristics must be present. The evidence for the existence of such heuristics, although not necessarily their form, is very strong: (1) People lose the verbatim content of messages very soon after hearing or reading the content although the gist (or essential meaning) is more lasting (Keenan, MacWhinney, & Mayhew, 1977; Stafford & Daly, 1984; Stafford, Burggraf, & Sharkey, 1987). (2) People often lose the behavioral facts that lead to trait descriptions while the trait descriptions remain as a part of the memory of an event (Allen & Ebbesen, 1981; Carlston, 1980; Ostrom, Lingle, Pryor, & Geva, 1980). (3) People respond to information overload with decreased processing, stress, and, in extreme cases, leaving the situation (Hamilton, 1983; Humphreys & Revelle, 1984). We believe that the existence of heuristics to guide processing of information-dense messages is indisputable. What is less clear is the form of these heuristics and how to discover them.

The third implication following as corollary of the second implication is that text models of messages are starkly different from mental models of messages. Remember that the fundamental difference between textual and mental models is the degree of homomorphism of the message. If one accepts the assumption that messages are too information-dense to process completely and that people must use some simplifying heuristics on them, then one cannot escape the claim that a representation of the message that is isomorphic with the message preserves too much of the complexity that people are trying to escape. But the solution to the complexity problem is not to provide a homomorphism for the text rather than an isomorphism but to discover and to postulate the homomorphism (or set of homomorphisms) that people use in representing messages to themselves; that is, to discover the mental models used in the psychological representation of messages. In the next section we will review some of the mental models used in the persuasion literature.

The fourth implication, then, must be that methods for discovering and studying the mental models that people have for messages (that is, for studying the mapping from message as objectively defined to message as represented mentally) need to be developed. Recent work by Palmer and Cunningham (1987) allows the study of the relationship between any coded feature (or set of features) of a message (whether written or oral) and any continuous, sequential judgment about that message as it unfolds. Consider the following scenario: One has a simple dialogue for which the following behaviors have been coded on a common time base: gestures, gaze, pitch, floor, smiles, posture, degree of verbal disagreement, and so on. Second, a group of judges (or the participants themselves) provide continuous on-line judgments in real time of their evaluation of how affiliative person A and person B are acting as the interaction unfolds on tape. The interesting question then becomes: Can one find a mapping from the domain of behaviors to the domain of judgments such that the variations in judgments are accounted for in terms of some function of the behaviors? Suggestive of the power of this technology is the fact that one can use any number of coded behaviors from vocal pitch to types of speech acts synchronously displayed on a common time base and any number of observer or participant judgments from "person A is being deceptive" to "the message is comprehensible" as input and output measures. The search for a mapping from coded behavior to output judgment is the search for a homomorphism that is the basis of mental modeling.

Finally, it is fair to ask what types of homomorphisms we can expect to find in the search for a mental model. This question is simply one of the types of mappings that could exist from behavioral codings to output judgments. (1) *Leveling:* A good deal of the information in messages could simply be ignored, contributing nothing to the variance explained in output judgments. This is the simplest heuristic but also represents a considerable loss of information. (2) *Salience:* A recent thought-provoking book by Sperber and Wilson (1986) argues that communication is essentially the making salient of certain assumptions by the speaker. In the language of mental models, salient events in the behavioral domain may explain much of the variance in output judgments (Hastie, 1980, 1984). These events may include attention-getting occurrences such as significant deviations from baseline behaviors or unusual events such as those occurring very infrequently. In this heuristic, novel, salient, and unusual events receive attention, deeper processing, and a more intense representation in the mental model (Taylor & Fiske, 1978). (3) *Incremental averaging:* Certain continuously changing behaviors may contribute to output judgments by an additive, averaging, moving average, or some more complex function (Hastie & Park, 1986). In this case, the heuristic involves a continuous updating of levels through some given algorithm. (4) *Inference making:* Information may not only be lost or summarized in the mapping from behavioral states to output judgments but may in fact be created. As Sperber and Wilson (1986) and Holland, Holyoak, Nisbett, and Thagard (1986) note, the process of inference-making is at the heart of the study of all forms of complex human behavior. Certainly the study of the mental representation of messages must account for the way in which hearers infer connections between parts of a message, infer connections between the message and its context, and infer new pieces of information not stated in the message. This heuristic may or may not be simplifying. In order to understand some messages, inferences are necessary. In this situation inference-making adds information (which is not simplifying) but adds it in such a way that what is present is made to cohere (and, therefore, it is simplifying). (5) *Unique stimulus combinations:* Certain special combinations of message features may explain variance in output representations because of some unique meaningfulness that their combination creates. For example, gaze aversion in the presence of verbal praise may create distinctive reactions that are not predictable from gaze alone or praise alone. Here the heuristic is one of uniqueness: certain special combinations receive preferential processing with others being ignored or grossly simplified through other heuristics.

Of course, we have no idea what undiscovered heuristics might simplify the mapping process from message characteristics to mental representations. The above represent some reasonable guesses that research must explore. What we do know, however, is that the study of messages cannot move forward in communication research unless the representation of those messages by audiences is understood, and, in turn, such understanding cannot come about without data representing the on-line judgments people make in relation to the objective character of the message itself.

MENTAL MODELS AND
MESSAGE EFFECTS

The concept of mental model sketched in the previous section can be applied to a wide variety of message-outcome situations. For example, the relationship between verbal and nonverbal behavior and judgments of dominance or affiliativeness by observers (Coker & Burgoon, 1987;

Shrout & Fiske, 1981); the relationship between informal conversational acts and on-line social judgments of job suitability, gender, sociability, intelligence (Hastie & Park, 1986); the relationship between media consumption and beliefs about social reality (Gerbner, Gross, Morgan, & Signorelli, 1980; Hawkins, Pingree, & Adler, 1987); the relationship between adjective descriptors and trait judgments of people (Anderson, 1981); and the relationship between information and decision making (Slovic & Lichtenstein, 1971) are just a few of the social and behavioral phenomena that fall under the broad umbrella of mental modeling work.

Certainly one of the most important phenomena, theoretically and practically, is attitude change or persuasion. Research in this tradition has a long and rich history that has been reviewed extensively by others (Eagly & Chaiken, 1984; Fishbein & Ajzen, 1975; Petty & Cacioppo, 1981). We will treat the persuasion literature briefly here in order to illustrate how the mental models approach informs and focuses questions within this tradition.

First, some caveats are in order. The brief review presented here will only focus on message factors and their effect on beliefs and attitudes. Clearly, other factors, such as credibility of the source, persuasibility of the audience, and so on, are relevant to the success of persuasive attempts. Such factors, however, are not relevant to message effects per se. In addition, we will focus only on the more recent, cognitively based effects theories. Many of the earlier attitude change theories were "closet" cognitive theories, having weak cognitive principles, and also mental models of messages that were simplistic. For example, the cognitive mechanisms were based primarily on balance or consistency principles and the mental representation of the message was a veridical translation of the attitude expressed by the source's communication (social judgment theory being an exception; Sherif, Sherif, & Nebergall, 1965). Although the earlier consistency perspectives produced a prolific and informative base of attitude research, the theories per se were uninformative about how audiences represented the delivered message in their mental storehouses.

To ascertain the mental model implicit in an effects theory, one needs to determine (a) how the external message is represented cognitively to the individual receiver and (b) the rule describing the combination of message features with prior attitudes and/or beliefs to produce an outcome mental state. Point (a) refers to what aspects of the message are made prominent in the theory and how those aspects are encoded cognitively. Point (b) refers to the probable recording of information abstracted from the message into a reduced form to be integrated with existing pertinent information according to the predictions of the theory. Message features must be combined and these results combined in turn with prior attitudes or beliefs.

Let us illustrate how mental models of persuasion have changed toward greater complexity and subtlety. Perhaps the earliest of the information processing approaches to attitude change is due to McGuire (1960). His model made the plausible assumption that attention led to comprehension, which led to yielding. The mental representation of the message in this case is the message "received" (that is, the message attended to and comprehended); presumably, the content and arguments of the message, once received, would result in yielding. The earlier, and more general, forms of the theory did not specify the nature of the yielding process. Later refinements of the theory (McGuire, 1981) did specify the relationship between major and minor premises in message and outcome propositions. The truth value of the conclusion was hypothesized to be the product of the truth value of the premises upon which it was based.

Wyer (1970, 1974) extended what has come to be called McGuire's probabilogical model to include propositions only indirectly related to the outcome proposition. In this extension, the subjective probability of the truth value of an outcome proposition is related to the subjective believability of beliefs related to the outcome proposition and to the contingent probability of the outcome given the belief related to it. The combination rules can be very complicated even in the restricted testing situations that characterize much of the work in this area. Chaiken and Eagly's (1984) review claims that the empirical evidence for Wyer's extension is quite good, although the context of application is one that has only a distant relationship to more realistic persuasive settings because simple outcome-belief relationships are considered.

A recent extension of this model to more realistic persuasive contexts has been carried out by Morley (1987; Morley & Walker, 1987) based in part on work by Hample (1977, 1978). These authors used Toulmin's (1964) model of argument, Wyer's probability rules, and theoretical definitions of importance, novelty, and plausibility to predict changes in attitude toward a claim from changes in data, warrants, backing, and support used in arguments to support a claim. The combination rules are much more complicated than those described by either McGuire or Wyer, but they are also applicable to more realistic, and hence more complex, persuasive settings.

Although differing in complexity, the above three approaches share similar mental models of messages. They all reduce messages to claims, propositions in support of claims, and warrants and backing for supportive propositions. The subjective probability (i.e., believability) of propositions, backings, and warrants is the second feature of the mental model of messages implicit in these theories. These two features together with the combination rules for propositions yield predictions of the subjective probability of the truth value of the claim. The mental model then is a cognitive representation of the message (claims, premises, warrants, data, support, backing, and their subjective probabilities) and a rule for linking parts of the message to produce an outcome effect (or judgment).

A second category of effects models treats messages in terms of the cognitive responses that the arguments in the messages produce in the minds of the receivers. Here contributions by Chaiken and Eagly (1983), Eagly & Chaiken (1984), Greenwald (1968), Petty, Ostrom, and Brock (1981), and Petty and Cacioppo (1986a, 1986b) have helped to define the approach. The argument is that the content of messages under certain conditions stimulates favorable and unfavorable thoughts in response to the issues and positions raised by the speaker's message. As more favorable thoughts are elicited, change in the direction of the position advocated by the speaker develops; as more negative thoughts are stimulated, no change or change away from the position of the message ensues. The cognitive response point of view becomes both theoretically and pragmatically useful as the conditions for attention to the arguments of the message (central routes to persuasion) and conditions for attention to the factors surrounding the message (peripheral routes to persuasion) are made specific. Perhaps the most detailed explication of these factors is the recent statement by Petty and Cacioppo (1986a, 1986b), under the name of the elaboration likelihood model (ELM).

The cognitive response analysis approach has followed hard on the heels on the cognitive revolution in the social and behavioral sciences and it involves the audience as a highly active component in the persuasion process. The mental model of the message presumed by this approach depends first of all on the ability and motivation of audience members to focus on the arguments in the message versus the superficial features of the message. When ability and/or motivation are high (see Petty & Cacioppo, 1986b, for factors related to ability and motivation), then the mental model of the message is the set of arguments inherent in the message and the favorability of the thoughts generated in response to the arguments. These might include responses to direct arguments and responses to inferences from the arguments. Thus the mental model of the message can include both direct translations of content and additions to that content.

When ability and motivation are low, then audience members presumably use other, simplifying heuristics as their cognitive responses. For example, Chaiken and Eagly (1984) note one common heuristic: "length equals strength." Here the message is reduced to a simple distal cue that allows the receiver to respond to the persuasive communication without the expenditure of much cognitive energy. In effect, the content of the message is bypassed in favor of a radical simplification.

The rule of change implicit in the mental model under conditions of high motivation and/or ability is one that accumulates the favorable and unfavorable thoughts generated by the audience. The more positive the mental responses to the message, the more favorable the resultant attitude; similarly for negative mental responses and unfavorability.

Although the CRA models have rekindled interest in the study of persuasion in the research community, in part due to their assumptions about audience activity, rules for combining audience-generated thoughts with prior attitudes are relatively weak and imprecise. Other models, not in the CRA tradition, have given a more thorough treatment of mental rules for aggregating bits of message-based information with prior attitudes. The most comprehensive of these models are the expectancy value models (Ajzen & Fishbein, 1977; Fishbein & Ajzen, 1975) and the information intégration models (Anderson, 1971, 1981).

Expectancy value models are based upon the assumption that beliefs are related to attitudes through the evaluative implications of the beliefs and the audience's subjective assessment of their truth value. An audience member's attitude is assumed to be the sum of the product of belief evaluations and belief probabilities. Thus the model of the message in this theory implicitly abstracts the message as a set of belief statements and their subjective truth value. Some of these beliefs will be new, some will bolster existing beliefs, and some will attack existing beliefs. Change results when the new attitude is more positive or more negative than the old attitude. What is unique here is the precision of statement relating beliefs and their truth value to the attitude issue. The sum of products rule and the mental model of the message (as belief positivity-negativity plus truth value) have been shown to be an effective predictor of attitude toward an issue (Ajzen & Fishbein, 1977).

Information integration models are the most precise of all the attitude models discussed here. They assume that attitudes are formed on the basis of the integration of prior attitude with the evaluated information that is new. The "evaluation" process specifically requires the valuation of the incoming information (usually an adjective item) on a positive-negative scale and a weight for that item in predicting the outcome judgment. The implicit mental model of the message requires the reduction of the message to a set of single word descriptors (usually trait adjectives) and their valuation on subjective scales of positivity-negativity. The integration rule is a weighted averaging principle in which the sum of the weighted scale values of the incoming information is averaged with the prior attitude on the issue, under the constraint that the weights sum to one. Although the integration rules may vary with the context of application, Anderson (1981, 1982) has shown that a straight averaging rule without interactions among informational items is sufficient for many applications.

In the review above none of the intricacies of the various positions has been considered. Rather we have tried to indicate that effects theories of messages make implicit assumptions, sometimes made explicit, about how the message is represented cognitively by the audience and, once represented, how the features of the message are integrated according to the specific rules of cognitive algebra hypothesized by the theory. What is obvious is that the message is radically transformed in each of these theories so that only limited features of the message are held in working memory. Additionally, the "effect" of the message is based upon a hypothesized combination rule pulling together the various components of the message (and sometimes the previously existing attitude). This combination rule is crucial because under some circumstances all that will be left as the mental representation of the message will be its effect. Hastie and Park (1986) have argued that certain tasks prompt judgment-making spontaneously (e.g., trait judgments about other people) while other tasks do not. When no on-line judgment is being made, then later judgments should be related to memory of the message content. In these cases, the mental model of the message is crucially important because retrieval of the information from memory for the purposes of predicting judgments will depend upon what is held in memory. When the judgment is on-line, then memory for items in the message seems to be unrelated to judgment. The message's effect in this case is predicted significantly by the on-line judgment, which, in turn, is determined by the combination rule for features of the message.

In sum, successful theories of message effects will need to be sensitive to several matters. Is the phenomenon to be predicted on-line or not? In the former case, the mental model is best treated as the effect produced by the message while it is being processed. In the latter case, memory for the message's content and, hence, its mental representation is crucial to predicting the message's effect. Is the mental model of the message congruent with the outcome judgment? For example, the pro-babilogical models discussed above are relevant to processes of assessing truth value of propositions but may not be directly relevant to predicting an audience's favorability toward an attitude issue. Such models may serve as input to combinatorial models such as expectancy value approaches in which believability of supportive propositions is one of the predictive components. Conversely, focusing on positive-negative evaluations of message components will have little utility for assessing the subjective truth value of a message's propositional structure.

Implicitly or explicitly, mental models of messages are the sine qua non of effects theories. Our research and theorizing needs to be sensitive to the mental representation of the message and to the combinatorial rule for message features that are being specified.

METHODOLOGICAL ISSUES IN
STUDYING MENTAL REPRESENTATIONS

Next we turn to some of the factors that alter the way in which audiences respond to messages. These include (a) the differential reaction of participants and observers, (b) the character of contrived messages, and (c) the use of restricted message channels. In each case the study of mental models can be radically affected by an inappropriate choice or a choice whose implications are not well understood. Thus the methods one uses to study mental representations can have a significant effect on the type of mental representation that results. It is imperative that we become aware of the impact of these methodological choices on the possible substantive conclusions.

PARTICIPANT-OBSERVER DIFFERENCES

The classical (though simplistic) approach for studying "message effects" is for the researcher to formulate messages differing on some dimension of interest (e.g., lexical diversity or speech rate), control for potentially confounding variables (e.g., accent or nonverbal behavior), present the message to a listener/reader who, after receiving the message, self-reports judgments of the speaker, attitude change, and so on. In effect, the receiver's role is that of an *observer* of the message as opposed to that of a *participant*. This difference is not problematic unless theorists borrow from message variable research using observers to formulate theoretical propositions about the perceptual and behavioral responses of interactants (see, e.g., Bradac, Bowers, & Courtright, 1980; Cappella & Greene, 1982; Giles & Street, 1985). The assumption, of course, is that findings using observers as receivers are applicable to interactants as well. This assumption is highly suspect for several reasons.

First, observers' tasks are traditionally ones of decoding; that is, they listen to and/or watch stimulus person(s) and subsequently make judgments about the target(s). Social participants, on the other hand, must direct cognitive and behavioral energy to accomplish an array of objectives such as monitoring self and others' behaviors, making appropriate conversational extensions, assessing partner characteristics and states, and producing behavioral responses given interaction goals and arousal levels (Farr & Anderson, 1983; Patterson, 1983; Street & Cappella, 1985).

Second, the nature of information available to observers is often qualitatively different from the information monitored by participants. Observers generally have access to only the speech, and occasionally the nonverbal behavior displays, of the participants. Participants not only perceive behavior but also have access to feelings, thoughts, and relational considerations, given past experiences with these or similar partners. Because of differences in their roles and in available information, actors and observers tend to attribute behavior to situational and dispositional factors, respectively (Jones & Nisbett, 1971; Kelley & Michela, 1980).

Third, during social interaction, person perception processes (including those utilizing communicative messages) are quite dynamic as interactants negotiate their social roles and identities (Swann, 1984). Thus what judgments participants produce early in an encounter may be unstable and eventually revised with the advent of future messages.

Given these differences in perspective and communicative responsibilities, participants and observers may produce different cognitive, affective, and behavioral responses to the same message. Several studies have reported few significant correlations between participants' and observers' attributions of similar communicators and/or messages (Allen, 1974; Montgomery, 1984; Street, 1985; Street, Mulac, & Wiemann, 1988). Still other studies have indicated that the same message features may elicit different relational and personal inferences from the perceptions of observers relative to those of interactants (Buller & Diez, 1984; Burgoon, Buller, Hale, & de Turck, 1984; Imada & Hakel, 1977; Street, 1985; Street et al., 1988). For example, participants usually evaluate their partners significantly more favorably than do observers (Street, 1985; Street et al., 1988). In fact-finding interview contexts, Street (1985) observed that participants' competence and sociability ratings of partners were partly correlated with *dyadic* speech measures such as the interactants' degree of speech rate and response latency similarity whereas similar judgments by observers were partly associated with the participants' *individual* rate and latency levels. Within conversational contexts, two studies (Street et al., 1988; Welkowitz & Kuc, 1973) have reported fewer significant correlations between speech behaviors and participants social-evaluative judgments of partners than between speech behaviors and observers' ratings of the same conversants.

Indirect evidence also implicates participant-observer response differences to similar messages. Receivers hearing audiotapes or reading transcripts have rated speakers with lexically diverse messages as more communicatively competent and effective, lower in anxiety, and higher in socioeconomic status than those producing redundant messages (Bradac et al., 1979; but see Giles, Wilson, & Conway, 1981). However, among participants, low lexical diversity has been linked to judgments of perceived influence in simulated juries (Scherer, 1979). Observers usually denigrate communicators with long response latencies (Lay & Burron, 1968; Scherer, London, & Wolf, 1973; Street, 1982), whereas participants have (Crown, 1982) and have not (Putnam

& Street, 1984; Street, 1984). Regarding nonverbal behaviors, Burgoon et al. (1984) reported that observers were strongly influenced by proximity when assessing relational characteristics of videotaped interactions. However, Buller and Diez (1984) did not find proximity to be a significant predictor of dyadic participants' judgments of relational features of their interactions. In addition, Buller and Diez observed that participants' judgments of partners were influenced by contextual considerations.

Thus there is ample evidence that observers and actors differ in their processing of and responses to similar communicative messages. We suggest two avenues for future inquiry. First, researchers can continue to use observers or participants as long as they *limit the generalizability of their findings either to the participant or observer roles.* Though most message perception takes place among cointeractants, individuals process many messages as "observers": listeningto the radio, listening/watching television, hearing a speech or an oral presentation, eavesdropping on a conversation, and perhaps even as an interactant as when an employment interviewer asks a question and then "observes" the applicants' responses without feeling compelled to formulate immediate responses.

Second, and perhaps more important, researchers should make actor-observer differences in message perception an object of empirical inquiry worthy of theoretical explication. The foundations have already been laid for such work. Farr and Anderson (1983) point out that the traditionally simple distinction between actor and observer is quite superficial as interactants can be actors and observers simultaneously. Swann (1984) has cogently argued that, among participants, person perception is dynamic and negotiated. Thus judgments of partners may not be limited to one message or an "average" message level. Finally, Street (1984) has proposed that observers may employ stereotypic or prototypic knowledge (e.g., educated people produce lexically diverse messages) when making person judgments whereas participants may rely upon relational features of messages (e.g., degree of communicative behavior similarity given conversants' mutual affiliative desires or appropriate communicative differences given participants' status differences). However, the two tests of this proposition have produced mixed results (Street, 1985; Street et al., 1988).

MESSAGE-EFFECT THRESHOLDS AND
CONTRIVED VERSUS NATURAL MESSAGES

Bradac (1986) has described some of the problems researchers face when studying elicited, purloined, and contrived messages. Rather than repeat his observations, we instead will elaborate on the issue of ecological validity when using experimenter-constructed messages.

Calling it the unnaturalness problem, Bradac (1986) has observed that, in their attempt to study theoretically interesting properties of messages, researchers often create highly unusual message products. That is, the manipulation of a message variable of interest (say, language intensity or speech rate) may create a message exhibiting extreme levels of that message feature that exceed normal limits produced by most communicators. A representative example of this problem is the research on speech rate effects. In experimental studies, the relationships between speech rate and judgments of competence and sociability are typically linear and curvilinear, respectively (Brown, 1980; Smith, Brown, Strong, & Rencher, 1975; Street & Brady, 1982; Street, Brady, & Putnam, 1983). However, the fast and slow rate extremes in these studies (e.g., 140 and 376 syllables per minute), which usually account for the speech rate effects, are probably beyond the rate levels normally exhibited by communicators. In natural discourse, these extreme rate levels are rarely present (i.e., communicators may be *avoiding* or *incapable of* speaking with these speech rates). The use of naturally occurring speech rates may account for the fact that, outside of experimental studies, speech rate effects on social judgments have (Crown, 1982; Siegman & Reynolds, 1982) and have not emerged (Putnam & Street, 1984; Street, 1984; Woodall & Burgoon, 1983).

Speech rate studies are not the only ones utilizing unnatural message manipulations. In Bradac and Mulac's (1984a) study of different types of powerless linguistic markers (e.g., hedges, hesitations, tag questions), each stimulus message contained numerous instances of a powerless speech marker and was written in paragraph form. The authors found that indeed these markers had varying effects on a communicator's perceived power. The question is, of course, does this finding indicate that powerless speech markers elicit perception of low power or that many powerless speech markers within a short, written transcript of talk produce these judgments? Bell, Zahn, and Hopper (1984) have provided some insight into this issue. In their study (observers rated conversants based on a reading of a transcript of conversation), it took four disclaimers within six utterances to lessen raters' perceptions of conversants' competence; six disclaimers within six utterances to affect judgments of conversants' certainty, and the maximum manipulation (six within six) had no effect on communicators' perceived character.

If message extremes are often responsible for significant message effects and if there is a wide array of acceptable, evaluatively indiscriminate message levels, then what theoretical construct can best describe these phenomena? Recently, several theorists have posited that individuals respond to messages according to *expectancy* (Cappella & Greene, 1982) or *preference* "ranges" (Street & Giles, 1982). Hence, varying message levels could be perceptually or evaluatively comparable as long as the message was within the expected or preferred range. Several studies support the existence of such threshold regions.

Street and Brady (1982) reported that speech rates between 197 and 324 syllables per minute were not evaluatively discriminated and were perceived as relatively similar to the receivers' own rates. However, listeners were highly aware of a speaker's fast (376 spm) and slow (140 spm) extremes (see also Street, 1982). Sereno and Hawkins (1967) observed that communicators were not denigrated for producing a small amount of disfluent speech but were evaluated negatively for moderate and high disfluency levels. Extrapolating from Bell, Zahn, and Hopper (1984) findings, one could posit that perceivers tolerate minimal to moderate usage of disclaimers but respond negatively to their frequent occurrence. Finally, regarding behavioral responses to expressive behaviors, Cappella and Greene (1982) reinterpret previous research to suggest that behaviors within the expectancy range are experienced as affectively positive and are reciprocated whereas behaviors outside expectancy regions generate negative affect and compensatory responses.

The notion of message acceptance or preference ranges also serves as a useful heuristic device for examining potential mediators of the "width" and "contents" of the range itself. For example, contextual, personal, and relational factors can influence what message levels interlocutors deem appropriate and the range of acceptable messages. Thus receivers may prefer some message levels in one context but different levels in another. For intimate topics, relatively slow speech is more acceptable, if not preferred, than relatively fast speech whereas the reverse is the case for nonintimate topics (Siegman, 1978; Siegman & Reynolds, 1982). Relative to informal conversation, listeners have reported that moderate speech rates (as opposed to fast speech) are more appropriate to employment interviews presumably because the latter context requires more deliberate, reflective speech (Street et al., 1983). Regarding the range of acceptable behaviors, formal or highly evaluative communicative events (e.g., courts of law, employment interviews, a formal speech) may call for a restricted or highly scripted range of communicative choices whereas in informal settings such as casual conversation a wide array of communicative styles may be appropriate. Street, Mulac, and Wiemann (1988) acknowledged this possibility to account for the data in their study in which, contrary to Street's (1985) findings in an interview setting, observers' judgments of conversants' personal attributes were frequently unrelated to the conversants' speech behaviors.

Personal characteristics of the perceiver may also mediate preferences for message levels. Cappella (1986) and Cappella and Greene (1984) have demonstrated that certain types of people—namely, high self-monitors and high sensation-seekers—will reciprocate (and thus presumably approve of) a wider range of partners' affiliative and speech behaviors than will other individuals—namely, low self-monitors and low sensation-seekers. Speech accommodation theorists (see Giles, 1977; Giles et al., 1987; Street & Giles, 1982) have posited, and provided some support for, the notion that, unless status or role differences dictate otherwise, interactants usually prefer partners with communicative styles similar to their own. Thus a receiver's message preference region may encompass behaviors within his or her own communicative repertoire (see, e.g., Giles & Smith, 1979; Street, 1984; Street et al., 1983).

Finally, relational factors may influence the expected behaviors of an interlocutor. Apparently, in England, higher-status individuals are expected to speak with more standard accents and with faster rates (and perhaps with greater lexical diversity) than lower-status persons (Thakerar & Giles, 1981; Thakerar, Giles, & Cheshire, 1982). Also, interactants often accept a wider range of communicative behaviors from interlocutors perceived as having high status or power than from their lower-status counterparts. Thus employment interviewers, supervisors, and other high-status persons are often allowed to speak more casually, touch more, speak more slowly, shift lexical styles more frequently, and have a more open, relaxed posture than interviewees, subordinates, and lower-status persons (Knapp, 1978; Patterson, 1983; Scotton, 1985; Street, 1986). From research in progress, Street and Buller (1986) have observed that, while many physicians verbally and nonverbally behave as effective listeners and instructors, some do not (i.e., use jargon, interrupt relatively frequently, avoid detailed explanations). Nevertheless, the 41 patients in the study perceived their doctors as having very affiliative and informative communicative styles. One explanation for this finding is that, because of the physicians' social prestige and power, patients will tolerate an extremely wide range of messages before making judgments questioning the doctor's medical or communicative competence.

In sum, the theoretical utility of message variable research that employs unnatural message manipulation remains questionable. However, the construct of acceptance or expectancy ranges may be a useful concept not only for explicating the effects of message extremes but also for explaining the impact of messages in natural discourse. In particular, a promising avenue for future research is the study of situational, personal, and relational factors that determine the content and scope of message preference regions.

RESTRICTING COMMUNICATIVE CHANNELS

Another characteristic of message-effects research is the effort by investigators to manipulate one or two message variables (say, accent and lexical diversity) and to control for other potentially influential variables such as message length, content, and nonverbal cues. Thus researchers have employed some of the following procedures: To examine speech rate effects, one speaker's voice utters the same message at varying rates (Giles & Smith, 1979; Smith et al., 1975; Street & Brady, 1982); to examine the effect of vocalics on listeners' judgments of communicators, listeners are exposed to content-filtered speech (Hall, Roter, & Rand, 1981; Hayes & Meltzer, 1972); to investigate the influence of nonverbal behavior on relational attributions, perceivers see but do not hear a simulated conversation (Burgoon et al., 1984); and to examine the consequences of different types of powerless speech markers, receivers may only listen to an interaction (Bradac & Mulac, 1984b) or read transcribed excerpts of an interaction (Bradac & Mulac, 1984a).

The underlying assumption for restricting communicative channels is that the message variable of interest has an *independent* effect on message outcomes. While sometimes acknowledging that message variables may interact with one another (see, e.g., Bradac et al., 1979; Giles & Smith, 1979; Street, 1982), researchers fail to realize that by controlling for theoretically uninteresting variables they may be *accentuating* the likelihood of a meaningful effect from the variable of interest. The accentuation effect conceivably exceeds what would be expected from normal communicative events.

For one thing, it is easy to see that the less information available to receivers, the greater the likelihood that the information that is available will influence receivers' responses. For example, if one is listening to an audiotape of a speaker with the verbal content filtered, then obviously vocal style will be the stimulus for any judgment one is asked to make. With increasing information (e.g., access to nonverbal behavior, verbal content), the vocal cues are likely to assume less salience and subsequent judgments based on the perception of vocal, verbal, and nonverbal behaviors may even *contradict* attributions based on speech alone. Hall et al. (1981) reported that observers' ratings (from reading transcripts of physician-patient interactions) of positive physician affect was *positively* related to patients' self-reports of contentment with health care. However, from another group of observers who listened to content-filtered speech of the same interactions, ratings of *negative* physician affect were related to patients' contentment.

In an investigation of this issue, Street et al. (1988) hypothesized that the relationships between noncontent speech behaviors (e.g., rate, pauses, turn duration) and social-evaluative judgments would be stronger in an audio-only observer condition than in face-to-face participant, audiovisual observer, and transcript reader conditions. This prediction received partial support regarding perceived communication satisfaction but no support for perceived sociointellectual status, aesthetic quality, and dynamism.

Aware of the interactive effect of certain messages, some researchers examine two or three message variables as independent variables and then construct designs examining various combinations of these variables (Giles & Smith, 1979; Street, 1982). As Bradac (1986) points out, while internally valid, these designs may create unusual message specimens such as a message that is simultaneously high in language intensity, high in immediacy, and low in lexical diversity.

The problem of restricted message channels is symptomatic of what we consider a more important problem: using the "channel" approach to examine message effects and message production. In other words, researchers often limit their research to one communicative channel such as verbal behavior (Bradac et al., 1979), speech behavior (Street, 1982, 1984), or nonverbal behavior (Burgoon et al., 1984; Shrout & Fiske, 1981). These researchers typically ignore the possibility that some behaviors in an extraneous channel can change the impact of behavior in the channel of interest (Cappella, 1983). For example, fast speech with negative facial effect and in a loud voice can signal anger or criticism whereas fast speech with positive facial affect and a moderately intense voice can signal enthusiasm and poise. Obviously, high levels of gaze can create impressions of intimacy, hate, or attentiveness depending on co-occurring verbal and nonverbal behaviors.

Thus we and others have recently proposed that message-variable research should employ a "functional" approach (Cappella & Street, 1985; Dindia, 1985; Patterson, 1983). Rather than dividing the behavioral stream horizontally by isolating communicative channels of interest, researchers should examine the vertical structure of communication by focusing on the collective behaviors—verbal, vocal, and nonverbal—that accomplish particular social interaction functions such as intimacy, coherence, control, and impression management. Researchers would then develop behavioral composites that relate to functional outcomes. Through the use of factor-analytic and clustering techniques, some investigators have been able to align numerous nonverbal, vocal, and verbal behaviors along a few functional dimensions such as intimacy, involvement, activity, and control (see, e.g., Burgoon et al., 1984; Cappella, 1986; Cappella & Greene, 1984). In addition to acknowledging and identifying functionally similar behaviors, a functional approach to communication is context-sensitive. That is, different situations will call for different interaction functions given interactants' goals and interpretations of behaviors. Because meanings and intentions are grounded in contextual considerations, behavioral groupings related to a certain function should also reflect contextual constraints.

CONCLUSION

We have briefly touched upon the nature of mental models of messages and their role in organizing thinking about the effects of messages. In conducting research on the nature of the mental representations of messages, several obstacles to the development of valid mental models were addressed. Nevertheless, we are optimistic about future prospects. The fact that this volume is dedicated to this topic underscores an awareness within our discipline of the importance of research on the representation of messages. Recent theoretical work in this realm is not only producing the best explanatory metaphors to date but these theories are "communicative" in nature. Obviously, a great deal more work needs to be done. Research on attitude change in the passive communication context has not given sufficient attention to how the complex messages that attend persuasion may be represented cognitively. Assumptions are made but little direct testing of the psychological validity of these assumptions is conducted. Much more work has been done in the interpersonal and person perception contexts as our review of methodological issues shows.

In our view, many good trends are reported in the literature. Researchers are increasingly shedding their reliance on self-reported and experimenter-manipulated behavior and, instead, are examining the natural occurrence of communicative messages. Given modern data processing technologies, the once laborious tasks of observing, categorizing, and quantifying data are now being accomplished with greater ease and in less time with mini- and microcomputer behavior-coding programs. As a result, we believe that theory construction and research on the mental modeling of messages will be both productive and useful.

REFERENCES

Ajzen, I., & Fishbein, M. (1977). Attitude-behavior relations: A theoretical analysis and review of empirical research. *Psychological Bulletin, 84*, 888-918.

Allen, J. (1974). When does exchanging personal information constitute "self-disclosure"? *Psychological Reports, 35*, 195-198.

Allen, R. B., & Ebbesen, E. B. (1981). Cognitive processes in person perception: Retrieval of personality trait and behavioral information. *Journal of Experimental Social Psychology, 17*, 119-141.

Anderson, N. H. (1971). Integration theory and attitude change. *Psychological Review, 78*, 171-206.

Anderson, N. H. (1981). *Foundations of information integration theory.* New York: Academic Press.

Anderson, N. H. (1982). *Methods of information integration theory.* New York: Academic Press.

Bell, R. A., Zahn, C. J., & Hopper, R. (1984). Disclaiming: A test of two competing views. *Communication Quarterly, 32*, 28-40.

Berger, C. R., & Bradac, J. J. (1982). *Language and social knowledge: Uncertainty in interpersonal relations.* London: Edward Arnold.

Bradac, J. J. (1986). Threats to generalization in the use of elicited, purloined, and contrived messages in human communication. *Communication Quarterly, 34*, 55-65.

Bradac, J. J., Bowers, J. W., & Courtright, J. A. (1979). Three language variables in communication research: Intensity, immediacy, and diversity. *Human Communication Research, 5*, 257-269.

Bradac, J. J., Bowers, J. W., & Courtright, J. A. (1980). Lexical variations in intensity, immediacy, and diversity: An axiomatic theory and causal model. In R. N. St. Clair & H. Giles (Eds.), *The social and psychological contexts of language* (pp. 193-224). Hillsdale, NJ: Lawrence Erlbaum.

Bradac, J. J., & Mulac, A. (1984a). A molecular view of powerful and powerless speech styles: Attributional consequences of specific linguistic features and communicator intentions. *Communication Monographs, 51*, 307-319.

Bradac, J. J., & Mulac, A. (1984b). Attributional consequences of powerful and powerless speech styles in a crisis-intervention context. *Journal of Language and Social Psychology, 3*, 1-19.

Brown, B. L. (1980). Effects of speech rate on personality attributions and competency ratings. In H. Giles, P. W. Robinson, & P. M. Smith (Eds.), *Language: Social psychological perspectives* (pp. 293-300). Oxford: Pergamon.

Burgoon, J. K., Buller, D. B., Hale, J. L., & de Turck, M. A. (1984). Relational messages associated with nonverbal behaviors. *Human Communication Research, 10*, 351-378.

Buller, D. B., & Diez, M. (1984). *Relational message interpretations in dyadic interactions.* Unpublished manuscript, Texas Tech University.

Cappella, J. N. (1983). Conversational involvement: Approaching and avoiding others. In J. M. Wiemann & R. P. Harrison (Eds.), *Nonverbal interaction* (pp. 113-148). Beverly Hills, CA: Sage.

Cappella, J. N. (1986). Violations of distance norms: Reciprocal and compensatory reactions for high and low self-monitors. In M. L. McLaughlin (Ed.), *Communication yearbook* (Vol. 9, pp. 359-376). Beverly Hills, CA: Sage.

Cappella, J. N., & Greene, J. O. (1982). A discrepancy-arousal explanation of mutual influence in expressive behavior for adult-adult and infant-adult interaction. *Communication Monographs, 49*, 89-114.

Cappella, J. N., & Greene, J. O. (1984). The effects of distance and individual differences in arousability on nonverbal involvement: A test of discrepancy-arousal theory. *Journal of Nonverbal Behavior, 8*, 259-286.

Cappella, J. N., & Street, R. L., Jr. (1985). A functional approach to the structure of communicative behavior. In R. L. Street, Jr., & J. N. Cappella (Eds.), *Sequence and pattern in communicative behavior* (pp. 1-29). London: Edward Arnold.

Carlston, D. E. (1980). The recall and use of traits and events in social inference processes. *Journal of Experimental Social Psychology, 16*, 303-328.

Chaiken, S., & Eagly, A. H. (1984). Communication modality as a determinant of persuasion: The role of communicator salience. *Journal of Personality and Social Psychology, 45*, 241-256.

Coker, D. A., & Burgoon, J. A. (1987). The nature of conversational involvement and nonverbal encoding patterns. *Human Communication Research, 13*, 463-494.

Crown, C. L. (1982). Impression formation and the chronography of dyadic interactions. In M. Davis (Ed.), *Interaction rhythms: Periodicity in communication behavior* (pp. 225-248). New York: Human Sciences Press.

Dindia, K. (1985). Affiliation and resource exchange: A functional approach to self-disclosure. In R. L. Street, Jr., & J. N. Cappella (Eds.), *Sequence and pattern in communicative behavior* (pp. 142-160). London: Edward Arnold.

Eagly, A. H., & Chaiken, S. (1984). Cognitive theories of persuasion. In L. Berkowitz (Ed.), *Advances in experimental social psychology* (Vol. 18, pp. 267-359). New York: Academic Press.

Farr, R. M., & Anderson, T. (1983). Beyond actor-observer differences in perspective: Extensions and applications. In M. Hewstone (Ed.), *Attribution theory: Social and functional extensions* (pp. 45-64). Oxford: Basil Blackwell.

Fishbein, M., & Ajzen, I. (1975). *Belief, attitude, intention, and behavior: An introduction to theory and research*. Reading, MA: Addison-Wesley.

Gerbner, G., Gross, L., Morgan, M., & Signorelli, N. (1980). The "mainstreaming" of America: Violence profile no. 11. *Journal of Communication, 30*, 10-29.

Giles, H. (1977). Social psychology and applied linguistics: Towards an integrative approach. *ITL: Review of Applied Linguistics, 33*, 27-42.

Giles, H., Mulac, A., Bradac, J. J., & Johnson, P. (1987). Speech accommodation theory: The next decade and beyond. In M. L. McLaughlin (Ed.), *Communication yearbook* (Vol. 10, pp. 13-48). Beverly Hills, CA: Sage.

Giles, H., & Smith, P. (1979). Accommodation theory: Optimal levels of convergence. In H. Giles & R. N. St. Clair (Eds.), *Language and social psychology* (pp. 45-65). Baltimore, MD: University Park Press.

Giles, H., & Street, R. L. (1985). Communicator characteristics and behavior. In M. L. Knapp & G. R. Miller (Eds.), *Handbook of interpersonal communication* (pp. 205-262). Newbury Park, CA: Sage.

Giles, H., Wilson, P., & Conway, T. (1981). Accent and lexical diversity as determinants of impression formation and employment selection. *Language Sciences, 3*, 92-103.

Greenwald, A. G. (1968). Cognitive learning, cognitive response to persuasion, and attitude change. In A. G. Greenwald, T. C. Brock, & T. M. Ostrom (Eds.), *Psychological foundations of attitudes*. New York: Academic Press.

Greenwald, A. G. (1981). Cognitive response analysis: An appraisal. In R. E. Petty, T. M. Ostrom, & T. C. Brock (Eds.), *Cognitive responses in persuasion* (pp. 127-134). Hillsdale, NJ: Lawrence Erlbaum.

Hall, J. A., Roter, D. L., & Rand, C. S. (1981). Communication of affect between patient and physician. *Journal of Health and Social Behavior, 22*, 18-30.

Hamilton, V. (1983). *The cognitive structures and processes of human motivation and personality*. Chichester: John Wiley.

Hample, D. (1977). Testing a model of value argument and evidence. *Communication Monographs, 44*, 107-120.

Hample, D. (1978). Predicting immediate belief change and adherence to argument claims. *Communication Monographs, 45*, 219-228.

Hastie, R. (1980). Memory for behavioral information that confirms or contradicts a personality impression. In R. Hastie, T. M. Ostrom, R. S. Wyer, Jr., D. L. Hamilton, & D. E. Carlston (Eds.), *Person memory: The cognitive basis of social perception* (pp. 155-178). Hillsdale, NJ: Lawrence Erlbaum.

Hastie, R. (1984). Causes and effects of causal attribution. *Journal of Personality and Social Psychology, 46*, 44-56.

Hastie, R., & Park, B. (1986). The relationship between memory and judgment depends on whether the judgment task is memory-based or on-line. *Psychological Review, 93*, 258-268.

Hawkins, R. P., Pingree, S., & Adler, I. (1987). Searching for cognitive processes in the cultivation effect: Adult and adolescent samples in the United States and Australia. *Human Communication Research, 13*, 553-577.

Hayes, D. P., & Meltzer, L. (1972). Interpersonal factors based on talkativeness: Fact or artifact. *Sociometry, 35*, 538-561.

Holland, J. H., Holyoak, K. J., Nisbett, R. E., & Thagard, P. R. (1986). *Induction: Processes of inference, learning, and discovery.* Cambridge: MIT Press.

Humphreys, M. S., & Revelle, W. (1984). Personality, motivation, and performance: A theory of the relationship between individual differences and information processing. *Psychological Review, 91*, 153-184.

Imada, A. S., & Hakel, M. D. (1977). Influence of nonverbal communication and rater proximity on impressions and decisions in simulated employment interviews. *Journal of Applied Psychology, 62*, 295-300.

Jones, E. E., & Nisbett, R. E. (1971). The actor and the observer: Divergent perceptions of the causes of behavior. In E. E. Jones et al. (Eds.), *Attribution: Perceiving the causes of behavior* (pp. 79-94). Morristown, NJ: General Learning Press.

Kahneman, D., Slovic, P., & Tversky, A. (Eds.). (1982). *Judgment under uncertainty: Heuristics and biases.* New York: Cambridge University Press.

Keenan, J. M., MacWhinney, B., & Mayhew, D. (1977). Pragmatics in memory: A study of natural conversations. *Journal of Verbal Learning and Verbal Behavior, 16*, 549-560.

Kelley, H., & Michela, J. (1980). Attribution theory and research. In M. R. Rosenweig & Porter (Eds.), *Annual reviews of psychology.* Palo Alto, CA: Annual Reviews.

Knapp, M. L. (1978). *Nonverbal communication in human interaction.* (2nd ed.). New York: Holt, Rinehart & Winston.

Lay, C. H., & Burron, B. F. (1968). Perception of the personality of the hesitant speaker. *Perceptual and Motor Skills, 26*, 951-956.

McGuire, W. T. (1960). Cognitive consistency and attitude change. *Journal of Abnormal and Social Psychology, 60*, 345-353.

McGuire, W. T. (1981). The probabilogical model of cognitive structure and attitude change. In R. E. Petty, T. M. Ostrom, & T. C. Brock (Eds.), *Cognitive responses in persuasion* (pp. 291-308). Hillsdale, NJ: Lawrence Erlbaum.

Montgomery, B. M. (1984). Behavioral characteristics predicting self and peer perceptions of open communication. *Communication Quarterly, 32*, 233-242.

Morley, D. D. (1987). Subjective message constructs: A theory of persuasion. *Communication Monographs, 54*, 183-203.

Morley, D. D., & Walker, K. B. (1987). *The role of importance, novelty, and plausibility in producing belief change.* Unpublished paper, University of Colorado at Colorado Springs, Department of Communication.

O'Keefe, D. (1987). *Describing messages.* Unpublished paper, University of Illinois at Urbana-Champaign, Department of Speech Communication.

Ostrom, T. M., Lingle, J. H., Pryor, J. B., & Geva, N. (1980). Cognitive organization of person impressions. In R. Hastie et al. (Eds.), *Person memory: The cognitive basis of social perception* (pp. 55-88). Hillsdale, NJ: Lawrence Erlbaum.

Palmer, M., & Cunningham, R. (1987). *MADCAP: A computer hardware and software system for the analysis of social interaction.* Unpublished paper, University of Wisconsin-Madison, Department of Communication Arts.

Patterson, M. L. (1983). *Nonverbal behavior: A functional perspective.* New York: Springer-Verlag.

Petty, R. E., & Cacioppo, J. T. (1981). *Attitudes and persuasion: Classic and contemporary approaches.* Dubuque, IA: William C. Brown.

Petty, R. E., & Cacioppo, J. T. (1986a). *Communication and persuasion: Central and peripheral routes to persuasion.* New York: Springer-Verlag.

Petty, R. E., & Cacioppo, J. T. (1986b). The elaboration likelihood model of persuasion. In L. Berkowitz (Ed.), *Advances in experimental social psychology* (Vol. 19, pp. 123-205). New York: Academic Press.

Petty, R. E., Ostrom, T. M., & Brock, T. C. (1981). Historical foundations of the cognitive response approach to attitudes and persuasion. In R. E. Petty, T. M. Ostrom, & T. C. Brock (Eds.), *Cognitive responses in persuasion* (pp. 5-30). Hillsdale, NJ: Lawrence Erlbaum.

Putnam, W. B., & Street, R. L., Jr. (1984). The conception and perception of non-content speech performance: Implications for speech accommodation theory. *International Journal of the Sociology of Language, 46,* 97-114.

Ryan, E. B., & Giles, H. (Eds.). (1982). *Attitudes towards language variation: Social and applied contexts.* London: Edward Arnold.

Scherer, K. R. (1979). Voice and speech correlates of perceived social influence in simulated juries. In H. Giles & R. N. St. Clair (Eds.), *Language and social psychology* (pp. 88-120). Baltimore, MD: University Park Press.

Scherer, K. R., London, H., & Wolf, J. J. (1973). The voice of confidence: Para-linguistic cues and audience evaluation. *Journal of Research in Personality, 7,* 31-44.

Scotton, C. M. (1985). What the heck, sir: Style shifting and lexical coloring as features of powerful language. In R. L. Street, Jr., & J. N. Cappella (Eds.), *Sequence and pattern in communicative behavior* (pp. 103-119). London: Edward Arnold.

Sereno, K. K., & Hawkins, G. J. (1967). The effects of variation in speakers' nonfluency upon audience ratings of attitude toward the speech topic and speakers' credibility. *Speech Monographs, 34,* 58-64.

Sherif, C. W., Sherif, N., & Nebergall, R. E. (1965). *Attitude and attitude change: The social judgment-involvement approach.* Philadelphia: W. B. Saunders.

Shrout, P. E., & Fiske, D. W. (1981). Nonverbal behaviors and social evaluation. *Journal of Personality, 49,* 115-128.

Siegman, A. W. (1978). The telltale voice: Nonverbal messages of verbal communication. In A. W. Siegman & S. Feldstein (Eds.), *Nonverbal behavior and communication* (pp. 183-243). Hillsdale, NJ: Lawrence Erlbaum.

Siegman, A. W., & Reynolds, M. (1982). Interviewee-interviewer nonverbal communication: An interactional approach. In M. Davis (Ed.), *Interaction rhythms: Periodicity in communication behavior* (pp. 240-278). New York: Human Sciences Press.

Slovic, P., & Lichtenstein, S. (1971). Comparison of Bayesian and regression approaches to the study of information processes in judgment. *Organizational Behavior and Human Performance, 6,* 649-744.

Smith, B. L., Brown, B. L., Strong, W. J., & Rencher, A. G. (1975). Effects of speech rate on personality perception. *Language and Speech, 18,* 145-152.

Sperber, D., & Wilson, D. (1986). *Relevance: Communication and cognition.* Cambridge, MA: Harvard University Press.

Stafford, L., Burggraf, C. S., & Sharkey, W. F. (1987, May). *Conversational memory: The effects of time, recall mode, and memory expectancies on remembrances of natural conversations.* Paper presented at the International Communication Association Meetings, Montreal, Canada.

Stafford, L., & Daly, J. A. (1984). Conversational memory: The effects of recall mode and memory expectancies on remembrances of natural conversations. *Human Communication Research, 10,* 379-402.

Street, R. L., Jr. (1982). Evaluation of noncontent speech accommodation. *Language and Communication, 2,* 13-31.

Street, R. L., Jr. (1984). Speech convergence and speech evaluation in fact-finding interviews. *Human Communication Research, 11,* 139-169.

Street, R. L., Jr. (1985). Participant-observer differences in speech evaluation. *Journal of Language and Social Psychology, 4,* 125-130.

Street, R. L., Jr. (1986). Interaction processes and outcomes in interviews. In M. L. McLaughlin (Ed.), *Communication yearbook* (Vol. 9, pp. 215-250). Beverly Hills, CA: Sage.

Street, R. L., Jr., & Brady, R. M. (1982). Speech rate acceptance ranges as a function of evaluative domain, listener speech rate, and communication context. *Communication Monographs, 49,* 290-308.

Street, R. L., Jr., Brady, R. M., & Lee, R. (1984). Evaluative responses to communicators: The effects of speech rate, sex, and interaction context. *Western Journal of Speech Communication, 48,* 14-27.

Street, R. L., Jr., Brady, R. M., & Putnam, W. B. (1983). The influence of speech rate stereotypes and rate similarity on listener's evaluations of speakers. *Journal of Language and Social Psychology, 2,* 37-56.

Street, R. L., Jr., & Buller, D. B. (1986). *Communicative patterns and outcomes in physician-patient interactions.* Unpublished manuscript, Texas Tech University.

Street, R. L., Jr., & Cappella, J. N. (1985). Sequence and pattern in communicative behavior: A model and commentary. In R. L. Street, Jr., & J. N. Cappella (Eds.), *Sequences and pattern in communicative behavior* (pp. 243-276). London: Edward Arnold.

Street, R. L., Jr., & Giles, H. (1982). Speech accommodation theory: A social-cognitive approach to language and speech behavior. In M. E. Roloff & C. R. Berger (Eds.), *Social cognition and communication* (pp. 193-226). Beverly Hills, CA: Sage.

Street, R. L., Jr., Mulac, A., & Wiemann, J. M. (1988). Speech evaluation differences as a function of perspective (participant versus observer) and presentational medium. *Human Communication Research, 14,* 333-363.

Swann, W. B., Jr. (1984). Quest for accuracy in person perception: A matter of pragmatics. *Psychological Review, 91,* 457-477.

Taylor, S. E., & Fiske, S. T. (1978). Salience, attention and attribution: Top of the head phenomena. In L. Berkowitz (Ed.), *Advances in experimental social psychology* (Vol. 11, pp. 249-288). New York: Academic Press.

Thakerar, J. N., & Giles, H. (1981). They are—so they speak: Noncontent speech stereotypes. *Language and Communication, 1,* 251-256.

Thakerar, J. N., Giles, H., & Cheshire, J. (1982). Psychological and linguistic parameters of speech accommodation theory. In C. Fraser & K. R. Scherer (Eds.), *Advances in the social psychology of language* (pp. 205-255). Cambridge: Cambridge University Press.

Toulmin, S. E. (1964). *The uses of argument.* Cambridge: Cambridge University Press.

van Dijk, T. A., & Kintsch, W. (1983). *Strategies of discourse comprehension.* New York: Academic Press.

Welkowitz, J., & Kuc, M. (1973). Interrelations among warmth, genuineness, empathy, and temporal speech patterns in interpersonal interaction. *Journal of Consulting and Clinical Psychology, 41,* 472-473.

Woodall, G. W., & Burgoon, J. K. (1983). Talking fast and changing attitudes: A critique and clarification. *Journal of Nonverbal Behavior, 8,* 126-142.

Wyer, R. S. (1970). Quantitative prediction of belief and opinion change. *Journal of Personality and Social Psychology, 16,* 559-570.

Wyer, R. S. (1974). *Cognitive organization and change: An information processing approach.* Hillsdale, NJ: Lawrence Erlbaum.

Chapter 3

METHODOLOGICAL ISSUES IN THE STUDY OF MESSAGE EFFECTS

Anthony Mulac and Dale Kunkel

COMMUNICATION RESEARCH AS WE KNOW IT today has its roots in a number of academic traditions and disciplines. Therefore, it is hardly surprising that communication as an empirical science encompasses a number of different focuses, perspectives, and emphases, all striving to explain and predict relationships among widely divergent types of variables. How do messages influence the distribution of knowledge, people's attitudes and behaviors, the spread of social change, the policies of government, and the social institutions of our culture? These are just a handful of the types of issues explored in communication-effects research that require the study of widely differing forms of variables.

Such diversity in the nature of the variables examined by communication scholars has led Paisley (1984) to label communication "a variable field," indicating that it focuses attention on one category of behavior, communication, across many levels of analysis. This perspective contrasts with "level fields" such as psychology or sociology that generally study a wide range of behaviors at only one primary level of analysis, in this case, that of the individual or of large groups. Communication researchers, therefore, must be capable of conceptualizing and measuring a wide range of disparate types of variables.

AUTHORS' NOTE: A preliminary version of this chapter was presented at the meeting of the Speech Communication Association, Chicago, November 1986.

This diversity in the focus of communication research has brought both problems and benefits to the field. The wide range of concerns embodied by communication science has probably served as an obstacle to the construction of any single theoretical perspective that might shape or guide exploration throughout the entire field. But it has also at times served as a vehicle to inspire cross-fertilization in research perspectives across the field's different subdomains.

One way by which studies of communicative behavior have been distinguished consistently over the years is according to the channel used to transmit the message—either interpersonal or mass. This approach parallels other dichotomies from the early days of the field, such as the direct effects perspective on the study of communication messages: namely, that influence must come from media or from people but not from both (McLeod & Blumler, 1987). But most other dichotomies associated with the field's earlier perspectives, for example, that the media have strong, direct effects or none at all, have long since disappeared. It is surprising, however, that the distinction between interpersonal and mass communication-effects research has remained remarkably resilient over the years. This is an irony because, to a large extent, both mass and interpersonal message-effects research share the same level of analysis—that of the individual (Chaffee & Berger, 1987; Hawkins, Wiemann, & Pingree, 1988), and thus should have much to gain from one another.

An awareness of the potential for shared perspectives in the study of both interpersonal and mass forms of communication was evident in the early work of Carl Hovland and his associates. Hovland's research examined the influence of various factors on the persuasive effects of messages and has been widely recognized as being among the most influential in establishing the discipline of communication research. After applying his knowledge of experimental social psychology to the exploration of attitude change via the mass media in a pioneering set of media effects studies (Hovland, Lumsdaine, & Sheffield, 1949), Hovland argued subsequently that "the ways in which words and symbols influence people" should cut across all types of communication (Hovland, Janis, & Kelly, 1953, p. 1). His call, then, was for an integrated approach to the study and understanding of the process of persuasion.

While Hovland's research group stressed the development of theory, Delia (1987, p. 63) notes that "the important influences that were to come from the Hovland program reflected its research practices rather than its general theory." The standard research approach involved the experimental manipulation of source and message factors (e.g., source credibility, fear appeals, order of arguments, channel of presentation) to observe their effect upon the audience's attitudes.

Hovland and his associates' preference for the experimental approach to scientific inquiry played a major role in shaping the early paradigm for communication research (Hovland, 1957; Hovland & Janis, 1959; Hovland, Janis, & Kelly, 1953; Hovland et al., 1949). Following the model established by this group, experimentation has been broadly adopted and applied to virtually all areas of communication study, reaching well beyond the parameters of attitude-change research. This paradigm remains largely intact today, which means that in many ways the research pursued by contemporary communication scholars closely resembles the work conducted in Hovland's laboratory.

It is worth noting that a longstanding, if small, niche in the field prefers qualitative approaches to research methodology. However, because quantitative methods clearly constitute the dominant approach to message-effects research, this chapter will concentrate exclusively on that perspective. For even if the dominant paradigm remains the same as in the Hovland period, it has certainly been supplemented by advances in research design strategies, measurement procedures, and statistical analysis techniques that now allow a greater diversity of approaches to the study of communication processes and effects.

What is the same and what is different in the means by which communication researchers pursue their studies today as compared with Hovland's day? What advances, both methodological and conceptual, allow message-effects research to explore issues well beyond what Hovland might have deemed possible? These questions provide the principal focus for this chapter. Our primary goal, however, is not to provide a historical account of the gains in research techniques and methodology since the early days of communication inquiry. Rather, the emphasis will center upon the evaluation of recent advances in the practice of communication research, with an occasional glance backward simply to allow us to place these developments in a context that helps to identify their value to the field.

THE LINK BETWEEN
THEORY AND RESEARCH

The purpose of message-effects research, or almost any scholarly research for that matter, is ultimately theory development. Hovland recognized the more applied or problem-centered approach to mass communication studies as a liability for the growth of knowledge, and this recognition led him to argue for more integrated and theory-driven perspectives in the pursuit of communication-effects research. While some projects that emphasize applied considerations certainly can be found in the literature today, they are clearly outnumbered by the efforts of those engaged in theory-building. If the primary purpose of research can be said to be the construction of theory, then it can also be said that the primary purpose of method is to help build, test, expand, and refine those theories.

Our colleagues in theoretical physics, in their quest to discover the manner in which the four forces fit in an orderly universe, are unable to test current theories by direct observation, the method so long the exemplar of the hard sciences (Crease & Mann, 1986). Instead, they must rely upon mathematical or, more to the point, purely indirect or theoretical means to test their conceptions. In contrast, message variable research does not suffer from this disparity between theory and method, which, of course, makes the often heard "physics-envy" syndrome so common in the behavioral sciences seem a bit ironic.

Advanced methodology that cannot be used to further theory would be meaningless. Methods do not exist for their own sake. Similarly, advanced theory (however that might be conceptualized) would be equally useless without some means to verify it. It follows, then, that the strength of our theories is in large part influenced by the ability of our methods to demonstrate support for them. Moreover, the strength of our methods is primarily evaluated in terms of their validity.

FOUR FORMS OF RESEARCH VALIDITY

Cook and Campbell (1979) have proposed a four-category model of validity for evaluating research design, measurement procedures, and data analysis that is useful for our analysis of methodological issues. These authors (1979, p. 37) note that they use "the concepts of *validity* and *invalidity* to refer to the best available approximation to the truth or falsity of propositions, including propositions about cause." Their four forms of research validity, based on Campbell and Stanley's (1966) earlier conceptualization of internal and external validity, raise four classes of issues or challenges to validity: (1) *Statistical conclusion validity*, which raises the question: Is there a relationship between the independent and dependent variables? (2) *Internal validity*, which asks: Given that a relationship exists, is it causal from one variable to the other? (3) *Construct validity*, which poses the question: Given that a causal relationship exists between independent and dependent variables, what are the cause and effect constructs represented by these variables? (4) *External validity*, which challenges: Given that there is a causal relationship between the constructs of the independent and dependent variables, how generalizable is it across persons, settings, and times?

These four forms of validity can be viewed as criteria that should be sequentially applied to the evaluation of research methodology of a given study. That is, the question of a causal link between independent and dependent variables (*internal validity*) is not raised if covariation between the two variables (*statistical conclusion validity*) has not been found. Similarly, if the operationalizations of independent and dependent variables do not stand for meaningful concepts (*construct validity*), the issue of generalizing findings to other persons, settings, and times (*external validity*) is not usefully considered.

Research on message effects, as in any other area of communication, is effective to the extent that it meets these four criteria. Where there have been improvements in methodology, their effects may be seen as benefiting one or more of these forms of validity. In addition, where research problems remain, new methods or new applications of established approaches can be effectively recognized from the perspective of this model. This fourfold model provides the structure for our discussion of methodological improvements, even though many procedures discussed under one criterion may also have implications for another.

STATISTICAL CONCLUSION VALIDITY

The first form of validity, *statistical conclusion validity,* views the extent to which "it is reasonable to presume covariation [between independent and dependent variables] given a specific alpha level and the obtained variance" (Cook & Campbell, 1979, p. 41). It involves finding relationships that exist between variables and deals with such matters as reliability of measurement and statistical power.

Since Hovland's day, the reliability of measurement of the dependent variable has benefited in a number of ways related to technological advances. The use of videotape to capture the *process* of communication for subsequent review and analysis has allowed more careful and extensive coding of variables than was possible in research settings limited to measurement during the actual event. For example, facial affect in response to specific message content can be unobtrusively recorded with videotape cameras and subsequently coded by comparing subjects' expressions to prototypical pictures associated with each of the six basic emotions (e.g., Ekman & Friesen, 1975, 1978; Izard, 1971; Izard, Dougherty, & Hembree, 1983). Such observations can achieve an acceptably high degree of reliability because coders can review the facial expressions as much as necessary to determine their proper categorization. Of course, these research methods require extensive coder training, and this training can also benefit from the use of videotape replay, thereby increasing reliability.

The greater the reliability of measures, the greater the chance that meaningful relationships that exist between variables can be identified. For example, in analysis of variance (ANOVA), unreliable measures can artificially inflate the within-group variance and hence the error term used as the denominator for the F ratio. Because there is no corresponding change in the between-group variance, given that errors are random and average to zero, the F ratio numerator remains the same, resulting in a diminished F and, therefore, a decreased likelihood of finding statistically significant differences.

A more recent development in message-effects research has been the increased emphasis placed on the power of the statistical tests employed in data analysis. Statistical power refers to the probability that a given analysis will yield statistically significant results, taking into account such factors as sample size, anticipated effect size, and the nature of the particular analytic technique (Cohen, 1977). Quantitative studies have always indicated the level of significance associated with the relationships identified by research. Until recent years, however, it was rare to see a study report the power of a statistical test that failed to yield a hypothesized relationship between the variables of interest.

Such information is valuable because it bears directly on the question of whether one should "accept" the null hypothesis or worry that the hypothesized relationship exists but, for whatever reason, simply was not found. The greater the power of the statistical test, the greater the confidence one can have in accepting the null hypothesis of no relationship among variables.

Recent studies published in two leading communication journals, *Communication Research* and *Human Communication Research,* have consistently included statistical power estimates where appropriate. Unfortunately, too many researchers wait until after collecting data to consider the power of the statistical tests they plan to employ. This may create a situation that makes it difficult to accept the null hypothesis when no significant relationships are found because of the limited power of the analysis. This issue is best resolved by consulting statistical power estimate tables (e.g., Cohen, 1977) prior to data collection to determine acceptable means of obtaining the desired level of power.

While early communication researchers such as Hovland had to rely upon simple critical ratios, t-tests and one-way F ratios, advances in analytic techniques allow contemporary scholars to employ approaches that are much more likely to identify important relationships among variables. For example, statistical power has been improved by the availability of the repeated measure ANOVA and MANOVA (multivariate analysis of variance). With its partitioning of the error term for the F ratio into between-subject and within-subject error terms, this statistical design generally has the effect of increasing the magnitude of the resulting F, although it does diminish degrees of freedom. Kellermann (1986), for example, employed this approach to test the extent to which conversation participants and observers changed their ratings of dyad partners across ten 30-second intervals. Burgoon and Hale (1988) utilized a repeated measure MANOVA design to test for differences in naive dyad participants' reactions to nonverbal expectancy violations by a friend and by a stranger. In addition to increasing statistical power and hence *statistical conclusion validity,* repeated measure designs can be useful in assigning variance to its appropriate source, thereby aiding *internal validity,* discussed in the next section.

Another source affecting *statistical conclusion validity* that is especially important in some interpersonal research involves the possible correlation of dyad partners' behavior, for example, eye gaze or amount of talk, during interactions. If a negative correlation exists, then any F

or *t* ratios computed with scores from individual interactants will be artificially diminished (Kraemer & Jacklin, 1979). On the other hand, if a positive relationships exists, the resulting *F*s or *t*s will be artificially inflated. It is only in cases where the relationship between the partners' scores is nonexistent that the statistical analysis is unaffected. Operationally, this is often taken as a Pearson product-moment correlation coefficient of < .30, either positive or negative. Kraemer and Jacklin (1979) have offered a procedure for computing *F* and *t* ratios when a relationship exists. Dindia (1987) demonstrated the utility of this approach to related interactant data in a study of male versus female conversational interruptions in same-sex and mixed-sex dyads.

INTERNAL VALIDITY

The second form of validity, *internal validity,* looks at the extent to which "statements can be made about whether there is a causal relationship from one variable to another in the form in which the variables were manipulated or measured" (Cook & Campbell, 1979, p. 38). This criterion addresses the issue of possible alternative or intervening causes for the measured effects on the dependent variable. It asks whether the results found are solely attributable to the independent variable or variables.

Although Hovland and his colleagues generally employed research designs that controlled effectively for extraneous factors that might affect the dependent variable, one aspect of their designs that can be faulted, and one that has generally diminished in current message research, is the use of pretest-posttest designs. It is now accepted that the pretest can, in and of itself, influence the posttest, hence reducing *internal validity.* For this reason, in cases where pretest measures are necessary to a research plan, they are often separated in time or place from the treatment manipulation.

Another way in which *internal validity* has benefited since the Hovland era has been through the use of statistical models that can isolate the effects of a number of variables acting together, as with statistical interactions in factorial designs, or the effects of a combination of weighted predictor variables, as with canonical functions in discriminant analysis. Even the classic 2 × 2 ANOVA, with its ability to determine the unique effect of the two independent variables acting in concert, was not used by Hovland and his associates 30 years ago.

Aside from the ubiquitous and important factorial model, it is now possible to assess the analogue of statistical interaction where the data are nominal in character through the use of log-linear analysis. For example, Witteman and Fitzpatrick (1986) used log-linear analysis of nominal data to show that various marital types utilize different patterns of compliance-gaining communication. Similarly, Zahn (1984) used the procedure to assess the effects of sequencing determinants and contextual determinants on the structure of conversational repair episodes.

Closely related to the issue of partitioning variance for the statistical interaction between independent variables is that of partitioning to assess the effects of potentially confounding variables. For example, Fitzpatrick and Dindia (1986) have noted that much of the early research on differences between husband-wife couples and unmarried, mixed-sex pairs confounded the effects of the person, the partner, and the relationship of the pair. A relatively new statistical model that permits the partitioning of variance attributable to each of these sources is the multivariate round-robin analysis of variance design (Kenny & LaVoie, 1984). Fitzpatrick and Dindia (1986) used this design to analyze talk-time data from dyadic interactions in which individuals conversed with their spouse and strangers of the same and opposite sexes. The parceling of the various causes of variance in the data permitted a clearer picture of the actual causes of the observed differences.

Another statistical procedure that can clarify the issue of what variables influence the dependent variable is analysis of covariance (ANCOVA), which can be used to control for one or more variables likely to affect the dependent variable. In a test of breadth, depth, and amount of self-disclosure by dual- and single-career couples, Rosenfeld and Welsh (1985) employed ANCOVA to control for respondents' age, years of marriage, number of children, age of youngest child, and highest educational degree obtained. The importance of using the procedure in this study was indicated by the fact that both number of children and highest degree obtained were significantly predictive of self-disclosure, the dependent variable. Therefore, the statistical control of these variables was important in terms of *internal validity*.

An additional procedure relevant to this form of validity is the statistical approach known as causal modeling (McPhee & Babrow, 1987) or path analysis, used to determine the extent to which variables are linked in a directional, cause/effect manner. Because the direction of the cause-effect relationship can be determined, this procedure has advantages over purely correlational methods such as partial correlation. This approach can be accomplished using estimation procedures such as LISREL (Jöreskog & Sörbom, 1985). Malamuth (1983) showed the utility of this method by demonstrating the effectiveness with which attitudes about rape led to laboratory aggression against women.

The most essential element in guarding against threats to internal validity is *randomization* of subject assignment to treatment groups, a technique used consistently by Hovland and associates. This precaution alone, however, does not guarantee the internal validity of a given study. A well-known experiment examining the effects of televised violence on children's subsequent aggressive behavior illustrates some of the problems that can emerge even when randomization is utilized.

Feshbach and Singer (1971) randomly assigned preadolescent and adolescent boys in institutional settings to one of two treatment conditions in which they were exposed to either a predominantly violent or a predominantly nonviolent television diet over a six-week period. Dependent measures indicated that the group assigned to the nonviolent television schedule evidenced much higher levels of aggression than the group that had viewed the violent programming. The researchers interpreted this outcome as support for the catharsis hypothesis, which holds that exposure to televised violence can vicariously purge an individual of the need to behave aggressively toward others.

An alternative explanation for this finding is that those in the non-aggressive treatment group became resentful and frustrated at their inability to view the programs of their preference (Liebert, Sobol, & Davidson, 1971). According to this interpretation, the frustration of the boys assigned to the nonaggressive treatment, who were unable to watch many of their favorite shows due to the violent nature of the content, may have accounted for this group's higher level of aggression.

Feshbach and Singer themselves reported that their subjects assigned more favorable ratings to aggressive than nonaggressive programs. Indeed, in an attempt to avoid frustration effects associated with subjects being unable to see their favorite program, the researchers acquiesced to the demands of three of their seven nonaggressive treatment groups that they be allowed to watch their favorite aggressive program, *Batman.* Thus, in this case, there are at least two principal threats to internal validity: the lack of consistency in manipulating the independent variable, caused by the accommodation of the requests to view *Batman,* and the presence of an alternative explanation aside from the treatment to account for differences observed in the dependent measure, aggressive behavior. Both of these factors undermine the confidence one can place in the results of this study, despite the proper use of random assignment of subjects to treatments.

As is sometimes the case in attempting to maximize research validity, the Feshbach and Singer study presents competing and perhaps irreconcilable issues. If subjects were allowed to choose their treatment, the benefits of randomization would be lost and threats to *internal validity* would be increased. But when researchers force exposure to messages that some individuals might never choose to receive (or, conversely, cut off access to their messages of choice), threats to *external validity* may emerge. This form of interrelationship, and occasional antagonism, among the validity criteria may involve any of the four primary types of research validity.

CONSTRUCT VALIDITY

The third form of research validity, what Cook and Campbell (1979) call *construct validity* of putative (or presumed) causes and effects, examines the extent to which "we can make generalizations about higher-order constructs from research operations" (Cook & Campbell, 1979, p. 38). Put another way, what do the operationalizations, both of independent and of dependent variables, stand for in the "real world"? This question addresses the very nature of reality as studied in message-effects research.

One of the issues raised in terms of the construct validity of any research design is that of the reactivity of the data collection environment. That is, to what extent has the communication behavior of interest been influenced by the presence of the researcher's process of collecting the data? For researchers who study language samples or nonverbal behavior, the use of low-light television cameras to record interactions through one-way glass may diminish the reactivity of the environment, as may concealed microphones and the simulation of familiar settings. Wiemann (1981) found that obtrusiveness of observation procedures did not affect out-of-consciousness behaviors (e.g., head nods); thus for such behaviors reactivity may not be a serious concern.

Even more obtrusive means of gathering data can sometimes overcome problems associated with subject reactivity. For example, a handful of studies have successfully placed time-lapse photographic or video recording equipment in subjects' homes to examine "real world" television viewing behavior (e.g., Allen, 1965; Anderson, Field, Collins, Lorch, & Nathan, 1985; Bechtel, Achelpohl, & Akers, 1972). Several precautions are typically employed to help ensure that this very intrusive measurement approach does not bias the results.

Once equipment is placed in the home, a period of time is usually allowed to pass before actual data collection begins. This permits subjects to acclimate and hopefully to return to their normal patterns of behavior should they be influenced by the presence of the devices. More important, comparisons can be made with control groups that do not have equipment in the home, both in terms of the demographics of participants and in terms of their viewing behaviors and responses. For example, Anderson et al. (1985) utilized three control groups for comparison purposes. One was recruited in the same manner as the experimental group (i.e., they agreed to place equipment in their homes, but were randomly assigned as a control), another was never told about the possibility of placing cameras in the home, and a third consisted of families who initially agreed but subsequently refused to allow the equipment in the home (but participated in all other aspects of the study). Subsequent analyses found no systematic differences between the families willing to accept the observational equipment and those serving as controls, nor in the reported viewing behaviors between the two (Anderson et al., 1985). These precautions allow much greater confidence to be placed in the results than would otherwise be the case, providing important findings gathered in the field that overcome many of the limitations traditionally associated with laboratory studies.

One of the most interesting results from the home observation studies is that substantial disparities occur between people's self-reported television exposure and their viewing behavior as measured by more direct means. Compared to the observational data, people using self-reports tend to overestimate their television viewing, often by 25% or more. At least a part of this disparity may be related to the lack of a clear definition of the construct of "watching" television (Salomon & Cohen, 1978).

Among the different operational definitions of viewing that have been applied over the years are the following: self-reports of having watched a program, given in surveys or interviews conducted after the behavior of interest; meter devices that indicate the television set in a home is on and tuned to a given channel; and videotaped observations of subjects in the same room with the TV on and eyes directed toward the screen. Each of these different approaches to the measurement of television viewing behavior tends to offer a higher degree of reliability than the one preceding it. It is clear, however, that these various approaches often reflect entirely different constructs of television viewing.

There are many different reasons for studying television viewing behavior. Interests vary from a focus on viewers' use of time, which might render information about specific program choices irrelevant, to concern with their attention to, or comprehension of, particular message content. The nature of the research determines the preferred construct, which in turn shapes the nature of the measurement to be used. The problem created by this lack of consistency in the construct of television viewing is that it is difficult to compare findings across various studies. This issue will be addressed again when we consider the topic of meta-analysis.

"Mono-operation bias" (Cook & Campbell, 1979), or the use of a single exemplar of each level of an independent variable, is probably the most common threat to the validity of message-effects research, whether interpersonal or mass. Reliance upon a single message to instantiate variables places a heavy burden upon the researcher to ensure that the example chosen is highly prototypical. A single example of the construct of interest may under- or overrepresent certain aspects of the target of interest, or even contain irrelevancies that distract from the anticipated effect. In fact, Jackson and Jacobs (1983, 1987) argue that a general norm of message-effects research is the use of a single message manipulated in various ways and that the results of such research can easily be idiosyncratic to the particular message.

At least two basic approaches can help to minimize this problem. If it is absolutely necessary to rely upon a single message to operationalize the independent variable, then a preliminary assessment asking a separate group of subjects to rate the typicality of that example would clearly be in order. A more desirable alternative is to employ multiple examples of the construct of interest. Analyses could then be initially conducted independently for each of the exemplars to assess the consistency of the effects observed, with the hope of combining responses if no systematic differences occur. While this approach can strengthen the generalizabilty of the findings, it exacts a potentially heavy cost in terms of the sample size required. Should disparities emerge across the multiple exemplars, the researcher must be capable of conducting final analyses for each one without combining data across the differing treatments.

Methodological improvements have also been shown in terms of *construct validity* of the dependent variable. Factor analysis of data from semantic differentials, among other measurement approaches, in order to determine the underlying factor structure of the items measured, has become commonplace. Multidimensional scaling procedures are now appearing with greater frequency. For example, Bell and Daly (1984) used multidimensional scaling to determine the multivariate structure of affinity-seeking; Wiseman and Schenck-Hamlin (1981) used it to test a taxonomy of compliance-gaining strategies.

Not only do these analyses permit a better understanding of the composition of the construct measured, they permit the comparison of factor structures of different groups using the same measurement instrument through procedures such as the "coefficient of congruence" (Mulaik, 1972) and confirmatory factor analysis (Jöreskog & Sörbom, 1985). For example, in a number of studies, the factor structures of male and female raters, as well as university student and older nonstudent raters, have been compared using the coefficient of congruence before combining their ratings (Mulac, Incontro, & James, 1985; Mulac & Lundell, 1980, 1981, 1982).

The sequential nature of conversation events has been assessed through such statistical procedures as Markov chain procedures, lag sequential analysis, and stochastic modeling. In their simplest form, these approaches can analyze, for example, adjacent pairs of statement-response turns to detect conversational patterns. Williamson and Fitzpatrick (1985) used Markov chain and lag sequential analyses to determine differences in the sequencing of control strategies used by different types of couples in conversations between spouses. Markov statistics were also useful in establishing changes over time in the sequential use of relational control strategies in developing relationships (Fisher & Drecksel, 1983). Without these procedures for analyzing the sequence of conversational events, this aspect of the communication process could not be examined.

Two other statistical procedures that have benefited *construct validity* are multiple regression analysis and discriminant analysis. Both determine the combination of variables that, when differentially weighted, predict with maximum accuracy the criterion variable. In this way they give the researcher a clearer understanding of the makeup and relative importance of the variables that combine to provide predictive utility. In the case of multiple regression analysis, the variable predicted is continuous in nature, for example, the degree of satisfaction with a dyad partner. In the case of discriminant analysis and multiple discriminant analysis, the criterion variable is dichotomous, for example, the sex of the interviewer. Of course, these sophisticated and complex procedures require the use of powerful computers that were not available to Hovland and his associates.

Another use of computers has made it possible to determine the mutual occurrence of events in dyadic interactions by lining up data coded in real time, much as event recorder data might be lined up manually. In one study (Mulac, Studley, Wiemann, & Bradac, 1987), trained observers entered on microcomputers their coding of videotaped dyadic interactions for participants' gaze and talk (i.e., four separate interactant states) in real time. After computing intercoder reliability and aggregating across coders, a computer was used to line up the "snapshots" of the gaze/talk states of the two interactants for every 1/5th second of the eight-minute interaction, yielding 2,400 data points for each dyad. In this manner, 108 dyadic interactions were coded and the data were transformed to give simultaneous dyad behavior in terms of 10 variables or states, such as *Mutual Gaze/Mutual Silence* and *One Gazes/Other Talks.* Measurement of the construct of simultaneous, moment-to-moment, gaze/talk of the dyad would have been virtually impossible in Hovland's era, without the use of computers for data collection and analysis.

EXTERNAL VALIDITY

The fourth form of research validity, *external validity,* examines the extent to which "conclusions are drawn about the generalizability of a causal relationship to and across populations of persons, settings, and times" (Cook & Campbell, 1979, p. 39). That is, to what other contexts can the results be generalized beyond the research setting in which they were found?

By and large, the procedure of using volunteer university subjects for experimental research on message variables has predominated at least since the Hovland era. The difficulty and costs involved in obtaining more diverse subject populations are the most common barriers to overcoming this practice. Also, because of their emphasis on theory development, most academic researchers show greater concern for the other three forms of validity than for external validity. Is this reliance upon convenience sampling cause for concern? The answer depends on the particular focus of the research.

Some topic areas would pose few potential problems, while others might raise rather troubling concerns. A handful of studies have addressed this issue directly by comparing the responses gathered from university students with findings generated from more heterogeneous subjects. For example, several studies on the effects of obscene language (Mulac, 1976), foreign and regional accent (Mulac, Hanley, & Prigge, 1974; Mulac & Rudd, 1977), and gender-linked language (Mulac, Blau, & Bauquier, 1983; Mulac & Lundell, 1980, 1981, 1982) have used both university student and older nonstudent raters to test for possible difference in reaction. Of the 18 potential statistical interactions between rater group and the independent variable of primary concern in these six studies (one for each of three dependent variables measured), only one showed an effect approaching statistical significance. In that case, older nonstudent raters denigrated speakers using obscenities more on *aesthetic quality* than did student raters (Mulac, 1976). Although this suggests that the potential bias was not especially important in these particular studies, the extent of concern about this issue will vary substantially from topic to topic, and there is little to guide the researcher in this domain. Each study must be individually evaluated to determine whether or not a "student bias" could be problematic and, therefore, whether expanding the respondent pool would be important.

Another common bias in message-effects research that also affects *external validity* might be termed "laboratory bias." For reasons of control, with its inherent value of strengthening *internal validity,* researchers have frequently chosen the laboratory as the setting for their data collection. This is often an appropriate trade-off, improving one form of validity at the expense of another. An alternative is the use of field studies, which offer the possibility of maintaining control of potentially confounding variables outside the laboratory. For example, Sykes (1983) studied the demographic and situational factors influencing the choice of communication partners by naval apprentice trainees during off duty hours at a large naval base. In another naturalistic setting study, Jones and Yarbrough (1985) used student participant observers to code the touch behavior they experienced in their daily interactions and to interpret the meanings they attached to those behaviors.

Cook and Campbell (1979, p. 73) provide a useful perspective regarding the means for improving *external validity:* "A case can be made . . . that external validity is enhanced more by a number of smaller studies with haphazard samples than by a single study with initially representative samples if the latter could be implemented." Thus it is appropriate to address the issue of generalizability of findings through replication of studies. Here replication can be seen as taking a variety of forms ranging along a continuum representing degree of duplication (Kelly, Chase, & Tucker, 1979).

CONSIDERING RESEARCH ACROSS STUDIES: METHODOLOGICAL DEBATES AND META-ANALYSIS

Most of this chapter has addressed issues pertaining to methodological concerns *within* a particular study. But the results of almost any single study are of limited value in advancing knowledge. Of far greater importance are the conclusions drawn when considering a collection of findings in a given area.

One way in which collections of findings have been assessed is through debates regarding the efficacy of particular research approaches or paradigms. When these appear in the same issue of a journal, they facilitate readers' careful consideration of contrasting arguments. For example, Jackson and Jacobs (1983) argued that message-effects research is plagued by two design flaws: (a) single message representation of message categories and (b) the "language-as fixed-effect fallacy." Counterarguments and discussion were provided in the same issue by Bradac (1983) and Hewes (1983).

Even sometimes acrimonious exchanges, such as has occurred between different research groups that study the effects of sexually explicit, violent media content (Christensen, 1987; Linz & Donnerstein, 1988; Zillmann & Bryant, 1987, 1988) can prove beneficial. These elaborate colloquies published by the *Journal of Communication* have allowed the various camps studying this topic to air their differences, suggesting factors that might account for disparities in findings. Such articles allow extensive, detailed arguments and discussion necessary to reconcile strongly divergent findings across studies in a given area. While the tone of these particular exchanges has been more hostile than is the norm for academic publications, they nevertheless have been grounded in discussions of fundamental methodological issues, such as the generalizability of sample populations and the possible influence of unmeasured mediating variables. More debates such as these would help critical readers to evaluate the relative merits of divergent findings and positions.

Another approach for evaluating research findings across studies involves the traditional literature review format. For Hovland's cohort, this task would likely have been conducted without the benefit of any systematic procedure. That is, the findings of various studies would be reviewed and a cumulative summary prepared in a literary format by an eminent scholar. Any weighting of the different pieces of evidence would be performed subjectively by the expert charged with analyzing the relevant research. Such a summary can, of course, be highly effective by, for example, synthesizing findings from diverse research paradigms.

In recent years, the approach called meta-analysis has gained prominence as an alternative to the traditional research review. Meta-analysis is defined as the synthesis of a collection of primary research results into more general conclusions at the theoretical level (Rogers, 1981). It involves recoding of statistics from original empirical studies into a standard form that allows comparisons using statistical techniques. Varying degrees of sophistication can be employed, depending on the focus and goals of the inquiry.

While the techniques required to perform meta-analyses have been available for quite some time, the work of educational researcher Gene Glass (1976, 1977; Glass, McGaw, & Smith, 1981) is widely recognized as having fostered its understanding and acceptance as a research tool. When properly conducted at an appropriate point in the growth of a body of research, meta-analysis can yield scientific information that cannot be obtained in any other way.

Rogers (1981) played an influential role in introducing this analytic technique to communication researchers in an International Communication Association presidential address. Since that time, communication scholars have pursued this type of research with growing vigor. Examples have emerged recently in such areas as television and social behavior (Hearold, 1986), children and media effects (Meadowcroft & McDonald, 1986), and effects of sequential-request persuasive strategies (Dillard, Hunter, & Burgoon, 1984).

As communication research continues to grow in both volume and scope, meta-analysis will become increasingly important as a tool to draw meaningful conclusions from the expanding body of relevant literature. This is not to say that this technique will in any way displace the more traditional approach to literature reviews. Such overviews require both more creativity and more flexibility in arriving at their conclusions. As such, they are capable of weighing the relative value of studies surveyed by considering many more factors than meta-analysis allows. The strength of meta-analysis lies in its precision in comparing results from an area that is clearly defined and somewhat narrow in scope.

SUMMARY

The examples of methodological advances in message variable research noted above are hardly representative of the diversity of the field of message-effects research. They are, however, indicative of the sorts of changes that have taken place over roughly the last three decades.

Since Hovland's day, we have seen important improvements in the ability of researchers to identify and address methodological issues that can weaken or undermine the validity of research. Three forms of research validity have benefited substantially from the advances during this period. *Statistical conclusion validity,* leading to the increased likelihood of establishing real relationships between independent and dependent variables, has advanced through the use of electronic recording devices for improved reliability of data coding and more powerful statistical procedures to locate existing relationships. *Internal validity,* permitting causal linking of independent and dependent variables, has benefited from statistical procedures that permit the assignment of variance to sources that might influence the dependent variable. *Construct validity,* permitting generalization to higher-order constructs from research operations, has improved primarily through procedures that have given researchers greater insight into the nature and multidimensional makeup of the dependent variables studied.

On the other hand, *external validity,* permitting generalization of findings to other persons, settings, and times, has not improved dramatically in this period. Meaningful improvement in this area remains difficult to accomplish. Because a given study's weakness in this form of validity can be addressed through repeated testing of findings with other samples in other contexts, this criterion appears to be less troublesome for researchers than the other three. Hence it is perhaps under-standable that little improvement can be seen here.

The effects of the methodological improvements noted have, we think, been generally positive, as the preceding discussion suggests. There have, of course, been cases where researchers have seemed more enthralled with the methodological wizardry involved in their study than in its theoretical implications. Sophisticated research methods have never ensured theoretical substance. But continued interest in the methods of obtaining data to establish and extend theory can only benefit the field.

We would conclude that message variable theory has benefited by recent advances in research methodology. It is, of course, difficult to predict those areas in which methodological breakthroughs and innova-tions will enhance theory-building and testing in the coming decades. We fully expect that 30 years from now, scholars in the field will point to substantial improvements they will have made on the "quaint" pro-cedures that they inherited from our era.

REFERENCES

Allen, C. (1965). Photographing the TV audience. *Journal of Advertising Research, 14*, 2-8.

Anderson, D., Field, D., Collins, P., Lorch, E., & Nathan, J. (1985). Estimates of young children's time with television: A methodological comparison of parent reports with time-lapse video home observation. *Child Development, 56*, 1345-1357.

Bechtel, R., Achelpohl, C., & Akers, R. (1972). Correlates between observed behavior and questionnaire responses on television viewing. In E. Rubinstein, G. Comstock, & J. Murray (Eds.), *Television and social behavior* (Vol. 4, pp. 274-344). Washington, DC: Government Printing Office.

Bell, R. A., & Daly, J. A. (1984). The affinity-seeking function of communication. *Communication Monographs, 51*, 91-115.

Bradac, J. J. (1983). On generalizing cabbages, messages, kings, and several other things: The virtues of multiplicity. *Human Communication Research, 9*, 181-187.

Burgoon, J. K., & Hale, J. L. (1988). Nonverbal expectancy violations: Model elaboration and application to immediacy behaviors. *Communication Monographs, 55*, 58-79.

Campbell, D. T., & Stanley, J. C. (1966). *Experimental and quasi-experimental designs for research.* Chicago: Rand McNally.

Chaffee, S., & Berger, C. (1987). What communication scientists do. In C. Berger & S. Chaffee (Eds.), *Handbook of communication science* (pp. 99-122). Newbury Park, CA: Sage.

Christensen, F. (1987). Effects of pornography: The debate continues. *Journal of Com-munication, 37*, 186-187.

Cohen, J. (1977). *Statistical power analysis for the behavioral sciences.* New York: Academic Press.

Cook, T. D., & Campbell, D. T. (1979). *Quasi-experimentation: Design & analysis issues for field settings.* Chicago: Rand McNally.

Crease, R. P., & Mann, C. C. (1986). The gospel of string. *Atlantic Monthly, 257,* 24-29.

Delia, J. (1987). Communication research: A history. In C. Berger & S. Chaffee (Eds.), *Handbook of communication science* (pp. 20-98). Newbury Park, CA: Sage.

Dillard, J. P., Hunter, J. E., & Burgoon, M. (1984). Sequential-request persuasive strategies: Meta-analysis of foot-in-the-door and door-in-the-face. *Human Communication Research, 10,* 461-488.

Dindia, K. (1987). The effects of sex of subject and sex of partner on interruptions. *Human Communication Research, 13,* 345-371.

Ekman, P., & Friesen, W. (1975). *Unmasking the face: A guide to recognizing emotions from facial clues.* Englewood Cliffs, NJ: Prentice-Hall.

Ekman, P., & Friesen, W. (1978). *Facial action coding system: Investigator's guide.* Palo Alto, CA: Consulting Psychologists Press.

Feshbach, S., & Singer, R. (1971). *Television and aggression: An experimental field study.* San Francisco: Jossey-Bass.

Fisher, B. A., & Drecksel, G. L. (1983). A cyclical model of developing relationships: A study of relational control interaction. *Communication Monographs, 50,* 66-78.

Fitzpatrick, M. A., & Dindia, K. (1986). Couples and other strangers: Talk time in spouse-stranger interaction. *Communication Research, 13,* 625-652.

Glass, G. (1976). Primary, secondary, and meta-analysis of research. *Educational Researcher, 5,* 3-8.

Glass, G. (1977). Integrating findings: The meta-analysis of research. *Review of Research in Education, 5,* 351-379.

Glass, G., McGaw, B., & Smith, M. (1981). *Meta-analysis in social research.* Beverly Hills, CA: Sage.

Hawkins, R., Wiemann, J. M., & Pingree, S. (Eds.). (1988). *Advancing communication science: Merging mass and interpersonal processes.* Newbury Park, CA: Sage.

Hearold, S. (1986). A synthesis of 1043 effects of television on social behavior. In G. Comstock (Ed.), *Public communication and behavior* (Vol. 1). New York: Academic Press.

Hewes, D. E. (1983). Confessions of a methodological Puritan: A response to Jackson and Jacobs. *Human Communication Research, 9,* 187-191.

Hovland, C. I. (Ed.). (1957). *The order of presentation in persuasion.* New Haven, CT: Yale University Press.

Hovland, C. I., & Janis, I. L. (Eds.). (1959). *Personality and persuasibility.* New Haven, CT: Yale University Press.

Hovland, C., Janis, I. L., & Kelly, H. H. (1953). *Communication and persuasion.* New Haven, CT: Yale University Press.

Hovland, C., Lumsdaine, A., & Sheffield, F. (1949). *Experiments on mass communication.* Princeton, NJ: Princeton University Press.

Izard, C. (1971). *The face of emotion.* New York: Appleton-Century-Crofts.

Izard, C., Dougherty, L., & Hembree, E. (1983). *A system for identifying affect expressions by holistic judgments.* Newark, DE: University of Delaware, Instructional Resources Center.

Jackson, S., & Jacobs, S. (1983). Generalizing about messages: Suggestions for design and analysis of experiments. *Human Communication Research, 9*, 169-191.

Jackson, S., & Jacobs, S. (1987, May). *The search for systematic message effects: Contributions of meta-analysis and better design.* Paper presented at the meeting of the International Communication Association, Montreal.

Jones, S. E., & Yarbrough, A. E. (1985). A naturalistic study of the meanings of touch. *Communication Monographs, 52*, 19-56.

Jöreskog, K. G., & Sörbom, D. (1985). *LISREL VI: User's guide.* Chicago: National Educational Resources.

Kellermann, K. (1986). Anticipation of future interaction and information exchange in initial interaction. *Human Communication Research, 13*, 41-75.

Kelly, C. W., Chase, L. J., & Tucker, R. K. (1979). Replication in experimental communication research: An analysis. *Human Communication Research, 5*, 338-342.

Kenny, D., & LaVoie, J. (1984). The social relations model. In L. Berkowitz (Ed.), *Advances in experimental social psychology* (Vol. 18, pp. 221-242). New York: Academic Press.

Kraemer, H. C., & Jacklin, C. N. (1979). Statistical analysis of dyadic social behavior. *Psychological Bulletin, 86*, 217-224.

Liebert, R., Sobol, M., & Davidson, E. (1971). Catharsis of aggression among institutionalized boys: Fact or artifact? In G. Comstock, E. Rubinstein, & J. Murray (Eds.), *Television and social behavior* (Vol. 5, pp. 351-358). Washington, DC: Government Printing Office.

Linz, D., & Donnerstein, E. (1988). The methods and merits of pornography research. *Journal of Communication, 38*, 180-184.

Malamuth, N. M. (1983). Factors associated with rape as predictors of laboratory aggression against women. *Journal of Personality and Social Psychology, 45*, 432-442.

McLeod, J., & Blumler, J. (1987). The macrosocial level of communication science. In C. Berger & S. Chaffee (Eds.), *Handbook of communication science* (pp. 271-322). Newbury Park, CA: Sage.

McPhee, R. D., & Babrow, A. (1987). Causal modeling in communication research: Use, disuse, and misuse. *Communication Monographs, 54*, 344-366.

Meadowcroft, J., & McDonald, D. (1986). Meta-analysis of research on children and the media: A typical development? *Journalism Quarterly, 63*, 474-480.

Mulac, A. (1976). Effects of obscene language upon three dimensions of listener attitude. *Communication Monographs, 43*, 300-307.

Mulac, A., Blau, S., & Bauquier, L. (1983, November). *Gender-linked language differences and their effects in male and female students' impromptu essays.* Paper presented at the annual meeting of the Speech Communication Association, Washington, DC.

Mulac, A., Hanley, T. D., & Prigge, D. Y. (1974). Effects of phonological speech foreignness upon three dimensions of attitude of selected American listeners. *Quarterly Journal of Speech, 60*, 411-420.

Mulac, A., Incontro, C. R., & James, M. R. (1985). A comparison of the gender-linked language effect and sex-role stereotypes. *Journal of Personality and Social Psychology, 49*, 1099-1110.

Mulac, A., & Lundell, T. L. (1980). Differences in perceptions created by syntactic-semantic productions of male and female speakers. *Communication Monographs, 47*, 111-118.

Mulac, A., & Lundell, T. L. (1981, November). *Effects of gender-linked language differences in male and female written communication.* Paper presented at the annual meeting of the Speech Communication Association, Anaheim, CA.

Mulac, A., & Lundell, T. L. (1982). An empirical test of the gender-linked language effect in a public speaking setting. *Language and Speech, 25,* 243-256.

Mulac, A., & Rudd, M. J. (1977). Effects of selected American regional dialects upon regional audience members. *Communication Monographs, 44,* 185-195.

Mulac, A., Studley, L. B., Wiemann, J. M., & Bradac, J. J. (1987). Male/female gaze in same-sex and mixed-sex dyads: Gender-linked differences and mutual influence. *Human Communication Research, 13,* 323-343.

Mulaik, S. A. (1972). *The foundations of factor analysis.* New York: McGraw-Hill.

Paisley, W. (1984). Communication in the communication sciences. In B. Dervin & M. Voight (Eds.), *Progress in the communication sciences* (Vol. 5, pp. 1-43). Norwood, NJ: Ablex.

Rogers, E. (1981, May). *Methodology for meta-research.* Presidential address at the annual conference of the International Communication Association, Minneapolis.

Rosenfeld, L. B., & Welsh, S. M. (1985). Differences in self-disclosure in dual-career and single-career marriages. *Communication Monographs, 52,* 253-263.

Salomon, G., & Cohen, A. (1978). On the meaning and validity of television viewing. *Human Communication Research, 4,* 265-270.

Sinsabaugh, B. A., & Fox, R. A. (1986). Reevaluating the SLIP paradigm: A research note. *Communication Monographs, 53,* 335-341.

Sykes, R. E. (1983). Initial interaction between strangers and acquaintances: A multivariate analysis of factors affecting choice of communication partners. *Human Communication Research, 10,* 27-53.

Wiemann, J. M. (1981). Effects of laboratory videotaping procedures on selected conversation behaviors. *Human Communication Research, 7,* 302-311.

Williamson, R. N., & Fitzpatrick, M. A. (1985). Two approaches to marital interaction: Relational control patterns and marital types. *Communication Monographs, 52,* 236-252.

Wiseman, R. L., & Schenck-Hamlin, W. (1981). A multidimensional scaling validation of an inductively-derived set of compliance-gaining strategies. *Communication Monographs, 48,* 251-270.

Witteman, H., & Fitzpatrick, M. A. (1986). Compliance-gaining in marital interaction: Power bases, processes, and outcomes. *Communication Monographs, 53,* 130-143.

Zahn, C. J. (1984). A reexamination of conversational repair. *Communication Monographs, 51,* 56-66.

Zillmann, D., & Bryant, J. (1987). A response. *Journal of Communication, 37,* 187-188.

Zillmann, D., & Bryant, J. (1988). A response. *Journal of Communication, 38,* 185-192.

Chapter 4

GOALS, PLANS, AND
DISCOURSE COMPREHENSION

Charles R. Berger

IT IS IRONIC THAT COMMUNICATION researchers have expended so little energy studying the processes involved in the understanding of spoken discourse and written text. During the 1950s and 1960s, when social influence research was king, models of persuasion frequently included message comprehension as a crucial prerequisite for attitude change. Hovland, Janis, and Kelley (1953) emphasized the importance of such factors as the learning of arguments and recommendations presented in persuasive messages in the production of attitude and behavior change; although, the more recent work of Petty and Cacioppo (1986a, 1986b) suggests that only under certain conditions is such learning necessary for attitude change to take place. While a few communication researchers have been concerned with issues relevant to discourse comprehension (Haslett, 1987; McLaughlin, 1984) or have studied how well persons remember conversations (Stafford & Daly, 1984), very little communication research has been done to understand the factors responsible for making discourse and texts more or less comprehensible to consumers. This oversight is difficult to understand given that comprehension is such a basic part of the communication process. From a practical point of view, many events labeled "communication breakdowns" involve comprehension failures. Not only is message comprehension a kind of message effect, it is perhaps the primary effect that message exchanges produce.

It is true that some communication researchers have shown interest in such topics as conversational cohesion (McLaughlin, 1984; Planalp, Graham, & Paulson, 1987); however, knowing the features of verbal exchanges that are responsible for producing cohesive conversations is only a first step in understanding how persons are able to comprehend conversations. A combination of textual cues and cognitive operations make discourse, including conversations, coherent and comprehensible. Meanwhile, over the past 15 years, cognitive scientists and artificial intelligence researchers have developed a number of models of discourse comprehension and discourse production. These models and the voluminous research that has been done to test them cannot be reviewed in detail here. Instead, this chapter will focus on three main issues. First, the question of why communication researchers have spent so little effort looking at comprehension will be explored briefly. Second, some basic assumptions underlying discourse processing models will be considered and several approaches to discourse understanding discussed. Third, the specific roles played by goals and plans in discourse comprehension will be explored. At the conclusion of the chapter the implications of these models for communication research will be discussed. We now turn to answering the question of why message comprehension has not been at the center of communication inquiry.

WHAT EVER HAPPENED TO
MESSAGE COMPREHENSION?

Even a cursory examination of the research published in communication journals during the past 20 years reveals a decided dearth of studies in which message comprehension is the main dependent variable. An exception is the occasional study examining memory for conversations or interaction sequences (Douglas, 1983; Stafford & Daly, 1984) or interpretation of spoken discourse (Bostrom & Waldhart, 1988). What is responsible for this intellectual "black hole" in the communication science literature? One potential answer to this question is based on findings generated in the persuasion research tradition of the 1950s and the 1960s. Early studies designed to explore the relationship between message comprehension and attitude change frequently yielded inconsistent findings. Many times attitude change was not found to be related to recall of arguments presented in the message (Petty & Cacioppo, 1981). The inability of message comprehension variables to predict attitude change consistently may have discouraged communication researchers from examining message comprehension further.

A second, and potentially more compelling, answer to this question rests upon the notion that communication researchers have in the past exploited and continue to use theories developed by social psychologists as heuristics for their research. During the golden age of persuasion research, theories of dissonance, reactance, and social judgment were frequently used as starting points for communication inquiry. Continued flirtations with more recent social psychological perspectives, such as attribution and social cognition theories, has led to the development of a long-term relationship between the two fields. Unfortunately, however, the cognitive orientation that swept social psychology during the past decade generally has not propelled social psychologists toward the study of discourse; rather, the focus of much cognitively oriented social psychological research has been upon the biases that plague social judgment makers and the strategies that might be used to ameliorate them (Kahenman, Slovic, & Tversky, 1982; Kunda & Nisbett, 1986; Nisbett & Ross, 1980). As a result, those communication researchers who traditionally have looked to social psychological theories for insights into communication processes have been lead away from the discourse processing literature.

A final answer to the question concerns the direction of verbal learning research in the 1960s and into the early 1970s. During this period, experimental psychologists interested in verbal learning shied away from using connected discourse as experimental stimuli for reasons of control. Instead, they employed nonsense syllables or word lists to deal with the problem of the differential meaningfulness of connected discourse. Although such a move was laudable from the standpoint of experimental control, it was difficult for communication researchers to see the relevance of much of this work to their interests, which, of course, were concerned with connected discourse. As a result, this earlier work exerted little influence upon communication research.

With increases in both the speed and the capacity of computers, natural language processing by computers was becoming more of a possibility in the 1970s, although crude systems for translating one language into another by computers (machine translation) had been developed during the 1960s, but with little success (Barr & Feigenbaum, 1981). By the early 1970s artificial intelligence researchers were seriously pursuing the goal of constructing computer software capable of understanding and producing natural language. This development was at least partially responsible for motivating those interested in verbal learning to move to the study of connected discourse. As a consequence, since the middle 1970s, researchers in such areas as computer science, linguistics, philosophy, and psychology have directed their efforts toward developing and testing a variety of models of discourse comprehension and production. Because this movement has been under way for over 15 years and has been focused on understanding processes that are basic to human communication, it is difficult to see why more communication researchers have not embraced these more recent approaches. Perhaps it is simply because communication scientists have not come into contact with the literature of these areas. If this is the case, the remainder of this chapter should provide enough contact so that the importance and value of these approaches will be appreciated.

MODELS OF TEXT COMPREHENSION

This section begins by discussing some basic assumptions underlying discourse comprehension. Then, three approaches to discourse comprehension are briefly described. In the final section, the specific role played by goals and plans in discourse processing is considered.

SOME BASIC ASSUMPTIONS

The approach taken here assumes that our understanding of the world around us, including various verbal and nonverbal communication inputs, is the joint product of incoming data and of knowledge that resides in memory. The ability of persons to understand the actions, texts, and discourse produced by others does not arise solely from these inputs themselves; rather, persons must have requisite knowledge about the physical and social world in order to comprehend meaningfully actions, texts, and discourse. Without such knowledge, actions and discourse may be perceivable but not necessarily comprehensible. This assumption raises the interesting paradox of how it is possible for persons to achieve understandings of events they have never experienced before. If relevant knowledge is necessary for understanding sense data, then how can one acquire the requisite knowledge for understanding a unique situation? Schank (1982) provides one answer to this seeming paradox with his theory of reminding. He suggests that persons understand new situations by finding similarities between the new situation and general features of situations that are available in long-term memory. As a consequence, the new situation may remind persons of similar situations they have witnessed in the past, thus providing them with a basis for understanding the present, unique situation.

Although the assumption that comprehension of the world arises from the interaction of incoming data with existing knowledge seems eminently reasonable, it is not necessarily endorsed in some quarters. For example, direct perceptionists (Gibson, 1966, 1979; Michaels & Carello, 1981) argue that the physical environment provides information to which perceivers must attune themselves so that they can behave adaptively. These theorists reject the idea that incoming information must be corrected by a cognitive system in order to achieve more veridical representations of the world. They assert that the construct of memory is not necessary to explain the facts of perception. The radio, with its ability to receive various frequencies in order to pick up different signals, is seen to be a more useful metaphor for describing perception than the computer metaphor that is frequently employed to describe information processing. This position cannot be described in detail; however, one should be mindful of the fact that the assumption advanced previously is viewed with skepticism by some theorists.

If the basic assumption that comprehension is the joint product of incoming data with existing knowledge is accepted, at least two implications about the nature of "message effects" follow. First, as noted earlier, old studies of persuasion and attitude change were done under the assumption that, if persons were informed by the message and learned its arguments, they would be persuaded. In view of the position advanced here, this approach was misguided because it failed to take into account the knowledge that message recipients brought with them to the persuasion situation. In fact, recent research in the cognitive response tradition (Petty, Ostrom, & Brock, 1981) has found that attitude change is rarely correlated with the acquisition of message arguments but is frequently related to the number of self-generated cognitive responses to messages. Persons who themselves generate more positive responses to the message are more persuaded by it; conversely, persons who generate more negative responses are less persuaded. Rather than simply providing "new" information, the persuasive communication may trigger extant knowledge. The triggering of this knowledge may be responsible for the persuasive effect. Cognitive response research demonstrates convincingly the important role played by prior knowledge in the processing of current inputs and the importance of assessing extant knowledge before attempting to predict message effects.

A second implication of the basic assumption is that because persons do not have identical experiences in their interactions with the world, including other persons, their world knowledge is somewhat idiosyncratic; thus their understandings of the "same message" are likely to show variation. Obviously, persons have many experiences in common that lead them to develop common knowledge. For example, children may be told from an early age that by being nice to others they can expect others to be nice to them. Most of the time, this relationship seems to hold. However, because the relationship does not hold all of the time for most persons, and for some persons may hold very little of the time, such as in the case of abused children, this piece of social knowledge is not invariant across persons. As a result, when this knowledge becomes relevant to the comprehension of text or discourse, individual differences in understanding are to be expected. In a sense, then, there are as many "message effects" as there are persons who are exposed to a message. While the individual differences in comprehension that flow from individual differences in knowledge have been emphasized here, it is important to note that, in many routine communication transactions, there is enough common knowledge derived from common experience so that the parties involved generally achieve some degree of mutual understanding.

Some communication researchers have argued that the appropriate focus of social interaction research should be on patterns of message transactions between persons rather than on the impact of messages themselves (Fisher, 1980; Rogers & Farace, 1975), although Hewes and Planalp (1987) have discussed the potential limitations of this position. While the study of patterns of message exchanges can tell us something about relationships between people, by itself it tells us very little about the basic processes involved in message comprehension. How persons in relationships comprehend the messages they exchange is vital to understanding how they will respond to each other. However, in order to understand how persons comprehend each other's messages, it is necessary to understand how they use their knowledge of the social world and each other to process their message exchanges. Simply charting patterns of message exchanges cannot tell us very much about the meanings that persons derive from their discourse. Rather, it is necessary to examine how cognitive structures and processes interact with message inputs to produce understanding or misunderstanding.

Having explicated these basic assumptions, attention now turns to specific models of discourse processing. While several of the models to be considered have focused on the processing of narrative discourse, it is not difficult to see how some of them might be generalized to encompass other types of discourse, including informal conversations. Some of the models, for example, van Dijk and Kintsch (1983), have been cast in sufficiently general terms to subsume both story processing and the processing of social interaction. However, much of the research done to test these various models has not examined the processing of conversations but has employed stories, newspaper reports, and other accounts of action sequences as experimental stimuli. As a result, the ability of these models to explain and predict how conversations are encoded, stored, and retrieved from memory remains undetermined. Nevertheless, the potential applicability of these models to conversational processing will become apparent.

STORY GRAMMARS

Story grammars break narratives into their constituents by applying a set of rewrite rules. For example, a basic rewrite rule is that a story consists of a setting and an event structure. Other rewrite rules specify the nature of settings and event structures. The terms used in these rewrite rules are specified further by additional rules (Mandler & Johnson, 1977). Using this approach, stories can be represented as hierarchies in which more abstract story units appear at the top of the hierarchy and the details of the story at the bottom. Through repeated exposure to stories containing similar structures, persons develop mental representations of story structure called story schemata. It is assumed that when persons are faced with the task of understanding a story, story schemata that contain the features represented in story grammars are instantiated in order to achieve comprehension. Story grammars are systems for describing narratives, while story schemata are mental structures used in the processing of these texts (Mandler & Goodman, 1982). Although a number of different story grammars have been developed (Johnson & Mandler, 1980; Mandler & Johnson, 1977; Rummelhart, 1975, 1977; Stein & Glenn, 1979; Thorndyke, 1977), empirical tests aimed at examining the effects of story schemata on the processing of narratives have yielded similar findings. For example, when persons read and then recall stories, they show better memory for story units that are more abstract or higher in the hierarchical representation of the text than units that are lower in the hierarchy (Mandler & Johnson, 1977; Meyer, 1975; Thorndyke, 1977). This phenomenon has been labeled the "levels effect" in story recall. Although recall of the lower-level details of stories is less likely than higher-level units, Yekovitch and Thorndyke (1979) found that, on recognition memory measures, persons could discriminate above chance levels among verbatim propositions, false propositions, and paraphrases of propositions from a story. This finding suggests that less abstract representations of text are not lost but may be more difficult to retrieve than are more abstract discourse units. Mandler and Goodman (1982) provided evidence for the psychological validity of story structure by demonstrating that arranging story constituents in unusual orders slowed reading times significantly at the points where the unexpected units were placed.

Some types of story units appear to be recalled consistently better than others. For example, in Stein and Glenn's (1979) story grammar, story episodes consist of the sequence of events: settings, initiating events, internal states (cognitions, emotions, and goals), attempts, consequences, and reactions (cognitions, emotions, and actions). Among these events, settings, initiating events, goals, and consequences are better recalled (Mandler & Johnson, 1977; Stein & Glenn, 1979). One explanation for this finding is that events that play an important part in organizing the story are better recalled than are categories of events that are not critical to the organization of the story. A second explanation is that events that are part of a causal chain tend to be better recalled than events that are not causally connected (Omanson, 1982). A final explanation for this effect is that event types that have more connections with other events in the story, because of their centrality, are more likely to be recalled than events with fewer connections. These three alternatives were contrasted in a study by Trabasso and van den Broek (1985), who found that whether or not an event was part of a causal chain, and the number of causal connections to the event, each alternative accounted for substantial common and unique portions of variance in immediate recall, delayed recall, summarization, and judged importance of the events. The Stein and Glenn (1979) story grammar categories contributed some unique variance but showed considerable overlap with the two causal variables. Trabasso and van den Broek (1985) concluded that a story event may be remembered because of its level in a hierarchy (levels effect), its causal or logical relations to other events in the story, or its role in the episodic structure of the story. These factors frequently covary together; however, sometimes they make independent contributions to recall and summarization.

Questions have been raised concerning the viability of the story grammar approach (Black & Wilensky, 1979; Garnham, 1983), although Black and Wilensky's (1979) analysis has been challenged by several investigators (Frisch & Perlis, 1981; Mandler & Johnson, 1980; Rummelhart, 1980). The details of these claims and counterclaims cannot be dealt with here; however, Mandler (1982, 1984) has attempted to clarify the limits of story grammars. She averred that the structural approach to story comprehension never claimed to account for all aspects of processing and that such features of stories as sentence structure, word frequency, and the emotive properties of the text might also influence story memory.

STRATEGIC DISCOURSE PROCESSING

A second approach to discourse comprehension has been advanced by Kintsch and van Dijk (1978), van Dijk (1980), and van Dijk and Kintsch (1983). Their approach contrasts in a number of ways with the story grammar perspective. First, the scope of their theory is considerably wider than that of the story grammar theorists in that it deals with the processing of several different types of discourse beyond the narrative. Second, while the story grammarians emphasize the role played by story structure in the processing of narratives, the strategic approach advocated by van Dijk and Kintsch (1983) is decidedly more concerned with the role played by semantic factors in the comprehension of text. Finally, the strategic approach contrasts with algorithmic, rule-governed perspectives. These latter approaches, like generative grammars, provide unique structural descriptions of sentences when the rules of the grammar themselves are correct and applied correctly. By contrast, the application of strategic processes does not guarantee a unique representation of the text. Because strategic analysis depends upon both the characteristics of the text and those of the language user, the language user's reconstructed meaning for the text may be the joint product of cues provided in the text itself, the context within which it is presented, and the meanings that are most relevant to the language user's own goals and interests (van Dijk & Kintsch, 1983).

According to van Dijk and Kintsch (1983), the overall goal of the text comprehender is the construction of a textbase. A *textbase* is the semantic representation of the input discourse in episodic memory. Textbases are defined in terms of propositions and the relationships among them. Atomic propositions, which correspond roughly to word meanings, are organized into a propositional schema on the basis of structural relations or functions. For example, the first noun or pronoun appearing in a sentence is the subject. When the subject is a person, that individual is assigned the role of agent before the rest of the sentence is processed. Language users attempt to establish the local coherence of text by searching for relationships between facts denoted by the propositions. Kintsch and van Dijk (1978) argued that local coherence is achieved by references to the same facts by different propositions; however, local coherence may be achieved by strategies other than coreference (Givon, 1979). Texts are understood not only locally but also at a more abstract level. To achieve this global understanding, macro propositions are developed in parallel with local propositions and similar strategies are used to search for global coherence among these macro propositions. Development of global coherence enables the discourse processor to infer what the text is about by processing only part of it, for example, knowing what a book "is about" by reading only a chapter or two. Evidence for the importance of macro propositions in text comprehension has been provided by Guindon and Kintsch (1984) and Kieras (1981). In addition, Brown and Day (1983) have shown that college students, in contrast to fifth- and seventh-graders, use more sophisticated macro rules for paraphrasing texts. They also found that college rhetoric teachers were better able to combine information across paragraphs and were more likely to summarize in their own words than were college freshmen, thus indicating that the rhetoric teachers used more efficient macro rules than their less experienced counterparts. In addition to macro propositions there are superstructures. These schemata represent conventionalized forms of discourse like narratives, journal articles, debates, and TV show formats. These superstructures provide the syntax for global coherence.

Theorists van Dijk and Kintsch (1983) posit a number of additional strategies that may be used to comprehend discourse. Stylistic strategies concern the alternative ways in which the same concept can be expressed and the potential effects of these variations on the meanings that might be constructed by the text consumer. Rhetorical strategies like figures of speech may draw special attention to certain aspects of the discourse. Conversational strategies including turn-taking may also make contributions to the comprehension of discourse. Finally, the nonverbal information made available in facial expressions, gestures, body position, and proximity may provide information that augments the semantic interpretation of discourse. Although none of these strategies may be represented uniquely in a textbase, their use may emphasize or deemphasize certain portions of the text to the point that both textbase and text comprehension are affected.

In addition to the development of a textbase, a situation model is also postulated in episodic memory. The situation model contains a cognitive representation of events, actions, persons, and situations that the text is about and is updated as text processing takes place. The situation model may also incorporate previous experiences in similar situations, as well as general knowledge about such situations. While the comprehension of discourse at the conceptual level rests upon its local and global coherence, the situation model is employed to assess what the discourse means referentially. The importance of situation models in the understanding of text has been demonstrated in a number of studies (Morrow, 1985a, 1985b; Morrow & Greenspan, 1987; Morrow, Greenspan, & Bower, 1987). For example, the latter study of this series found that objects located in a room in which a story character desired to be were more accessible in readers' memories than·were objects located in other rooms. As the distance from the location room to the probed room increased, objects tended to become less accessible to readers. These findings indicate the potential importance of the spatial and temporal information contained in situational models to the interpretation of narratives.

KNOWLEDGE STRUCTURES

This approach to discourse comprehension differs, along a number of dimensions, from both story grammars and the strategic approach just discussed. First, in contrast to story grammars, the role of text structure is deemphasized. Second, in the knowledge structures approach, it is assumed that various categories of linguistic elements can be represented in the form of relatively few conceptual categories (Schank, 1975). For example, all verbs of physical movement may be

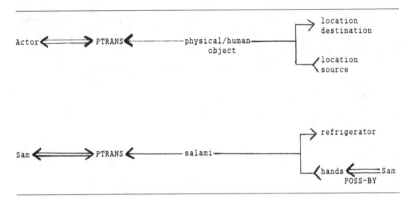

Figure 4.1 PTRANS CD Frame

represented by the expression PTRANS. Such verbs as *move, push, pull, put, walk,* and *go to* would be subsumed by this ACT. Another generic ACT in this system is MTRANS. This ACT refers to the transfer of information through communicative and cognitive acts. For example, activities like *tell, show, ask, remember, see, hear,* and *notice* are subsumed under the MTRANS conceptual primitive. Associated with each of these generic ACTS are frames that specify the arrangement of slots that are typically associated with ACTS. Figure 4.1 shows the PTRANS CD frame and how that frame would represent the sentence, "Sam put the salami in the refrigerator." As the example in Figure 4.1 shows, the conceptual dependency representation is highly general in that it can plausibly and parsimoniously represent a wide array of sentences in a single CD frame. Other CD frames, containing varying numbers of slots, are built around each of the other ACT conceptual primitives.

Schank and Abelson (1977) argued that the part of the knowledge necessary to understand such texts as narratives and news stories is organized in the form of plans and scripts. Plans are sequences of actions for achieving goals. They are relatively flexible in that there may be a number of alternative ways to reach a particular goal. Scripts are action sequences that have been enacted so frequently that they become habitual and carried out with minimal attention. They are relatively inflexible and evolve from plans over time (Galambos, Abelson, & Black, 1986; Schank & Abelson, 1977). As was previously suggested, stories almost always involve characters striving to achieve goals. Because story characters may follow plans and scripts to achieve their goals, it is assumed that understanders use their knowledge, organized as plans and scripts, to understand the intentions, motives, and actions of story characters. While the main focus of the knowledge structure work has been on story understanding, knowledge organized as plans and scripts can be used to comprehend the actions of others in ongoing social situations.

There is considerable evidence to support the psychological validity of the script construct. For example, in a series of experiments, Bower, Black, and Turner (1979) developed short stories representing such routine activities as getting up in the morning, going grocery shopping, and attending a lecture. They found that, when a story was presented out of sequence, subjects tended to recall it in its canonical order. In addition, subjects' recall errors frequently involved recalling actions that were part of the usual script underlying the story but that were not actually presented in the story itself. The tendency for persons to reorganize stories with out-of-sequence actions into more coherent sequences at recall suggests that a scriptlike knowledge structure must be involved in the process at some point. Similarly, the tendency to recall actions that are part of a script as if they were actually present in a story representation of a script suggests that persons may employ scripts to make inferences in order to fill gaps in the input text as it is encoded in memory and later recall those inferences, or they may use a script to aid recall at the time of retrieval. In either case, the tendency to fill gaps in an input text with material that is part of a habitual action sequence suggests the operation of scripts.

Other support for the psychological validity of the script construct comes from studies of differential memory discrimination for actions that are typical of scripts versus actions that deviate from script expectations. Specifically, when persons attempt to recall action sequences that are part of a script, they should have difficulty discriminating between those that were actually part of the action sequence from those that were not but are normally part of the script. By contrast, actions that deviate from scripted expectations should be more easily remembered at a later time. For example, at their 25th college reunion, alumni should show better memory for the time Professor Jones fell off the platform while lecturing than for the usual events that occurred during the professor's lectures. Research has demonstrated that persons have better discrimination accuracy for script-deviant events than for script-congruent events (Bower, Black, & Turner, 1979; Graesser, Gordon, & Sawyer, 1979).

Script actions are not only organized temporally but they also bear a causal relationship to each other; that is, events that occur earlier in the script enable later events. For example, in a restaurant script, being given a menu enables ordering, ordering enables eating, and eating enables paying the check and leaving a tip. Haberlandt and Bingham (1984) reasoned that if the causal order of script actions were reversed, processing of the out-of-order actions would be impeded. They found that target sentences describing actions were read faster when they were in the usual causal sequence than when they were arranged in a backward order. In a related study, Black and Bern (1981) reported that persons remembered sentences that were causally related better than sentences that were not causally related. Finally, the Trabasso and van den Broek (1985) study discussed previously revealed that persons showed better memory for events that were part of causal chains than those that were not. These findings provide general support for the idea that script knowledge is organized in terms of causal dependencies among script actions.

Since Schank and Abelson's (1977) formulation was advanced, the conceptualization of various knowledge structures has been altered and elaborated (Schank, 1982). In this more recent incarnation of the theory, scenes are generalized action sequences that can take place in a variety of situations. For example, the paying scene can take place in a wide variety of contexts from department stores to restaurants. Scenes are organized into coherent sequences by memory organization packets (MOPs). Thus the MOP for taking a bus might include the scenes of boarding, paying, being seated, and deboarding. Each of these scenes consists of generalized actions that may be modulated to some extent by the specific situation. For example, paying to board a bus is in some ways different from paying the check at a restaurant. Boarding a train is in some ways different from boarding a plane. The actions that are unique to each of these contexts constitute scripts that are attached to each scene. Thus, in this more recent formulation, scripts are no longer sequences of scenes; rather, MOPs organize scene sequences, and scripts provide actional details that allow contextual variations within particular scenes.

GOALS, PLANS, AND UNDERSTANDING

The previous discussion of knowledge structures focused mainly on the role played by scripts in discourse comprehension. The focus now turns to the ways in which goals and plans influence the processing of discourse. The line between plans and scripts can be somewhat fuzzy; however, it is generally acknowledged that in contrast to scripts, plans are more flexible in that they allow for alternative ways to reach goals (Galambos, Abelson, & Black, 1986). For example, because there are numerous ways to get from Chicago to Los Angeles, it is difficult to talk about *the* plan to get from one city to the other, as if there were only one way in which to accomplish the goal. Moreover, in developing plans to reach goals, persons often may have to develop subplans to reach subgoals that enable them to reach superordinate goals.

WHAT ARE PLANS?

Since the seminal work of Miller, Galanter, and Pribram (1960), the concept of plan has received considerable attention from both artificial intelligence researchers and cognitive psychologists. In their work, Miller et al. (1960) saw plans as cognitive structures responsible for guiding the production of goal-directed action. In this and later work (Schank & Abelson, 1977; Wilensky, 1983), the plan concept has been defined in similar ways, leading Berger (1988, p. 96) to propose the following summary definition:

> A plan specifies the actions that are necessary for the attainment of a goal or several goals. Plans vary in their levels of abstraction. Highly abstract plans can spawn more detailed plans. Plans can contain alternative paths for goal attainment from which the social actor can choose.

Wilensky (1983) has argued that plans are implicated in the processing of action in at least two ways. First, plans are the basis for the production of action, although Brand (1984) has pointed out that plans themselves are not sufficient to account for the production of human action. He asserts that a motivational component must also be invoked to explain action that is goal-directed; that is, it is not enough to know how to achieve a goal, one must also have the desire to achieve it. Second, persons frequently achieve their understanding of others' actions by inferring the goals that others are pursuing and the plans they are using to reach their goals. This inferencing process is not limited to perception of ongoing action; it can also be involved in the comprehension of spoken discourse and written text as well (Abbott & Black, 1986; Bruce, 1980; Lichtenstein & Brewer, 1980; Seifert, Abelson, & McKoon, 1986; Schank & Abelson, 1977; Schmidt, 1976; Wilensky, 1983). Some research has been directed toward understanding the role played by plans in the production of action (Berger, 1988; Berger & Bell, in press; Kreitler & Kreitler, 1987) and AI researchers have implemented planners to guide robot arms (Sacerdoti, 1977); however, considerably more work has been done to explore how goals and plan structures influence the processing of both observed actions and text. It is this latter body of theory and research that will be the focus here.

GOALS, PLANS, AND DISCOURSE COMPREHENSION

The central role played by goals and plans in the comprehension of both event sequences and narrative prose has been demonstrated by Lichtenstein and Brewer (1980) in a series of experiments. These researchers videotaped two different situations in which an individual was either going through the process of writing a letter or setting up a slide projector. Both situations depicted a single individual acting alone and contained no verbalizations of any kind. In a norming study, persons watched the tapes and listed, in as much detail as possible, all of the actions in which the person engaged. From the lists provided by the observers, a consensus list of actions was developed. In general, observers showed relatively high levels of agreement concerning the actions that constituted the event sequence they observed. In a second study, another group of participants was given the task of identifying actions that were performed *in order to* achieve other actions. For example, in the letter writing situation, the subordinate actions "opens desk drawer," "takes envelope from drawer," and "puts envelope in typewriter" were performed in sequence in order to achieve the superordinate goal action "types address," and the superordinate goal action of "pressing the stamp on the envelope" was preceded by the subordinates "takes wallet from pocket," "takes stamp booklet from wallet," "opens stamp booklet," "tears stamp out," and "licks stamp." Using this technique, both superordinate and subordinate actions were identified for each of two situations. These patterns of superordinate and subordinate actions were then arranged into a plan hierarchy for each of the two situations. Also, the use of this technique identified actions that were not directly related to the achievement of superordinate goals. For example, putting the stamp booklet on the desk after taking it from the wallet is simply a side action that is enabled by the stamp booklet being taken from the wallet; however, placing the stamp booklet on the desk is not directly related to pressing the stamp on the envelope. By contrast, in order to place the stamp on the envelope, the stamp booklet must be taken from the wallet.

Having identified the plan hierarchies for both situations, the researchers then had a new group of participants view the videotapes. These persons were asked to recall, in as much detail as possible, the actions that the person on the tape performed. The recall results revealed a number of interesting patterns. First, persons consistently showed better recall for superordinate actions over subordinate actions. Second, probabilities of recall of superordinate actions given the recall of subordinate actions were significantly greater than the probabilities of recall of subordinate actions given the recall of superordinate actions. Third, actions that were not directly related to the achievement of the goal were recalled less frequently than either superordinate or subordinate actions. Finally, non-goal-directed actions also tended to be recalled later than goal-directed actions. These findings support the conclusion that the knowledge used to understand goal-directed action sequences is organized in the form of hierarchical plans rather than in the form of temporal associative chains in which each action is an associative cue for the retrieval of a subsequent action in the sequence. Although the simple associative cuing model for action sequence memory can be rejected on the basis of these findings, there are a number of alternative explanations for the recall findings. For example, persons might show better memory for superordinate actions because the plan schema directs more attention to these events while they are being encoded into memory. Alternatively, the plan schema could direct memory search at recall, thus biasing retrieval in favor of superordinate events. While these findings do not discriminate between these alternatives, they do support the notion that knowledge in the form of hierarchical plans is critical to the understanding of goal-directed action sequences.

Additional experiments in this series revealed that actions depicted in the videotaped sequences that were placed out of their canonical order, as determined by the plan schema, were placed in the wrong order more frequently at recall than were actions that were presented in the plan schema sequence. Moreover, persons who were presented with the noncanonical actions frequently recalled them as taking place in the order represented in the plan schema. This reorganization phenomenon is similar to the one reported by Bower et al. (1979) in their work on scripts. Finally, Lichtenstein and Brewer (1980) reasoned that, because narratives frequently contain characters who pursue goals by constructing action plans (Mandler & Johnson, 1977; Stein & Glenn, 1979; Thorndyke, 1977), narrative representations of the videotaped sequences should produce the same patterns of recall as those produced by the videotaped sequences themselves. They tested this hypothesis by constructing story representations of the two videotaped episodes and conducting recall tests. The results of these studies replicated those obtained for the videotaped enactments, including those obtained in the noncanonical versions of the situations. These findings indicate that action plan hierarchies, like those investigated by Lichtenstein and Brewer (1980), are implicated in the processing of both generic experience and symbolic representations of such experience. Moreover, these plan hierarchies exert similar effects on comprehension despite differences in input modalities, although one might expect modality differences under certain circumstances.

Other research has demonstrated the central role played by goals, plans and goal-directed actions in memory for narrative texts. Black and Bower (1979) reported that goal-oriented narrative episodes are stored as separate chunks in the memory representation of stories. Black and Bower (1980) found that characters' actions that were successful in reaching goals were better remembered than actions that failed to reach goals. In addition, actions that were abandoned before goal attainment were less well remembered than those that were completed. Actions that were higher in an action hierarchy were better remembered than were actions lower in hierarchies. Owens, Bower, and Black (1979) reported that persons who were given information concerning a story character's motives before reading a mundane narrative about the character recalled more episodes in the narrative than did persons who read the mundane narrative but did not receive the motive information. However, persons who were given the motive information also showed higher levels of distortion in their recall of the mundane narrative; that is, their knowledge of the character's motives induced them to embellish their recall of the story beyond the story material actually presented to them. Persons not given motive information before reading the story showed fewer memory distortions.

In order to comprehend text and spoken discourse successfully, readers and listeners must "fill in" gaps left by writers and speakers. Making inferences to "fill in" these gaps makes texts and spoken discourse coherent. Writers and speakers cannot possibly provide all of the necessary detail while pursuing their discourse goals. Thus, in order to make texts and discourses understandable, persons must generate inferences while they are reading or listening. Persons cannot wait until the text or discourse is over before they make such inferences; they must be made while the particular input is being processed. Thus, while the Owens et al. (1979) study showed that persons make inferences about story characters' actions, the fact that these inferences were collected as part of recall protocols says little about the kinds of inferences that are made while text or discourse is being processed. This issue was addressed by Seifert, Robertson, and Black (1985). These researchers found that when goal, plan, and action statements were omitted preceding target sentences in stories, thus making the reader draw an inference about a goal, plan, or action, reading times for the target sentences increased. By contrast, when sentences describing states of being were omitted preceding target sentences, reading times for the target sentences did not increase. Also, recognition memory tests revealed high false alarm rates for goal, plan, and action inferences, but not for states. These findings demonstrate that persons make goal, plan, and action inferences while they read and that these inferences, together with information explicitly stated in the text, are incorporated in memory. Apparently, the inferences become an indistinguishable part of the memory representation for the narrative. This does not apply to state inferences, however.

Abbott and Black (1986) have argued that world knowledge organized in the form of source-goal-plan (SGP) units plays a central role in the comprehension of narratives. The statement "Joe had been lost in the woods for three months" might be considered the source for the goal: "Joe wanted to talk to as many people as possible." The statement indicative of a plan in this case might be "Joe decided to go to the party." Thus, because Joe was deprived of human contact for so long, he wanted to talk with as many people as possible. In order to accomplish this goal, he planned to go to the party. Abbott and Black assert that knowledge organized in the form of these SGP units is so extensive that it is frequently brought to bear when persons attempt to comprehend narrative discourse. They contrasted the recall of stories constructed on the basis of SGP units with recall for sets of sentences that were related by simple repetition of concepts. They reasoned that, if SGP units serve to organize memory, recalling one of the sentences of the unit should raise the probability of recalling the other two sentences representing the unit. By contrast, in the case of concept repetition, a similar facilitating effect should not occur. Conditional probabilities of recall showed a large advantage for the stories written in the SGP format. These results suggest that recalling the goal that a particular story character had in a story should lead to the recall of the source of the goal and the plan that the character used to reach the goal. Although the results do not differentiate between memory structure and retrieval strategy explanations, Abbott and Black provide additional evidence suggesting that SGP units are represented in memory.

The research reviewed in this section strongly suggests that memory structures built around goals and plans are implicated in the comprehension of narrative discourse and goal-oriented action sequences observed in everyday life. These structures are organized into subgoal hierarchies. Actions represented as superordinate goals in these hierarchies are better remembered than are subordinate actions that are performed in order to reach higher-level goals, and actions that are not implicated in goal achievement are less well remembered. Actions that achieve goals are better remembered than actions that fail to reach goals. As persons process narrative texts, they make inferences concerning the goals, plans, and actions of story characters. These inferences become indistinguishable from the information provided in the text, and both inferences and information are merged in the memory representation of the text. The goals that story characters are believed to be following strongly influence the ways text consumers interpret characters' mundane actions.

IMPLICATIONS FOR COMMUNICATION RESEARCH

The theories and research reviewed in this chapter demonstrate the utility of approaching the study of communication from a cognitive perspective, as advocated by some communication researchers (Hewes & Planalp, 1987; Planalp & Hewes, 1982). The mechanisms responsible for the comprehension and generation of both spoken discourse and texts are critical ingredients in the communication process. Regardless of whether knowledge is represented in the form of story schemata, atomic and macro propositions, or scenes, scripts, and plans, the important point is that world knowledge interacting with information provided by discourse and the context within which the discourse is presented are responsible for producing comprehension. Thus, in order to understand how persons comprehend discourse, one cannot simply focus upon attributes of the text or the discourse itself; rather, one must study the relationships between discourse attributes on the one hand and cognitive structures and processes on the other. Moreover, to manipulate message attributes in order to determine how they influence various judgments without a simultaneous concern for the role that cognitive structures and processes play in transforming message inputs into judgments is to engage in what is essentially a theoretically vacuous enterprise. Explaining how message inputs eventuate in judgments of communicator competence or attractiveness, for example, requires some theorizing about intervening cognitive processes; simply providing correlations between message attributes and judgments does not explain how these transformations occur.

Although much of the research reviewed in this chapter employed narratives as stimulus materials, there is reason to believe that findings derived from these studies might be generalized to comprehension processes in social interaction situations. For example, Lichtenstein and Brewer (1980) found that verbal representations of action sequences produced patterns of recall that were similar to those produced by observers of the sequences themselves. Moreover, many everyday social interaction situations are organized around goals. Persons may interact to achieve such goals as gathering information, making an acquaintance, establishing a friendship, or getting help (McCann & Higgins, 1988). And persons develop plans to achieve such goals (Berger, 1988). Once persons in social interaction situations understand the goals that others are pursuing, and perhaps why they are pursuing them, they can instantiate, from a long-term store, a plan hierarchy that enables them to predict and to comprehend the actions of others in the situation. Furthermore, the plan hierarchy helps to determine how the individual will play his or her role in the interaction; that is, the plan will serve to guide actions. This plan schema may be little different from one that would be used to process a story involving the pursuit of a similar social goal. Thus plan-based theories of social interaction may go a long way toward explaining why persons act the way they do in social interaction situations. Of course, such theories must take into account the ways in which cointeractants' inferences about each other's plans influence their individual plans (Bruce & Newman, 1978; Hobbs & Evans, 1980).

At the beginning of this chapter it was pointed out that there has been a decided dearth of communication research aimed at understanding how persons comprehend discourse. Communication researchers seemingly have done about as much as they can do to avoid studying this crucial process, in spite of the fact that early communication researchers recognized the central importance of such constructs as understanding and meaning in the study of communication (Berlo, 1960). It is one thing to assert in introductory communication textbooks that the meanings people arrive at for the actions and the symbolic representations of actions of others are important determinants of their responses to these actions and their representations. It is quite another thing to understand precisely what cognitive structures and processes are responsible for the achievement of this meaning. Instead of focusing on these basic processes, communication researchers have devoted considerable energy to studying the relationships between various nonverbal and paralinguistic cues emitted by sources and a variety of social and personal judgments listeners make based on these cues, while completely ignoring how the content of what is being said is being understood or misunderstood. This is not to say that nonverbal cues of various kinds are unimportant in the discourse comprehension process; discourse processing researchers themselves have suggested the importance of nonverbal factors in comprehension (van Dijk & Kintsch, 1983). However, in the comprehension of written texts, such cues are either absent or play a minor role and, in some face-to-face interactions, their influence may be minimal—for example, when persons pay very close attention to what the other person is saying.

In response to this line of argument one might counter, for example, that it is these nonverbal cues that pave the way for the acceptance or rejection of a message in a social influence situation, as Petty and Cacioppo (1986a, 1986b) suggest in their discussion of peripheral message processing in the elaboration likelihood model of persuasion. Certain nonverbal cues may act to increase or to decrease an audience's perceptions of a source's credibility, thus influencing the ultimate acceptance of the message. Notice, however, that this hypothetical response presupposes that the audience comprehends at some level what the source has to say, unless one is willing to take the position that nonverbal cues of various kinds *completely* determine persuasive effectiveness. Moreover, when sources attempt to achieve other communication goals such as informing or entertaining, comprehension becomes even more central. Persons cannot be informed unless they comprehend what sources are saying, and jokes are not funny unless they are understood in a particular way. Nonverbally well-polished sources who present gibberish may not be able to make audiences understand no matter how many times they gesticulate and smile.

What is called for is a balanced approach that examines simultaneously the roles played by both content factors and noncontent factors in discourse comprehension. Certainly, nonverbal signals and other stylistic features can serve to emphasize certain portions of the content of discourse, thus influencing the amount of both processing capacity and processing time that are devoted to these segments. These differentials, in turn, might affect memory for discourse in systematic ways and influence interpretations of discourse. While these are very real possibilities, to date little research of this kind has been done by those interested in discourse processing. It is this kind of research niche into which communication researchers are eminently qualified to fit.

REFERENCES

Abbott, V., & Black, J. B. (1986). Goal-related inferences in comprehension. In J. A. Galambos, R. P. Abelson, & J. B. Black (Eds.), *Knowledge structures* (pp. 123-142). Hillsdale, NJ: Lawrence Erlbaum.

Barr, A., & Feigenbaum, E. A. (1981). *The handbook of artificial intelligence* (Vol. 1). Los Altos, CA: William Kaufmann.

Berger, C. R. (1988). Planning, affect, and social action generation. In L. Donohew, H. E. Sypher, & E. T. Higgins (Eds.), *Communication, social cognition, and affect* (pp. 93-116). Hillsdale, NJ: Lawrence Erlbaum.

Berger, C. R., & Bell, R. A. (in press). Plans and the initiation of social relationships. *Human Communication Research.*

Berlo, D. K. (1960). *The process of communication.* New York: Holt, Rinehart & Winston.

Black, J. B., & Bern, H. (1981). Causal coherence and memory for events in narratives. *Journal of Verbal Learning and Verbal Behavior, 20,* 267-275.

Black, J. B., & Bower, G. H. (1979). Episodes as chunks in narrative memory. *Journal of Verbal Learning and Verbal Behavior, 18,* 309-318.

Black, J. B., & Bower, G. H. (1980). Story understanding as problem solving. *Poetics, 9,* 223-250.

Black, J. B., & Wilensky, R. (1979). An evaluation of story grammars. *Cognitive Science, 3,* 213-230.

Bostrom, R., & Waldhart, E. (1988). Memory models and the measurement of listening. *Communication Education, 37*, 1-16.

Bower, G. H., Black, J. B., & Turner, T. J. (1979). Scripts in memory for text. *Cognitive Psychology, 11*, 177-220.

Brand, M. (1984). *Intending and acting: Toward a naturalized theory of action*. Cambridge: MIT Press.

Brown, A. L., & Day, J. D. (1983). Macrorules for summarizing texts: The development of expertise. *Journal of Verbal Learning and Verbal Behavior, 22*, 1-14.

Bruce, B. C. (1980). Plans and social actions. In R. J. Spiro, B. C. Bruce, & W. F. Brewer (Eds.), *Theoretical issues in reading comprehension* (pp. 367-384). Hillsdale, NJ: Lawrence Erlbaum.

Bruce, B., & Newman, D. (1978). Interacting plans. *Cognitive Science, 2*, 195-233.

Douglas, W. (1983). Scripts and self-monitoring: When does being a high self-monitor really make a difference? *Human Communication Research, 10*, 81-96.

Fisher, B. A. (1980). *Small-group decision-making* (2nd ed.). New York: McGraw-Hill.

Frisch, A. M., & Perlis, D. (1981). A re-evaluation of story grammars. *Cognitive Science, 5*, 79-86.

Galambos, J. A., Abelson, R. P., & Black, J. B. (1986). Goals and plans. In J. A. Galambos, R. P. Abelson, & J. B. Black (Eds.), *Knowledge structures* (pp. 101-102). Hillsdale, NJ: Lawrence Erlbaum.

Garnham, A. (1983). What's wrong with story grammars. *Cognition, 15*, 145-154.

Gibson, J. J. (1966). *The senses considered as perceptual systems*. Boston: Houghton Mifflin.

Gibson, J. J. (1979). *The ecological approach to visual perception*. Boston: Houghton Mifflin.

Givon, T. (1979). *On understanding grammar*. New York: Academic Press.

Graesser, A. C., Gordon, S. E., & Sawyer, J. D. (1979). Recognition memory for typical and atypical actions in scripted activities: Tests of the script pointer + tag hypothesis. *Journal of Verbal Learning and Verbal Behavior, 18*, 319-332.

Guindon, R., & Kintsch, W. (1984). Priming macropropositions: Evidence for the primacy of macropropositions in the memory for text. *Journal of Verbal Learning and Verbal Behavior, 23*, 508-518.

Haberlandt, K., & Bingham, G. (1984). The effect of input direction on the processing of script statements. *Journal of Verbal and Verbal Behavior, 23*, 162-177.

Haslett, B. J. (1987). *Communication: Strategic action in context*. Hillsdale, NJ: Lawrence Erlbaum.

Hewes, D. E., & Planalp, S. (1987). The individual's place in communication science. In C. R. Berger & S. H. Chaffee (Eds.), *Handbook of communication science* (pp. 146-183). Newbury Park, CA: Sage.

Hobbs, J. R., & Evans, D. A. (1980). Conversation as planned behavior. *Cognitive Science, 4*, 349-377.

Hovland, C. I., Janis, I. L., & Kelley, H. H. (1953). *Communication and persuasion*. New Haven, CT: Yale University Press.

Johnson, N. S., & Mandler, J. M. (1980). A tale of two structures: Underlying and surface forms in stories. *Poetics, 9*, 51-86.

Kahenman, D., Slovic, P., & Tversky, A. (1982). *Judgment under uncertainty: Heuristics and biases*. New York: Cambridge University Press.

Kieras, D. E. (1981). The role of major referents and sentence topics in the construction of passage macrostructure. *Discourse Processes, 4*, 1-15.

Kintsch, W., & van Dijk, T. A. (1978). Toward a model of text comprehension and production. *Psychological Review, 85*, 363-394.

Kreitler, S., & Kreitler, H. (1987). Plans and planning: Their motivational and cognitive antecedents. In S. L. Friedman, E. K. Scholnick, & R. R. Cocking (Eds.), *Blueprints for thinking: The role of planning in cognitive development* (pp. 110-178). New York: Cambridge University Press.

Kunda, Z., & Nisbett, R. E. (1986). The psychometrics of everyday life. *Cognitive Psychology, 18*, 195-224.

Lichtenstein, E. H., & Brewer, W. F. (1980). Memory for goal directed events. *Cognitive Psychology, 12*, 412-445.

Mandler, J. M. (1982). Some uses and abuses of story grammar. *Discourse Processes, 5*, 305-318.

Mandler, J. M. (1984). *Stories, scripts, and scenes: Aspects of schema theory.* Hillsdale, NJ: Lawrence Erlbaum.

Mandler, J. M., & Goodman, M. S. (1982). On the psychological validity of story structure. *Journal of Verbal Learning and Verbal Behavior, 21*, 507-523.

Mandler, J. M., & Johnson, N. S. (1977). Remembrance of things parsed: Story structure and recall. *Cognitive Psychology, 9*, 111-151.

Mandler, J. M., & Johnson, N. S. (1980). On throwing out the baby with the bathwater: A reply to Black and Wilensky's evaluation of story grammars. *Cognitive Science, 4*, 305-312.

McCann, C. D., & Higgins, E. T. (1988). Motivation and affect in interpersonal relations: The role of personal orientations and discrepancies. In L. Donohew, H. E. Sypher, & E. T. Higgins (Eds.), *Communication, social cognition, and affect* (pp. 53-79). Hillsdale, NJ: Lawrence Erlbaum.

McLaughlin, M. (1984). *Conversation: How talk is organized.* Beverly Hills, CA: Sage.

Meyer, B. J. F. (1975). *The organization of prose and its effects on memory.* Amsterdam: North-Holland.

Michaels, C. F., & Carello, C. (1981). *Direct perception.* Englewood Cliffs, NJ: Prentice-Hall.

Miller, G. A., Galanter, E., & Pribram, K. H. (1960). *Plans and the structure of behavior.* New York: Holt, Rinehart & Winston.

Morrow, D. G. (1985a). Prominent characters and events organize narrative understanding. *Journal of Memory and Language, 24*, 304-319.

Morrow, D. G. (1985b). Prepositions and verb aspect in narrative understanding. *Journal of Memory and Language, 24*, 390-404.

Morrow, D. G., & Greenspan, S. L. (1987). Situation models and information accessibility. In N. Sharkey (Ed.), *Advances in cognitive science* (Vol. 2). Norwood, NJ: Ablex.

Morrow, D. G., Greenspan, S. L., & Bower, G. H. (1987). Accessibility and situation models in narrative comprehension. *Journal of Memory and Language, 26*, 165-187.

Nisbett, R. E., & Ross, L. (1980). *Human inference: Strategies and shortcomings of social judgment.* Englewood Cliffs, NJ: Prentice-Hall.

Omanson, R. C. (1982). The relation between centrality and story category variation. *Journal of Verbal Learning and Verbal Behavior, 21*, 326-337.

Owens, J., Bower, G. H., & Black, J. B. (1979). The "soap opera" effect in story recall. *Memory and Cognition, 7*, 185-191.

Petty, R. E., & Cacioppo, J. T. (1981). *Attitudes and persuasion: Classic and contemporary approaches.* Dubuque, IA: William C. Brown.

Petty, R. E., & Cacioppo, J. T. (1986a). *Communication and persuasion: Central and peripheral routes to attitude change.* New York: Springer-Verlag.

Petty, R. E., & Cacioppo, J. T. (1986b). The elaboration likelihood model of persuasion. In L. Berkowitz (Ed.), *Advances in experimental social psychology* (Vol. 19, pp. 123-205). New York: Academic Press.

Petty, R. E., Ostrom, T. M., & Brock, T. C. (Eds.). (1981). *Cognitive responses in persuasion.* Hillsdale, NJ: Lawrence Erlbaum.

Planalp, S., Graham, M., & Paulson, L. (1987). Cohesive devices in conversations. *Communication Monographs, 54,* 325-343.

Planalp, S., & Hewes, D. E. (1982). A cognitive approach to communication theory: *cogito ergo dico?* In M. Burgoon (Ed.), *Communication yearbook* (Vol. 5, pp. 49-77). New Brunswick, NJ: Transaction.

Rogers, L. E., & Farace, R. V. (1975). An analysis of relational communication in dyads: New measurement procedures. *Human Communication Research, 1,* 222-239.

Rummelhart, D. E. (1975). Notes on a schema for stories. In D. G. Bobrow & A. Collins (Eds.), *Representation and understanding: Studies in cognitive science* (pp. 211-236). New York: Academic Press.

Rummelhart, D. E. (1977). Understanding and summarizing brief stories. In D. LaBerge & S. J. Samuels (Eds.), *Basic processes in reading: Perception and comprehension* (pp. 265-303). Hillsdale, NJ: Lawrence Erlbaum.

Rummelhart, D. E. (1980). On evaluating story grammars. *Cognitive Science, 4,* 313-316.

Sacerdoti, E. D. (1977). *A structure for plans and behavior.* New York: Elsevier.

Schank, R. C. (1975). *Conceptual information processing.* New York: American Elsevier.

Schank, R. C. (1982). *Dynamic memory: A theory of reminding and learning in computers and people.* New York: Cambridge University Press.

Schank, R. C., & Abelson, R. P. (1977). *Scripts, plans, goals, and understanding: An inquiry into human knowledge structures.* Hillsdale, NJ: Lawrence Erlbaum.

Schmidt, C. F. (1976). Understanding human action: Recognizing the plans and motives of other persons. In J. S. Carroll & J. W. Payne (Eds.), *Cognition and social behavior* (pp. 47-67). Hillsdale, NJ: Lawrence Erlbaum.

Seifert, C. M., Abelson, R. P., & McKoon, G. (1986). The role of thematic knowledge structures in reminding. In J. A. Galambos, R. P. Abelson, & J. B. Black (Eds.), *Knowledge structures* (pp. 185-210). Hillsdale, NJ: Lawrence Erlbaum.

Seifert, C. M., Robertson, S. P., & Black, J. B. (1985). Types of inferences generated during reading. *Journal of Memory and Language, 24,* 405-422.

Stafford, L., & Daly, J. A. (1984). Conversational memory: The effects of recall mode and memory expectancies on remembrances of natural conversations. *Human Communication Research, 10,* 379-402.

Stein, N. L., & Glenn, C. G. (1979). An analysis of story comprehension in elementary school children. In R. Freedle (Ed.), *New directions in discourse processing* (pp. 53-120). Norwood, NJ: Ablex.

Thorndyke, P. W. (1977). Cognitive structures in comprehension and memory of narrative discourse. *Cognitive Psychology, 9,* 77-110.

Trabasso, T., & van den Broek, P. (1985). Causal thinking and the representation of narrative events. *Journal of Memory and Language, 24,* 612-630.

van Dijk, T. A. (1980). *Macrostructures.* Hillsdale, NJ: Lawrence Erlbaum.

van Dijk, T. A., & Kintsch, W. (1983). *Strategies of discourse comprehension*. New York: Academic Press.

Wilensky, R. (1983). *Planning and understanding: A computational approach to human reasoning*. Reading, MA: Addison-Wesley.

Yekovitch, F. R., & Thorndyke, P. W. (1979). An evaluation of alternative functional models of narrative schemata. *Journal of Verbal Learning and Verbal Behavior, 20*, 454-469.

Chapter 5

INFERENCE-GENERATING KNOWLEDGE STRUCTURES IN MESSAGE PROCESSING

Kathy Kellermann and Tae-Seop Lim

THROUGHOUT OUR LIVES we are literally bombarded with messages that seek to have an effect on us in some way—influencing our attitudes, opinions, or behaviors; adding to our knowledge; creating an emotional reaction (pain, fear, suffering, joy); recognizing our existence; and so on. Regardless of the specific effect(s) sought in a particular message, one constant in the production of these effects is the role of message processing and comprehension. In other words, actual messages (e.g., text and dialogue) *of and by themselves are insufficient* for changing attitudes, letting us learn new information, or having us laugh at a joke. Messages must be *processed* cognitively if *message* effects are to occur. Without cognitive processing, the symbols in the message would have no meaning; the symbols would be no different than chicken scratches or meaningless sounds.

However, assigning meaning to a message involves far more than processing the symbols by searching through memory and locating their definitions. The processing of messages requires the making of inferences that go beyond the message itself. Grice (1969) notes that what a speaker means by an utterance may not be closely related to the literal meaning of that utterance at all. Similarly, Searle's (1975, p. 60) discussion of indirect speech acts explicitly relies on the idea that "the speaker communicates to the hearer more than he actually says." For example, left largely implicit in utterances are the interpersonal aspects of meaning (Hildyard & Olson, 1978). We take as a given, as does Levinson (1983, p. 21), that "above all, understanding an utterance involves the making of *inferences* that will connect what is said to what is mutually assumed or what has been said before."

This chapter explores the role of inference-making in the occurrence of message effects. We take as a given that inferences are required when people process messages and that message effects will rest on the inferences that are made. We are *not* claiming that message effects only stem from *comprehension* of the message; rather, we are claiming that message effects stem from *inferences* made about the message *whether or not* comprehension occurs. In specific, we will explore *how* inferences are made and how various *types* of inferences affect persons' comprehension and evaluation of messages.

THE MAKING OF INFERENCES

It is well documented that persons abstract meanings from messages that are not directly available in the symbols used in those messages. Persons often know more than an utterance specifies directly (Kintsch, 1972) and often report information and ideas not directly stated in discourse they perceived (Bransford, Barclay, & Franks, 1972; Bransford & Franks, 1971; Brewer, 1977; Harris, 1974; Johnson, Bransford, & Solomon, 1973). Not all possible inferences about a given message will be made, however. Most messages would permit a *very* large number of inferences to be generated (Charniak, 1975; Clark, 1975) though the limitations on our processing capabilities reduce the number actually generated (Singer, 1980). For example, only "important" inferences are drawn in message comprehension where relevance is the criterion for importance (Crothers, 1978); that is, these inferences are required for conceptual connectivity between utterances (Graesser & Clark, 1985). Similarly, less than 50% of the possible ("correct") inferences are made by persons when faced with a conditional statement (Kellermann, Lim, Kang, Burrell, & Mulcrone, 1987). Such findings have led some researchers to suggest that the inference-making process is directed by both message producers and recipients. These researchers rely on Grice's (1975) theory of conversational implicatures that states that persons should only state what they need to state, providing neither more nor less than what is needed. Consequently, production of utterances is based on an assumption of cooperative decoding that "standard assumptions" are operating unless interlocutors expressly specify otherwise. In other words, inferences are *invited* by persons under the maxims regulating message production (Geis & Zwicky, 1971; Rips & Marcus, 1977; Rumain, Connell, & Braine, 1983). The real issue here is not whether inferences are made or that only some subset of inferences are made, but *how those inferences can even occur*. It is known, for example, that text-based inferences (those available only from the symbols in the message) are insufficient, by themselves, to guarantee the generation of inferences that permit understanding (Bower & Cirilo, 1985; Krulee, Fairweather, & Bergquist, 1979). The answer to this issue is that perceivers are using their own knowledge base to generate inferences *and* that producers of messages are *presuming* that perceivers will do so.

The knowledge being employed can come in many forms though two seem most pertinent to the making of inferences: the knowledge might be organized as a schema or it might involve use of some heuristic. Schemas are cognitive structures that represent some domain (e.g., persons, social roles, event sequences, or contexts) and organize one's knowledge about that domain. Schematic processing of messages has been demonstrated to influence inferences that are generated about those messages (Bransford & McCarrell, 1974; Dooling & Lachman, 1971; Johnson, 1970; Sanford & Garrod, 1982; Spiro, 1977). Heuristics are "rules of thumb" that provide a way of "guesstimating" inferences. For example, if a message argues that Black Monday is similar to the stock market crash before the Great Depression, a representativeness heuristic is likely to lead us to estimate the likelihood of a recession or depression to be quite high. In this case we are using a judgment of *similarity* to infer *probability*. These two knowledge structures— schemas and heuristics—provide abstractions of our experiences and knowledge that aids us in making inferences about messages.

An important point to understand, however, is that message producers and perceivers *may or may not* be using the same knowledge structures to generate inferences about a message. For any given message, a *number* of different schemas might be applied to the message to aid in the inference process. For example, persons could process a paid political spot by using a politician schema, a candidate schema, a person schema (for the particular person), various contextual schemas (for issues, locations, and so on), and the like (Louden, 1985). The "subset" of all possible inferences that can be drawn about a message will be influenced by the knowledge structures actually used to process it.

Two lines of research are pertinent to the role knowledge structures play in the generation of inferences: point of view or perspective studies and framing studies. The point of view studies typically focus on schematic approaches to processing messages while the framing studies typically focus on heuristic approaches to processing messages. Regardless, both lines of research confirm that the knowledge structures actually used to process a message alter the inferences persons will make.

Many studies have indicated that altering one's perspective, approach, or viewpoint on some message leads to an alteration in comprehension and memory of that message (Anderson, Reynolds, Schallert, & Goetz, 1977; Anderson, Spiro, & Anderson, 1978; Bower, 1978; Pichert & Anderson, 1977; Schallert, 1976). Zadny and Gerard (1974) provide a vivid demonstration of how inference and meaning is dependent on schematic processing. These researchers made a videotape of two persons searching through an apartment. Subjects in the study were variously told that they would see a videotape of persons (a) preparing for a drug bust by removing their illicit drugs, (b) engaging in burglary, or (c) waiting for friends. Events and features relevant to the schema employed for processing were better remembered, indicating that the schema that is *activated* affects the comprehension that occurs. Similarly, the activated schema will affect *judgments* one makes. Langer and Abelson (1974) prepared an audiotape of an interaction, instructing one group of listeners that it was a tape of a job interview and another group that it was a psychiatric intake interview. Therapists served as subjects in the study. Therapists using an intake interview schema found significantly more pathology in the behavior of the interviewee than did therapists using the job interview schema due to distortions in recall that were schematically driven. Two different schemas were used to process this discourse with significantly different outcomes in terms of assessment of the mental health of the interviewee.

While research on framing is less developed due to its more recent introduction (Fischoff, 1983; Kahneman & Tversky, 1979, 1984; Meyerowitz & Chaiken, 1987; Tversky & Kahneman, 1981, 1986), it makes much the same point. Kahneman and Tversky's (1979) prospect theory argues that persons encode messages in terms of potential gains or losses from their "anchored" position. When an action is in the domain of potential *gains*, persons will opt for more *certain* though perhaps less beneficial outcomes; when an action is in the domain of potential losses, persons will opt for more *risky* though perhaps more disadvantageous outcomes. For example, if offered a choice, most persons would prefer a sure gain of $100 to a 50% chance to gain $200 and a 50% chance to gain nothing; that is, when an outcome is in the domain of gains, persons are risk averse and will opt for the certain outcome, forgoing possible more beneficial outcomes. By contrast, if offered a choice, most persons would reject a sure loss of $100 to a 50% chance of losing nothing and a 50% chance to lose $200; that is, when an outcome is in the domain of losses, persons are risk-takers and will opt for the risky choice, even though it may have more disadvantageous outcomes (Tversky & Kahneman, 1986).

The thrust of this framing research is that it suggests that how a message is framed will affect its acceptability and/or persuasiveness. It is known, for example, that persons will prefer policies that either certainly save lives or offer the opportunity (probability) to avoid the loss even though more lives could potentially be saved or fewer lives would certainly be lost if alternative policies were adopted (Tversky & Kahneman, 1981). Such risk aversion in the domain of gains and risk-taking in the domain of losses obtained by simple linguistic changes ("saving lives" to "losing lives") can also be demonstrated in the framing of day-to-day economic messages. For example, a difference between two prices can be labeled as a surcharge or a discount—if the anchor point is the lower price, the difference between the two prices would be seen as a surcharge, while having the anchor point being the higher price permits the price difference to be labeled a discount. The framing of this difference in terms of the anchor point is critical in that the surcharge is then placed in the domain of losses while the discount is then placed in the domain of gains. Moreover, a surcharge would be seen as a certain loss (one would have to pay this increased amount of money if one wanted the product) while a discount would be seen as an uncertain gain (one could chose to pay the discount price or wait for the price to return to its normal anchor point). It is more acceptable to forgo the uncertain gain than it is to experience the certain loss; consequently, the difference between two prices is typically labeled as a discount (Thaler, 1980). In other words, a surcharge is seen as price-gouging by merchants while a discount is seen as providing the consumer a "good deal." It is important, however, that such a relatively minor framing difference has major effects on the inferences persons will make.

Similarly, tax policy provides *exemptions* for families with children rather than labeling the difference in tax rates as a *tax premium* for childless couples. The "exemption" is a *risky gain* forgone (consistent with acceptability in the domain of gains) while the tax premium is a *certain* loss (inconsistent with acceptability in the domain of losses). Meyerowitz and Chaiken (1987) investigated the influence of the framing heuristic in terms of persuasive message construction. These researchers found that messages arguing for a behavioral change because persons would experience *certain loss* otherwise were more persuasive than messages stressing the *less certain gains* of the behavioral change. In other words, persons are likely to find messages more persuasive if they are framed in terms of avoidance of certain losses rather than as gaining uncertain benefits.

It would seem, then, that the effect of a message would hinge on which schema or heuristic is activated for processing. What is recalled, what inferences are made, and what options are seen as acceptable are often dependent on the knowledge structures employed for message processing. What is most critical to note here is that the activation of these knowledge structures is not *strictly* perceiver-based. Certainly a message producer could try to cue particular knowledge structures or heuristics (Kellermann & Sleight, 1989). For example, cohesive devices have been argued to serve an information processing function by cuing appropriate knowledge structures for the processing of discourse (Badzinski, 1985; Planalp & Tracy, 1980). Preindexing, topic identification, and the topical relevance of utterances can also serve as cues to knowledge structure activation (Beach & Dunning, 1982; Bransford & Johnson, 1972; Krulee, Fairweather, & Bergquist, 1979). A message could be framed that argued for the *certainty* of some positive outcome from Plan A (the preferred outcome) versus the *uncertainty* of the more "beneficial" Plan B. In other words, message effects hinge on *both* the message *and* its cognitive processing by perceivers.

The remainder of this chapter will not distinguish between these two possibilities of knowledge structure activation (perceiver or message producer); rather it will be assumed that either the message or the perceiver (or both) are involved in activating a particular knowledge structure. Particular types of inferences will be examined in terms of how they arise from knowledge structures and what their occurrence implies. It should be recognized that the inferences that arise are *per se* message effects, *and* any behavioral, cognitive, or emotional outcomes these inferences foster are indirect effects of messages. As noted previously, message processing is necessary for the occurrence of message effects, and comprehension is a process that inherently requires the making of inferences. Consequently, the study of message effects would seem to require a focus on message comprehension and inference-making as these effects seem to be the primary effects of many messages.

TYPES OF INFERENCES

Many different types of inferences exist, three of which will be examined here due to their central role in the processing of messages. The role of knowledge structures in generating *causal, probabilistic,* and *evaluative* inferences from messages will be explored with the purpose of understanding what specific inferences will be made, when those inferences will be made, and how those inferences influence other behavioral, cognitive, and emotional outcomes.

CAUSAL INFERENCES

Several researchers have emphasized the role of causal relationships in representing and comprehending messages (Black & Bern, 1981; Glenn, 1978; Graesser, Robertson, & Anderson, 1981; Lehnert, 1977; Singer & Ferreira, 1983). Most of these researchers argue that the causal links underlying meaning are generally implicit or missing, necessitating causal inferences to ensure comprehension of the message. In other words, causal inferences help "bridge the gap" between otherwise seemingly unrelated utterances. Consider the following example:

Person A: Mike was injured in the accident.
Person B: Carol was up all night.

Generally, persons will make a *causal* inference (Carol was up all night *because* Mike was injured in the accident) in order to connect these statements. Indeed, comprehension of a message increases as more utterances are causally connected (Haberlandt & Bingham, 1978; Keenan, Baillet, & Brown, 1984). Furthermore, persons will take time in order to establish causal inferences when processing messages (Bower, Black, & Turner, 1979). Persons will go so far as to perceive causal relations between events even when they know that the relation between those events is completely spurious (Michotte, 1963). "It is a psychological commonplace that people strive to achieve a coherent interpretation of the events that surround them, and that the organization of events by schemas of cause-effect relations serves to achieve this goal" (Tversky & Kahneman, 1982, p. 117).

The generation of causal inferences exceeds the simple connection of utterances or sentences in a message. Slot-filling, different from text-connection, occurs when an action, event, or state is given in the message but its motivation or cause is unspecified and the perceiver attempts to fill it in. Several investigators who studied people's recall of schema-based text found that people retrieved some information that had not been in the text (Belleza & Bower, 1982; Haberlandt & Bingham, 1984; Owens, Bower, & Black, 1979; Walker & Yekovich, 1984). This information, which seemed to help construct causal chains, was so essential in comprehending the text that people could not distinguish between this inferred information and the information actually presented in the text.

These causal inferences are often schematically driven. Schematic processing offers a means for *ordering* events and filling in slots so that a "proper" causal sequence can be maintained. Stories with their paragraphs randomly ordered take people longer to read, though summaries of these stories follow the *causal* order of the action sequence (Kintsch & van Dijk, 1975). Such reorganization of a message or text to match the causal sequencing of the schema is common (Bower, Black, & Turner, 1979; Kintsch, Mandel, & Kozminsky, 1977; Stein & Nezworski, 1978). Consequently, persons not only generate causal inferences but they use these inferences to "properly organize" an event sequence in a message.

What specific causal inferences will be made? Causal inferences can be directed both forward and backward. Backward inferences (Just & Carpenter, 1978; Singer & Ferreira, 1983; Thorndyke, 1976) are similar to Clark's (1975) concept of "bridging" and link the current utterance/statement with previous utterances/statements. Consequently, the ability to make backward causal inferences enhances the meaningfulness of a message and, therefore, its perceived coherence. Forward inferences (Nicholas, 1976; Reiger, 1974; Trabasso & Nicholas, 1977) refer to predicting possible subsequent events in the message. In other words, forward inferences occur when persons infer consequences on the basis of stated causes. Forward inferences do not contribute to the perceived coherence of a message, but instead aid in comprehension of the message by activating relevant schemas.

Causal inferences are often cued by connectives (i.e., use of such words as *then, after,* and the like). For example, consider the following part of a message: "John kissed Sue then Sue fainted." The use of the connective "then" tends to cue the causal inference that Sue fainted because of the wonder or horror of John's kiss. Causal inferences need not be overtly cued, however. Because messages can only be produced in a serial manner (one word after another; one sentence after another), the *ordering* of words or sentences tends to encourage causal inferences. For example, say you were talking about the recent loss of your favorite football team and you said, "We fumbled the ball. They scored." A common causal inference would be that your team's fumbling of the ball was the reason why the other team scored, which was the reason your team lost. In addition, the nature of the words one uses will affect causal inferences. General action verbs like *destroy* are more likely to generate causal inferences related to one's intentions than are more specific action verbs like *tear up* (Kanouse, 1972). Despite such cuing, ordering, and word choice effects, however, causal inferences are also influenced in *direction* by grammatical features of subjects and objects. The subject of a sentence is much more likely to be seen as the cause of some event than is an object of a sentence. The sentences "The book was bad" and "I hated the book" spark very different causal inferences about why you gave the book away.

In sum, then, causal inferences are influenced by the nature of the message (the extent and types of cues, the fact that language is produced serially, the fact of choosing a subject of a sentence, and so on) as well as by the nature of the knowledge structure employed to process the message. These inferences serve to aid comprehension as well as to predict what will come next.

PROBABILISTIC INFERENCES

Probabilistic inferences are inferences about the likelihood or probability of some outcome. These inferences are typically made via recourse to judgmental heuristics wherein some criterion is used to *estimate* likelihood. For example, judgments that two events are *similar* might lead a person to judge the likelihood of one event to be equivalent to that of the other. A number of different heuristics are employed when forming probabilistic inferences: the representativeness heuristic, availability heuristic, anchoring heuristic, and simulation heuristic (Kahneman, Slovic, & Tversky, 1982).

Representativeness. The representativeness heuristic is a rule of thumb that uses *similarity* to estimate probability. Typically, an instance or object will be seen as more similar to a *class* of instances or objects than the class will to the instance (Tversky, 1977). In other words, asymmetry exists in the use of this heuristic. For example, a particular person will seem more similar to a general stereotype (librarian, extrovert, and so on) than the stereotype will seem to the person. Nonetheless, the more similarity evidenced, the more *likely* a given outcome will seem.

How might the representativeness heuristic affect processing of messages? The assessment of similarity might lead a perceiver to believe that the simultaneous occurrence of two events is more likely than the occurrence of the least probable event (Tversky & Kahneman, 1983). For example, persons producing messages that attempt to *explain* their behavior will often offer multiple reasons (or excuses!). The probability that the "joint" explanation is "true" is often seen as being higher than the probability that one of the offered reasons, taken alone, is true (Leddo, Abelson, & Gross, 1984). Now the fact of the matter is that the joint explanation can have no higher a probability than the *least likely* reason. To understand this principle, consider the following example adapted from Locksley and Stangor (1984, p. 473):

John D. committed suicide. Why did he do so?

1. John was depressed, lost his job, and his wife left him.
2. John was depressed.
3. John lost his job.
4. John's wife left him.

Typically, people will assign a higher probability to reason 1 than to some of the other reasons. However, if reason 2 has only a 10% chance of being true, then reason 1 can mathematically have *no higher* than a 10% chance of being true. The reason the mathematical rule of conjunction is violated is that the reasons, *taken together*, seem more *similar* to the situation of a person who commits suicide than a given reason might taken alone. Locksley and Stangor (1984) discovered that this "conjunction fallacy" is most likely to occur when the outcome is rare (e.g., committing suicide) instead of common (e.g., getting married). This conjunction fallacy in the inference patterns of message perceivers is particularly important in a legal setting where the prosecution is attempting to lay out a *series* of specific motives for a crime and the defense is attempting to rebut those motives. In essence, one would expect that multiple motives would lead juries to more decisions of guilt than single motives *even though, objectively speaking*, multiple motives can be more likely than the *least likely* motive. Indeed, the occurrence of the conjunction fallacy in jury decision making has been demonstrated (Goldsmith, 1978).

Much of the reason for this "inappropriate" inference pattern leading to the conjunction fallacy stems from message perceivers' *indifference* to the distinction between conjunctive statements and conditional statements (Fillenbaum, 1978; Taplin & Staudenmayer, 1973). Linguists have long been aware that the connective *and* is often used in daily discourse in ways that deviate substantially from the mathematical concept of conjunction (see, e.g., Lakoff, 1971). The connective *and* has been related to such connectives as *and then, but,* and *and also.* Each of these interpretations presupposes a *conditioning* of one event's occurrence on another rather than a conjunction. Indeed, Taplin and Staudenmayer (1973, p. 532) found that persons are "unable to discriminate a conditional sentence (i.e., if p, then q) from a conjunctive sentence (p and q)." This indifference to conditional versus conjunctive phrasing has been identified in terms of persons' understanding of threats, warnings, promises, and tips (Fillenbaum, 1978). Most important, this linguistic indifference has been found to underlie the occurrence of the conjunction fallacy (Kellermann, Burrell, Mulcrone, Lim, & Kang, 1987). Consequently, the use of the representativeness heuristic is likely when a message contains statements about similarity, and the use of that heuristic is likely to lead to inappropriately elevated probability judgments when *multiple* events, excuses, characteristics, motives, and so on are assessed. Employment of the connective *and* is what permits the functioning of the conjunction fallacy in such instances.

Availability and simulation. The availability heuristic is also a rule of thumb that helps in the assessment of probability, although in this case the probability of some specific event is assessed as a function of how easy it is to bring to mind particular instances or occurrences of the event (Tversky & Kahneman, 1973). For example, a person may assess the likelihood of being a victim of crime by considering past crime victims the person has known or heard about from friends or the media. The easier it is to recall such events, the higher the probability a person will provide an estimate of his or her chance of being a victim of crime.

One immediate implication of the availability heuristic is in terms of the inferences that will be drawn when a message actively attempts to aid the recall of such instances versus leaving this recall process up to the perceiver. When the recall process is left to the perceiver, far more *variance* might be expected in estimates of the likelihood of some outcome (nuclear war, floods, earthquakes, and the like). By contrast, when the recall process is *aided* by the message through the provision of specific instances, the estimates of probability are likely to be higher due to convergence in the estimation process brought on by "similar" levels of ease of recall across persons. It is interesting that life, fire, health, and other insurance industry salespersons seem to be intuitively aware of this principle; messages to buy insurance often focus on aiding the recipients' recall by "nudging" it with specific examples of catastrophe. It is interesting that tornadoes, floods, and fires are among the most *overestimated* causes of death (Slovic, Fischhoff, & Lichtenstein, 1980), suggesting the insurance industry has done an excellent job in making particular events *available* in memory for recall.

A heuristic closely related to availability is the simulation heuristic. This is a rule of thumb to estimate probability from the ease with which a scenario can be constructed by a person. While availability deals with ease of *recall* of events to estimate probability, the simulation heuristic focuses on the ease with which a mental image/scenario can be *constructed*. The easier it is to construct an image/scenario, the higher the estimate of probability of the event. Probably the most timely example of the operation of this heuristic is the estimation of the likelihood of nuclear war. At this point in time, various messages from the media and friends have provided sufficient *detail* so that *imagining* a nuclear war is within the capabilities of most people. Consequently, the estimates for the likelihood of nuclear war are probably too high. The role of messages in the production of distorted estimates of one's risk of dying through various means is particularly interesting. There is a strong relationship between the amount of newspaper coverage of a given type of cause of dying and persons' perceptions of the likelihood of that cause. For example, homicides tend to be reported three times as much as death through all types of diseases in newspapers, and persons' estimates of their chance of being murdered are higher than their estimates of their chance of dying due to a disease, despite the fact that diseases take about 100 times as many lives as do homicides (Slovic, Fischoff, & Lichtenstein, 1980). The key here is that these types of highly reported life-threatening events become *imaginable* and perhaps, eventually, *recallable*.

Anchoring. Typically, when persons are exposed to a message they have some opinion on the topic prior to hearing the message. That opinion may range from strongly opposed to neutral to strongly in favor, but the point is that few people are "opinionless" on very many topics. The anchoring heuristic is a rule of thumb that helps guide persons in the revision of their opinions. The anchoring heuristic states that adjustments should be made from the point at which a person currently is rather than trying to adopt a tabula rasa approach and generate an opinion after the receipt of each message. While this heuristic, like the others, can often be quite useful (think of where learning would be without it), it is nonetheless the case that adjustments to opinions are typically insufficient when new information is received (see, for review, Kahneman, Slovic, & Tversky, 1982; Nisbett & Ross, 1980). In particular, the conservatism effect references the willingness of individuals to alter their opinions upon the receipt of new information, with the alteration typically being in the "right" direction though not "far enough" (Edwards, 1968). In fact, the more diagnostic (e.g., useful) the new information, the more conservatism is evidenced (Slovic & Lichtenstein, 1971). Persons are anchored too strongly to their initial position. Two to nine presentations of new information are often necessary to create the opinion revision that should occur with one presentation (Peterson, Schneider, & Miller, 1965; Phillips & Edwards, 1966).

Messages having the goal of persuasion are thus faced with an important constraint given the anchoring heuristic. For each unit of opinion change desired, 10 "bits" of information need to be provided to obtain the unit of change anticipated by the first "bit." However, the importance of producing multiple messages on the same topic is highlighted by this same effect. As individuals are conservative in processing information, exposing them multiple times to different bits of information is necessary. Small group decision making thus takes on an important role. While small group decisions have often been labeled risky or cautious in comparison to *individual* decision making, the fact is that small groups tend to generate those 10 bits of information (arguments) needed to create the opinion change that should have occurred with the first bit. In other words, small groups are neither risky *nor* cautious; rather, they help compensate for the conservatism of individuals stemming from use of the anchoring heuristic (Kellermann & Jarboe, 1987).

Summary. Our examination of probabilistic inference has identified a number of heuristics persons employ in the processing of messages. Linguistic variations, the incorporation of examples, and variance in information provided are all message elements that affect the generation of probabilistic estimates. The point is, however, that these estimates need *not* reflect actual reality for persons to make them or find them persuasive. Even in the absence of specific message cuing, the similarity between two objects, events, or people, the availability of instances in memory, the ability to imagine outcomes, and the "anchor" point for opinion revision will still stimulate probabilistic inferences though the specific inference made will depend solely on the perceiver.

EVALUATIVE INFERENCES

When people process messages, more than just causal and probabilistic inferences are generated. Persons also make *judgments* of either the content or the totality of the message and these judgments are what we are calling evaluative inferences. These judgments are inferences about the *nature* of the message and not the message producer. Certainly, judgments about message producers (e.g., status, attractiveness) are frequently made by message recipients; however, evaluations of the content of messages are also quite common and are the focus of this section. While many evaluative inferences are made about messages, two seem particularly important: informativeness and coherence.

Informativeness. Messages often contain a great deal of information that varies in its relevance to a given claim, topic, or person. Message perceivers tend to use only a small percentage of the information available to them.

> The voter who examines a candidate, the clinician who diagnoses the cause of some trouble, and the admissions officer who assesses a student's prospects of success must all select the information they consider to be relevant or diagnostic for their judgments. Often, they must extract the diagnostic information from a broad data base that also contains other information that is nondiagnostic, or devoid of any predictive value for that specific judgment. (Zukier, 1982, p. 1163)

In other words, it is the rare message that would be judged to contain 100% diagnostic information.

So, how do people sort information for its diagnosticity or informativeness and how does variously diagnostic information affect judgments? Initial research on sorting diagnostic from nondiagnostic information in a message concluded that nondiagnostic information weakened the impact of diagnostic information (Nisbett, Zukier, & Lemley, 1981; Zukier, 1982). This research was conducted by presenting people with messages containing varying degrees of diagnostic information and then having them make predictions about some outcome (e.g., how much shock a person could withstand given certain background information about the person; how many movies a person would attend given background information; the likelihood that a person was a child abuser). The initial conclusion was that, when information was provided that was diagnostic of a person withstanding shock, going to movies, or being a child abuser, persons did utilize this information; however, including nondiagnostic information about the target of judgment tended to reduce perceptions of the likelihood of the person withstanding shock, going to movies, or being a child abuser. According to this early research, such "diluting" of diagnostic information by nondiagnostic information should not occur; the judgment should remain the same as persons should "sort out" and ignore information that is nondiagnostic.

Ironically, other research had already found that persons made predictions that were too extreme when they were provided only with diagnostic information and that persons were overly confident of these extreme predictions (Kahneman & Tversky, 1972, 1973). Consequently, it was *unclear* whether nondiagnostic information reduces an extremity bias of diagnostic information or whether it biases predictions downward so much that accurate predictions are *bounded* by these two cases. Nisbett, Zukier, and Lemley (1981, pp. 275-276) present a telling description of this problem:

> It is important to note some of the implications of the present work for decisions such as those made by social workers and other institutional "gatekeepers." Many years ago, Goffman (1961) pointed to the dangerous potential of case records, for mental patients and other "deviants," which contain only "diagnostic" information about the individual. Goffman's concern was that predictions based on such highly selected, exclusively diagnostic information might be too extreme and yield too confident a

judgment of deviance. Research . . . provides strong evidence favoring Goffman's presumption. . . . The present research, however, suggests that the complementary danger may also arise. If the case record, or other information available to the gatekeeper, contains large amounts of information which, taken singly, would be believed by *the judge himself* to be valueless for purposes of prediction, extreme predictions, *even when correct*, may be set aside in the context of the complete file of information. As a consequence, individuals who are a danger to themselves or others might be likely to be untreated, released, or paroled, simply as a function of the amount of worthless information about the individual which the gatekeeper happens to possess.

Consequently, the judgment of informativeness or diagnosticity of messages is an important one for it will determine what information will be retained as well as what information might be used further by a person to guide other cognitions, behaviors, or emotions.

Research that followed these initial studies provided a key breakthrough in understanding the role of nondiagnostic information on predictions. The *typicality* of the nondiagnostic information was found to determine whether it was used or ignored when making predictions (Zukier & Jennings, 1983-1984). The idea behind this research was that a pattern of *typical* behavior (even though supposed to be nondiagnostic) would be inconsistent with an extreme (i.e., atypical) outcome, hence diluting predictions of the likelihood of that outcome. So, for example, knowing that a person is a good worker, has many friends, and is a mother would be taken as being inconsistent with her being a child abuser even though each of these pieces of information, by itself, is nondiagnostic of child abuse. The key is that the *pattern* of behavior is *typical* so that the *atypical* behavior of child abuse seems inconsistent.

The movement from nondiagnosticity to *typicality* as the basis of understanding what information will be employed in judgments is particularly important given a related line of research that has explicitly attempted to determine the causes of informativeness. This research has centered on a phenomenon called the "negativity effect" (see, for review, Fiske, 1980; Kanouse & Hanson, 1972; Kellermann, 1984, 1988). The negativity effect is defined as the disproportionate weighting of negative information in comparison to equidistantly valenced positive information in the formation of judgments. In other words, the negativity effect occurs when one negative characteristic seems to be more important than an equally positive characteristic.

The central explanation generated for this effect was that negative information was less *typical* than positive information and, consequently, more informative. Kellermann (1984, 1988) argued that a "positivity effect" or a "symmetry effect" might also occur whenever positive information was less typical than or equally typical to negative information. In other words, it is the *typicality* of information that determines its informativeness. Kellermann (1988) found that observers of conversations relied on *typicality* of information, regardless of its negative or positive valence, for their judgments of informativeness. Participants in conversations used typicality as a cue to informativeness but to a significantly weaker extent than observers. Reminiscent of this finding is the *Doonesbury* cartoon where a professor finally gains the attention of a history class when he produces utterances that label various patriotic American presidents and other figures of stature as communists, Marxists, and other counterintuitive (atypical, unexpected, novel) names. Consequently, *typicality* is a key determinant of informativeness for message perceivers in an observational role (which would include listeners in some cases). In other words, message perceivers will "sort" and "process" a message according to the typicality of its statements or utterances and find *informative* those elements that are atypical.

Coherence. While informativeness is a judgment that is concerned with the importance or relevance of either the parts or the whole of a message, coherence is a judgment of the meaningfulness of a message (Kellermann & Sleight, 1989). Coherence is a critical judgment of messages, witnessed not only by the frustration of persons when they perceive a message to be incoherent but also by the extensive research conducted on the topic to date. Coherence is of critical importance because people communicate with a "coherence expectation"; that is, people are motivated to produce coherent discourse and expect that others will also produce coherent discourse (Brown & Yule, 1983). Of course, people will not always produce discourse that is judged to be coherent nor will they always judge others' discourse as coherent; rather, people *expect* themselves and others to produce coherent discourse. Consequently, even when a person produces intentionally obscure or unusual discourse, it is often judged to be coherent (Grice, 1975, 1978). In fact, persons are so reluctant to judge discourse as completely incoherent, they will often engage in considerable cognitive work to come up with an interpretation that can be judged to be at least minimally coherent (Charolles, 1983).

So how is this judgment of coherence made? While coherence has often been confused with relevance (the significance or importance of various parts of the message), cohesion (devices used to link utterances together), and other concepts, coherence is nothing more and nothing less than a *judgment*. Coherence does not reside *in* a message; rather, it is an evaluation of the state of some message. This evaluation stems from the message *meeting* message expectations, which are driven by schematic knowledge structures (Kellermann & Sleight,1989). Various knowledge structures that could apply to a given message (which could include role structures for the speaker, situation structures for the context, content structures for the message topic, and so on) are used to generate expectations for the message. If these expectations are met, then the message will be judged to be coherent.

A critical implication of this perspective is that messages need not be comprehended in order to be judged coherent. For example, most people would not judge a message produced in a foreign language as being incoherent; rather, we would presume our own lack of knowledge of that foreign language to be the reason why we fail to comprehend the speaker (i.e., we would not *expect* to understand the speaker) *and* we would presume that, given the coherence expectation, the speaker is probably being coherent. Such a judgment would be reinforced if other listeners were responsive, attentive, or otherwise indicating comprehension (an expectation of what should occur if other listeners understand the foreign language). Consequently, when failure to comprehend a message is attributed to oneself, the message will not be judged as incoherent as long as *other* expectations driven by knowledge structures are met (Kellermann & Sleight, 1989).

Similarly, a highly technical message on a topic with which we have no familiarity may not be judged to be incoherent. If, because of the situation we are in, we *expect* we will not understand a message, there is no reason for us to judge it incoherent; in fact, there is every reason (due to *matching* of expectations generated by our knowledge structures to the message) to judge it coherent. For example, consider what you would think if your spouse, who is a doctor while you are not, dragged you to a medical conference on genetic engineering. Various knowledge structures might let you infer that (a) most of the presentations will be beyond you grasp, (b) most of the presenters will use words you have never heard of let alone know how to spell, (c) most of the speakers will be highly trained medical professionals, and (d) most of the audience, being other medical professionals interested in genetic engineering, will understand the presentations. The point here is that because the actual presentations *match* what you expect to happen, you would not only have no grounds to judge the presentations as incoherent *but* you would have sufficient grounds to judge them as coherent (but beyond you). Again, the attribution of responsibility for failure to comprehend is assigned to oneself, and other inferences from schematic knowledge structures about the speakers, content of the presentations, and so on *match* what occurs in the presentations. In other words, you judge the presentations to be *meaningful* though you are incapable of determining that meaning.

Now, certainly, people are not as willing to assign blame for failure to comprehend a message to themselves as they are to assign it to a speaker. People routinely prefer to avoid taking responsibility for failure (Ross, 1977). Consequently, comprehension and a judgment of coherence are positively correlated; it is only important to remember that comprehension is not a necessary condition for a judgment of coherence. Neither is comprehension a sufficient condition for a judgment of coherence. Consider the case where two perceivers use *different* knowledge structures to comprehend the message. These knowledge structures may permit "equal amounts of" comprehension (though different interpretations perhaps) though they may also *match* the nature, structure, content, and context of the message to varying degrees. One perceiver may have had to work considerably harder than the other to "comprehend" the message vis-à-vis the instantiated knowledge structure. Consequently, one would expect different judgments of coherence from these two perceivers. It is important to note, however, that both perceivers will work hard, *if they have to*, to try to judge the message as coherent. An initial judgment of incoherence is likely to lead to further efforts to comprehend the message until the responsibility for the failure is attributed to the speaker.

CONCLUSION

Throughout this chapter we have noted the role of knowledge structures—schemas and heuristics—in the processing of messages. One's frame or point of view is critical. In addition, we have examined the making of causal, probabilistic, and evaluative inferences. These inferences affect what parts of a message may be processed, what the message will "mean" to the perceiver, and what those meanings may then generate in terms of other cognitions, behaviors, or emotions. In all cases, it is apparent that the particular knowledge structure employed is a function *both* of the message *and* the perceiver. Messages can be tailored to cue or otherwise activate various knowledge structures and thereby direct the inferential process, *and* perceivers can self-activate these structures and consequently generate meanings that may or may not be intended by the message producer.

Not considered throughout the discussion was the role motivation plays in message processing. To some extent, implicit throughout the chapter was the presumption that persons wanted to process a message, at least to some degree. In the absence of any motivation to process a message, many of these message effects probably would not occur. Under such conditions, the message recipient is unconcerned with comprehension and will fail to exert effort to produce understanding of the message. Consequently, fewer inferences are likely to be generated. In addition, when motivation is low, it is likely that only those knowledge structures directly cued by the message will be used, thus restricting effects to those solely desired by the message producer (or least contained in the message). On the other hand, high motivation may lead to the *interactive* (producer and perceiver) determination of knowledge structure use, perhaps attenuating *or* augmenting particular *desired* effects (from the perspective of the message producer).

Aside from ignoring the role of motivation in message processing, the chapter focused on effects stemming from knowledge structures that were already in place in the minds of perceivers. Messages can also *create* knowledge structures, given sufficient information, time, and/or repetition. For example, mass media messages can provide sufficient information, even with minimal processing motivation, to have perceivers construct knowledge structures (Kellermann, 1985). This "drip effect" is a cumulative reaction to similar message structures over time (Himmelweit et al., 1958) and can occur not only with entertainment programming but with commercial advertising (Krugman, 1965). The acquisition of such knowledge structures begins early in childhood (Collins, 1979) in response to the highly structured nature of most media messages, particularly television messages.

> All television products are framed in this sense, and what they accomplish is not just a portrayal of this or that scene and event and the display of this

or that set of characters. The frame, the format, the style, the time limit, and so forth all communicate the significance of the components and the meaning of their relationships, sequence, outcomes, and interactions. It is this structuring that adds communicated content to the episodes and elements of television products. It may well be that these organizations of content are more important characteristics of the messages of television than the components taken alone. (Withey, 1980, p. 13)

At issue here is the ability of message producers to create the very knowledge structures that will then provide the inferences in processing future messages. Research support exists consistent with the principle that repetitive message structuring is learned and subsequently used to comprehend mediated messages (Baggett, 1979). While these construction effects are important, a paucity of information exists on knowledge structure acquisition. Consequently, the role of messages in producing such structures is difficult to identify at present. One provocative study on this issue was conducted by Arons and Katsch (1977) in which they analyzed TV crime shows, finding numerous instances of constitutional violations and other improper police actions. These violations, however, typically went undetected by viewers of the programs, leading Arons and Katsch to conclude that the "crime/arrest procedure" knowledge structure acquired from television has "softened up" public opinion by making illegal and often brutal police behavior more acceptable. Such evaluative inferences stemming from the acquisition of knowledge structures created by messages are an important area for future research to explore and for which, at present, few valid conclusions can be drawn.

We can draw the following conclusions, however. First, one's frame and point of view will affect knowledge structures that will be employed, recall of the message, inferences that will be made, and evaluations of the message and/or the message producer. Second, causal inferences are critical to message processing and can be guided by a number of different message features. Third, when similarity is used to assess likelihood, inappropriate inferences are likely to be generated that could have serious consequences (e.g., if made as a member of a jury). Fourth, when ease of recall or simulation is used as a basis to assess likelihood, distortions can arise due to the message aiding recall/simulation or by a series of messages providing sufficient information to affect the ease of simulation/recall. Fifth, conservatism in processing of information suggests that multiple pieces of information must be provided perceivers in order for them to have a "final" opinion close to what should have occurred with far less information. Sixth, informativeness of a message is almost solely a function of typicality for observers or listeners. Seventh, coherence is a judgment of meaningfulness and not of meaning or relevance. It is clear that knowledge structures play a role in all of these message effects and it is clear that one may or may not want these effects to occur. It is certainly within the capability of the message producer to countermand many of these inferences through explicit verbal statements. For example, a message producer could provide a description of a person that makes the person sound like a librarian and then explicitly countermand the inference that there is a high probability the person is a librarian. However, the cooperative assumption of language use makes such comprehensive and continual countermanding potentially inappropriate. It seems that message producers should instead understand the likely inferences that will be made by recipients and then adapt their messages so that the intended recipients will make the inferences the message producers prefer.

REFERENCES

Anderson, R. C., Reynolds, R. E., Schallert, D. L., & Goetz, E. T. (1977). Frameworks for comprehending discourse. *American Educational Research Journal, 14*, 367-381.

Anderson, R. C., Spiro, R., & Anderson, M. C. (1978). Schemata as scaffolding for the representation of information in connected discourse. *American Educational Research Journal, 15*, 433-440.

Arons, S., & Katsch, E. (1977, March 19). How TV cops flout the law. *Saturday Review, 4*, 10-18.

Badzinski, D. (1985, November). *The functions that cohesive devices serve in conversations.* Paper presented at the annual meeting of the Speech Communication Association, Chicago.

Baggett, P. (1979). Structurally equivalent stories in movie and text and the effect of the medium on recall. *Journal of Verbal Learning and Verbal Behavior, 18*, 333-356.

Beach, W. A., & Dunning, D. G. (1982). Preindexing and conversational organization. *Quarterly Journal of Speech, 68*, 170-185.

Belleza, F. S., & Bower, G. H. (1982). Remembering script-based text. *Poetics, 11*, 1-23.

Black, J. B., & Bern, H. (1981). Causal coherence and memory for events in narratives. *Journal of Verbal Learning and Verbal Behavior, 20*, 267-275.

Bower, G. H. (1978). Experiments on story comprehension and recall. *Discourse Processes, 1*, 211-231.

Bower, G. H., Black, J. B., & Turner, J. T. (1979). Scripts in text comprehension and memory. *Cognitive Psychology, 11*, 177-220.

Bower, G. H., & Cirilo, R. K. (1985). Cognitive psychology and text processing. In T. A. van Dijk (Ed.), *Handbook of discourse analysis: Vol. 1. Disciplines of discourse* (pp. 71-105). London: Academic Press.

Bransford, J. D., Barclay, J. R., & Franks, J. J. (1972). Sentence memory: A constructive versus interpretive approach. *Cognitive Psychology, 3,* 193-209.

Bransford, J. D., & Franks, J. J. (1971). The abstraction of linguistic ideas. *Cognitive Psychology, 2,* 331-350.

Bransford, J. D., & Johnson, M. K. (1972). Contextual prerequisites for understanding: Some investigations of comprehension and recall. *Journal of Verbal Learning and Verbal Behavior, 11,* 717-726.

Bransford, J. D., & McCarrell, N. S. (1974). A sketch of a cognitive approach to comprehension. In W. B. Weimer & D. S. Palermo (Eds.), *Cognition and the symbolic processes.* Hillsdale, NJ: Lawrence Erlbaum.

Brewer, W. F. (1977). *Memory for the pragmatic implications of sentences* (Technical report no. 65). Urbana: University of Illinois at Urbana-Champaign, Center for the Study of Reading.

Brown, G., & Yule, G. (1983). *Discourse analysis.* Cambridge: Cambridge University Press.

Charniak, E. (1975). Organization and inference in a framelike system of common knowledge. In R. Schank & B. Nash-Webber (Eds.), *Theoretical issues in natural language processing: An interdisciplinary workshop* (pp. 46-55). Cambridge, MA: MIT Press.

Charolles, M. (1983). Towards a heuristic approach to text-coherence problems. In F. Neubauer (Ed.), *Coherence in natural language texts* (pp. 1-16). Hamburg: Buske.

Clark, H. H. (1975). Bridging. In R. Schank & B. Nash-Webber (Eds.), *Theoretical issues in natural language processing: An interdisciplinary workshop* (pp. 188-193). Cambridge, MA: MIT Press.

Collins, A. (1979). Children's comprehension of television programs. In E. Wartella (Ed.), *Children communicating: Media and development of thought, speech, and understanding* (pp. 21-52). Beverly Hills, CA: Sage.

Crothers, E. J. (1978). Inference and coherence. *Discourse Processes, 1,* 51-71.

Dooling, D. J., & Lachman, R. (1971). Effects of comprehension on retention of prose. *Journal of Experimental Psychology, 88,* 216-222.

Edwards, W. (1968). Conservatism in human information processing. In B. Kleinmuntz (Ed.), *Formal representations of human judgment* (pp. 17-52). New York: John Wiley.

Fillenbaum, S. (1978). How to do some things with if. In J. W. Cotton & R. L. Klatzky (Eds.), *Semantic factors in cognition* (pp. 169-214). Hillsdale, NJ: Lawrence Erlbaum.

Fischoff, B. (1983). Predicting frames. *Journal of Experimental Psychology: Learning, Memory, and Cognition, 9,* 103-116.

Fiske, S. T. (1980). Attention and weight in person perception: The impact of negative and extreme behavior. *Journal of Personality and Social Psychology, 38,* 889-908.

Geis, M. L., & Zwicky, A. M. (1971). On invited inferences. *Linguistic Inquiry, 2,* 561-566.

Glenn, C. G. (1978). The role of episodic structure and of story length in children's recall of simple stories. *Journal of Verbal Learning and Verbal Behavior, 17,* 229-247.

Goffman, E. (1961). *Asylums: Essays on the social situation of mental patients and their inmates.* Garden City, NY: Doubleday.

Goldsmith, R. W. (1978). Assessing probabilities of compound events in a judicial context. *Scandinavian Journal of Psychology, 19,* 103-110.

Graesser, A. C., & Clark, L. F. (1985). *Structures and procedures of implicit knowledge.* Norwood, NJ: Ablex.

Graesser, A. C., Robertson, S. P., & Anderson, P. H. (1981). Incorporating inferences in narrative representations: A study of how and why. *Cognitive Psychology, 13*, 1-26.

Grice, H. P. (1969). Utterer's meaning and intentions. *Philosophical Review, 78*, 147-177.

Grice, H. P. (1975). Logic and conversation. In P. Cole & J. L. Morgan (Eds.), *Syntax and semantics: Vol. 3. Speech acts* (pp. 41-58). New York: Academic Press.

Grice, H. P. (1978). Further notes on logic and conversation. In P. Cole (Ed.), *Syntax and semantics: Vol. 9. Pragmatics* (pp. 113-127). New York: Academic Press.

Haberlandt, K., & Bingham, G. (1978). Verbs contribute to the coherence of brief narratives: Reading related and unrelated sentence triples. *Journal of Verbal Learning and Verbal Behavior, 17*, 419-429.

Haberlandt, K., & Bingham, G. (1984). The effect of input direction on the processing of script statements. *Journal of Verbal Learning and Verbal Behavior, 23*, 162-177.

Harris, R. J. (1974). Memory and comprehension of implications and inferences of complex sentences. *Journal of Verbal Learning and Verbal Behavior, 13*, 626-637.

Hildyard, A., & Olson, D. R. (1978). Memory and inference in the comprehension of oral and written discourse. *Discourse Processes, 1*, 91-117.

Himmelweit, H., Oppenheim, A., & Vince, P. (1958). *Television and the child.* London: Oxford University Press.

Johnson, M. K., Bransford, J. D., & Solomon, S. K. (1973). Memory for tacit implications of sentences. *Journal of Experimental Psychology, 98*, 203-205.

Johnson, R. E. (1970). Recall of prose as a function of the structural importance of the linguistic units. *Journal of Verbal Learning and Verbal Behavior, 9*, 12-20.

Just, M. A., & Carpenter, P. A. (1978). Inference processes during reading: Reflections from eye fixations. In J. Senders, D. F. Fisher, & R. Monty (Eds.), *Eye movements and the higher psychological functions* (pp. 157-174). Hillsdale, NJ: Lawrence Erlbaum.

Kahneman, D., Slovic, P., & Tversky, A. (Eds.). (1982). *Judgment under uncertainty: Heuristics and biases.* Cambridge: Cambridge University Press.

Kahneman, D., & Tversky, A. (1972). Subjective probability: A judgment of representativeness. *Cognitive Psychology, 3*, 430-454.

Kahneman, D., & Tversky, A. (1973). On the psychology of prediction. *Psychological Review, 80*, 237-251.

Kahneman, D., & Tversky, A. (1979). Prospect theory. *Econometrica, 47*, 263-292.

Kahneman, D., & Tversky, A. (1984). Choices, values, and frames. *American Psychologist, 39*, 341-350.

Kanouse, D. E. (1972). Language, labeling, and attribution. In E. E. Jones et al. (Eds.), *Attribution: Perceiving the causes of behavior* (pp. 121-135). Morristown, NJ: General Learning Press.

Kanouse, D. E., & Hanson, L. R. (1972). Negativity in evaluations. In E. E. Jones et al. (Eds.), *Attribution: Perceiving the causes of behavior* (pp. 1-16). Morristown, NJ: General Learning Press.

Keenan, J. M., Baillet, S. D., & Brown, P. (1984). The effects of causal cohesion on comprehension and memory. *Journal of Verbal Learning and Verbal Behavior, 23*, 115-126.

Kellermann, K. (1984). The negativity effect and its implication for initial interaction. *Communication Monographs, 51*, 37-55.

Kellermann, K. (1985). Memory processes in media effects. *Communication Research, 12*, 83-131.

Kellermann, K. (1988, May). *The negativity effect in interaction: It's all in your point of view*. Paper presented at the annual meeting of the International Communication Association, New Orleans.

Kellermann, K., Burell, N., Mulcrone, J., Lim, T. S., & Kang, K. H. (1987, November). *Representativeness and the conjunction fallacy: It's Linda, Linda, and Linda*. Paper presented at the annual meeting of the Speech Communication Association, Boston.

Kellermann, K., & Jarboe, S. (1987). Conservatism in judgment: Is the risky shift-ee really risky, really? In M. L. McLaughlin (Ed.), *Communication yearbook* (Vol. 10, pp. 259-282). Newbury Park, CA: Sage.

Kellermann, K., Lim, T. S., Kang, K. H., Burrell, N., & Mulcrone, J. (1987, November). *Conditional inference and knowledge: If you know, then we won't tell*. Paper presented at the annual meeting of the Speech Communication Association, Boston.

Kellermann, K., & Sleight, C. (1989). Coherence: A meaningful adhesive of discourse. In J. Anderson (Ed.), *Communication yearbook* (Vol. 12, pp. 95-129). Newbury Park, CA: Sage.

Kintsch, W. (1972). Notes on the structure of semantic memory. In E. Tulving & W. Donaldson (Eds.), *Organization of memory* (pp. 247-308). New York: Academic Press.

Kintsch, W., Mandel, T., & Kozminsky, E. (1977). Summarizing scrambled stories. *Memory and Cognition, 5*, 547-552.

Kintsch, W., & van Dijk, T. A. (1975). Recalling and summarizing stories. *Languages, 40*, 98-116.

Krugman, H. (1965). The impact of television advertising: Learning without involvement. *Public Opinion Quarterly, 29*, 349-356.

Krulee, G. K., Fairweather, P. G., & Bergquist, S. R. (1979). Organizing factors in the comprehension and recall of connected discourse. *Journal of Psycholinguistic Research, 8*, 141-163.

Lakoff, R. (1971). If's, and's, and but's about conjunction. In C. Fillmore & D. T. Langendoen (Eds.), *Studies in linguistic semantics* (pp. 115-150). New York: Holt, Rinehart & Winston.

Langer, E. J., & Abelson, R. P. (1974). A patient by any other name . . . Clinical group differences in labeling bias. *Journal of Consulting and Clinical Psychology, 42*, 4-9.

Leddo, J., Abelson, R. P., & Gross, P. H. (1984). Conjunctive explanations: When two reasons are better than one. *Journal of Personality and Social Psychology, 47*, 933-943.

Lehnert, W. (1977). Human and computational question-answering. *Cognitive Science, 1*, 47-73.

Levinson, S. C. (1983). *Pragmatics*. Cambridge: Cambridge University Press.

Locksley, A., & Stangor, C. (1984). Why versus how often: Causal reasoning and the incidence of judgmental bias. *Journal of Experimental Social Psychology, 20*, 470-483.

Louden, A. (1985, May). *Schematic processing and political advertising: Explaining "spot" effects*. Paper presented at the annual meeting of the International Communication Association, Honolulu.

Meyerowitz, B. E., & Chaiken, S. (1987). The effect of message framing on breast self-examination: Attitudes, intentions, and behavior. *Journal of Personality and Social Psychology, 52*, 500-510.

Michotte, A. (1963). *The perception of causality*. New York: Basic Books.

Nicholas, D. A. (1976). *Toward a taxonomy of linguistic inferences in children's story understanding.* Princeton, NJ: Princeton University, Department of Psychology Library, Junior Project.

Nisbett, R., & Ross, L. (1980). *Human inference: Strategies and shortcomings of social judgment.* Englewood Cliffs, NJ: Prentice-Hall.

Nisbett, R. E., Zukier, H., & Lemley, R. E. (1981). The dilution effect: Nondiagnostic information weakens the implications of diagnostic information. *Cognitive Psychology, 13*, 248-277.

Owens, J., Bower, G. H., & Black, J. B. (1979). The "soap opera" effect in story recall. *Memory and Cognition, 7*, 185-191.

Peterson, C. R., Schneider, R. J., & Miller, A. J. (1965). Sample size and the revision of subjective probabilities. *Journal of Experimental Psychology, 69*, 522-527.

Phillips, L. D., & Edwards, W. (1966). Conservatism in a simple probability inference task. *Journal of Experimental Psychology, 72*, 346-357.

Pichert, J. W., & Anderson, R. C. (1977). Different perspectives on a story. *Journal of Educational Psychology, 69*, 309-315.

Planalp, S., & Tracy, K. (1980). Not to change the topic but . . .: A cognitive approach to the management of conversation. In D. Nimmo (Ed.), *Communication yearbook* (Vol. 4, pp. 237-258). Brunswick, NJ: Transaction.

Reiger, C. J., III (1974). *Conceptual memory: A theory and computer program for processing the meaning content of natural language utterances.* Unpublished doctoral dissertation, Stanford University.

Rips, L. J., & Marcus, S. L. (1977). Suppositions and the analysis of conditional sentences. In M. H. Just & P. A. Carpenter (Eds.), *Cognitive processes in comprehension* (pp. 185-220). Hillsdale, NJ: Lawrence Erlbaum.

Ross, L. (1977). The intuitive psychologist and his shortcomings: Distortions in the attribution process. In L. Berkowitz (Ed.), *Advances in experimental social psychology* (Vol. 10, pp. 173-220). New York: Academic Press.

Rumain, B., Connell, J., & Braine, M. D. S. (1983). Conversational comprehension processes are responsible for reasoning fallacies in children as well as adults: *If* is not the biconditional. *Development Psychology, 19*, 471-481.

Sanford, A. J., & Garrod, S. C. (1982). Towards a processing account of reference. In A. Flammer & W. Kintsch (Eds.), *Discourse processing* (pp. 100-110). New York: Elsevier Science.

Schallert, D. L. (1976). Improving memory for prose: The relationship between depth of processing and context. *Journal of Verbal Learning and Verbal Behavior, 15*, 621-632.

Searle, J. R. (1975). Indirect speech acts. In P. Cole & J. L. Morgan (Eds.), *Syntax and semantics: Vol. 3. Speech acts* (pp. 59-82). New York: Academic Press.

Singer, M. (1980). The role of case-filling inference in coherence of brief passages. *Discourse Processes, 3*, 185-201.

Singer, M., & Ferreira, F. (1983). Inferring consequences in story comprehension. *Journal of Verbal Learning and Verbal Behavior, 22*, 437-448.

Slovic, P., Fischhoff, B., & Lichtenstein, S. (1980). Perceived risk. In R. C. Schwing & W. A. Abers (Eds.), *Societal risk assessment: How safe is safe enough?* (pp. 181-214). New York: Plenum.

Slovic, P., & Lichtenstein, S. (1971). Comparison of Bayesian and regression approaches to the study of information processing in judgment. *Organizational Behavior and Human Performance, 6*, 649-744.

Spiro, R. J. (1977). Remembering information from text: Theoretical and empirical issues concerning the "state of schema" reconstruction hypothesis. In R. C. Anderson, R. J. Spiro, & W. E. Montague (Eds.), *Schooling and the acquisition of knowledge* (pp. 137-165). Hillsdale, NJ: Lawrence Erlbaum.

Stein, N. L., & Nezworski, T. (1978). The effects of organization and instructional set on story memory. *Discourse Processes, 1*, 177-194.

Taplin, J. E., & Staudenmayer, H. (1973). Interpretation of abstract conditional sentences in deductive reasoning. *Journal of Verbal Learning and Verbal Behavior, 12*, 530-542.

Thaler, R. H. (1980). Towards a positive theory of consumer choice. *Journal of Economic Behavior and Organization, 1*, 39-60.

Thorndyke, P. W. (1976). The role of inferences in discourse comprehension. *Journal of Verbal Learning and Verbal Behavior, 15*, 436-446.

Trabasso, T., & Nicholas, D. W. (1977). *Memory and inferences in the comprehension of narratives*. Paper presented at the Conference on Structure and Process Models in the Study of Dimensionality of Children's Judgment, Kassel, Germany.

Tversky, A. (1977). Features of similarity. *Psychological Review, 84*, 327-352.

Tversky, A., & Kahneman, D. (1973). Availability: A heuristic for judging frequency and probability. *Cognitive Psychology, 5*, 207-232.

Tversky, A., & Kahneman, D. (1981). The framing of decisions and the psychology of choice. *Science, 211*, 453-458.

Tversky, A., & Kahneman, D. (1982). Causal schemas in judgments under uncertainty. In D. Kahneman, P. Slovic, & A. Tversky (Eds.), *Judgment under uncertainty: Heuristics and biases* (pp. 117-128). Cambridge: Cambridge University Press.

Tversky, A., & Kahneman, D. (1983). Extensional versus intuitive reasoning: The conjunction fallacy in probability judgment. *Psychological Review, 90*, 293-315.

Tversky, A., & Kahneman, D. (1986). Rational choice and the framing of decisions. *Journal of Business, 59*, S251-S278.

Walker, C. H., & Yekovich, F. R. (1984). Script-based inferences: Effects of text and knowledge variables on recognition memory. *Journal of Verbal Learning and Verbal Behavior, 23*, 357-370.

Withey, S. B. (1980). An ecological, cultural and scripting view of television and social behavior. In S. B. Withey & R. P. Abeles (Eds.), *Television and social behavior: Beyond violence and children* (pp. 9-16). Hillsdale, NJ: Lawrence Erlbaum.

Zadny, J., & Gerard, H. B. (1974). Attributed intentions and informational selectivity. *Journal of Experimental Social Psychology, 10*, 34-52.

Zukier, H. (1982). The dilution effect: The role of the correlation and the dispersion of predictor variables in the use of nondiagnostic information. *Journal of Personality and Social Psychology, 43*, 1163-1174.

Zukier, H., & Jennings, D. L. (1983-1984). Nondiagnosticity and typicality effects in prediction. *Social Cognition, 2*, 187-198.

Chapter 6

MESSAGES AND PERSUASIVE EFFECTS

Michael Burgoon

REVIEW OF ISSUES IN MESSAGE-EFFECTS RESEARCH IN THE SOCIAL INFLUENCE LITERATURE

In their 1978 review of persuasion and message design, Miller and Burgoon discussed the apparent decline of interest in persuasion research in general and message research in particular. Although the reasons for this decline were advanced a decade ago, they seem as viable today as when initially formulated. First, they argued that in the field of communication there appeared to be more interest in faddish methodological techniques than in whether the data generated by those techniques had any isomorphism with theory, past research, or common sense. Although Miller and Burgoon were referring to the abuse of factor-analytic techniques, one need only observe the recent overuse and misuse of meta-analytic techniques to realize that this concern about methodologically driven research efforts is as valid today as it was 10 years ago.

Second, Miller and Burgoon (1978) advanced the argument (more forcefully offered by Burgoon, in press) that some researchers in the

AUTHOR'S NOTE: Acknowledgments to three doctoral students at the University of Arizona are gratefully extended. Roxanne Parrott and Brian Bateman made intellectual contributions that substantially improved an earlier draft of this chapter. Beth Le Poire provided valuable assistance in compiling original articles for this literature review. Thomas Birk provided assistance by condensing the findings and conclusions of previously published review articles on this topic area.

field believed that it was more fruitful to engage in the difficult and important task of describing "talk" or "conversation" than to do relatively trivial and "easy" systematic research with the goal of explaining and predicting more traditional concerns. Even today, some scholars seem to believe that the concern with isolating message effects does not contribute greatly to our knowledge base because of the complexity with which variables interact in naturally occurring situations. To bolster their argument, these scholars point out that the message-effects research literature in the area of social influence is replete with examples of confounded and confusing findings. Part of this confusion is the result of less than careful research methods that have been used to generate knowledge on message effects. For example, a quick perusal through the evidence literature shows that much of the early research often suffered from inadequate manipulations of critical message components (see Hample, 1978) or did not adequately separate out the effects of other variables (see McCroskey, 1969). Given that interactions between message characteristics and other uncontrolled variables are still quite common, it seems desirable to better design studies looking at message characteristics as main-effect variables.

·Another antecedent condition leading to the present state of knowledge is that too much research has been strictly variable-analytic and unguided by theoretical concerns. Careful, systematic, explanatory research in the area of message effects is essential to understanding human communication. As I have argued, one must recognize that building data sets and building theory are not synonymous (Burgoon, in press). A final related problem, which has been partially corrected but is still true to some extent, was the myopic conceptual view of people engaged in persuasion research. Miller and Burgoon (1978) argued that the tendency for most scholars to view persuasive transactions as a one-to-many, unidirectional communicative activity concerned only with measures of attitude change placed much of the research on message effects out of touch with current theorizing in the area.

Much of the research on message effects in social influence has operated at a micro level of analysis, which is the focus of this chapter. The first part of the chapter considers variables studied as part of the "rational" construction of messages designed to influence others. The body of knowledge is voluminous, if not consistent and interpretable. A second genre of research has examined variables designed to appeal to the emotions or the "psycho-logic" of intended persuadees. Here the concern shifts to examining variables with certain drive-producing properties. Like the wealth of material on rational appeals, the *pathos* strategies are full of conflicting findings, controversies, and problems. However, the body of literature is substantial enough that generalizations about message effects at the micro level of analysis can be offered. Each section will conclude with such empirical generalizations.

MICRO-LEVEL MESSAGE ANALYSIS:
AN ANALYTIC FRAMEWORK

Many treatises on social influence rely on overt expression of attitudinal or behavioral change as the sole index of persuasive effects. However, successful influence does not necessarily imply the modification or reversal of an overt behavior, nor does it always indicate change in the valence or relative attractiveness of an attitudinal statement. Sometimes, the intent of our message strategies is to strengthen an already existing attitude in receivers or increase the frequency of desired behaviors. Moreover, if we can make people more resistant to future persuasive attempts contrary to our positions, then our messages will have the desired effects, and our influence will be successful. Reinforcing existing attitudes and behaviors and inducing resistance to future persuasion are important goals of persuasion that have been neglected by the tradition of singular concern with the *effects of attempts to change people*.

Before beginning the sojourn into message-effects research literature, it is essential to provide a conceptualization of the persuasive process in order to consider what "effects" messages are constructed to achieve. First, the process of persuasion will be examined, as displayed in Figure 6.1 (see also Burgoon & Miller, in press).

It is useful to discuss this graphic display of the persuasive process for it provides the foundation for subsequent discussion of micro-level analyses of message effects. In this view, a source decides on a general issue and must determine the precise goal that will represent suasory success. This expanded view of the persuasion process recognizes that multiple effects define the success or failure of any given influence attempt. The source constructs messages comprising various propositions that are directed at different psychological processes embedded

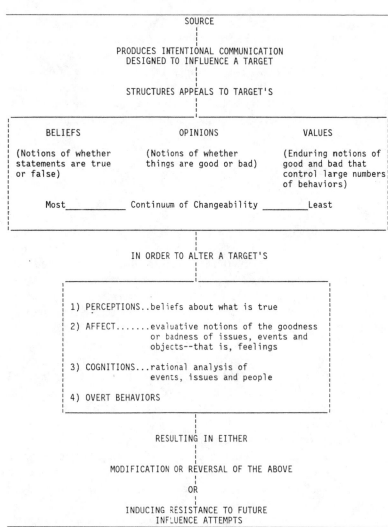

Figure 6.1 Model of Persuasive Communication

in receivers. A proposition is the verbal manifestation of the attitude that a persuader might want the receiver to accept.

The model delineates three different components of attitudes that merit the attention of persuasive communicators. First, there is a system of *beliefs* that represent receivers' views of reality or notions of the truth or falsity of propositions. The statement that careful, systematic research in the area of message effects is essential to our understanding of human communication is a statement of belief. Accepting that statement into our system of beliefs says nothing about our evaluation of that belief. *Opinions* are affective reactions. They are evaluative statements about what is good or bad, desirable or undesirable.

Values, the third component of the model, represent more enduring notions of goodness and badness that guide behavior in a variety of contexts. Values typically have been inculcated over a number of years and are usually resistant to change attempts. Because our values control so many of our opinions and behaviors, a change in one value might dictate a change in a large number of beliefs, opinions, and behaviors. Although values are very resistant to most change attempts, success in changing such enduring traits probably produces a very permanent change in people.

When using propositions to establish or modify beliefs, *perceptions* about what is true or false in the world can be altered. When appealing to *affect*, reliance upon emotional responses toward events, issues, and people is common. At other times, we appeal to the more rational side of people to change their *cognitions* or the way they analyze problems. Finally, we may be less interested in perceptions, affect, or cognition and merely concerned with whether we can obtain overt behavioral compliance with our requests. Given the goal of the communicator, any of the above can be considered successful outcomes of a given persuasive attempt.

The next stage of the model is critical to this chapter, because it identifies the possible alterations in receivers that result from persuasive communication. In other words, it identifies the range of effects expected as a result of persuasive messages. There are two possible end results of successful persuasion. As the model depicts, persuasive success may be defined either as the modification or reversal of previously held beliefs, opinions, and values or changes in overt behaviors, or as the induction of resistance to future persuasive attempts.

One of the most fundamental questions in communication is whether a persuader is best advised to construct messages appealing to people's rationality or to their emotions. We are imbued with the importance of constructing our messages to be "logical" and "rational," but just how rational must one be to secure meaningful persuasive effects? This basic argument can be traced back to the ancient Greek philosophers and stems from a fundamental difference in the way people view others. A strict rationalist would argue that humans are truly rational animals who respond most to well-constructed, logical arguments. Others claim that humans are essentially emotional beings, swayed most by messages constructed to appeal to psychosocial values.

Actually, very few scholars interested in message effects would be completely comfortable with either extreme position. Although, by convention, many writers like to characterize messages as either emotional or logical, the problem with such a bifurcation of message appeals is that it leads to the conclusion that messages are either logic-based or emotion-based. Few logic-based messages carry no emotional overtones and vice versa. Humans are psychosocial animals, and it may well be that the most effective messages combine characteristics of both types of appeals. But the question persists as to whether the best advice one can give a prospective persuader is to structure messages so as to emphasize rational appeals or appeals made to various emotions.

It should be noted that several reviews (for example, Bettinghaus & Cody, 1987; Bostrom, 1983; Burgoon, in press; Burgoon & Burgoon, 1975; Burgoon & G. Miller, 1985; Burgoon & M. Miller, in press) have examined the body of research literature in attempts to answer this question. Rather than debate what is considered a specious argument, this conventional distinction will be used only as an organizing principle to provide a synthesis of the major empirical findings concerning the use of both rational and emotional message appeals. A format and organizational pattern that has varied slightly since the early review chapter by Burgoon and Burgoon (1975) will be used, beginning with a basic examination of the questions a persuader must ask when designing "rational" appeals—that is, appeals that rely on logic, organization, and evidence for their persuasive efficacy.

MICRO-LEVEL MESSAGE ANALYSIS: QUESTIONS OF CONCERN

Several issues relating to message organization, structure, and logical arrangement have spawned interesting and useful research programs. While not exhaustive, the following questions have generated much of the micro-level analyses and previously cited literature reviews concerning the effectiveness of rational appeals in social influence attempts.

(1) What is the effect of message organization on outcomes associated with persuasive success?

(2) Are there any specific organizational patterns that are more effective in securing outcomes associated with persuasive success?

(3) Where should the strongest, most important, or most interesting arguments be placed within a persuasive message?

(4) Should a source present a small number of arguments in favor of a position or should a persuader present all possible arguments to a receiver?

(5) How often should persuasive messages be presented to be maximally effective?

(6) Are people affected by logical inconsistencies in messages?

(7) Is it most effective to draw the conclusions of arguments explicitly or implicitly in persuasive messages?

(8) Should persuasive communicators present both sides of an issue or only the side that the source advocates?

(9) Is the inclusion of evidence in messages a necessary condition for successful influence?

MICRO-LEVEL MESSAGE ANALYSIS: ORGANIZATION OF APPEALS TO RATIONALITY

Organized versus unorganized messages. One of the few areas that yields some fairly clear findings concerns the effects of message structure on behavior. When interested in belief and attitude formation as persuasive outcomes, there is some evidence that organized messages produce more comprehension and retention than do unorganized messages and thus should facilitate belief and attitude formation.

Although some studies have concluded that a structured message may be no more effective than an unstructured one, most of the research findings suggest that structured messages are more effective than unstructured ones, although this research is somewhat inconclusive about the precise effects of message organization. Beighly first (1952a) suggested that research data on verbal messages was somewhat inconclusive. However, in his review of the literature on written messages, Beighly (1952b) found clear support for the conclusion that comprehension was greater for organized than for disorganized messages. Two other investigations found that sequentially organized messages increased retention of a written message (Darnell, 1963; Kissler & Lloyd, 1973), although total sentence by sentence disorganization was required to produce these differences (Darnell). Spicer and Bassett (1976) constructed a chronologically ordered message that described the game rules of "Risk" and an unorganized message in which rules were nonsequentially rearranged. Receivers hearing the first message had higher scores on the subsequent learning task than subjects hearing the disorganized message. Investigation of verbal organization's impact on retention found that highly structured messages produced more learning than messages with less structure (Whitman & Timmis, 1975). Baird's (1974) use of summaries also found a positive effect for retention.

The majority of research has examined the impact of organization on the processes of comprehension and retention because these factors are considered the antecedent conditions of attitudinal and behavioral formation and change. However, less evidence attests to the direct impact of these variables on attitude change. Sencer's (1965) results showed that grammatical errors in messages did not affect learning but did adversely affect attitude change. In varying message comprehensibility, Eagly (1974) found that subjects in the high comprehensibility condition recalled more arguments about the topic *and* were persuaded more.

Bettinghaus and Cody (1987, pp. 141-142) reviewed the above material and agreed with the conclusion of Burgoon and Miller (in press) that, as a general rule, some use of organized structure in messages will aid in the comprehension and retention of messages. While it appears that disorganization may need to reach some critical threshold before negatively affecting comprehension and retention, lesser amounts of disorganization seem to result in decreased attitude change toward the position advocated by the source. The persuasive impact of organized versus unorganized messages on attitude change is more uncertain, perhaps because the impact on attitude change is indirect, mediated through attributions of source credibility.

Source credibility as an outcome of persuasion is often treated as a mediating variable because of its connection with more traditional outcomes such as attitude and behavioral change. Much of our persuasive time is spent modifying and changing people's beliefs and attitudes about ourselves. It follows that examining how message structure and organization affects source credibility should be important to communicators both because of its association with more traditional outcomes and as an *end product of the persuasive process* worthy of study in its own right. McCroskey and Mehrley's (1969) literature review on attitude change and organization reports that a disorganized message lowers the credibility of a highly credible source, while an organized message increases the credibility of a moderately credible and possibly a less credible source. McCroskey and Mehrley conclude that message organization may affect attitude change by leading receivers to perceive sources as more or less competent, which should be causally related to various measures of persuasive success such as attitudinal shifts and/or behavioral changes.

In conclusion, organized messages seem to result in greater comprehension and retention of the message, more positive attributions of source credibility, and—because of the mediating factors—greater attitudinal and behavioral change. If some organization is preferable to no organization, the next question is whether there are any patterns or arrangements of material that are more effective than others. For example, is the use of a problem-solution pattern more effective than a cause-effect pattern? When is it advisable to employ a deductive versus inductive pattern of organization? Although prescriptive dictums abound, systematic research efforts to answer such questions are not abundant in the social science research literature.

Organizational patterns. The next area of concern is the specific organizational pattern's effectiveness in securing outcomes associated with persuasive success. The task of selecting an organizational pattern is complicated by the quantity of available patterns (e.g., see Bettinghaus & Cody, 1987; Burgoon & Ruffner, 1974) and whether or not the selection of one pattern over another could make a qualitative difference on various outcomes. Gulley and Berlo (1956) examined inductive and deductive patterns, and compared climactic, anticlimactic, and pyramidal organization. No differences in retention were found, although some differences were obtained on specific attitude change measures.

For a long time, there has been little scientific evidence regarding the relative effectiveness of any of the *specific patterns* of organization discussed above. There is still an insufficient data base to claim conclusively that message organization is totally uncorrelated with persuasive success. Much of the research that has been done does not directly test the patterns discussed; instead, some organized pattern is usually tested against no organization at all. Darnell (1963) concluded that the critical variable in the choice of organizational pattern was familiarity—that is, any organizational pattern would be acceptable as long as it was one that had some degree of familiarity to the audience. It follows that some organizational patterns may be more familiar than others to receivers and some may seem more or less appropriate given the specific contingencies of the message.

More recently, Burgoon (in press) and Burgoon and Miller (1985) persuasively argued for the utility of expectancy theory as a theoretical calculus for examining the multitude of message effects data. The logic outlined in the original formulation of Expectancy Theory, one of the few extant message-based theories of persuasion, argues that because language is a rule-governed symbolic system, people develop sociological norms and expectations for the contextual appropriateness of language choices in persuasive messages. As Burgoon and Miller clearly state, in many communication transactions, language usage conforms to and confirms those norms, often enhancing the normative status of individuals who engage in specific kinds of language behavior. In other words, relatively rigid norms of appropriateness develop in a given language community. When an advocate attempts to alter, maintain, or reinforce the attitudes and/or behaviors of people and intentionally or accidentally negatively violates social norms governing language usage, expectations of targets are violated, inhibiting receptivity to persuasive messages.

Contingent on a number of mediating variables, such violations of expectations may enhance or inhibit the persuasive efficacy of a message, depending on whether the violation is perceived positively or negatively. Language behavior viewed as culturally or socially inappropriate represents a *negative violation* of expectations and predictably inhibits a target's receptivity to the advocated position. If a change in attitudinal position and/or behavior is advocated, the consequences of a negative violation include (a) lack of attitudinal change and/or modification of behaviors, or (b) actual movement of attitudes and modification of behaviors in the opposite direction from that desired by the advocate. If a source conforms more closely than expected to established norms, or behaves in an unexpectedly more competent manner than past history would suggest, a positive violation of expectations occurs and attitude and/or behavioral change is enhanced.

It follows that, if receivers come to expect certain basic types of organizational patterns for certain kinds of messages, then the efficacy of persuasive messages may be undermined if the organizational structures of these messages deviate from these expected patterns. For example, a policy speech advocating the adoption of a specific policy as a solution to a problem would likely follow the familiar and expected problem-solution pattern (Bettinghaus & Cody, 1987, p. 145). To the extent a source selects a less appropriate, familiar, or expected pattern, the potential success of the message may be compromised.

Receivers may also come to expect a certain degree of organization in messages as a function of the credibility of the source. On one hand, a moderately or less credible source who constructs an articulate, well-organized message may positively violate receiver expectations, increasing the effectiveness of the message. On the other hand, a highly credible source who delivers a disorganized message may negatively violate expectations, thereby decreasing the effectiveness of the message. A parsimonious explanation of the McCroskey and Mehrley (1969) findings is possible with this theoretical perspective. Simply stated, the source of a message should strive not to violate the expectations of the audience with regard to the structure or specific pattern employed and should attempt to develop lucid, well-organized messages.

A pattern of organization that has received comment but limited research attention focuses on intraindividual decision making (Bettinghaus & Cody, 1987, p. 145). Toulmin (1958) argues that people make decisions based on a fairly limited repertoire of available argumentative patterns. According to Toulmin, the strength of this representation of argument lies in its isomorphism with human cognition. Research aimed at delineating the kinds of arguments people actually use would provide the basis for identifying, on an a priori basis, argument structures that would be predicted to be positive or negative violations of expectations.

To summarize, there seems to be very little evidence to suggest that any one organizational pattern is inherently superior to any other. However, an abundance of evidence suggests that some organizational structure is superior to none. What is needed is an examination of how much of the variance in behavior is a result of message organization, the source, or interactions between the two. It could be that under certain conditions the persuasive effect of the source is enhanced by the message, or that the persuasive effect of the message is enhanced by the credibility of the communicator.

Regardless of the pattern selected to organize suasory discourse, most messages are composed of multiple arguments, claims, and kinds of supporting statements. Thus within any message there are usually some points that are stronger, more important, or more interesting than the others. Given that there may be qualitative differences in the arguments that can be used to support the main thesis of any persuasive message, the persuasive communicator must ask the question: Where should the strongest, most important, or most interesting arguments be placed within a persuasive message?

Message (argument) order. One question that has spawned a considerable amount of research activity is where the strongest argument should be placed. The answer to this question depends on whether one believes that material will be remembered best if presented first (a primacy effect), or conversely, that material will be remembered best, and most effectively, if presented last (a recency effect).

Evidence for a primacy effect was found by Knower (1936), while Hovland et al.'s (1957) investigation of the primacy-recency question obtained inconclusive results. Others have examined the more theoretically interesting question of whether communicators can predict when there will be a recency or primacy effect. Rosnow and Robinson (1967), for example, discovered a primacy effect with interesting, familiar topics, and when the message deals with controversial topics. It was reasoned that, in these situations, targets' interest is initially high and then decreases over the course of the message. Lind (1982) demonstrated that a primacy effect is likely to obtain when the receiver's primary goal is to make a decision about a person's character. This is consistent with the first-impression literature, which indicates that judgments of others are formed rapidly and based on limited information (Burgoon & Saine, 1978).

Kanouse and Abelson (1967) varied the use of positive and negative statements in persuasive communication, as well as the strength of these statements, and found no significant effects associated with strength and valence of the statements. However, when a message had a strong negative argument and a weak positive argument, an effect was obtained for placing the strong negative argument first. When the message combined a weak negative argument and a strong positive argument, the strong positive argument was more effective delineated second.

Summarizing past investigations of message-order effects, Bettinghaus and Cody (1987), Burgoon and Bettinghaus (1980), and Burgoon and M. Miller (in press) have all concluded that both climactic and anticlimactic order is more preferable to pyramidal order, but the majority of studies indicate no main effect due exclusively to primacy versus recency. Order effects, however, are only one of a host of variables that seem to affect receivers' attention, comprehension, and degree of yielding to messages. In summary, the above review articles found recency effects when receivers are evaluating general issues, or when issues are less interesting, unfamiliar, but important. Primacy effects are expected for more interesting or familiar material, less important issues, and controversial topics. For the latter, motivation to attend to message is maximal during early stages of the message but decreases over time.

The first question a persuader must ask, given multiple arguments of unequal quality, is where to put the strongest, most important, or most interesting arguments within the message? Given that there are often multiple arguments varying in degree of interest, relevance, and salience to receivers, a closely related question is this: Should a source present a small number of high-quality arguments in favor of a position or should a persuader present all possible arguments to a target?

Number of arguments. The number of arguments in a message has been found to increase the reader's level of comprehension (Stone, 1983). However, it is less clear whether these arguments were also qualitatively different. One would suspect that the inclusion of less relevant, less salient, and uninteresting arguments just for the sake of quantity might distract from the message and decrease receivers' comprehension.

Petty and Cacioppo (1984) found that message quality interacted with receiver involvement to affect attitude change. Subjects low in involvement were persuaded more by messages with a greater number of arguments, whereas high-involvement subjects found fewer, high-quality arguments more persuasive. This supports the quality over quantity approach for highly involved subjects while the obverse appears in cases with low-involvement targets. Norman (1976) found that when the source of a message was perceived to be an "expert," the inclusion of a larger number of arguments significantly increased the amount of attitude change. When the source was perceived as physically attractive, however, increasing the number of arguments did not significantly affect attitude change scores.

To summarize, it appears that, when receivers are highly involved in an issue, suasory effectiveness is enhanced by emphasizing quality over quantity of arguments. When receivers are less involved (and, therefore, less motivated to think about and evaluate each argument), then messages are more likely to be persuasive if messages are composed of multiple arguments. In addition, to the extent that expert sources are expected to provide adequate arguments and evidence to support their positions, then the omission of such arguments can undermine persuasive success. Future research is warranted to examine speculations that less credible sources, or highly attractive nonexperts, may achieve success with quantitatively fewer or qualitatively inferior arguments.

Another closely related question awaiting investigation deals not with the number of arguments in the message but with the number of exposures to the message. In other words, how often should persuasive messages be presented to be maximally effective?

Repetition of message components. The studies of Cacioppo and Petty (1979, 1980), Grass and Wallace (1969), Gorn and Goldberg (1980), Greenberg and Suttoni (1973), Krugman (1968), Mayeux (1984), Miller (1976), Ray and Sawyer (1971), Ray, Sawyer, and Strong (1971), and Wilson and Miller (1968) conclude that multiple exposure to persuasive messages is superior to a single exposure but, at some point (around five), a satiation point is reached and a diminishing returns syndrome occurs. In some research, this was manifested in increased retention but decreased attitude change. With few exceptions, the majority of research on frequency effects has been conducted in the areas of advertising and marketing in which reach and frequency are crucial theoretical and practical considerations. However, political campaigners and wellness promoters may be well advised to consider the issue of message repetition, and systematic research is needed to recommend the optimal number of exposures to such messages.

Another general issue in determining how to structure messages is whether appeals should follow a *strictly* logical pattern; in other words, to what extent are people affected by logical inconsistencies in messages?

Logical inconsistencies. It has long been assumed that people are capable of recognizing logically valid arguments and are, indeed, rational enough to be persuaded by such logically presented persuasive messages. There is some evidence to support the former presumption.

Nesdale, Tunmer, and Clover (1985) showed that children as young as five years of age can detect logical inconsistencies in messages, provided the communication does not exceed their processing capacity. Stewart (1961) has shown that people have at least a general idea as to what constitutes a logical argument, although errors in judging validity seem to increase with the complexity of the logical arrangement (Steinfatt, Miller, & Bettinghaus, 1974).

The research evidence indicates, however, that logical validity does not lead to more persuasion than messages containing logical inconsistencies. Miller (1969), in a review of the literature, claimed that people have a tendency to accept arguments that the formal rules of logic would declare invalid, while others argue that persuasive effectiveness may be contingent upon the appearance, rather than the actual presence, of logic. In attempting to explain why prior attitude toward the topic is more important than pure logical structure, McGuire (1960) argues that in making logical judgments people try to maintain attitudinal consistency. This explanation is supported by Lefford (1946), who demonstrated that individuals' mistakes in judging the validity of syllogisms are biased toward the concluding statement in the direction they initially held.

If McGuire's explanation is correct, not only should illogical arrangements be selectively perceived as a function of prior attitude but the acceptance of logically valid messages should also be influenced by the desire to maintain attitudinal consistency. Feather (1964) found that people judged a formal syllogism to be logically valid when they agreed with the conclusion. Several studies concur with the findings of Feather (Janis & Frick, 1943; Morgan & Morton, 1953; Thouless, 1959) that prior attitudes are potent predictors of how people are likely to respond to logical and illogical messages. Again, the use of logic appears to interact with perceptions of the source. For example, Bettinghaus, Miller, and Steinfatt (1970) found that more attitude change occurred when syllogistic reasoning is attributed to a positive source than when it is attributed to a negative source.

Overall, the bulk of the research seems to support the view that, if prior attitudes or beliefs of the audience are in agreement with the position advocated in the message, then logically valid arrangement may be less important because people may develop "psycho-logical" structure in order to arrive at conclusions that are consistent with their prior attitudes. However, if the audience holds prior attitudes that are discordant with the position advocated, then a simple, logically valid argument attributed to a positive source may be most effective. It may be that credible sources are expected to play by the rules of formal logic; if their messages do not meet formal logical standards, persuasive success may be hindered. Less credible sources may be obligated to use logical appeals in order to be seen as competent communicators.

In developing a persuasive argument, the source has the choice of explicitly drawing the conclusions of arguments or using implicit conclusions that allow the audience to arrive at the conclusion through their own logical processes. Thus a salient question is this: Is it better to draw the conclusions of arguments explicitly or implicitly?

Implicit or explicit conclusions. The issue of whether to draw explicit conclusions at the end of a speech was examined in an often cited study by Hovland and Mandell (1952), who discovered that explicit were more effective than implicit conclusions. Others have found that drawing explicit conclusions was more effective regardless of prior audience commitment (Tubbs, 1968; Weiss & Steenbock, 1965). Thistlewaite, de Haan, and Kamenetzky (1955) discovered, however, that when understanding of the message was held constant, drawing explicit conclusions was not an important factor. One function of explicit conclusion drawing, it appears, is to help the target *understand* exactly what claim or course of action is being advocated by the would-be persuader.

When using implicit conclusions, persuaders must be cautious in assuming the audience will draw the "correct" conclusion from the data. It follows from the discussion of logical inconsistencies that, when sources use implicit conclusions, receivers may selectively draw conclusions that are consistent with their own attitudes and inconsistent with the desired course of action being advanced by the advocate. If there is potential for receivers to make incorrect conclusions, and explicit conclusions appear to be more effective regardless of initial position, one might conclude that explicit conclusion-drawing should be the strategy of choice. The core issue, however, is whether receivers will negatively react to the explicit restatement of "self-evident" conclusions. With the use of explicit conclusions, there is potential for receivers to perceive that the source is "talking down" to them, thereby producing reactance. In summary, then, the best advice regarding the use of implicit or explicit conclusions is to proceed with some caution.

If the conclusions that should be drawn from arguments appear self-evident and receivers are in agreement with the position advocated in the message, then the use of implicit conclusions may be most effective. If, however, the message contains complex arguments or claims that may be discordant with beliefs and attitudes of receivers, it may be advisable to draw explicit conclusions for receivers.

No message exists in a persuasive vacuum. Almost all arguments and positions advocated by individuals have opposite justifiable positions advanced by others. Thus another issue of concern is whether the source of a persuasive message should present both sides of an issue or only the side advocated by the would-be persuader.

Message-sidedness. Given that persuasive claims may be argued from two sides, the location of opposing arguments is vital to the structuring of messages. The Hovland group at Yale conducted several class studies on military personnel during World War II and discovered that a one-sided presentation was more persuasive for men with lower educational attainment, and for men who were initially in agreement with the position advocated by the message, while two-sided messages were more effective with men with at least some high school education (Hovland, Lumsdaine, & Sheffield, 1949). Lumsdaine and Janis (1953) followed this research with a study revealing that people in agreement with the claim being advanced were more persuaded by one-sided messages. Conversely, two-sided messages were more persuasive for people who were initially in opposition to the position advocated by the message.

Recent research by Chebat and Picard (1985) found that personal involvement was the mediating variable in consumers' confidence about a product and one-sided messages about price. Varying the message-sidedness has also been tested to investigate the extent to which print ads are informative (Earl & Pride, 1980). Weston (1967) argued that a two-sided message is most effective if audience members have information about the opposing sides, or if it is possible that they will become aware of opposing arguments.

The multitude of findings to date lead to several generalizations that summarize the research concerning message-sidedness (Bettinghaus & Cody, 1987; Burgoon & M. Miller, in press). Two-sided messages tend to be more effective with people who have more formal education, regardless of their initial position. In addition, two-sided messages tend to be more effective when the audience initially disagrees with the persuader's position. If the audience has been previously exposed to opposing arguments, or if they will be exposed to opposing arguments, then a two-sided message is more likely to be persuasive. When constructing two-sided messages it is more effective to present supporting arguments first and then refute opposing arguments. One-sided messages are more effective when the receiver is in agreement with the source, provided that the receiver is not likely to be exposed to later messages opposing the position advocated in the previous one-sided message.

Some would argue that it is a myth to believe that the inclusion of evidence in itself will necessarily increase the persuasiveness of a message. Thus a persuader must consider whether the inclusion of evidence in messages is a necessary condition for successful influence.

Evidence. There is relatively little research that directly tests the relationship between use of evidence and persuasive success in the existing literature. Reviews by McCroskey (1969) and McGuire (1969) include less than two dozen studies. McCroskey's (1969) review led to the erroneous, or at least less than useful, conclusion that the relationship between the use of evidence and attitude change was so complicated as to defy valid conclusions. McCroskey suggested that the previous evidence research had produced no definitive answers concerning the effects of evidence on attitude change. However, most of the studies reviewed by McCroskey have major theoretical or methodological shortcomings. Many of these studies employed college students as a data base, examined evidence as a secondary theoretical concern, employed overly complicated designs that undermined the interpretability of the findings, and/or the potential main effects of evidence were overridden by interactions with other variables.

Another source of confusion considers the repeated use of "no evidence" manipulations. However, Hample (1978) has since pointed out that any argument without the explicit use of evidence inherently has implied evidence that is provided by receivers. Thus many of the early studies were comparing the explicit use of source-provided evidence with implicit use of evidence constructed by targets rather than the purported "no evidence" manipulations.

Recognizing these flaws, McCroskey, to his credit, engaged in programmatic research to provide more detailed analysis of the effects of evidence. This program of research as well as evidence taken from prior research resulted in six generalizations about the effective use of evidence to produce both short- and long-term attitudinal effects (see McCroskey, 1969, pp. 175-176).

A more current and detailed review by Reynolds and Burgoon (1983) concurs with, adds to, and takes exception with previous conclusions about the effective use of evidence. The following propositions advanced by Reynolds and Burgoon represent a current articulation of the state of the knowledge about the effective use of evidence in persuasive messages. The first propositions concerned the simple effects of including evidence in persuasive messages. They claim research support for the conclusion that the use of evidence produces more attitude change than either the use of no evidence or the use of simple source assertions.

In addition to the research on attitude change, several studies have reported that use of evidence enhances advocate credibility. The citation of evidence by a moderate to low credibility advocate increases the advocate's credibility and success in persuasion. In addition, use of evidence from a highly credible source will, over time, further increase an advocate's credibility.

A second set of propositions deals with the use of citations attributed to various kinds of sources. Concerning the use of citations as evidence and their impact on persuasive outcomes, Reynolds and Burgoon advanced several propositions. In reviewing this literature, they concluded that the use of irrelevant evidence from poorly qualified sources will produce counter to advocated attitude change, regardless of the credibility of the advocate. Moreover, failure to use relevant evidence by qualified sources may produce counter-to-advocated attitude change for low to moderately credible advocates.

In sequential message situations, failure to include evidentiary citations in a message following a prior message containing evidence and expressing opposing views will result in lowered credibility ratings for the last advocate. Also, the use of evidence citations produces more attitude change when the evidence source and the evidence source's qualifications are provided, or when evidence is presented without a source citation, than when evidence is presented with just the source identification. Finally, placing citations of less credible evidence sources after the evidence improves acceptance of a message more than when citing less credible sources prior to presentation of evidence.

Some inconsistent findings in early studies were purportedly a result of receivers' prior knowledge or attitudes toward topics. Subsequent research demonstrated that use of evidence results in attitude change when receivers have no prior knowledge of the evidence. It was also discovered that the use of evidence increases attitude change over time—regardless of the credibility of the advocate—and use of evidence results in attitude change over time only when receivers hold extreme attitudes on the issue.

Several of the studies reviewed by Reynolds and Burgoon (1983) examined variables that may influence receivers' evaluations of support used in persuasive communication or evaluations of the message overall. They found that credibility of an advocate is positively related to evaluation of the message, and clarity of evidence citations is positively related to evaluations of evidence and the advocate.

Finally, some research has examined individuals' ability to evaluate evidence per se. Propositions concerning these findings are that people tend to evaluate evidence consistent with their own attitudes, regardless of the quality of the evidence. Moreover, evidence that is inconsistent with the major propositions being advanced is more difficult to decode accurately than is irrelevant evidence or evidence from unqualified sources.

Miller (1966, p. 25) has defined evidence as "those data that are intended to induce a sense of belief in the proposition which the data purportedly support." It follows that evidence, then, is often essential for persuasive success, especially when the goal of communication involves altering beliefs of receivers. Florence (1975) demonstrated that the effects of evidence are primarily on belief systems of intended receivers. Current theorizing by Morley (Morley, 1987; Morley & Walker, 1987) has generated interesting research data indicating that perceived importance, novelty, and plausibility may be necessary conditions for evidence to produce belief change. Previous research has treated each of these factors as separate and independent contributors to the efficacy of evidence in persuasion. Suffice it to say that attempts to use evidence to form, change, or reinforce the evaluations of targets are likely to fail if belief systems of receivers cannot support such evaluations.

MICRO-LEVEL ANALYSIS:
ORGANIZATION OF APPEALS TO EMOTIONS

As mentioned earlier, since ancient times, it has not been assumed that humans are solely or even predominantly intellectual/cognitive beings, rather that they are a complex blend of intellectual and emotional attributes. This is the reason that a purely rational or logical appeal, regardless of organizational structure and evidence, may fail to have the desired persuasive impact. Thus it is crucial to examine message appeals that function more to stimulate than to convince the receiver to behave in certain ways. These emotional appeals attempt to link the proposition of messages with drive-producing mechanisms of human psychology. Emotional appeals attempt to persuade receivers by playing on their feelings of fear, guilt, happiness, pride, or other affective states. Researchers and advertisers have found a number of emotionally oriented messages that are effective in achieving goals essential to persuasive success. In this section, specific types of emotional appeals that have received research attention, including humor, highly intense or opinionated message appeals, obscene language, and fear-arousing messages will be examined.

The literature on emotional appeals has received a great deal of recent attention. In-depth reviews (Burgoon, in press; Burgoon and Bettinghaus, 1980; Burgoon & G. R. Miller, 1985; Burgoon & M. Miller, in press) have recently been published. Burgoon and his associates have synthesized much of the research on emotional appeals and reinterpreted the findings from an Expectancy Theory framework. Space limitations preclude an exhaustive review of that voluminous body of knowledge here. However, selected message variables have been sufficiently studied to warrant inclusion in a brief summary of research on message strategies to appeal to emotions.

Humor. Bettinghaus and Cody (1987, p. 156) claim that "humor may not be able to change attitudes or overcome resistance on the part of issue-involved receivers but humor does have a place in persuasion." To buttress such a claim, they reviewed two important pieces of advertising research examining the effects of humor. First, Madden and Weinberger (1984) surveyed advertising practitioners and found that most believed that humor can be used to draw attention to a product; aid name recall; increase retention of simple, but not complex, copy; persuade consumers to switch brands; and create a positive mood that may enhance persuasion. Consumer nondurables and business services are perceived to be best promoted by humor while corporate advertisements and industrial products are least well served by the use of humor. It was further suggested that humor should be related to the product, should not be used with sensitive goods or services, and is more appropriately used with younger, better educated, affluent, male, and professional targets. It is believed that humor is better suited to the medium of radio and TV than it is to print or direct mail advertisements (see Bettinghaus & Cody, 1987, p. 156).

Humor appeals did not produce different results from a straightforward information treatment in Brooker's (1981) investigation. Lammers, Leibowitz, Seymour, and Hennessey (1983) found that there is a delayed response to humor with receivers first experiencing the humor and then over time thinking about the message content (i.e., they reach what cognitive theorists call the elaboration stage). In this research effort, men generated more positive thoughts about the product while women thought of more counterarguments. On the other hand, a nonhumorous message produced an immediate impact and then the effects began to decay following a forgetting curve.

Based on a much more detailed review of the literature by Gruner (1985), other generalizations can be offered concerning the use of humor in persuasive communications. For example, a moderate amount of apt, relevant humor in *informative* discourse may produce favorable audience reaction toward the source of the message. Humor that is self-disparaging may further enhance person perception of moderately credible communicators (Chang & Gruner, 1981; Gruner, 1982; Smith & Powell, 1988). If a message contains factors other than humor that increase interest, then the addition of humor seems to have little suasory impact. There is also some evidence that, to the extent that humor increases interest in the message, it may aid recall of the content of the message.

A study by Mette, Hrelec, and Wilkins (1971) demonstrates that receiver expectations may mediate receptivity to humor in certain situations, although the authors did not frame the predictions from such a theoretical perspective. Students were led to believe that an otherwise competent professor's one fault was either that he was a "frustrated comedian" or that he had a "dry" and "humorless" demeanor. When students were induced to believe that the professor was a frustrated comedian and he delivered a serious lecture, his ratings were more positive. Moreover, when the professor was expected to be humorless and attempted to use jokes, his ratings were more positive. Such empirical data are consistent with Expectancy Theory propositions articulated earlier, in that both experimental manipulations represent a systematic positive violation of expectations leading to more positive evaluations of source characteristics.

In summary, it appears that humor may be used to gain the attention of receivers, especially in the absence of other interest-provoking message factors, and individuals often recall humorous material better than nonhumorous material. In addition, we may be less resistant to persuasion when humor is used because humor often serves as a distraction making people more, not less, vulnerable to the persuasive content of the message (see Markiewicz, 1974; Powell, 1977). Beyond these few empirical indicators, past research offers little in the way of prescriptions about the effective use of humor in influence attempts. Additional research on the use of varying forms of humor as antecedent to changes in source perception, attitudinal shifts, and behavioral modification would be a valuable addition to knowledge of message effects.

Appeals varying in intensity. Language intensity can be conceptualized as the degree to which a persuasive message deviates from neutrality. The intensity of language choices can be manipulated within sentences by the use of future tense verbs, adverbial qualification, and sex and death metaphors. Other forms of intense language include the use of opinionated and obscene language.

Bowers (1963) found a boomerang effect such that messages using relatively low levels of intense language were more persuasive than messages arguing very intensely. Burgoon and King (1974), among others, presented evidence that people react somewhat negatively to messages that are perceived as too intense. Jones and Burgoon (1975) found that people under stress were especially likely to be receptive to messages employing low levels of language intensity while tending to reject highly intense messages.

Burgoon and Stewart (1975) discovered another factor that mediates the effects of language intensity in the persuasion process. They were among the first to suggest that people develop expectations about what is "appropriate" communicative behavior. At least in this culture, males can apparently use much more intense language and still be successful in their .influence attempts; females are more effective when they use language relatively low in intensity. Burgoon (1975) reported that highly credible sources, perhaps because they are expected to be force-ful and dynamic, can be effective with highly intense language while their low-credibility counterparts cannot.

Burgoon and his associates provide compelling evidence of a general superiority of low-intensity encoding in the passive message reception paradigm, a situation in which audiences receive messages delivered by some active would-be persuader. In the active participation para-digm where speakers delivered messages that were counter to their prior beliefs (i.e., counterattitudinal advocacy) different results obtained. In the active encoding situations, the more intense the language used by speakers, the more they changed their private beliefs to conform to the position advocated (Burgoon & King, 1974).

Opinionated language. I have repeatedly suggested that the use of opinionated language represents a special case of the use of intense language. Research indicates that opinionated statements are perceived as more intense than nonopinionated statements. Opinionated language can convey two separate types of information: (a) the claim of the source and (b) the source's attitude toward those who agree or disagree with the claim. A message that derogates those who disagree is an opinionated rejection statement; a message that praises those who agree is an opinionated acceptance statement. Miller and Lobe (1967) and Miller and Basehart (1969) found that highly credible sources could use opinionated rejection statements more effectively than could sources low in credibility. Mehrley and McCroskey (1970) reported that opin-ionated rejection statements were more effective than nonopinionated language when receivers were neutral on the issue being discussed. However, when people are highly involved and hold intense attitudes toward the topic, nonopinionated language is significantly more persuasive.

Obscene language. Another method of indicating intensity is through the use of obscene language. A limited amount of evidence exists on the relationship between obscenity and persuasion. Research has shown that the source's use of obscenity adversely affects listeners' ratings of confidence in the source but does not affect the speech's persuasive effectiveness (Bostrom, Basehart, & Rossiter, 1973). Use of obscenity also negatively affects evaluation of the speaker (Mulac, 1976), perhaps a reflection of the old adage that people who use obscenity are not intelligent enough to find another way of expressing themselves. These two pieces of research are generally cited as the extant base of reliable information about the relationship between obscenity and persuasion.

A review by Bradac, Bowers, and Courtright (1979) generated a number of generalizations concerning the use of intense, opinionated, and obscene language.

(1) Cognitive stress is inversely related to the language intensity of sources.

(2) Language intensity is directly related to receivers' attributions of internality to sources.

(3) Obscenity is inversely related to the amount of attitude change produced by messages (at least when the source is a male).

(4) Obscenity is inversely related to postcommunication ratings of source competence.

(5) Language intensity of a nonobscene type in attitudinally discrepant messages is inversely related to postcommunication ratings of source competence.

(6) For highly aroused receivers (at least when the basis for arousal is irrelevant to the message), language intensity is inversely related to attitude change.

(7) Language intensity and initial receiver agreement with the proposition of a message interact in the production of attitude reinforcement or change in such a way that intensity enhances the effect of attitudinally congruent messages but inhibits the effect of attitudinally discrepant messages.

(8) Language intensity in an initial message that supports receiver attitudes is inversely related to amount of attitude change produced by a subsequent persuasive attack of moderate intensity.

(9) Language intensity and initial source credibility interact in the production of attitude change in such a way that intensity enhances the effect of credible sources but inhibits the effect of less credible sources.

(10) The relationship between initial source credibility, intensity, and attitude change is strengthened when receivers are high in need for approval.

(11) Language intensity and "maleness" interact in the production of attitude change in such a way that intensity (of a nonobscene type) enhances the effect of male but inhibits the effect of female sources.

(12) Language intensity and target participation in encoding are positively related to attitude change.

(13) Language intensity and initial agreement with the proposition of the message interact in the production of receiver attributions in such a way that intensity in congruent messages enhances, but in discrepant messages inhibits, attributions of source similarity (Bradac, Bowers, & Courtright, 1979, pp. 259-261).

Appeals based on fear. Another type of appeal might be conceptualized as a special case of intensity: the use of fear to change attitudes and/or behaviors. A fear appeal claims that harm will befall the listener or someone important to him or her if the claim is not adopted. A fear appeal is an argument of the following form, according to Boster and Mongeau (1984, p. 371):

... You (the listener) are vulnerable to a threat.

... If you are vulnerable, then you should take action to reduce your vulnerability.

... If you are to reduce your vulnerability, then you must accept the recommendations contained in this message.

... Therefore, you should accept the recommendations contained in this message.

The early research on fear appeals is replete with conflicting findings. Many early studies (DeWolfe & Governale, 1964; Goldstein, 1959; Janis & Feshbach, 1953; Janis & Terwilliger, 1962) reported that lower levels of fear were more effective in changing attitudes. Other studies found the reverse or report mixed findings concerning level of fear in persuasive messages (Chu, 1966; Miller & Hewgill, 1964, 1966; Snider, 1962). Boster and Mongeau (1984) present a more recent detailed meta-analysis of the fear appeal literature that lends support to the claim that the results are still confusing and confounded.

Insko, Arkoff, and Insko (1965), Leventhal and Niles (1965), Leventhal, Watts, and Pagano (1967), Burnett and Wilkes (1980), and Calatone and Warshaw (1985) showed high fear appeals to be effective. Hewgill and Miller (1965) demonstrated that highly credible sources could effectively use high levels of fear while sources of low credibility were more effective using low levels of fear. They also found that the success of fear appeals depended on the perceived relevance of the topic to the receivers.

The *topic* of the persuasive message seems to be a factor that might explain these conflicting findings. It has been argued by others (see Burgoon & Bettinghaus, 1980) that, if sense is to be made of the morass of empirical data concerning the effective use of message features, designs must be created to control for the interaction of theoretical variables of import with the topic of the message.

It has been argued elsewhere (Burgoon & Bettinghaus, 1980) that McGuire's (1969) argument for the existence of a nonmonotonic, inverted "U-shaped" curve is the best description of the relationship between arousal/anxiety and subsequent attitude. He posits an interaction between the receiver's level of anxiety (arousal) and opinion change such that both high and low fear appeals can be effective in specific situations. This interaction suggested by McGuire (1969) was found in some studies (Leventhal & Watts, 1966; Millman, 1965; Niles, 1964; Powell, 1965) prior to the publication of McGuire's review article. Unfortunately, subsequent research has not provided further insight regarding the relative ineffectiveness of moderately worded fear appeals nor has there been a satisfactory expansion of this descriptive claim focusing upon why the inverted U-shaped curve tends to occur. Moreover, other than in this very limited number of instances, this nonmonotonic function has not been replicated in well-executed research efforts.

More recent research has lead me to abandon my earlier embracing of McGuire's explanation. In fact, I have recently (Burgoon, in press) argued that the evidence suggests that strong fear appeals are generally more effective than weak ones in suasory attempts (Baron & Byrne, 1977; Higbee, 1969). In support of that claim, the argument has been made that two different theoretical paradigms might explain the relative superiority of strong fear appeals:

> The general cognitive consistency paradigm (Festinger, 1957; Heider, 1948; Osgood & Tannenbaum, 1955) addresses issues related to an advocate's use of language to arouse fear and how such arousal affects persuasion. Variations on the consistency model suggest that fear appeals should utilize explicit, rather than mild language to emphasize the harmful consequences of non-compliance. Strong language about the consequences of not following the advocate's prescriptions for behavior should increase stress and/or inconsistency in the target and motivate compliance in order to restore cognitive consistency. A reasonable person would obviously want to act in a manner that avoids harmful consequences and maintains a perception of rationality. A competing, perhaps more parsimonious explanation for the relative superiority of strong fear appeals is a drive-reduction explanation (Higbee, 1969; Baron & Byrne, 1977). The drive-reduction model assumes that strong fear appeals lead to an increased state of arousal in the receiver. When presented with recommendations for how negative outcomes can be avoided (acceptance of the claim) the receiver is reassured and the arousal is reduced. This reduction in negative forms of arousal is reinforcing and enhances the probability

an advocate's claims and suggestions will be accepted, thus inducing
attitude change (Baron & Byrne, 1977) and/or behavioral modification.
Other findings (Leventhal & Niles, 1964, 1965; Niles, 1964; Singer, 1965)
report a similar positive relationship between level of fear arousal and
attitude change (Burgoon, in press).

In the same review, some generalizations involving the effective use
of fear appeals are offered. Fear appeals that point out immediate and
severe consequences of noncompliance are more effective than those
that focus on more long-term or delayed effects. Strong fear appeals
supported with evidence are more likely to be effective than those
without evidence. Highly credible communicators can effectively use
fear appeals when low-credibility communicators cannot. Finally, fear
appeals linking noncompliance to harm befalling a receiver's loved one
are likely to be more effective than appeals where threats are directed
only at the target.

DISCUSSION AND CONCLUSION

The importance of message variables is recognized by those concerned with social influence processes and evidenced by the voluminous amount of empirical research on message variables that affect the
alteration of attitudes and/or behaviors. Burgoon (in press) has articulated concerns about the entire body of message behavior research, and
these concerns seem appropriate as closing comments for this chapter.
There has been a lag in the development of explanatory theoretical
models that incorporate functional statements about the relationship
between message variables and social influence. This lack of theoretical
development has had unfortunate consequences for those interested in
communication and social psychology because (a) research over the
past decade on language choices, message strategies, and persuasion
has been relatively moribund; (b) extant research has been dismissed
by many as hopelessly confused and confounded; and (c) recent theoretical models have simply ignored the large body of classic studies that
attest to the suasory power of micro-level message variables.

The variable-analytic tradition of communication and social psychology prior to this decade contributed heavily to the present discon-
tent with the quality of knowledge claims emanating from various

research efforts. Without theoretical guidance, the prevailing research paradigm has been an inductive, exhaustive examination of a single message variable and its relationship to persuasion. Much of this research focused on messages designed to appeal to the emotions as a vehicle to facilitate change in attitudinal positions or to modify behavior. When main-effect findings demonstrated relationships between the selected variable and some measure of attitude/behavior change, additional variables such as source characteristics, power, and receiver variables were investigated.

In many studies, main-effect findings were not replicated or interaction effects overrode conclusions about the impact of the selected message variable. It was not uncommon for claims advanced about the impact of message choices on attitude change to be immediately challenged by null findings or, in many cases, by research reporting the obverse. The fear appeal literature is but one area of social influence replete with confounded claims and conflicting conclusions. Bodies of research dealing with language intensity, obscenity, opinionated language, and humor present similar often uninterpretable findings.

The problems identified with this research tradition are not limited to the language of emotional appeals. Research on logical appeals and message organization has been undertaken within the same paradigm of mechanistic empiricism, resulting in equally confounded accumulations of evidence. Programs of research investigating the relationship between logical consistency, evidence, message structure, and message organization manifest a similar pattern. Disputed main-effect findings, confusing interactions, and lack of functional explanatory mechanisms have precluded informed conclusion-drawing about logic, language, and organization in the attitude-change process.

One approach to this conceptual muddle, taken by such researchers as Petty and Cacioppo (1986) with their development of the Elaboration Likelihood Model, is simply to ignore this wealth of empirical data and relegate persuasive message variables to the status of unobserved intervening variables. The labeling of arguments as central or peripheral is often derived from inferring antecedents from consequents, or a teleological method or explanation. Thus *if* specific outcomes occur (e.g., attitude change), then certain kinds of intrapsychic message processing had to have occurred. Such an explanatory mechanism is relatively unproductive for people interested in the social effects of message strategy choices. The more appropriate approach is to specify a priori how message variables affect the persuasive process.

The argument I have advanced in this chapter is that much could be gained by examining related, but distinct, lines of research in a different organizational format. An analytic framework can be constructed to explain the relationship between message variables and social influence by focusing on micro-level message variable choices to offer empirical generalizations, provide a theoretical umbrella under the general rubric of expectancy-based propositions, and offer suggestions for needed research.

REFERENCES

Baird, J. (1974). A comparison of distributional and sequential structure in cooperative and competitive group discussion. *Speech Monographs, 41*, 226-232.

Baron, R., & Byrne, D. (1977). *Social psychology*. Boston, MA: Allyn & Bacon.

Beighly, K. C. (1952a). The effect of four speech variables on comprehension. *Speech Monographs, 19*, 249-258.

Beighly, K. C. (1952b). A summary of experimental studies dealing with the effect of organization and skill of speakers on comprehension. *Journal of Communication, 2*, 58-65.

Bettinghaus, E. P., & Cody, M. J. (1987). *Persuasive communication*. New York: Holt, Rinehart & Winston.

Bettinghaus, E., Miller, G. R., & Steinfatt, T. (1970). Source evaluation, syllogistic content, and judgement of logical validity of high- and low- dogmatic persons. *Journal of Personality and Social Psychology, 16*, 238-244.

Boster, F., & Mongeau, P. (1984). Fear-arousing persuasive messages. In R. N. Bostrom (Ed.), *Communication yearbook* (Vol. 8, pp. 330-375). Beverly Hills, CA: Sage.

Bostrom, R. N. (1983). *Persuasion*. Englewood Cliffs, NJ: Prentice-Hall.

Bostrom, R. N., Baseheart, J. R., & Rossiter, C. M. (1973). The effects of three types of profane language in persuasive messages. *Journal of Communication, 23*, 461-475.

Bowers, J. W. (1963). Language intensity, social introversion and attitude change. *Speech Monographs, 30*, 345-352.

Bradac, J. J., Bowers, J. W., & Courtright, J. A. (1979). Three language variables in communication research: Intensity, immediacy, and diversity. *Human Communication Research, 5*, 257-269.

Brooker, G. W., Jr. (1981). A comparison of the persuasive effects of mild humor and mild fear appeals. *Journal of Advertising, 10*, 29-40.

Burgoon, J. K., & Saine, T. (1978). *The unspoken dialogue: An introduction to nonverbal communication*. Boston: Houghton Mifflin.

Burgoon, M. (1975). Empirical investigations of language intensity: III. The effects of source credibility and language intensity on attitude change and person perception. *Human Communication Research, 1*, 251-256.

Burgoon, M. (in press). Language and social influence. In H. Giles & P. Robinson (Eds.), *Handbook of language and social psychology*. London: John Wiley.

Burgoon, M., & Bettinghaus, E. P. (1980). Persuasive message strategies. In M. E. Roloff & G. R. Miller (Eds.), *Persuasion: New directions in theory and research* (pp. 141-169). Beverly Hills, CA: Sage.

Burgoon, M., & Burgoon, J. K. (1975). Message strategies influence attempts. In G. J. Hanneman & W. J. McEwen (Eds.), *Communication and behavior* (pp. 149-163). Reading, MA: Addison-Wesley.

Burgoon, M., & King, L. B. (1974). The mediation of resistance to persuasion strategies by language variables and active-passive participation. *Human Communication Research, 1*, 30-41.

Burgoon, M., & Miller, G. R. (1985). An expectancy interpretation of language and persuasion. In H. Giles & R. St. Clair (Eds.), *Recent advances in language, communication, and social psychology* (pp. 199-229). London: Lawrence Erlbaum.

Burgoon, M., & Miller, M. D. (in press). Communication and influence. In G. L. Dahnke & C. F. Collado (Eds.), *Communication as social science: An introductory survey*. Belmont, CA: Wadsworth.

Burgoon, M., & Ruffner, M. (1974). *Human communication*. New York: Holt, Rinehart & Winston.

Burgoon, M., & Stewart, D. (1975). Empirical investigations of language intensity: I. The effects of sex of source, receiver, and language intensity on attitude change. *Human Communication Research, 1*, 224-248.

Burnett, J. J., & Wilkes, R. E. (1980). Fear appeals to segments only. *Journal of Advertising Research, 20*, 21-24.

Cacioppo, J. T., & Petty, R. E. (1979). Effects of message repetition and position on cognitive response, recall, and persuasion. *Journal of Personality and Social Psychology, 37*, 97-109.

Cacioppo, J. T., & Petty, R. E. (1980). Persuasiveness of commercials is affected by exposure frequency and communication cogency: A theoretical and empirical analysis. In J. H. Leigh & C. R. Martin (Eds.), *Current issues and research in advertising*. Ann Arbor: University of Michigan.

Calatone, R. J., & Warshaw, P.R. (1985). Negating the effects of fear appeals in election campaigns. *Journal of Applied Psychology, 70*, 627-633.

Chang, M., & Gruner, C. R. (1981). Audience reaction to self-disparaging humor. *Southern Speech Communication Journal, 46*, 419-426.

Chebat, J. C., & Picard, J. (1985). The effects of price and message-sidedness on confidence in product and advertisement with personal involvement as a mediator variable. *International Journal of Research in Marketing, 2*, 129-141.

Chu, G. C. (1966). Fear arousal, efficacy and imminency. *Journal of Personality and Social Psychology, 5*, 517-524.

Darnell, D. (1963). The relation between sentence order and comprehension. *Speech Monographs, 30*, 186-192.

DeWolfe, A. S., & Governale, C. M. (1964). Fear and attitude change. *Journal of Abnormal and Social Psychology, 69*, 119-123.

Eagly, A. H. (1974). Comprehensibility of persuasive arguments as a determinant of opinion change. *Journal of Personality and Social Psychology, 29*, 758-773.

Earl, R. L., & Pride, W. M. (1980). The effects of advertisement structure, message-sidedness, and performance test results on print advertisement. *Journal of Advertising, 9*, 36-44.

Feather, N. T. (1964). Acceptance and rejection of arguments in relation to attitude strength, critical ability and intolerance of inconsistency. *Journal of Abnormal and Social Psychology, 59*, 127-137.

Festinger, L. (1957). *A theory of cognitive dissonance.* Palo Alto, CA: Stanford University Press.

Florence, T. (1975). An empirical test of the relationship of evidence to belief systems and attitude change. *Human Communication Research, 1*, 145-158.

Goldstein, M. J. (1959). The relationship between coping and avoiding behavior and response to fear arousing propaganda. *Journal of Abnormal and Social Psychology, 58*, 247-252.

Gorn, G. J., & Goldberg, M. E. (1980). Children's responses to television commercials. *Journal of Consumer Research, 6*, 421-424.

Grass, R., & Wallace, W. H. (1969). Satiation effects on TV commercials. *Journal of Advertising Research, 9*, 3-8.

Greenberg, A., & Suttoni, C. (1973). Television commercial wearout. *Journal of Advertising Research, 13*, 47-54.

Gruner, C. R. (1982). *Speaker ethos, self-disparaging humor, and perceived "sense of humor."* Paper presented at the Third International Conference on Humor, Washington, DC.

Gruner, C. (1985). Advice to the beginning speaker on using humor: What the research tells us. *Communication Education, 34*, 142-147.

Gulley, H., & Berlo, D. (1956). Effects of intercellular and intracellular speech structure on attitude change and learning. *Speech Monographs, 23*, 288-297.

Hample, D. (1978). Predicting immediate belief change and adherence to argument claims. *Communication Monographs, 45*, 219-228.

Heider, F. (1948). Attitudes and cognitive organization. *Journal of Psychology, 21*, 107-112.

Hewgill, M., & Miller, G. (1965). Source credibility and response to fear-arousing communications. *Speech Monographs, 32*, 95-101.

Higbee, K. (1969). Fifteen years of fear arousal: Research on threat appeals: 1953-1968. *Psychological Bulletin, 72*, 426-444.

Hovland, C. I., Lumsdaine, A. A., & Sheffield, F. D. (1949). *Experiments in mass communication: Studies in social psychology in World War II* (Vol. 3). Princeton, NJ: Princeton University Press.

Hovland, C., & Mandell, W. (1952). An experimental comparison of conclusion drawing by the communicator and the audience. *Journal of Abnormal and Social Psychology, 48*, 581-588.

Hovland, C., Mandell, W., Campbell, E. H., Brock, T., Luchins, A. S., Cohen, A. R., McGuire, W. J., Janis, I. L., Feierabend, R. L., & Anderson, N. H. (1957). *Order of presentation in persuasion.* New Haven, CT: Yale University Press.

Insko, C., Arkoff, A., & Insko, V. (1965). Effects of high and low fear-arousing communications upon opinions toward smoking. *Journal of Experimental Social Psychology, 1*, 256-266.

Janis, L. L., & Feshbach, S. (1953). Effects of fear-arousing communications. *Journal of Abnormal and Social Psychology, 48*, 79-92.

Janis, I., & Frick, F. (1943). The relationship between attitudes toward conclusions and errors in judging logical validity of syllogisms. *Journal of Experimental Psychology, 33,* 99-114.

Janis, L. L., & Terwilliger, R. (1962). An experimental study of psychological resistance to fear-arousing communication. *Journal of Abnormal and Social Psychology, 65,* 403-410.

Jones, S. B., & Burgoon, M. (1975). Empirical investigations of language intensity: II. The effects of irrelevant fear and language intensity on attitude change. *Human Communication Research, 1,* 248-251.

Kanouse, D., & Abelson, R. (1967). Language variables affecting the persuasiveness of simple communications. *Journal of Personality and Social Psychology, 7,* 153-163.

Kissler, G., & Lloyd, K. (1973). Effect of sentence interrelation and scrambling on the recall of factual information. *Journal of Educational Psychology, 64,* 187-190.

Knower, F. (1936). Experimental studies of changes in attitude: A study of the effect of printed argument on changes in attitude. *Journal of Abnormal and Social Psychology, 30,* 522-532.

Krugman, H. E. (1968). Processes underlying exposure to advertising. *American Psychologist, 23,* 245-253.

Lammers, H. B., Leibowitz, L., Seymour, G. E., & Hennessey, J. E. (1983). Humor and cognitive responses to advertising stimuli: A trace consolidation approach. *Journal of Business Research, 11,* 173-185.

Lefford, A. (1946). The influence of emotional subject matter on logical reasoning. *Journal of General Psychology, 34,* 127-151.

Leventhal, H., & Niles, P. (1964). A field experiment on fear arousal with data on the validity of questionnaire measures. *Journal of Personality, 32,* 459-479.

Leventhal, H., & Niles, P. (1965). Persistence of influence for varying durations of exposure to threat stimuli. *Psychological Reports, 16,* 223-233.

Leventhal, H., & Watts, J. C. (1966). Sources of resistance of fear-arousing communications on smoking and lung cancer. *Journal of Personality, 34,* 155-175.

Leventhal, H., Watts, J., & Pagano, F. (1967). Effects of fear and instructions on how to cope with danger. *Journal of Personality and Social Psychology, 6,* 313-321.

Lind, E. A. (1982). The psychology of courtroom procedure. In N. L. Kerr & R. M. Bray (Eds.), *The psychology of the courtroom* (pp. 13-38). New York: Academic Press.

Lumsdaine, A., & Janis, I. (1953). Resistance to "counterpropoganda" produced by one-sided and two-sided propaganda presentations. *Public Opinion Quarterly, 17,* 311-318.

Madden, T. J., & Weinberger, M. G. (1984). Humor in advertising: A practitioner view. *Journal of Advertising Research, 24,* 23-29.

Markiewicz, D. (1974). Effects of humor on persuasion. *Sociometry, 37,* 407-422.

Mayeux, R. (1984). *Repetition effects: A proposal.* Unpublished paper, University of Southern California, Department of Communication Arts and Sciences.

McCroskey, J. C. (1969). A summary of experimental research on the effects of evidence in persuasive communication. *Quarterly Journal of Speech, 55,* 169-176.

McCroskey, J., & Mehrley, S. (1969). The effects of disorganization and nonfluency on attitude change and source credibility. *Speech Monographs, 36,* 13-21.

McGuire, W. J. (1960). A syllogistic analysis of cognitive relationships. In C. J. Hovland & M. J. Rosenberg (Eds.), *Attitude organization and change* (pp. 65-111). New Haven, CT: Yale University Press.

McGuire, W. J. (1969). The nature of attitudes and attitude change. In G. Lindzey & E. Aronson (Eds.), *The handbook of social psychology* (Vol. 3, pp. 136-314). Reading, MA: Addison-Wesley.

Mehrley, S., & McCroskey, J. (1970). Opinionated statements and attitude intensity as predictors of attitude change and source credibility. *Speech Monographs, 37*, 47-52.

Mette, D. R., Hrelec, E. S., & Wilkins, P. C. (1971). Humor as an interpersonal asset and liability. *Journal of Social Psychology, 85*, 51-64.

Miller, G. R. (1966). Evidence and argument. In G. R. Miller & T. R. Nilsen (Eds.), *Perspective on argumentation* (pp. 24-49). Chicago: Scott, Foresman.

Miller, G. R. (1969). Some factors influencing judgements of the logical validity of arguments: A research review. *Quarterly Journal of Speech, 55*, 276-286.

Miller, G. R., & Basehart, J. (1969). Source trustworthiness, opinionated statements, and responses to persuasive communications. *Speech Monographs, 36*, 1-7.

Miller, G. R., & Burgoon, M. (1978). Persuasion research: Review and commentary. In B. D. Ruben (Ed.), *Communication yearbook* (Vol. 2, pp. 29-47). New Brunswick, NJ: Transaction.

Miller, G. R., & Hewgill, M. A. (1964). The effects of variations in nonfluency on audience ratings of source credibility. *Quarterly Journal of Speech, 50*, 36-44.

Miller, G. R., & Hewgill, M. A. (1966). Some recent research on fear-arousing message appeals. *Speech Monographs, 33*, 377-391.

Miller, G. R., & Lobe, J. (1967). Opinionated language, open- and closed-mindedness and response to persuasive communications. *Journal of Communication, 17*, 333-341.

Miller, R. L. (1976). Mere exposure, psychological reactance and attitude change. *Public Opinion Quarterly, 40*, 229-233.

Millman, S. (1965). *The relationship between anxiety, learning and opinion change.* Unpublished doctoral dissertation, Columbia University.

Morgan, W., & Morton, A. (1953). Logical reasoning: With and without training. *Journal of Applied Psychology, 37*, 399-401.

Morley, D. D. (1987). Subjective message constructs: A theory of persuasion. *Communication Monographs, 54*, 183-203.

Morley, D. D., & Walker, K. B. (1987). The role of importance, novelty, and plausibility in producing belief change. *Communication Monographs, 54*, 436-442.

Mulac, A. (1976). Effects of obscene language upon three dimensions of listener attitude. *Communication Monographs, 43*, 300-307.

Nesdale, A. R., Tunmer, W. E., & Clover, J. (1985). Factors influencing young children's ability to detect logical inconsistencies in oral communications. *Journal of Language and Social Psychology, 4*, 39-49.

Niles, P. (1964). *The relationships of susceptibility and anxiety to acceptance of fear-arousing communications.* Unpublished doctoral dissertation, Yale University.

Norman, R. (1976). When what is said is important: A comparison of expert and attractive sources. *Journal of Experimental Social Psychology, 12*, 294-300.

Osgood, C. E., & Tannenbaum, P. H. (1955). The principle of congruity and the prediction of attitude change. *Psychological Review, 62*, 42-55.

Petty, R. E., & Cacioppo, J. T. (1984). The effects of involvement and responses to argument quantity and quality: Central and peripheral routes to persuasion. *Journal of Personality and Social Psychology, 46*, 69-81.

Petty, R. E., & Cacioppo, J. T. (1986). *Communication and persuasion: Central and peripheral routes to attitude change.* New York: Springer-Verlag.

Powell, F. A. (1965). The effects of anxiety-arousing messages when related to personal, familial and interpersonal referents. *Speech Monographs, 32,* 102-106.

Powell, L. (1977). Satirical persuasion and topic salience. *Southern Speech Communication Journal, 42,* 151-162.

Ray, M. L., & Sawyer, A. G. (1971). Repetition in media models: A laboratory technique. *Journal of Marketing Research, 8,* 20-28.

Ray, M. L., Sawyer, A. G., & Strong, E. C. (1971). Frequency effects revisited. *Journal of Advertising Research, 11,* 14-20.

Reynolds, R. A., & Burgoon, M. (1983). Belief processing, reasoning, and evidence. In R. Bostrom (Ed.), *Communication yearbook* (Vol. 7, pp. 83-104). Beverly Hills, CA: Sage.

Rosnow, R., & Robinson, E. (1967). *Experiments in persuasion.* New York: Academic Press.

Sencer, R. (1965). *An investigation of the effects of incorrect grammar on attitude and comprehension in written English messages.* Unpublished doctoral dissertation, Michigan State University.

Singer, R. P. (1965). *The effects of fear arousing communication on attitude change and behavior.* Unpublished doctoral dissertation, University of Connecticut.

Smith, C. M., & Powell, L. (1988). The use of disparaging humor by group leaders. *Southern Speech Communication Journal, 53,* 279-292.

Snider, M. (1962). The relation between fear-arousal and attitude change. *Dissertation Abstracts, 23,* 1802.

Spicer, C., & Bassett, R. (1976). The effect of organization on learning from a message. *Southern Speech Communication Journal, 41,* 290-299.

Steinfatt, T., Miller, G., & Bettinghaus, E. (1974). The concept of logical ambiguity and judgements of syllogistic validity. *Speech Monographs, 41,* 24-25.

Stewart, D. (1961). Communication and logic: Evidence for the existence of validity patterns. *Journal of General Psychology, 64,* 304-312.

Stone, D. J. (1983). The effects of format and number of arguments on comprehension of text by college undergraduates. *Resources in Education, 18,* 35.

Thistlewaite, D., deHaan, H., & Kamenetsky, J. (1955). The effects of "directive" and "nondirective" communication procedures on attitudes. *Journal of Abnormal and Social Psychology, 51,* 107-113.

Thouless, R. (1959). Effects of prejudice on reasoning. *British Journal of Psychology, 50,* 290-293.

Toulmin, S. (1958). *The uses of argument.* New York: Cambridge University Press.

Tubbs, S. (1968). Explicit versus implicit audience conclusions and audience commitment. *Speech Monographs, 35,* 14-19.

Weiss, W., & Steenbock, S. (1965). The influence on communication effectiveness of explicitly urging action and policy consequences. *Journal of Experimental Social Psychology, 1,* 396-406.

Weston, J. R. (1967). *Argumentative message structure and message sidedness and prior familiarity as predictors of source credibility.* Unpublished doctoral dissertation, Michigan State University.

Whitman, R., & Timmis, J. (1975). The influence of verbal organizational structure and verbal organizing skills on select measures of learning. *Human Communication Research, 1*, 293-301.

Wilson, W., & Miller, H. (1968). Repetition, order of presentation, and timing of arguments and measures as determinants of opinion change. *Journal of Personality and Social Psychology, 9*, 184-188.

Chapter 7

MESSAGE EFFECTS VIA INDUCED CHANGES IN THE SOCIAL MEANING OF A RESPONSE

Robert E. Sanders

IN FACE-TO-FACE INTERACTIONS, messages almost always have some connection to each other, combining to form a large whole (or at least the beginnings of one)—a conversation, quarrel, negotiation, courtship, collaboration, or the like. Moreover, it would be anomalous, even pathological, for (adult) people engaged in a face-to-face interaction to produce messages that did not combine to form some such larger whole. This is partly because they could not otherwise coordinate their respective contributions in anticipation of the consequences of the interaction for each participant.

Messages in social interactions cohere on either or both of two bases. First, many face-to-face interactions are scripted (Schank & Abelson, 1977), that is, they proceed from the interactants' knowledge structures about practices and procedures that have been established within particular institutions (especially service providers, from schools to hospitals to stores). Second, when interactions are not scripted, the separate contributions to them are progressively constrained by an emergent set of structural relations and meaning relations. (We can consider that an interaction is unscripted when there is no institutional protocol for it, and when its goals or constituent topics or the social issues that concern the interactants have not previously been *jointly* dealt with by them.) This latter, unscripted, type of discursive construction—and the interconnections among their constituents by which they cohere—is of particular interest here.

It follows from this that, in unscripted face-to-face interactions, *the effect of a given message on what the partner subsequently says and does is at least in part a consequence of the way that the message limits what can subsequently be contributed relevantly, coherently, to the discursive construction being produced*, given the structural relations and meaning relations that have already developed among messages produced in the interaction.

Research and theory about structural relations and meaning relations among the messages that form discursive constructions thus apply to the study of message effects. This work makes clear that, to make strategic decisions about the content, style, and medium of messages produced to achieve certain effects, communicators need to know not just about respondents' cognitions and dispositions but also about key constituents and their interconnection in the "discourse context." (Hereafter I will refer to an interactant who produces a message in order to elicit some response as "the communicator" and the interactant to whom that message is addressed as "the respondent." These roles are, of course, reversible in face-to-face interactions, with particular interactions varying as to whether one interactant acts as "communicator" and the other as "respondent" throughout the interaction, whether both take on the role of "communicator" at the same time, or whether they exchange roles from one segment of the interaction to the next.)

A case can be made that communicators with knowledge about the "discourse context" alone, without knowing anything about the particular respondent being addressed except that he or she is a member of the speech community, have as good or perhaps a better chance of producing a message that will constrain the respondent in the intended way than do communicators who have knowledge about the respondent's personal characteristics but not the discourse context in which responses will be made. And it happens that in practice communicators often are in precisely this circumstance—knowing about the discourse context, especially in face-to-face interactions, and not about the cognitions and dispositions of the respondent (except for what is progressively revealed by disclosure and inference during the interaction).

Attention to the structural relations and meaning relations in discursive constructions sheds light on *communication* constraints on the production of messages and the responses to them. Such constraints arise from what is required to produce messages that are coherent within the discursive constructions to which they are contributed—apart from the psychological and social dispositions to produce certain messages and responses that arise from the mental states and/or role requirements felt by actors.

This applies only marginally to discursive constructions that arise from scripted interactions. An individual can produce utterances and behaviors by following a script without there having to be any obvious structural relations or meaning relations among them. Hence, in interactions of this kind it is something of a misnomer to speak of message effects at all; each interactant's willingness to follow the script has a much greater influence on what they say and do than does the structural role and social meaning of any particular message that either interactant produces.

This chapter is about research and theory on the structural relations and meaning relations that cohere messages into discursive constructions, as that is informative about message effects. The pertinent sections of the chapter, respectively, are as follows: (a) a narrative synopsis detailing the relevance of this work to the study of message effects and examining its generalizability beyond face-to-face interactions to certain types of social interaction between communicators and large publics, as well as to social interactions between people in remote locations linked by some communications medium; (b) an examination of work on structure in discursive constructions as that constrains message effects; (c) an examination of work on meaning relations in discursive constructions as those constrain message effects; and (d) an extension of this work to a consideration of the difference that the medium of communication makes to the formation of structural relations and meaning relations in discursive constructions.

TWO PREMISES ABOUT MESSAGE EFFECTS

THE CLASSICAL PREMISE

The ancient Greeks took for granted that an orator's discourse will affect an audience's actions (their speech or behavior) regarding some matter only insofar as it changes their thinking about it, that is, their beliefs, attitudes, or feelings regarding that matter. (For the sake of economy of expression, I have coined the term *CogsWorld*, from "cognitions about the world," to refer globally to mental representations and orientations that are formed and changed through communication in

```
Message → CogsWorld
              |
         CogsWorld → Action
```

Figure 7.1

regard to the objects, events, situations, and relationships in the physical and social worlds: beliefs and knowledge structures—including scripts and other social cognitions—and also attitudes and feelings. But I do not include under the rubric "CogsWorld" native knowledge of "methods" of message production, such as rules of language, or the possible structural relations and meaning relations in discursive constructions, mainly because it is not obvious that communication can produce changes in such cognitions.)

I will refer to the idea that message effects are mediated by changes in CogsWorld as the classical premise. The interrelations on this premise between messages, the respondent's CogsWorld, and actions are depicted in Figure 7.1. The classical premise continues to dominate the study of message effects despite recent controversy about whether it is justified empirically to regard CogsWorld as being sufficient or even necessary antecedents of what individuals say and do (Deutscher, 1973; Fishbein, 1967; Goffman, 1959; Larson & Sanders, 1975; Steinfatt & Infante, 1976). It is on the classical premise that research on cognition and cognitive processes—of belief formation, attitude change, knowledge structures, information processing, and so on—is such a central aspect of research and theory on message effects.

But it is not my purpose here to debate the merits of the classical premise—and certainly not to dispute the great strides that have been made recently in our understanding of the effect of messages on cognition and cognitive processes. Rather, my purpose is just to detail factors other than psychological and social dispositions that bear on the effects of messages on what respondents then say and do.

Nonetheless, this could be viewed as a *de facto* presentation of a premise about message effects that competes with the classical premise, even though this alternate premise actually complements and qualifies the classical one. Accordingly, after the following overview of this alternate premise—which for expository purposes I have had to state partly in terms of its contrasts with the classical premise—I will outline briefly the relation to each other of these two premises about message effects.

AN ALTERNATE PREMISE ABOUT
MESSAGE EFFECTS

In recent years research and theory have started to appear about the relationship between messages and what respondents subsequently say and do that is not founded on the classical premise. Instead of coming about as a reaction against the classical premise, this work has emerged independently in an entirely different intellectual context. The concern has not been with message effects. Rather, it has been to identify the types and levels of connections that the components of discursive constructions must have to each other to form a coherent whole, and the devices available to interactants to monitor and coordinate their respective contributions to the interaction.

To apply this perspective to the study of message effects, we first have to accept that it is artificial to make a category distinction between *messages* (that which is communicated that produces an effect on the respondent's CogsWorld) and *responses* (that which respondents do as a result of the change that has been effected in their CogsWorld). *The actions that people take in response to a message are themselves messages* (utterances or behaviors with social meanings). As such, respondent actions/messages combine with the communicator's message, or other messages in the local context, to form a larger whole, such as a dialogue or an argument, and are constrained accordingly.

The social meaning, and therefore the social utility, of messages in unscripted interactions does not result simply from rules and conventions about how to interpret and respond to a message with these or those particular constituents and organization, produced in this context or that. Rather, a message's social meaning and utility in such interactions depend on its interconnections with others of the messages that have already been contributed (Edmondson, 1981; Goodwin, 1981; Jacobs & Jackson, 1983; Pearce & Cronen, 1980; Reichman, 1985; Sanders, 1987a; Sigman, 1987; Tannen, 1984; Tracy, 1982; van Dijk, 1980). Therefore, the meaning and corresponding social utility of the respondent's action/message arises from the way it combines with the communicator's message (and/or with other messages in whatever discursive construction is salient when the respondent acts).

Not every one of the actions/messages that a respondent is capable of producing as a function of his or her CogsWorld about the matter at hand will necessarily be *coherent* and be a *response* to the communicator's message, that is, will be *relevant*. For example, if a traveler asks someone for directions to a neighboring town, Pleasantville, the request may not only make salient for the respondent beliefs about how to get to Pleasantville but such CogsWorld as his or her belief that Pleasantville's tax base is eroding or his or her animus toward Pleasantville's rival high school football team. Of course, actions/messages expressing these latter CogsWorld would not be coherent responses to the traveler's request.

Respondent actions/messages (RMs) that are *expressive* of CogsWorld but *irrelevant* in the current discursive construction are socially dysfunctional because there is no reliable basis for their interpretation or effect on the subsequent actions/messages of others (Sanders, 1987a). Conversely, RMs that are relevant in the current discursive construction are socially functional regardless of whether they express CogsWorld accurately or at all.

Let us posit that, because of the social functionality of producing RMs that satisfy the constraints of the structural relations and meaning relations in discursive constructions, respondents have a generalized disposition to produce RMs that cohere in the present social interaction.

In that case, an actor's speech and behavior are potentially the product of two distinct dispositions that can either complement each other or conflict. On one hand, an actor's CogsWorld dispose him or her to speak and behave in some ways rather than others; on the other hand, the actor has a generalized disposition to speak and behave in ways that cohere in the discursive construction then being created. Generally, these dispositions are complementary: speech and behavior expressive of CogsWorld are often relevant in the discursive construction. But there is a potential, theoretically, for respondents to experience subjective conflicts between dispositions to produce RMs that are relevant and thus socially functional at a given juncture but not expressive of CogsWorld, and dispositions to produce RMs that are expressive of the actor's CogsWorld but either are not relevant or are not relevant in such a way as to acquire desired meanings in the present context.

(An important qualification is needed here. The idea that there is a potential for actors to produce RMs that do not express any of their CogsWorld does not—cannot—entail the absurd claim that people are able to say or do things for which there is no cognitive basis at all. To avoid opening the door to that claim, we have to suppose that in addition to the beliefs, attitudes, and feelings that an actor actually has—CogsWorld$_A$—there are numerous other beliefs, attitudes, and feelings that an actor knows or imagines that it is possible to have—CogsWorldp—that he or she can express linguistically and behaviorally. However, CogsWorld$_A$ have dispositional force, and CogsWorldp do not. It is not entirely ad hoc to make this distinction; without it we could not account for jokes, lies, insincerity and hypocrisy, fantasy and myth, and so forth.)

Because it is socially dysfunctional to produce RMs that are irrelevant in the unfolding discursive construction, and respondents are therefore disposed against doing so, then all else being equal, among the full set of RMs that express either CogsWorld$_A$ or CogsWorldp, those RMs that are relevant to CM (or other antecedents and consequents in the interaction) are more *probable* than RMs that are not. In addition, there may be differences in the probability of RMs within that subset, insofar as its members differ in the extent of their relation to CM.

Moreover, we can expect that among possible RMs that are relevant to CM, those are more probable that have a socially desirable meaning as a function of (a) the basis of their relevance to CM, and/or of (b) the basis of their relevance to what others have said or done in the immediate social context of RM's display, or of (c) the basis of their relevance to what the respondent projects others in that context could say or do subsequently because of RM. This is a secondary, more restrictive effect that structural relations and meaning relations within discursive constructions have on the probabilities of occurrence among the alternative RMs that are relevant in the present interaction. However, this secondary effect also depends on the respondent's CogsWorld$_A$, on whether he or she differentially values the meanings and social utility of the alternative RMs that are relevant in the present interaction.

In light of the above *it is theoretically possible, contrary to the classical premise, for a message to change what the respondent's later actions/messages would otherwise have been regarding the matter at hand without producing any change in CogsWorld regarding that matter*—as long as the message changes the structural relations or meaning relations between such later actions/messages and their antecedents or consequents, and thus changes the relevance and social meaning of those later actions/messages. The converse also follows. If the message does not change either the structural relations or the meaning relations that certain later actions/messages would have with their antecedents, on the basis of which those actions/messages would be irrelevant or have undesirable meanings, then *the message may not*

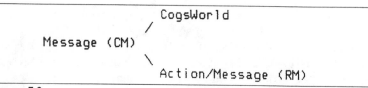

Figure 7.2

elicit those actions even if it does change CogsWorld about the matter at hand so as to psychologically dispose the actor toward taking them. The interrelations this presupposes between messages, CogsWorld, and actions are depicted in Figure 7.2.

This alternate premise entails that messages that influence respondent's CogsWorld need not influence actions/messages, and vice versa. Therefore, on this premise, for a communicator to produce messages that influence a respondent's actions/messages (as opposed to CogsWorld), he or she must know the principles by which utterances and behaviors are relevant to each other, and acquire their social meanings and social utility. On that basis, a communicator (and respondents as well) can project what consequences alternate selections of message content, form, medium, and timing will have for (a) what his or her message is understood to mean and (b) what actions/messages will be relevant subsequently—and, therefore, more probable—and which will not.

GENERALIZATION OF THE ALTERNATE PREMISE BEYOND FACE-TO-FACE INTERACTION

The alternate premise applies whenever the action/message produced in response to a communicator's message contributes to a discursive construction, in the context of which that response acquires a particular social meaning that has consequences for the outcome of the interaction, as well as for the ability of the communicator and the other(s) with whom he or she is interacting to coordinate the subsequent contributions each makes. This is obviously the case in face-to-face interactions, where both the communicator and the respondent are jointly engaged in producing a discursive construction and both are able to monitor the meanings and coherence of their respective contributions to it.

In contrast, when the communicator addresses a large public, or transmits the message to a remote location through some medium, the respondent generally is not and cannot be engaged with the communicator in the production of a discursive construction (except when communicator and respondent are utilizing a medium that enables a one-on-one interaction, such as a telephone or a computer link). But this does not mean that what the respondent says or does in regard to the communicator's message makes no contribution to a discursive construction. What respondents in large publics and in remote locations say and do in regard to a communicator's message is likely either to be produced in the course of a face-to-face interaction with others locally or to be witnessed by others with whom there is a potential for the respondent to interact in the future.

The social meaning of what the respondent says or does in regard to the communicator's message, based on the way in which the respondent's action/message is relevant to the communicator's, has a direct bearing on what it does (or can potentially) contribute to the social interactions in which the respondent is locally engaged or in which he or she anticipates being engaged. In that case, the strategic problem for a communicator who seeks certain responses from members of large publics, or from others in remote locations, is to produce a message such that the way in which sought-after responses would be relevant gives those responses a social meaning that it would be desirable for respondents to express *in other interactions, ones they are likely to have in other, local contexts.*

For example, even though Richard Nixon went on national television (in 1952) to respond to allegations of corruption engendered by discovery of a "slush fund" some businessmen had created for him, only 15% of his text is explicitly about that matter. The bulk of the speech presented a dramatistic portrait of Nixon and his career in which the allegations of corruption were represented as consequences of his anti-Communism. As a result, when he asked viewers at the end to communicate to the Republican National Committee whether they thought he should resign as Eisenhower's running mate, Nixon had shifted ground in such a way that expressions of support or opposition would be relevant to his record of anti-Communism, not to his conduct regarding that "slush fund" (for greater detail, see Sanders, 1987a, pp. 234-236). The social meaning that respondents' expressions of support would thereby acquire (vicarious anti-Communist acts) would probably have seemed far more desirable to produce during or in anticipation of local social interactions than the social meaning that expressions of support would otherwise have had (acts of blind faith or naive trust in the honesty of a self-interested politician).

Along these same lines, it is more and more characteristic of television advertisements, and some print ads as well, that they provide little or no information about the material and utilitarian qualities of the product, but rather depict the relevance of the product in stylized contexts—thereby giving the product a social meaning that it would presumably be desirable for the respondent to express (by virtue of visibly consuming the product) in local contexts.

THE RELATIONSHIP OF THE
TWO PREMISES TO EACH OTHER

The classical and alternate premises about message effects make considerably different empirical predictions about both the conduct of respondents to messages and also the conduct of producers of messages. Yet there is corroborating evidence for each premise, although it is indirect and not conclusive in either case. Two important conclusions follow. First, the available evidence requires that the alternate premise be taken as seriously as the classical premise has been. Second, the fact that there is evidence for both premises indicates that they are not contraries and that they can be reconciled conceptually.

The empirical support for each premise. The key difference in the empirical predictions of the two premises is this: The classical premise predicts that people will act in a consistent way across social contexts in regard to some matter, until and if new experiences or messages regarding that matter produce a change in their CogsWorld$_A$. In contrast, the alternate premise predicts that respondents (and actors generally) can be expected to vary what they say or do regarding some matter from one social context to another independent of changes in CogsWorld, insofar as those contexts present antecedents or possible consequents that change what relevance and social meaning particular utterances and behaviors regarding that matter will have.

Evidence that bears out the key prediction of the classical premise—that individual conduct varies as a function of CogsWorld$_A$—is relatively sparse simply because little research has been carried out on long-term patterns of speech and behavior about particular matters relative to changes in CogsWorld$_A$. The most systematic data available have been obtained in the context of studies of "public service" campaigns. Consistent with the classical premise, some communication campaigns have succeeded in producing stable, long-term behavior changes regarding smoking cessation, family planning practices, heart disease risk reduction, and so on (Rice & Paisley, 1981).

On the other hand, much of that research on communication campaigns shows that creating belief and attitude change alone often was not sufficient to produce these behavior changes. It was common to have to supplement the mass media campaigns that did achieve belief and attitude changes by providing opportunities for face-to-face interaction between campaign representatives and respondents. These interactions sometimes were devised to give respondents opportunities to practice the skills needed to make the sought-after change, but invariably they offered respondents opportunities for interaction about the sought-after changes outside their ordinary social contexts, in socially supportive ones (where the sought-after change could be guaranteed to have utility and a desirable social meaning). Moreover, this was particularly important when the behavior change being sought ran counter to the values or norms of the actor's reference group (e.g., campaigns against smoking among teens or for the adoption of family planning practices run counter to peer values and norms). In accordance with the alternate premise, this suggests that what individuals say or do depends on its utility and meaning in their local social contexts.

A second empirical prediction of the alternate premise about message effects is that some portion of the content of compliance-gaining (persuasive) messages can be expected not to be informative about the matter at hand, but instead to recast the basis of the relevance of desired responses within the discursive construction(s) in which they will occur, in order to change their social meaning and utility. Recent taxonomies of compliance-gaining strategies (Marwell & Schmitt, 1967; Wiseman & Schenck-Hamlin, 1981) are consistent with this. Constituent strategies, such as proffering rewards or punishments as inducements, inviting conformity with a reference group, or making interpersonal obligations salient, can be differentiated more by the basis they establish for the relevance and thus the social meaning of desired responses than by any change they are likely to induce in respondents' CogsWorld about the matter at hand. More telling, perhaps, a close inspection of the content of actual persuasive messages will reveal in many cases material that is uninformative about the matter at hand but that functions to recast the basis of the relevance of sought-after actions/messages within the discursive constructions in which they are expected to occur so as to attach certain social meanings to those actions/messages. This was the case, for example, in Nixon's "Checkers" speech, as described above.

A CONCEPTUAL INTEGRATION OF THE CLASSICAL AND ALTERNATE PREMISES

Both premises have in common the view that $CogsWorld_A$ are subject to formation and change by communication. The main difference between the two premises involves what cognitions and cognitive processes are taken as being formative of speech and behavior.

From the perspective of the classical premise, speech and behavior are neutral instruments for expressing or externalizing $CogsWorld_A$ that are salient in the present instance. Depending on one's motivation and ability to do so, others' messages are processed for the information they have encoded about the subjective conditions and environmental states of affairs that those others are experiencing or know about. This processing is based on knowledge structures that discriminate new from old information, and it results in changes in $CogsWorld_A$. Such changes in $CogsWorld_A$ are presumed to foster changes in speech and behavior.

The alternate premise reverses this. It treats $CogsWorld_A$ and $CogsWorld_P$ as resources to use in giving messages content and form sufficient to promote desired outcomes or inhibit undesired ones in social interactions. Others' messages are processed for the interaction outcomes and relational orientations that their production makes more or less probable. This processing is based on rules and principles for identifying structural relations and meaning relations in discursive constructions, and it fosters changes in one's expectations of the outcomes of interactions, the goals and agendas of others with whom one interacts, the social treatment one can expect from others, and so on. Such changes in one's expectations are presumed to foster changes in one's speech and behavior.

In these terms, the two premises are independent and nonexclusive, not contrary. Like the classical premise, the alternate premise takes as given that what actors say and do is an expression of $CogsWorld_A$, or at least $CogsWorld_P$, and that changes in CogsWorld will correspond to changes in the respondent's speech and behavior—but the alternate premise qualifies the classical premise by treating this as not being necessarily so, and not at every juncture. In contrast to the classical premise, the alternate premise entails that when and whether such changes in CogsWorld are registered in speech and behavior depends on whether and how they are relevant in the discursive construction to which their expression would contribute. Accordingly, the real difference between the classical and alternate premises is not about whether the changes that messages produce in CogsWorld will ultimately result in changes in speech and behavior—the real difference is about when such changes will manifest themselves, and how reliably across contexts, given the constraints of discursive constructions on what actors say and do.

To approach this from another angle, the alternate premise carries with it the idea that the relative probability of a possible action/message depends on the way it is relevant to its antecedents, because the basis of its relevance gives it a social meaning that it will be more or less socially desirable to express. But the social desirability of expressing some meaning is a function of CogsWorld$_A$. Thus messages that produce changes in CogsWorld$_A$ can correspondingly change the respondent's subjective estimate of the desirability of producing a given action/message, and thereby the probability of its production—but only at those junctures when it is relevant to produce that action/message at all. As above, this entails that the real difference between the classical and alternate premises is not whether changes that messages induce in CogsWorld$_A$ will have tangible consequences but when and how frequently and reliably those changes in CogsWorld$_A$ will correspond to changes in what respondents say and do.

STRUCTURAL RELATIONS IN DISCURSIVE CONSTRUCTIONS

We can consider that a discursive construction—like any object—is structured if it is formed from the combination of distinct parts. Such parts are structurally optional when the discursive construction can be made complete regardless of whether they are included (e.g., including examples in a classroom lecture is structurally optional). Such parts are structurally obligatory when making the discursive construction complete or whole depends on their inclusion (e.g., the bringing in of a verdict in a trial). When it is structurally obligatory to contribute a message, then not contributing one would be a conspicuous omission that at minimum will interfere with achieving closure, and in addition may be interpreted as an action, generally an antisocial one.

Because it usually is socially costly not to contribute a message that is structurally obligatory, communicators can make the production of messages subsequent to their own more probable if they make subsequent messages structurally obligatory. This is the key to the role of structure in message effects.

Sigman (1987) has postulated that what people say and do is structured on one or more of three distinct levels. One is the *semiotic* level, on which constituents are structurally obligatory to produce complete (i.e., interpretable) utterances and behaviors. A second is the *interaction* level, on which constituents are structurally obligatory to complete (i.e., make progress and achieve the goals of) the interaction. And the third is the *social* level, on which constituents are structurally obligatory to complete institutional "forms of life" (i.e., define situations, establish role identities, and so on).

In terms of the concern here with message effects, structure on the semiotic level is irrelevant because that generally involves the structural obligatoriness of contributions *within* a message. Structure on the social level does have behavioral consequences that are relevant here— communicators can undertake to increase the probability of certain subsequent messages by making them structurally obligatory as part of some form of life. However, much research has detailed the dispositional force that institutional structures have (by way of procedures, roles, and norms) in regard to individual actions, and there is little to be gained from rehashing that work here. Hence, the focus of this section is upon structure on the interaction level, which has behavioral consequences—but not ones that have been made explicit as such.

RESEARCH ON STRUCTURE IN INTERACTIONS

To the extent that it has been demonstrated that interactions are structured at all, research has revealed structures in the weak sense (e.g., Edmondson, 1981; Frentz & Farrell, 1976; Goodwin, 1981; Jacobs & Jackson, 1983; Reichman, 1978, 1985; Rumelhart, 1975; Schegloff, 1968; Schegloff & Sacks, 1973; Sinclair & Coulthard, 1975; van Dijk, 1980; Ventola, 1987). Objects are structured in the weak sense if they are formed by a combination of discrete parts (from among a closed set of theoretically possible parts), which are not ordered in any particular way—not mechanically, hierarchically, or syntactically. Objects that are structured in the weak sense are neither well-formed nor ill-formed, but are either complete (i.e., whole) or incomplete.

Attention to structure in interactions is a derivative concern that has emerged in two separate research contexts as a way of solving certain theoretical problems in each: in discourse analysis and language pragmatics on one hand, and ethnomethodology and conversation analysis on the other. However, there has been far more success in ethnomethodology (conversation analysis) than in discourse analysis and language pragmatics in demonstrating that interactions are structured such that certain constituents are structurally obligatory.

Work on structure in discourse analysis and language pragmatics. The research of interest here largely has a structuralist orientation: elements at each of a succession of levels of analysis up to and beyond single sentences are regarded as combining to form complex units that function in turn as elements at the next, higher level of analysis (e.g., Edmondson, 1981; Sinclair & Coulthard, 1975; van Dijk, 1980). The thrust of this work is to provide an alternative to Searle's (1969) action-theoretic (goal-centered) account of the social meanings of utterances. This alternative explains such meanings in terms of the function of utterances within structural units rather than as instrumental to the social purposes of actors.

However, Edmondson (1981) showed that the structural categories and levels specified in such work are ad hoc at best. The data do not justify the claims made about what the particular structural units of interactions (and, more generally, discourse) are, or claims that any constituents of such units are obligatory. Ventola (1987) has made the same objection, this time including Edmondson's analysis in the indictment.

The problem is that much of this work contains a fatal circularity. The data are equivocal as to whether interactions comprise structural units such that the social meanings and meaning distinctions of utterances are a function of the structural units they belong to—or the reverse, whether utterances have social meanings such that the meaning relations among them create structural divisions in the interaction.

Only Reichman's (1978, 1985) work and Ventola's (1987) are unequivocal in this regard. But both of them provide data that support the latter claim, that the meaning relations among utterances coheres them so as to create structural divisions in the interaction. Hence, both Reichman's and Ventola's work are valuable for the details of inflection and phrasing they reveal that mark the organization of talk into structural divisions. But neither provides any data that support claims that interactions are structured in particular ways or have certain obligatory structural components.

Work in conversation analysis of structure. Conversation analysis focuses on the communication resources and methods that individuals use to coordinate their respective contributions to interactions. The organization of the elementary constituents of interactions into subparts facilitates the coorientation of interactants to what has to be accomplished at each point, and accordingly what the function of their respective entries is (or will be construed as being). For example, Goodwin (1984, p. 241) observed an actor who was serving himself soup during the telling of a story at the dinner table, and found "that his serving activities are in fact being organized quite precisely with reference to the emerging structure of the story," in particular, that this listener started and stopped the movements of the ladle from tureen to soup bowl depending on whether "background" segments or "focal" segments of the story were being told.

Critical evidence that discursive constructions have structural units inherently such that certain contributions are structurally obligatory was provided by Schegloff's (1968) account of a notable regularity in telephone calls. Schegloff observed that the person who answers the telephone speaks first (at least in the United States). The caller then initiates an exchange of greetings (structurally optional), before introducing a topic or purpose of conversation (obligatory). But there was one exceptional instance in Schegloff's data, when the answerer did not speak upon picking up the handset; instead there was a silence and then the caller spoke first. But instead of just proceeding, the caller only said "hello" and stopped. The answerer did not then initiate greetings or introduce a topic, but also said "hello" and stopped. The conversation proceeded from there as usual, but in the third turn at speaking, not the second.

Schegloff proposed that a single structural description for conversational openings applies both to the regular openings in telephone conversations he observed and to the exception described above. Openings comprise a pair of functional elements: (a) a *summons* to interact and (b) an *answer* that confirms readiness to do so (Sacks, 1972; Nofsinger, 1975, described a parallel organization in openings of certain face-to-face interactions). Schegloff further proposed that, in the telephone conversations he examined, the answerer's initial utterance is the second, concluding part of the opening sequence (the "answer"); the ringing of the telephone is the first part (the summons). In that case, the initial silence of the answerer in the deviant case had the consequence of leaving the summons-answer sequence structurally incomplete, and so the caller restarted the sequence and got it completed before going on:

> summons (ring)
> 0-answer (handset is picked up, silence)
> summons (caller "calls to" answerer)
> answer (answerer acknowledges the summons)

Schegloff (1972, 1980, 1982), Jefferson (1972), and Schegloff and Sacks (1973) went beyond this to propose that there are a variety of pragmatically bound pairs in addition to a summons-answer sequence and that such *adjacency pairs* are the minimal structural units of discursive constructions. These pairs comprise utterances such that the meaning of the first pair part is that it is an act that is prefatory to a particular follow-up (i.e., in question-answer pairs, the meaning of a question is in part that it is an act that is prefatory to an answer; the meaning of an apology is in part that it is prefatory to forgiveness; and so on for request-comply/deny pairs, rebuke-repair pairs, greeting-greeting pairs, and the like). The utterance of the first pair part of an adjacency pair makes the second pair part structurally obligatory.

In addition to opening sequences and adjacency pairs, other structural units have been identified in this research context—presequences (Sacks, 1972) and prerequests (Jacobs & Jackson, 1983), closings (Schegloff & Sacks, 1973), and repair sequences (Schegloff, Jefferson, & Sacks, 1977). However, it has to be recognized that not all of the constituents of discursive constructions are members of such structural units. Many of the constituents of discursive constructions must be considered structurally optional. In fact, only the end parts of adjacency pairs, presequences, repair sequences, openings, and closings are structurally obligatory.

THE APPLICATION OF WORK ON STRUCTURE TO STUDIES OF MESSAGE EFFECTS

Hitherto, only Jacobs and Jackson (1983) have considered how structural relations in discursive constructions contribute to message effects. They provide a number of data regarding indirect requests and presequences that instantiate the general idea that making certain responses structurally obligatory increases the probability that they will be made. The more general form of this idea is that if a communicator produces a message that is the first pair part of an adjacency pair, repair sequence, opening, or closing, he or she thereby makes a certain follow-up message structurally obligatory.

Increasing the rate of respondent contributions by making them structurally obligatory entails an increase by chance alone in the overall number of cooperative (agreement) responses. But, in addition, it can be speculated that, when messages are structurally obligatory, there is a "structural preference" for cooperative responses; that is, prosocial responses tend to be responded to as fulfilling the structural obligation and achieving closure, whereas antisocial responses tend not to be. In that case, increasing the probability that a response will be made at all by making it structurally obligatory would create a disproportionate increase in the probability of prosocial responses.

This explains, for example, why face-to-face solicitations of respondent cooperation generally have greater success than the same solicitations through "noninteractive" media such as television or mail (e.g., Rice & Paisley, 1981). The explanation is that in face-to-face interactions an action/message from respondents can be made structurally obligatory far more readily than it is possible to do through "noninteractive" media. In face-to-face interactions, just engaging the respondent in an exchange of greetings and introduction of a topic or purpose often is enough to produce a discursive construction of the length and complexity needed to begin making certain respondent contributions structurally obligatory, whereas getting to that point through "noninteractive" media is far more problematic.

It is consistent with this that one often finds components of messages through "noninteractive" media that are dedicated to making certain responses structurally obligatory, or at least to inducing respondents to make themselves available for a subsequent face-to-face interaction. For example, Nixon did not depend simply on the effect of his "Checkers" speech on the dispositions of his audience to induce them to actively respond. Rather, at the end of his speech he explicitly asked his audience to communicate to the Republican National Committee their assessment of his viability as Eisenhower's running mate. By doing this, Nixon theoretically made such calls and telegrams structurally obligatory, and (even discounting a structural preference for prosocial responses) thereby fostered a net increase in the overall size of the public response on his behalf. Similarly, some commercial solicitations I have recently gotten through the mail attempt to make a response structurally obligatory by directing the addressee (often by name) to call a certain telephone number during certain hours in order to proceed with a transaction already started by the company.

MEANING RELATIONS IN INTERACTIONS AND OTHER DISCURSIVE CONSTRUCTIONS

Insofar as a set of constituent messages form a larger whole (an interaction or other type of discursive construction), it is true by definition that their meanings will be relevant to each other, that is, there will be a particular meaning relation among those messages (at least within each structural division). Reciprocally, as a discursive construction is produced, a particular meaning relation will emerge among its constituent messages as a function of the basis on which they are relevant to each other (e.g., Craig & Tracy, 1983; Dascal, 1977; Grice, 1975; Halliday & Hasan, 1976; Haslett, 1987; Jackson, Jacobs, & Rossi, 1987; Planalp, Graham, & Paulson, 1987; Sanders, 1987a; Sperber & Wilson, 1986; van Dijk, 1980).

As an interaction or other discursive construction unfolds, the range of meanings that subsequent messages can relevantly have narrows. The probability thus increases that the next message (within that structural division) will have certain meaning elements—or at least will tend to be interpreted as having them, given Grice's (1975) postulate that interpreters presume relevance and tend to interpret messages accordingly. There is laboratory evidence that supports this claim in terms of the specific meaning relations detailed below (Sanders, 1987a, pp. 101-125).

I will refer to the meaning relations that interconnect messages to form a structural division within some discursive construction as their *ground of coherence*. If the ground of coherence among constituents in a sequence results, for example, from their content being about the qualities of some particular experience, the probability increases that the content of the next message (within that structural division) will also be about that experience and its qualities, or be so construed. This is consistent with Reichman's (1978, 1985) analysis of the structural divisions ("context spaces") in discursive constructions. Her data indicate that expressions that are not intended to be relevant within a given structural division, but initiate a change in the ground of coherence (and thus begin or resume a different structural division), generally are marked as such with certain prefatory expressions.

Therefore, if communicators produce messages that establish a certain ground of coherence in the interaction (or other discursive construction), they will thereby increase the probability that the meanings of the messages respondents produce will have certain elements, namely, the elements that figure in that antecedent ground of coherence. This can be the communicator's goal in and of itself, to make it more probable that respondents' messages will have certain meaning elements, as when there are topics that the communicator wants the respondent's messages to be about (or not be about).

But making it more probable that the meanings of respondents' messages will have certain elements can instead be instrumental rather than a goal in its own right. It can become more likely that the respondent will produce a certain message because he or she is disposed (given his or her CogsWorld$_A$) to express the meaning elements that his or her message will have as a function of the basis of the relevance that the communicator has established for it.

For example, in addition to making responses structurally obligatory at the end of his "Checkers" speech, Nixon also made responses relevant in terms of particular meaning elements. The later part of the speech created a ground of coherence that interconnected his anti-Communist activities and the attacks being made upon him by constructing them as social action and reaction. This made respondents' messages supporting or opposing Nixon's candidacy relevant as—and thereby were more likely to be interpreted as—(re)actions toward his antiCommunism. The goal in this case would not have been to make it more probable that respondents' messages would have a certain content (in this case, about anti-Communism). The goal would have been to make it more probable that respondents' messages would have an illocutionary force if they had a certain content, such that respondents would be motivated to produce the message. Given the general social bias in the United States in the early 1950s in favor of anti-Communist acts, Nixon's making respondents' messages relevant as actions for or against his anti-Communism increased the social costliness of messages whose content opposed his candidacy, and thereby made messages more probable whose content was supportive of his candidacy.

Linguistic expressions have three distinct types of meaning, and they can be relevant to each other in terms of any one of them (Sanders, 1987a):

(1) *propositional content*—the expression's specification of an empirical state of affairs that the expression asserts or denies, requests information about, or directs the hearer to change (Katz & Fodor, 1963; Kempson, 1977; Raskin, 1985, pp. 59-98);

(2) *illocutionary force*—the social purpose it serves between the particular speaker and hearer to produce that utterance with its particular content and form (Austin, 1962; Bach & Harnish, 1979; Searle, 1969); and

(3) *conversational implicature*—the state of affairs that is implicated by the speaker's production of an utterance with that content at that juncture in an information exchange, given that the utterance's content does not provide the information needed at that juncture (Grice, 1975).

Meaning relations between the constituents of discursive constructions have generally been studied under the rubrics of "text cohesion" (e.g., Halliday & Hasan, 1976) and "coherence" (e.g., Craig & Tracy, 1983). That work has generally been about grounds of coherence based on the propositional content of constituent expressions, particularly in regard to topic management. Grounds of coherence based on illocutionary force or conversational implicature have gotten less attention, but they are no less possible ways of interconnecting messages in discursive constructions.

In regard to the study of message effects, however, only grounds of coherence based on propositional content or illocutionary force are of interest. Nothing is added by taking into account the grounds of coherence that make responses relevant in terms of what they implicate. This is because the antecedents that make messages relevant in terms of what they implicate do not make probable any meaning elements in respondents' messages that satisfy different communicator goals than antecedents that make messages relevant in terms of their propositional content (Sanders, 1987a, pp. 185-190).

GROUNDS OF COHERENCE BASED ON PROPOSITIONAL CONTENT

Grice (1975) describes the purpose of conversation as information exchange, thus entailing that the utility of constituents arises from the information they provide, that is, from their propositional content.

Grice moreover specifies that a message is "cooperative" in an ongoing conversation insofar as its content meets the information need at that point; that is, it is (a) topically relevant and (b) the speaker believes that it is true, (c) it provides the amount of information needed, and (d) it is precise and unambiguous. Related to this, Sperber and Wilson (1986) conceive of grounds of coherence as being a function of the interpreter's "knowledge base" about some state of affairs to which the propositional content of the expressions of discursive constructions are relevant insofar as they effect a change in that knowledge base.

This suggests that a ground of coherence based on propositional content generally involves more than the presence of common elements in the content of expressions within a structural division. In addition, as Haslett (1987) proposes, each subsequent expression is constrained to have relevant content that meets the information need at that point, that *adds to* what has already been said or achieves *progress* in the interaction (but see Heritage & Watson, 1979, for exceptions). Schank (1977) has pointed out that topically relevant expressions are anomalous whose propositional content is wholly redundant or was presupposed by an antecedent:

> (3) A: Let's go see a movie tonight.
> ? B: Each frame of a movie is a still photograph.

Related to this, Tracy (1982) has distinguished between the "issue" that the propositional content of a sequence of expressions is about (i.e., the commonalities in their content that constitute the ground of coherence between them) and the array of constituent "events" to which those expressions collectively refer. Tracy's laboratory data indicate that, generally, respondents were rated as being less communicatively competent if the content of the message they added to such a sequence was relevant to an antecedently named "event" rather than the "issue."

It follows that if the ground of coherence established by a communicator is based on propositional content—so that respondent messages will be relevant in terms of their content, for example, in terms of what they assert or deny about some state of affairs—then the probability that respondent messages will include references or claims in regard to a given state of affairs can be diminished by making such claims redundant. This is consistent with laboratory findings that communicators' messages are more effective for longer terms if they explicitly mention undesired responses, thus "inoculating" respondents against them (McGuire, 1961). Moreover, given the "issue" the communicator establishes in the discursive construction, the inclusion of certain content in respondent messages is more or less probable depending on whether that content is relevant to the "issue," or beside the point—relevant merely to incidental referents. Finally, whether content about specifics of a state of affairs is more or less likely to be included in respondents' messages depends on what specifics of a state of affairs the communicator refers to (Sanders, 1984).

GROUNDS OF COHERENCE BASED ON ILLOCUTIONARY FORCE

For an utterance to have a certain illocutionary force, to count as a particular social action, certain conditions—felicity conditions—have to be met regarding its form and content and the social circumstances under which it is produced. For example, for an utterance to be an insult, its content must be about qualities of the hearer (or of relatives, friends, or possessions of the hearer); the referent must unequivocally have those qualities; and those qualities must be undesirable ones by community standards. Having this content is a necessary but not sufficient condition for an utterance to have the force of an insult (e.g., utterances with such content could instead have the force of teasing). In addition, an utterance with that content must be uttered by someone with an established social animus toward the hearer in a conflict situation.

Utterances that have a certain illocutionary force—count as a particular social action—can thus be relevant to the following:

(1) antecedents whose content asserts or directs the creation of one or more of the felicity conditions for an utterance to have that force;

(2) antecedents whose content explicitly directs or requests that the respondent perform the action accomplished by an utterance with that force; or

(3) antecedent actions or sequences of actions that are conventional reciprocals of the present action or projections of subsequent actions that are reciprocals of the present action, corresponding to the idea of adjacency pairs—for example, answers are relevant to antecedent questions, thanking is relevant to an antecedent compliment, a refusal is relevant to an antecedent imperative or offer (Sanders, 1987a, pp. 88-91).

The likelihood that a respondent will perform some social act depends on his or her psychological dispositions toward it and whether it is a normatively approved act according to community standards (Fishbein & Ajzen, 1975), or on whether it is an act that is necessary to establish or preserve the actor's social front (Goffman, 1959). But the probability that what a respondent says and does will *have* a certain illocutionary force—or more precisely, that certain target messages will count as certain social acts—depends on which one or more of the above types of antecedent the communicator includes in his or her messages(s).

For example, suppose that a student wants to increase the probability that some instructor will assent to his or her request to turn an assignment in late. Suppose also that the student believes that this instructor values student initiative and originality, and that the instructor would be more likely to assent to a request to turn the assignment in late if that assent counted as the social act of sponsoring initiative/originality (or a denial had the force of suppressing it). The student could then present antecedents of the first kind, above, by citing the existence of felicity conditions for such an act, for example, by describing an opportunity he or she had found for taking an original approach to the assignment, but an opportunity that became available at a time that conflicted with the deadline for the assignment. Or the student could present antecedents of the second kind, above, by directly asking the instructor to sponsor initiative/originality by extending the deadline for the assignment to give the student the time needed to do the assignment in a more creative way. Or the student could present antecedents of the third kind, above, by describing to the instructor a series of actions the student had undertaken in the past, in other courses, to achieve more original work, and the series of failures in that regard he or she had experienced because of repressive and rigid (re)actions by other, rule-bound instructors.

THE ROLE OF COMMUNICATION MEDIA IN MESSAGE EFFECTS

Presumably as a consequence of the apparent force and wide use of the mass media in information, political, commercial, and development campaigns, there has been concern for some time with the role of communication media in the creation of message effects. However, much of the research and theory in this regard that is relevant to the concerns here is sociological in orientation, focused primarily on the effect that messages have when those are communicated through media with enough *massness* to produce a wholesale change in a community's social construction of reality (Sigman & Fry, 1985; van Dijk, 1985).

A more recent incentive for a concern with the role of communication media in message effects is the rapid growth in the use of new information technologies in private and public sector organizations. These technologies give a new role to print/graphics media (through computer linkages), audio-only media (voice linkages), and audio-video media (video conferencing) in task coordination, decision making, networking, information-pooling, and so on.

These innovations foster a consideration of properties of communication media other than their massness. They make salient what personal experience and anecdotal evidence indicate has been true for some time, that individuals who have choices among media (e.g., between conducting interactions face-to-face, by telephone, or in writing) tend to have preferences for one medium or another depending on what the communication problem is. Related to this, the medium of communication evidently can contribute directly to message effects, given, for example, the finding that group decision making carried on via channels in a computer network resulted in equally good decisions compared with group outcomes achieved through face-to-face interaction, but a greater level of unresolved conflict (Hiltz, Johnson, & Turoff, 1986).

From the perspective of work on structural relations and meaning relations in discursive constructions, there are two principal ways in which the properties of different media have a role in message effects. The first of these has already been considered in the section on structural relations in discursive constructions. It is easier in interactive than in noninteractive media to involve respondents in the production of discursive constructions of enough length and complexity to make responses structurally obligatory.

The second way in which media differ from this perspective involves their capacities to transmit nonverbal displays and, more important, their capacity to interconnect utterances and nonverbal displays temporally. In this regard, media fall along a continuum, with face-to-face interaction at one pole, audio-video media nearer that pole than the other, voice-only media in the middle, and print media at the opposite pole. I have detailed elsewhere that nonverbal displays can contribute to the establishment of grounds of coherence based on illocutionary force (Sanders, 1987a, pp. 198-199, 1987b). This is because felicity conditions for achieving some particular illocutionary force generally involve the social attitudes of the actor regarding the situation and the respondent, and these are readily and commonly expressed nonverbally. However, this role for nonverbal displays requires that they occur at a particular place in a sequence of messages. Given an utterance whose content could have the force of an insult (e.g., "You still don't know how to tell the difference between good ideas and bad ones"), its interpretation as an insult is not warranted if the communicator smiles before and during the utterance, but its illocutionary force is equivocal if the communicator smiles afterward, but not before or during the utterance.

It follows from this that media differences are not significant (except in terms of massness or cost) when the communicator has an *informational agenda*, that is, seeks to constrain the content of respondents' messages. It also follows that media differences do have a role in message effects when the communicator has an *interpersonal agenda*, that is, seeks to constrain the social actions toward the communicator or others that respondents' messages count as. This is consistent with the finding cited above that through print media, in contrast to face-to-face interaction, the quality of group decisions was relatively the same (informational agenda), but there was less success in resolving conflict (interpersonal agenda).

This is also consistent with much of the research on communication campaigns (Rice & Paisley, 1981). That research indicates that, in terms of constraining the content of respondents' messages in regard to either expressed beliefs or attitudes, the various media are roughly equivalent (leaving aside differences in accessibility, massness, and cost-effectiveness). However, in terms of constraining behavior—that is, social actions—there are differences in the media. Specifically, the probability of behavior change is greatly increased when a campaign makes a provision for face-to-face interaction in addition to delivering communicators' messages through other media.

GAINS FOR THE STUDY OF
MESSAGE EFFECTS

The study of message effects stands to gain in two ways from taking into account work on structure and meaning in discourse, interaction, and other discursive constructions. First, there is a considerable gain in theoretical parsimony if we do not have to account for details of message content, style, media, and timing in terms of their effect on respondents' dispositions, but can account for them instead in terms of their contribution to structural relations and meaning relations in discursive constructions. There is also a gain in theoretical parsimony if situational variability in what individual respondents say and do regarding some matter does not have to be explained in terms of indirect and complex relationships between cognitions and behavior but can be explained instead in terms of changes in the basis of the relevance of those messages to antecedents in particular contexts.

Second, taking into account work on structure and meaning in discursive constructions greatly enriches our ability to explain the fact that communicators seem to have a general strategic ability to produce influential messages even in the absence of accurate or complete information about respondents' CogsWorld, and sometimes having none. Research and theory on discourse and interaction make clear that, in any speech community, there exists a general set of principles by which messages combine in discursive constructions so as to make subsequent messages structurally obligatory, and to make it more probable that subsequent messages will include certain meaning elements. Therefore, on the basis of "knowing" those principles, and without any specific knowledge about the CogsWorld of individual respondents, it should be possible for any member of a speech community to produce messages that to some minimal extent will constrain the responses of other members of that same community, more so than would be achieved in the absence of the communicator's messages.

REFERENCES

Austin, J. (1962). *How to do things with words.* New York: Oxford University Press.
Bach, K., & Harnish, R. M. (1979). *Linguistic communication and speech acts.* Cambridge, MA: MIT Press.

Craig, R. T., & Tracy, K. (Eds.). (1983). *Conversational coherence: Form, structure, and strategy.* Beverly Hills, CA: Sage.

Dascal, M. (1977). Conversational relevance. *Journal of Pragmatics, 1*, 309-328.

Deutscher, I. (Ed.). (1973). *What we say/what we do: Sentiments & acts.* Glenview, IL: Scott, Foresman.

Edmondson, W. (1981). *Spoken discourse: A model for analysis.* London: Longman.

Fishbein, M. (1967). Attitude and the prediction of behavior. In M. Fishbein (Ed.), *Readings in attitude theory and measurement* (pp. 477-490). New York: John Wiley.

Fishbein, M., & Ajzen, I. (1975). *Belief, attitude, intention and behavior: An introduction to theory and research.* Reading, MA: Addison-Wesley.

Frentz, T. S., & Farrell, T. B. (1976). Language-action: A paradigm for communication. *Quarterly Journal of Speech, 62*, 333-349.

Goffman, E. (1959). *The presentation of self in everyday life.* Garden City, NY: Doubleday.

Goodwin, C. (1981). *Conversational organization: Interaction between speakers and hearers.* New York: Academic Press.

Goodwin, C. (1984). Notes on story structure and the organization of participation. In J. M. Atkinson & J. Heritage (Eds.), *Structures of social action: Studies in conversation analysis* (pp. 225-246). Cambridge: Cambridge University Press.

Grice, H. P. (1975). Logic and conversation. In P. Cole & J. L. Morgan (Eds.), *Syntax and semantics: Vol. 3. Speech acts* (pp. 41-58). New York: Academic Press.

Halliday, M. A. K., & Hasan, R. (1976). *Cohesion in English.* London: Longman.

Haslett, B. (1987). *Communication: Strategic action in context.* Hillsdale, NJ: Lawrence Erlbaum.

Heritage, J. C., & Watson, D. R. (1979). Formulations as conversational objects. In G. Psathas (Ed.), *Everyday language: Studies in ethnomethodology* (pp. 123-162). New York: Irvington.

Hiltz, S. R., Johnson, K., & Turoff, M. (1986). Communication process and outcome in face-to-face versus computerized conferences. *Human Communication Research, 13*, 225-252.

Jackson, S., Jacobs, S., & Rossi, A. (1987). Conversational relevance: Three experiments on pragmatic connectedness in conversation. In M. McLaughlin (Ed.), *Communication yearbook* (Vol. 10, pp. 323-347). Newbury Park, CA: Sage.

Jacobs, S., & Jackson, S. (1983). Strategy and structure in conversational influence attempts. *Communication Monographs, 50*, 285-304.

Jefferson, G. (1972). Side sequences. In D. Sudnow (Ed.), *Studies in social interaction* (pp. 294-338). New York: Free Press.

Katz, J. J., & Fodor, J. (1963). The structure of a semantic theory. *Language, 39*, 170-210.

Kempson, R. (1977). *Semantic theory.* Cambridge: Cambridge University Press.

Larson, C. U., & Sanders, R. E. (1975). Faith, mystery, and data: An analysis of "scientific" studies of persuasion. *Quarterly Journal of Speech, 61*, 178-194.

Marwell, G., & Schmitt, D. (1967). Dimensions of compliance-gaining behavior: An empirical analysis. *Sociometry, 30*, 350-364.

McGuire, W. J. (1961). The effectiveness of supportive and refutational defenses in immunizing and restoring beliefs against persuasion. *Sociometry, 24*, 184-197.

McLaughlin, M. (1984). *Conversation: How talk is organized.* Beverly Hills, CA: Sage.

Nofsinger, R. E. (1975). The demand ticket: A conversational device for getting the floor. *Speech Monographs, 42*, 1-9.

Pearce, W. B. (1977). Naturalistic study of communication: Its function and scope. *Communication Quarterly, 25*, 51-56.

Pearce, W. B., & Cronen, V. (1980). *Communication, action, and meaning: The creation of social realities.* New York: Praeger.

Philipsen, G. (1977). Linearity of research design in ethnographic studies of speaking. *Communication Quarterly, 25*, 42-50.

Planalp, S., Graham, M., & Paulson, L. (1987). Cohesive devices in conversations. *Communication Monographs, 54*, 325-343.

Raskin, V. (1985). *Semantic mechanisms of humor.* Dordrecht: Reidel.

Reichman, R. (1978). Conversational coherency. *Cognitive Science, 2*, 283-327.

Reichman, R. (1985). *Getting computers to talk like you and me: Discourse content, focus, and semantics (an ATN model).* Cambridge: MIT Press.

Rice, R. E., & Paisley, W. J. (Eds.). (1981). *Public communication campaigns.* Beverly Hills, CA: Sage.

Rumelhart, D. (1975). Notes on a schema for stories. In D. Bobrow & A. Collins (Eds.), *Representation and understanding: Studies in cognitive science* (pp. 211-236). New York: Academic Press.

Sacks, H. (1972). On the analyzability of stories by children. In J. J. Gumperz & D. Hymes (Eds.), *Directions in sociolinguistics: The ethnography of communication* (pp. 329-345). New York: Holt, Rinehart & Winston.

Sanders, R. E. (1984). Style, meaning, and message effects. *Communication Monographs, 51*, 154-167.

Sanders, R. E. (1987a). *Cognitive foundations of calculated speech: Controlling understandings in conversation and persuasion.* Albany: SUNY Press.

Sanders, R. E. (1987b). The interconnection of utterances and nonverbal displays. *Research on Language and Social Interaction, 20*, 141-170.

Sanders, R. E. (in press). The conversation about conversation. In H. Simons (Ed.), *The rhetorical turn: Invention and persuasion in the conduct of inquiry.* Chicago: University of Chicago Press.

Schank, R. (1977). Rules and topics in conversation. *Cognitive Science, 1*, 421-441.

Schank, R., & Abelson, R. (1977). *Scripts, plans, goals, and understanding: An inquiry into human knowledge structures.* Hillsdale, NJ: Lawrence Erlbaum.

Schegloff, E. A. (1968). Sequencing in conversational openings. *American Anthropologist, 70*, 1075-1095.

Schegloff, E. A. (1972). Notes on a conversational practice: Formulating place. In D. Sudnow (Ed.), *Studies in social interaction* (pp. 75-119). New York: Free Press.

Schegloff, E. A. (1980). Preliminaries to preliminaries: "Can I ask you a question?" *Sociological Inquiry, 50*, 104-152.

Schegloff, E. A. (1982). Discourse as an interactional achievement: Some uses of "uh huh" and other things that come between sentences. In D. Tannen (Ed.), *Analyzing discourse: Text and talk* (Georgetown University Roundtable on Languages and Linguistics; pp. 71-93). Washington, DC: Georgetown University Press.

Schegloff, E. A., Jefferson, G., & Sacks, H. (1977). The preference for self-correction in the organization of repair in conversation. *Language, 53*, 361-382.

Schegloff, E. A., & Sacks, H. (1973). Opening up closings. In R. Turner (Ed.), *Ethnomethodology* (pp. 233-264). Baltimore: Penguin.

Searle, J. R. (1969). *Speech acts: An essay in the philosophy of language.* London: Cambridge University Press.

Sigman, S. J. (1987). *A perspective on social communication.* Lexington, MA: Lexington.

Sigman, S. J., & Fry, D. L. (1985). Differential ideology and language use: Readers' reconstructions and descriptions of news events. *Critical Studies in Mass Communication, 2,* 307-322.

Simons, H. (Ed.). (in press). *The rhetorical turn: Invention and persuasion in the conduct of inquiry.* Chicago: University of Chicago Press.

Sinclair, J. M., & Coulthard, R. M. (1975). *Towards an analysis of discourse.* London: Oxford University Press.

Sperber, D., & Wilson, D. (1986). *Relevance: Communication and cognition.* Oxford: Basil Blackwell.

Steinfatt, T. M., & Infante, D. A. (1976). Attitude-behavior relationships in communication research. *Quarterly Journal of Speech, 62,* 267-278.

Tannen, D. (1984). *Conversational style: Analyzing talk among friends.* Norwood, NJ: Ablex.

Tracy, K. (1982). On getting the point: Distinguishing "issues" from "events," an aspect of conversational coherence. In M. Burgoon (Ed.), *Communication yearbook* (Vol. 5, pp. 279-301). New Brunswick, NJ: Transaction.

van Dijk, T. A. (1980). *Macrostructures: An interdisciplinary study of global structures in discourse, interaction, and cognition.* Hillsdale, NJ: Lawrence Erlbaum.

van Dijk, T. A. (Ed.). (1985). *Discourse and communication: New approaches to the analysis of mass media discourse and communication.* Berlin: Walter de Gruyter.

Ventola, E. (1987). *The structure of social interaction: A systemic approach to the semiotics of service encounters.* London: Francis Pinter.

Wiseman, R. L., & Schenck-Hamlin, W. (1981). A multidimensional scaling validation of an inductively derived set of compliance-gaining strategies. *Communication Monographs, 48,* 251-270.

Chapter 8

TELEVISION COMMERCIALS AS MASS MEDIA MESSAGES

Esther Thorson

TELEVISION COMMERCIALS ARE a unique form of the persuasive mass media message. Commercials have existed as a form of media message for only 40 years, nevertheless, they must now be assigned a significant role in discussions of cultural, social, and individual effects of the mass media.

Commercials are perceived, evaluated, and studied in a variety of ways. Some philosophers, historians, and social commentators (e.g., Bell, 1976; Boorstin, 1962; Commager, 1950; Galbraith, 1967; Nouwen, 1980; Pollay, 1986; Potter, 1954) see commercials as pervasive, psychologically invasive, and generally damaging in many ways to individuals and society. In contrast, some social scientists see television commercials as an art form (Feasley, 1984; Levitt, 1970). Advertisers value television commercials to the extent of willingness to spend an average of $145,600 on producing each one of them ("Cost of TV Spot," 1989) and as much as $750,000 for 30 seconds of air time (1988 Super Bowl prices) to present them. Consistently for the last decade, two-thirds of a national sample of consumers have agreed with the statement that commercials are insulting to the intelligence (*DDB Needham Lifestyles Study,* 1987). At the same time, however, there are few ordinary people who don't report having a favorite commercial—whether claymation raisins who "heard it through the grapevine," Michael Jackson gyrating for Pepsi, or Bartles and James sharing the down-home problems of running a wine cooler operation. Finally—and, many argue, most important—the presence of commercials on the air waves pays the bills for nearly 100% of commercial television programming.

The dimensional complexity of commercials guarantees that, regardless of whether one likes, hates, or is indifferent to them, it is important to understand what they are and how they affect their audiences. The goal of the present chapter is a review and analysis of a variety of approaches to these two problems.

THE SEDUCTIVE SIMPLICITY OF COMMERCIALS AND THEIR STUDY

Although the television viewer may think of commercials as hardly more than 30-second interruptions containing mostly irritating puffery and subtle misrepresentation, the information processing researcher recognizes commercials as highly complex mass media phenomena. Indeed, as this review progresses, the seductive simplicity that many may initially attribute to commercials will be shown to be incorrect. Commercials are made up of music, colors, movement, language, characters, stories, acting, camera work, edited features, information, and meanings. In fact, one could continue for some time adding to this list of even very grossly defined attributes of commercials. The obvious question is this: "Which of these many facets should the researcher examine?" It will be argued here that the answer depends, at least to an extent, upon what questions are being asked about commercials, that is, which dependent variables are the focus of the research. But even after one has decided whether to examine how commercials are remembered, or how they influence the probability of purchase, or how they change adolescent self-images, identification and selection of dimensions along which to describe and sample commercials remains a knotty problem. It is only fair to own up to the fact that this review contains no answers to the question of how best to characterize commercials. Instead, it attempts to overview the main alternative strategies for describing commercials and measuring their impact, and to provide some evaluation of how those alternatives have panned out in research thus far.

Not only are commercials themselves complex, studying them in such a way as to be able to generalize to "commercials" (as opposed to slice-of-life commercials for Tide, or, less general yet, to a particular execution for a particular brand) is a dilemma. Thousands of commercials exist or have existed and, like people, more are born each day. Of course, studies that examine only one commercial from among those thousands do not provide any generalizable information (Jackson & Jacobs, 1983). (Unfortunately, not all editors have come to terms with this fact.)

Second, although filming one's own commercials and making simple and minute changes so that individual aspects of the commercials can be studied experimentally sounds great in theory, anyone who has seen the final products of filming carried out in a university broadcast laboratory knows that these products are not "true" commercials. Making a commercial that could run on prime time is simply not a matter for the budgets of academic researchers. Therefore, experimental manipulation of commercials as stimulus objects, although in some limited cases possible, is not a generally feasible or advisable strategy.

A third strategy, and one that holds some promise, involves taking existent commercials and editing them so as to create the desired stimulus variation. Splicing together scenes from similar commercials, manipulating voice-overs, and cutting 60-second commercials to 15 seconds are all possible without great loss of a professional look. Indeed, this method has been used in a number of studies. Schumann (1986) edited commercials to be either less or more interesting. Thorson, Reeves, and Lometti (1984) took children's toy commercials that contained questionable representations of the toys with animation techniques and created a "matched" set of commercials with the animation sequences replaced with reasonable footage from similar commercials. If researchers have access to editing equipment, these kinds of changes in commercials are possible, even for those without professional editing skills.

The remaining method, and one currently the most popular in the advertising literature, involves representative sampling of commercials. Under this approach, the researcher samples commercials for study, just as he or she would sample subjects to watch those commercials. Unfortunately, although there are generally agreed upon strategies for sampling people, there are no such strategies for sampling commercials. Indeed, in the studies that have sampled commercials, the hows and wherefores of the sampling process are usually not mentioned. The reason is that there is no agreed upon taxonomy for describing and categorizing commercials. (See Thorson & Leavitt, 1986, for an initial attempt at such a taxonomy.) Researchers believe that adults 25 to 55 are usually significantly different from those over 55, but it is not clear whether commercials for shelf products are different from those for big ticket items. It is not clear whether problem-solution commercials are different from image commercials. Or whether commercials that describe product attributes are different from those that create an atmosphere for the brand. Until the critical dimensions of commercials are known, believing that a sample of commercials is representative of all commercials must remain a leap of faith.

It becomes clear, then, that not only are commercials multifaceted and complex but determination of which ones to use when attempting to study them is equally difficult. The problem seems to boil down to the need to know how to describe commercials before it is possible to get a very accurate picture of their effects. The fact that most studies have not dealt with the problem of what kinds of commercials are being studied should be kept in mind when evaluating all the research reviewed in upcoming sections.

CAVEATS AND LIMITATIONS OF THE REVIEW

Like all reviews, the present one has important coverage limitations and boundary conditions. Articulation of five of these seems particularly helpful.

A first limitation is that most of the literature cited is experimental. The effects of commercials are sometimes studied by surveying respondents, as, for example, when people are questioned about which political commercials they remember and believe to have affected them (Faber & Storey, 1984). It is difficult, if not impossible, however, to connect specific commercial structure attributes with their effects using survey methodology. The first reason is that there is no control over or way to ascertain exposure accurately. The second reason is that there is no opportunity to manipulate occurrence of commercial structural variables and thereby determine their unique impact, much less to compare their impact. In general, then, most research on television commercials has used experimental methodologies, and it is that literature that will be emphasized here.

A second caveat is that the literature cited here was mainly designed to investigate intended effects of commercials, that is, their persuasive, cognitive, and memorial impact. Unintended effects (Pollay, 1986), such as creating or reinforcing materialism, increasing personal dissatisfaction with life, changing or damaging self-perceptions, trivializing language and politics, stereotyping, disparaging authority figures, or encouraging a preoccupation with personal appearance or sexual activity, are not examined. The reason for this is not that these are unlikely effects or that they are uninteresting but simply that only a handful of studies have examined them. Perhaps in future reviews of the structure and impact of commercials, it will be feasible to focus equally on intended and unintended effects.

Third, the present review analyzes effects only at the level of the individual consumer. Sociological, anthropological, political, financial, and economic effects of television commercials are, again, not ignored because they are unimportant or uninteresting but simply because these dimensions of effects form areas in need of review in and of themselves.

Fourth, the present review focuses on the impact of commercials, independent of attributes of their audiences. There is a burgeoning literature in advertising that verifies the rather intuitive assumption that the impact of a commercial will vary as it is exposed to different segments of consumers. For example, the extent and sophistication of consumer knowledge is a major determinant of the processing of commercials (see Alba & Hutchinson, 1987, for an excellent review). Need for cognition is also important (Haugtvedt, Petty, Cacioppo, & Steidley, 1987), as is interpersonal anxiety (Hill, 1987). Many dimensions of people/product relations also affect the ways commercials affect individuals. A few examples include involvement with a product category, loyalty to brands, ability to differentiate brands, information seeking propensities, patterns of communication with others, interest in price, and decision-making attributes (Cushing & Douglas-Tate, 1985). Aspects of audiences that mediate the impact of commercials are not forsaken in the present review for any reason except that their inclusion would demand an additional 30 pages of text. It should be noted, however, that one area of the theories that will be reviewed does refer to consumer involvement and hence the claim that there is no treatment of audience variables is not completely true. Rather there is omission of most, but not all, of this important consideration.

A final caveat is that the present review treats commercials as individual entities, ignoring their role in the flow of the television experience. This fact means that there is no discussion of the effects of repeating commercials (Batra & Ray, 1986b), compressing them

(Schleuder, Thorson, & Reeves, 1988; Schlinger, Alwitt, McCarthy, & Green, 1983), ordering them in particular ways (Thorson & Wells, 1987; Webb & Ray, 1979), or embedding them in particular kinds of programming (Schumann & Thorson, 1987). Again, each of these areas constitutes a large and important research enterprise and these omissions should be recognized.

SUMMARY OF THE REVIEW

With these limitations and omissions in mind, the reader is probably wondering what is left for review in the present document. Fortunately, there remains a large and growing literature to explore. If commercial structure and individual effects are to be linked, a critical first step is development of a *taxonomy of commercial structures*. Such a taxonomy would provide a vocabulary of descriptors of commercials, as well as a system for categorizing each and every commercial as an exemplar of some genus or species of persuasive message.

A second step in linking commercial structure and individual effects is construction of a *taxonomy of dependent measures*. This enterprise involves identifying and categorizing measures of consumer response to commercials. Such a taxonomy is better developed than the taxonomy of commercial structures, and generally includes the categories of cognitive, attitudinal, emotional, memorial, and conative (behavioral) effects of viewing commercials.

A third step is to catalog *theories about commercial structure-effect links*. Seven major areas of theory development will be overviewed here.

Although each of the three endeavors is receiving considerable attention in the literature on processing television commercials, the research in each area remains in an initial and incomplete phase. Primitive though it is, current research on processing television commercials is not, however, uninformative. It will be argued here that the study of commercials and their effects provides an excellent analogue for the study of any kind of mass media message and that many of the commercial structure-effect links discovered in the advertising literature may generalize to the impact of other media messages.

A TAXONOMY OF WAYS TO
DESCRIBE COMMERCIALS

Hundreds of thousands of commercials exist and new ones are constantly being created. How can these messages be described, catalogued, compared, and contrasted? There is virtually an infinite number of possible systems for describing commercials, and perhaps a decision about which one to use depends upon which system best allows prediction of commercial effects.

DESCRIBING COMMERCIALS IN TERMS OF
WHAT THEY INTEND TO SELL

One of the most basic and global ways to categorize commercials is in terms of what they are meant to sell. The most frequently occurring category of this type is product and service commercials. In these, the focus is a product brand (Pepsi, Solo) or a generic product (e.g., milk, cheese, coffee) or a service (AT&T long distance service, Breeno's Lawn Mowing).

A second category is public service commercials. These messages focus on information that is generally thought to be of value to consumers. "Take a Bite Out of Crime," safe sex campaigns against the spread of AIDS, and anti-drunk driving campaigns are examples of public service commercials. Issue advertising focuses on positions taken by corporations, individuals, or institutions on controversial issues. Examples would be commercials by Gun Control, Inc., endorsing passage of a gun control law in Congress, commercials sponsored by Planned Parenthood and arguing against making abortions more difficult for teenagers to get, or commercials sponsored by R. J. Reynolds and arguing for smokers' rights.

Corporate commercials are those that tout the favorable qualities of companies themselves. Examples would be Texaco's claim that they are searching for new sources of oil to free consumers from the tyranny of the Arab countries, and General Electric's bringing good things to light for consumers.

Finally, there are political commercials. These focus on reasons to vote for one or several individuals running for political office.

Although there has been little, if any, research on the comparative impact of these categories of commercials, it seems likely that product commercials are processed much differently from political commercials, or public service commercials, or issue or corporate commercials. Categorization of commercials in terms of what they intend to persuade about may, then, have significant processing importance.

DESCRIBING COMMERCIALS IN TERMS OF EXECUTIONAL STYLE

A second common way to describe commercials is in terms of their "executional style." Teachers of the creative process in advertising— that is, those who attempt to teach people how to create commercials— typically differentiate commercials in terms of executional styles. Such a differentiation involves a rather gross characterization of commercials in terms of their predominant arguments about whatever is advertised.

Although there are as many lists of executional styles as there are textbooks on copy and layout, a few examples should suffice to characterize the majority of them. Book and Carey (1970) list nine executional styles, including (a) tells a story, (b) presents a problem and then a solution, (c) presents a mood through special effects and relates this to the product, (d) testimonial, (e) satire, (f) spokesperson, (g) demonstration of the product, (h) slice of life, and (i) fantasy that is related to the product. To this list, Nelson (1973) adds song and dance extravaganzas. Hilliard (1976) adds the category of humorous commercials.

Relying more on structural than content attributes, Reid, Lane, Wenthe, and Smith (1985) compared U.S. and foreign commercials in terms of the following executional styles: (a) information presentation; (b) argument, motivation with psychological appeals; (c) repeated assertion; (d) command; (e) brand familiarization; (f) symbolic association; (g) imitation; (h) obligation; and (i) habit-starting. Similarly, Hefzallah and Maloney (1979) list six psychological executional styles: (a) association of the product with pleasant experiences, (b) demonstration of the product, (c) informative approaches to the product, (d) plots in which the product answers the problem presented in the plot, (e) staging of action in which the product is used to the consumer's satisfaction, and (f) testimonial.

In attempts to simplify the variety of executional categories, Puto and Wells (1984) suggested that all commercials are transformational, informational, or a blend of the two. Informational commercials specify product attributes. Transformational commercials are designed to change the consumer's experience with a product ("This is not just hair coloring, it's a new and better you"). In a related but more recent approach, Wells (1987) suggested that all commercials can be characterized as lectures, dramas, or mixtures of the two. A lecture talks at the viewer and provides information for him or her. A drama attempts to draw the viewer into the screen by creating a play.

Most of the executional style taxonomies were developed to enable discussion of the variety of kinds of commercials, or to help link marketing plan specifications with optimal selection of commercial executions. For example, Percy and Rossiter (1980) suggest that when a product is to be introduced, the heavy informational content of testimonials, product demonstrations, and executions where the product solves a problem are most effective.

Although there are many discussions of how and when these various executional types should be used to carry out a particular marketing strategy (Percy & Rossiter, 1980), there is virtually no research that examines their differential effects on viewers. (The one exception is transformational-informational commercials, which Puto, 1986, has studied.) Nevertheless, it may be that these gross categories of commercial structure make a difference to the viewing individual. This possibility remains for future research.

OBJECTIVE AND DESCRIPTIVE
TAXONOMIES OF COMMERCIALS

There are two additional broad, descriptive approaches to commercial structure, however, which have received significant empirical investigation (Thorson & Leavitt, 1986). One of these approaches will be referred to as *objective* taxonomies of commercial structure; the other as *subjective* taxonomies. Objective descriptions depend upon direct and often micro-level measurement of commercial attributes. Subjective descriptions depend upon characterization of commercial structure in terms of how it is perceived and described by viewers. In other words, viewer responses to a commercial serve as a surrogate for characterization of the actual structure of the commercial itself. Each of the these approaches will be discussed in turn.

Both the objective and the subjective approaches can be further subdivided into theory-free and theory-driven analyses. Theory-free descriptions are those that articulate no specific mechanisms of how commercials are processed. Theory-driven descriptions are those that hypothesize psychological mechanisms that assign importance to particular aspects of commercials or viewer characterizations of commercials. The distinction between theory-free and theory-driven description will become clearer in the examples discussed below.

Theory-free objective descriptions of commercial structure. Objective descriptions of commercials are based either on attributes that can be measured with "pointer readings" (e.g., number of scene changes, brand name mentions, number of people appearing on the screen at a particular moment, or the presence of music), or that can be estimated by experts (e.g., degree of product-narrative integration, type of emotional tenor that is emphasized, or the quality of the product attribute arguments). Theory-free descriptions are those that ignore cognitive or information processing models of how the commercial structure variables might affect viewers, and instead rely on common knowledge in advertising circles or on personal intuitions.

There have been a number of studies that used theory-free objective descriptions of commercials to try to predict consumer response. Although some of the variables did emerge from specific theoretical orientations, most of them were generated by intuition or from commonly held notions of advertising practitioners.

Several points are important to keep in mind when evaluating these studies. The first is that the sample of commercials that is used to test the effectiveness of the objectively defined variables is undoubtedly critical. As noted in the discussion above, only if a sample that somehow captures the wide variation in commercial types is used will the results be generalizable to "commercials" in general. Some of the studies reviewed here did indeed aim for this variation in their test sample. Others used only a handful of commercials and a small number of products or executional styles. Generalizations from these latter studies should, therefore, be treated cautiously.

A second point to keep in mind is that the kind of consumer response that one wants to predict will also determine which objectively defined variables are most successful. Because neither the effect of sample type or extensiveness nor the impact of using various dependent variables has been explored, the studies described below must be interpreted only as preliminary attempts to identify some attributes of commercial structure that are important.

One of the earliest studies using a theory-free objective description of commercial structure was that of Haller (1972). He used experts to judge commercials on four dimensions: (a) the extent to which the visual elements aided the audio elements in getting the message across,

(b) the stopping power of the message, (c) the clarity of the commercial, and (d) the extent to which the message spoke personally to the viewer. These dimensions, estimated by experts, were then used to predict consumer memory for six commercials for cigarettes. With the four commercial structure variables, Haller was able to account for about 20% of the variation in memory.

In another theory-free approach, Aaker and Norris (1981) correlated (a) product class of advertised products, (b) whether their commercials used a hard or soft sell, (c) whether a problem was posed, and (d) price and product test mentions to predict how informative viewers rated commercials as being. They were able to account for about 50% of the variance in ratings of commercial informativeness. They also found that informative commercials were rated as convincing, effective, and interesting, and that these commercials were discriminable from those that were disliked, entertaining, and warm.

Haley, Richardson, and Baldwin (1985) generated 510 variables in 17 categories of nonverbal variables and found that 132 of the variables were significantly related to a pre-post persuasion measure of attitudinal responses to products advertised in 47 commercials. Categories of nonverbal variables measured in the study included voice characteristics, eye contact, distances between on-screen individuals, body motion, stance, and use of gestures. There has not yet been a published report of the amount of variance in the dependent variables Haley et al. were able to predict.

Stout and Leckenby (1988) identified a number of musical attributes of commercials and used them to predict Viewer Response Profiles (VRP; a dependent variable scale developed by Schlinger, 1979, and described below) of a sample of commercials. Music was coded in terms of its presence or absence, major or minor mode, volume, tempo, and whether there was a distinct melody. The variables major and minor mode, tempo, and melody accounted for the greatest portion of the variance in the Viewer Response Profile scales.

Using the largest sample of commercials yet examined in a single study of commercial structures and their impact, Stewart and Furse (1985, 1986) defined 155 structural variables in 1059 commercials, and used them to predict the Research System Corporation's (ARS) three main commercial effect measures: recall, key message comprehension, and persuasion. After removing the differences associated with product category, Stewart and Furse were able to account for 13% to 26% of the variance in recall of the commercials, 8% of the variance in key message comprehension, and 9% to 11% of the variance in persuasion. The descriptive variables used to categorize the commercials were divided into the following categories: (a) information content, (b) brand/product identification, (c) setting, (d) visual and auditory devices, (e) promises/appeals/propositions, (f) tone/atmosphere, (g) product comparisons, (h) music and dancing, (i) structure and format, (j) characters, and (k) timing and counting measures (e.g., length of the commercial or the number of times the brand name was shown). It is interesting to note that several of these categories overlap with the general executional styles defined at the beginning of this chapter. It should be kept in mind, however, that the actual descriptive variables used were more micro level than the executional categories, and this fact distinguishes Stewart's approach from the earlier ones.

In a last example of the theory-free objective taxonomic systems, Thorson, Heide, and Page (1987) defined six categories of micro-level variables in commercials and used them to predict responses to the Viewer Response Profile (Schlinger, 1979). The first category of stimulus variable was psycholinguistic, involving variables based on theoretically developed measures of language in the commercial (described in detail in the following section). The second category was emotional, and included expert ratings of the occurrence of six types of emotional stimuli in individual scenes (e.g., warmth, disgust, drive-surgency, calm, funny, upbeat), one nonemotional category (neutral), and measures of the percentage of scenes identified as emotion-inducing. The third category identified character content in each scene (people, children, animals, animated characters, and puppets). The fourth category identified the occurrence and duration of pans and zooms. The fifth category identified attributes of the music (presence or absence, pace, whether it was instrumental only or had words, and the percentage of the verbal content that was sung). The last category was labeled visual. It included simple measures of visual content, including the number of scenes, the amount of time the brand was shown on-screen, the number of supers, and the number of times brand attributes verbally described were demonstrated visually (e.g., "cooks up less greasy" would be accompanied by a closeup of lean bacon frying in a pan).

The structures of 98 commercials were analyzed along the dimensions defined above. All of the resulting variables were stepped into seven regressions, each one predicting one of the Viewer Response

Profile (VRP) dimensions of consumer response (relevance, novelty, gentleness, organization, character likability, entertainment, and believability). The variance accounted for ranged from 23% to 52%. The emotional, music, and psycholinguistic variables showed the strongest and most consistent relationships to the VRP scales. The number of scenes, visual demonstration of brand attributes, and time spent showing the product were individual variables that were also good predictors of VRP responses.

Theory-driven objective descriptions of commercial structure. In the next series of studies of commercial structure, the objective characterization of attributes is again used. In these studies, however, the commercial attributes are selected according to psychological or psychophysiological theories of how people process information. There are only a handful of studies that have been theoretically driven.

One of the earliest attempts to describe commercials in terms relevant to models of how people might process commercials was the work of Thorson and her colleagues (Thorson, 1983; Thorson & Rothschild, 1983; Thorson & Snyder, 1984). The model used was Kintsch and van Dijk's (1978) propositional text analysis. This model suggests that underlying all language comprehension are hierarchically arranged idea units, or propositions. The complexity and arrangement of the propositions are hypothesized to predict how well information will be remembered. Analysis of the propositional structure of samples of television commercials demonstrated that about 33% of the variance in both immediate and delayed recall of the content of commercials was indeed predictable from the propositional analyses. In the Thorson, Heide, and Page (1987) study cited earlier, the propositional variables were identified in a sample of 98 commercials and their impact compared with a variety of nontheoretically defined variables. It was interesting that the propositional variables accounted for significant variance in the VRP responses, which are primarily affective and evaluative rather than memorial.

There are two additional research streams (Deighton, 1984; Kehret-Ward, 1987) that have used psycholinguistic models to define commercial structure and then used that structure to predict effects, but both of them have been applied only to print advertising and not to television commercials.

There have also been theoretically based attempts to characterize commercials in terms of their expected psychophysiological effects. In the psychophysiological laboratory at the University of Wisconsin, there have been numerous attempts to describe commercials in this way. Reeves and his colleagues (Reeves et al., 1985) demonstrated that the occurrence of edits and central figure movement on the screen were associated with suppression of the alpha frequency in the EEG patterns of viewers. (Suppression of alpha is generally an indication of increased attention.) There was also evidence that commercials with more edits and central figure movement were better remembered. Rothschild, Hyon, Reeves, Thorson, and Goldstein (1988) showed that audio events (onsets of voices or music) in commercials were associated with alpha suppression in the parietal cortex (where audio information is processed), and that visual events were associated with alpha suppression in the occipital cortex (where visual information is generally processed). This study also showed differences in alpha patterns in the two brain hemispheres. These patterns were consistent with the notion that the right hemisphere processes spatial information and the left hemisphere processes verbal information.

In another psychophysiological approach, Alwitt (1985) defined a number of categories of variables in commercial structures and showed that many of them were correlated with alpha and beta EEG patterns. Alwitt's variables included many of those already seen in earlier studies (camera movement, music presence, brand name and product attribute mentions, visual shots of brand in use, supers, and voice-overs). She also, however, included depictions of human reactions, including a measure of when two or more people were engaged in a relationship, touching, looked like real people, or experienced an emotional or humorous moment. Alwitt found that visuals of the brand in use were most consistently related to EEG activity. She concluded that commercial impact on brain wave responses was primarily due to brand/message events.

Theory-free viewer-evaluated (subjective) descriptions of commercials. In contrast to approaches that attempt to measure commercial structure directly, viewer-evaluated approaches rely upon analyses of how viewers respond to commercials to characterize commercial structure. Several studies that have used such an approach are again theory-free, that is, they are based on intuitions about what variables are important, rather than on psychological theory that identifies significant variables.

Marketing researcher Clark Leavitt has been a major proponent of the use of subjective descriptions of commercials. An early example of his work was a study (Leavitt, 1970) in which he first collected a list of 525 words that had been used by consumers in focus groups to describe commercials. From this list, Leavitt selected words as a function of how often consumers had used them. In all, 45 words were retained and found to load onto three commercial-descriptive factors: stimulating, personally relevant, and familiar. These dimensions were not used to predict other aspects of consumer response to commercials, but recently Lastovicka (1983) showed that the relevance dimension was reliable and correlated with lack of irritation with commercials, as might be expected if the measure were externally valid.

In an approach similar to Leavitt's, McEwen and Leavitt (1976) gathered 293 sentences and phrases, and reduced them to 90 key-element items that loaded onto 12 factors: empathetic product integration, announcer integrated into commercial, demonstration by people, pleasant liveliness, confusion, new product introduction, structured product story, problem solution, animation, unpleasant, persuasive, and opening suspense. Again, the factors have not been correlated with other measures of consumer response to commercials to establish their external validity.

Schlinger (1979) developed another consumer-based system, one already referred to above. The Viewer Response Profile (VRP) was formed from an initial 600 descriptive statements culled from consumer playback data, and then reduced to 49 sentences about commercials. These sentences loaded on seven factors: entertainment, confusion, relevant news, brand reinforcement, empathy, familiarity, and alienation.

Both Leavitt's and Schlinger's systems have been extensively used and revised by advertising practitioners, and in the ad industry remain the most common descriptive systems for characterizing commercials. It should be noted, however, that the systems have tended to be used more as dependent measures than as tools for predicting other consumer responses to commercials.

Theory-driven viewer-evaluated (subjective) descriptions of commercials. Analogous to the objective descriptions of commercials, psycholinguistic theory has been the main theoretical staple in development of theory-driven subjective descriptions of commercials. Also analogously, there are few theoretical studies.

Leavitt (1968) is also responsible for developing a psycholinguistic analysis of viewer free recall protocols to characterize commercials. The primary measure in Leavitt's system was the number of related references made by viewers to parts of commercials. A *related reference* is defined as a statement about relationships between any two objects, acts, or ideas in a commercial (e.g., "Solo cleans and softens"). Related references in viewer protocols predicted the order of recall strength for a number of commercials that Leavitt sampled. In an extension of this work, McConville and Leavitt (1968) further divided related references into those with narrative emphasis only, with product-narrative integration, and with product-claim integration. They found that product narrative integration occurring in viewer protocols was the best predictor of recall of commercials. In a third related approach, Leavitt, Wadell, and Wells (1970) coded viewer protocols for personal product responses, that is, viewer comments relating the product to favorable personal behavior. They were able to demonstrate that the measure correlated well with both recall and eventual report of having purchased the product.

Miscellaneous isolated measures of commercial structure. All of the preceding measures of commercial structure have been embedded in systems of describing commercials. The literature on processing commercials also contains individual dimensions of commercial structure that have been related to consumer response. One of the most active research areas has involved the characterization of kinds of emotional structure in commercials (objective characterization). These include frequent use of the trichotomy, rational elements, emotional elements, and a mixture of rational and emotional elements (Choi & Thorson, 1983; Pechmann & Stewart, 1989; Stout & Leckenby, 1986). There are also many studies that characterize commercials in terms of the emotional responses consumers have to them. These vary from identification of one emotional response (Aaker, Stayman, & Hagerty, 1986); a handful of emotions (Batra & Ray, 1986a; Friestad & Thorson, 1985; Stephens & Russo, 1987; Thorson & Friestad, in press); to scores of emotions (Batra & Holbrook, 1987; Holbrook & Westwood, 1989).

Other examples of limited characterizations of commercial structure include vividness (Kisielsus & Sternthal, 1986); using versus not using celebrity endorsers (Atkin & Block, 1983); comparative versus noncomparative advertising (Gorn & Weinberg, 1983); and one- versus two-sided arguments in commercials (Belch, 1985). None of these characterizations has as yet been integrated into the systems for describing commercials, but certainly that potential exists and would be a fruitful enterprise.

A TAXONOMY OF INTENDED
EFFECTS OF COMMERCIALS

A second step to be taken in this chapter is the categorization of dependent measures used to index the intended effects of commercials. It should be noted that all of the viewer-evaluated (subjective) methods of categorizing commercials described above can and do serve as dependent measures as well as independent measures. For example, categorization of commercials as being "emotional" can be either a method of categorizing a commercial or a measure of the commercial's effect. Indeed, most subjective characterizations would belong in the category listed below of viewer perceptions and evaluations of commercials.

One of the oldest and, until recently, most popular indices of commercial effects is memory. Free recall—or, as it is sometimes called, proven recall—is measured by asking viewers either to list all the commercials they have recently seen or that they have seen during a particular program. Recognition memory is measured by presentation of aspects of commercials (often including false positives) and requesting that the viewer discriminate aspects encountered from those that were not. Both recall and recognition can be measured immediately after viewing or after various delays.

One of the most common recall measures was devised and implemented by the Burke Market Research company. Their 24-hour recall measure involves calling viewers the day after a test commercial has been aired and determining how many of them who watched the program in which the commercial appeared can either freely recall it or recall it after being prompted with a product category or a brand name cue.

A second dependent measure is one borrowed from the social psychological literature. Cognitive response measures were developed in the 1960s (Brock, 1967; Greenwald, 1968; Petty, Ostrom, & Brock, 1981). These measures are gathered by asking viewers to "list all the thoughts and feelings that went through your mind as you watched." In an early application of the method to the study of commercials, Wright (1973) coded three kinds of thoughts in the protocols: support arguments, counterarguments, and source derogations. These measures predominated until 1982, when Lutz and MacKenzie added the categories execution derogation and bolstering to characterize responses to the commercials themselves. Since then, several additional categories have been added, including positive affective responses (Batra & Ray, 1986a), other categories of affective response (Edell & Burke, 1987), and positive and negative viewer-oriented responses (Stephens & Russo, 1987). In all of these measures, the assumption is that a person's "cognitive" responses to the content of a commercial will serve as the source of attitude change or resistance to attitude change, and hence their importance.

A third area of dependent measures concerns involvement with commercials. In the advertising literature, Krugman (1965) originated the measure, suggesting that involvement could be indexed by the number of "bridging connections" viewers made between the content of viewed material and their own experience. The concept of involvement rapidly expanded to include estimates of situational involvement (Petty & Cacioppo, 1979), often measured as the number of positive, negative, and neutral thoughts listed after viewing; enduring involvement (Houston & Rothschild, 1977; Sherif & Cantril, 1947); product involvement (scales have been developed by Laurent & Kapferer, 1988; Kapferer & Laurent, 1986; Zaichowsky, 1985, 1987); and executional involvement (Gardner, Mitchell, & Russo, 1985).

Attitudinal responses to commercials composes a fourth category of dependent measures. Attitude toward a brand is typically measured by semantic differential items like pleasant-unpleasant, useful-useless, best-worst. Attitude toward products and commercials is measured by similar items.

Conative responses to commercials compose a fifth category of dependent measures. Intention to purchase is the most frequent index of conation and is generally indexed by semantic differential items such as the anchors, definitely would buy/definitely would not buy. A handful of studies (Smith & Swinyard, 1982, 1983) provide actual opportunities to choose among brands. Universal product code scanners installed in retail stores have allowed data to be collected on actual purchases of products, and these data can be related to electronically recorded data about viewing behavior in the home. Unfortunately, most of these data have remained proprietary and are not available in the literature (Carefoot, 1982).

A sixth category includes dependent measures that focus on viewer attention to commercials. Research cited earlier (Reeves et al., 1985; Rothschild et al., 1986) has used suppression of the alpha frequency of EEG as an indicator of increased attention. Lang (1987) used the orienting response pattern of heart rate to index attention to onsets and other attention-enhancing structural elements in commercials. Several other research streams have focused on measurement of viewer eyes-on-screen to indicate selective attention to television to the exclusion of other stimulus opportunities (Anderson, 1987; Horn & Atkin, 1987; Thorson & Zhao, 1987; Thorson, Zhao, & Friestad, 1987). Finally, a number of studies have relied on self-reported levels of attention to commercials (e.g., Friestad & Thorson, 1987; Nowak & Thorson, 1986).

A seventh dependent measure is emotional response. Several of the viewer response scales have involved emotional categories (Aaker & Bruzzone, 1981; Schlinger, 1979; Wells et al., 1971). Stout and Leckenby (1986) used three categories of coding viewer responses to emotional messages. Holbrook and Westwood (1989) developed a commercial-emotion scale based on Plutchik's (1980) four polar pairs of human emotions (acceptance/disgust, fear/anger, joy/sadness, and anticipation/surprise). Edell and Burke (1987) used upbeat, negative, and warm. Batra and Holbrook developed a scale for the emotions pleasure, arousal, and domination. Allen, Machleit, and Marine (1987) adapted Izard's Differential Emotions Scale to commercials. Friestad and Thorson (1985) used a dial-turning measure to index the pattern of emotional valence (positive and negative) and intensity over the duration of commercials. And Aaker, Stayman, and Hagerty (1986) used pencil tracings of warmth level across the duration of commercials to measure emotional response.

THEORIES OF COMMERCIAL
IMPACT ON VIEWERS

Most theories of how people respond to commercials are psychological in origin, and most of them take an information processing viewpoint. Although there are many individual models of consumer processing of commercials, the present review will examine only seven specific models or categories of models. These models clearly dominate the literature. Most of them are applied to both print and television advertising, although, consistent with the rest of this chapter, our focus will be on models that have been specifically applied to television commercials.

HIERARCHICAL MODELS OF COMMERCIAL EFFECTS

Hierarchical models assume that, for a commercial to be successful, it must be the initiating cause of people progressing through an ordered series of psychological processes. The earliest hierarchy model was introduced by E. St. Elmo Lewis (1898, cited in Preston, 1982). He suggested the critical steps included attention to the commercial, interest in the product, desire for the product, and action (e.g., purchase). Lavidge and Steiner (1961) assumed the same ordered set of processes, but replaced Lewis's steps with the stages of commercial awareness, product knowledge, product liking, product preference (over competitors), conviction of the judiciousness of purchase, and purchase. McGuire (1969) suggested the hierarchy should include attention, comprehension, yielding to the conclusion, retention of the new information, and behavior (purchase).

In an attempt to make the hierarchy concept more consistent with what is known about commercial processing (Preston, 1982; Preston & Thorson, 1984), it was assumed that each of the three main stages of the classic hierarchy, that is, perceiving the commercial, evaluating the brand, and becoming stimulated to respond to it, could be subdivided into (a) a *prior* state of the stage (before the commercial was encountered), (b) a change in response of that stage to the *product* because of experience with a commercial, and (c), as a result, an *integration* of the prior state and new response. This change meant that the full hierarchy was hypothesized to include the following subprocesses: awareness of an ad, perception of the advertised brand (prior, product, and integrated), evaluation of the brand (prior, product, and integrated), stimulation toward the brand (prior, product, and integrated), and, finally, action.

The power in the hierarchy models is that they are concerned with a whole family of responses stretching from exposure to a commercial to, eventually, an action response to it. The problem with the models is that they are so broad that they are difficult to test. It is also difficult to determine when all the succeeding stages would be expected to occur.

If they all occurred immediately after an ad exposure, it is not clear what measures could be used to index them or how one would tell which response came first. In addition, the hierarchy models assume a high level of conscious, cognitive response to commercials. This assumption is inconsistent both with intuition about watching television commercials and with a mounting literature on "low-involvement processing," a theoretical concept that will be discussed in detail below.

THE MULTIATTRIBUTE MODEL OF PROCESSING COMMERCIALS

For 20 years, the most influential model of commercial processing was the Fishbein-Ajzen (Fishbein & Ajzen, 1975) multiattribute model. This model suggests that a consumer's attitude toward any brand (or service) is determined by a summing of the consumer's evaluative response toward each individual product attribute (e_i), multiplied by a subjective estimate of the probability that the brand in question actually possesses attribute i (b_i). This relationship is represented by the well-known equation: $A_0 = b_i e_i$, where A_0 is the attitude toward the object (the brand).

According to this attitude change model, a commercial changes brand attitude either by changing a person's perception of the probability that a brand has some attribute, or by changing a person's evaluative beliefs about the attribute. The multiattribute model, like the hierarchies, assumes a conscious, cognitive orientation toward commercials. People are assumed to watch commercials, and constantly update their A_0 values. To repeat, the evidence that people are unlikely to maintain so high a level of involvement with commercials argues against such an approach, and it may well be that for print ads the model works better than for television commercials where less processing energy is necessary from the consumer.

INVOLVEMENT MODELS OF PROCESSING COMMERCIALS

Sherif and Cantril (1947) defined ego involvement in terms of attitudes closely integrated with people's egos. Ego-involved attitudes are those that people identify with and consider important aspects of their selves. Sherif and Hovland (1961) defined task involvement as a fleeting importance attached to particular situations because of external demands on people. An example would be an individual's involvement with a test when a teacher stresses the importance of performing well on it. In 1965, Krugman introduced the notion that television is an activity that involves few "bridging experiences," that is, personal links the viewer makes between what is being watched and his or her own experience. All three of these notions of involvement—ego, task, and personal, as well as many others—have come to play an important role in theories about how advertising is processed. Although there are many models of commercial processing that depend upon the concept of involvement, this review will examine only two of the most influential: Ray's Hierarchies of Effects Model and the Elaboration Likelihood Model of Petty and Cacioppo.

Ray's (1973) model, as its name indicates, is a hierarchy model of the type discussed earlier. The model appears in this section, however, because it violates the most basic notion of the classical hierarchies. It allows the stages to occur in several orders rather than in a single fixed one. For Ray, the three basic stages of responses to commercials include cognition, attitudes, and behavior. Like the hierarchies, Ray's model posits that, when people are motivated to learn from commercials (high involvement), they learn about a product, develop attitudes toward it, and may even eventually purchase it. But sometimes people are not motivated to learn. Then changes in cognitions precede changes in behavior, and changes in attitudes are the last occurrence. This order of the stages is called the low-involvement hierarchy. (There is a third hierarchy, dissonance attribution, but it is not relevant to message processing.)

An analysis and critique of Ray's model and its tests are not feasible here (see Salmon, 1986, for a complete review of the involvement concept). It is important, however, to note that the basic concept in the model is that the processing of commercials depends upon whether individuals are high- or low-involved. Indeed, Ray's model appears to be basically dichotomous. A consumer is in either one state or the other.

Probably the most influential model of consumer processing of commercials is the Elaboration Likelihood Model (ELM). It was first articulated by Petty and Cacioppo (1979) and has since undergone numerous changes and fine-tunings. Basically, the model suggests that attitudes are formed by two different routes. The central route focuses on message arguments, examining them for quality, and on the generating of thoughts (cognitive responses and evaluations) in reaction to them. This, of course, is the high-involvement condition. When it occurs, elaboration probability is said to be a high.

But under some circumstances, consumer involvement is low. When this is so, the peripheral route occurs. The consumer associates positive or negative cues with the advertised brand, or he or she infers things about the brand based on superficial analysis of cues in the commercial. There is little or no elaboration of the arguments. Motivation and ability to process information are antecedents that determine whether central or peripheral processing is likely to occur. Although it is generally treated as a dichotomous-state model—one either processes centrally or peripherally—Petty, Cacioppo, and Kasmer have recently (1987) suggested that the involvement response is continuous, and blends of central and peripheral processing can occur. (See Stiff, 1986, for a critique of the ELM, and Petty, Kasmer, Haugtvedt, & Cacioppo, 1987, for a response.)

There are a number of variations on the two involvement-dependent models discussed here. A list of them would include Batra and Ray's (1986b) Motivation, Ability, and Opportunity to Respond Model; Burnkrant and Sawyer's (1983) Information Processing Intensity Model; Greenwald and Leavitt's (1984) Involvement Model; and Gardner, Mitchell, and Russo's (1985) Brand-Nonbrand Processing Model.

ATTITUDE-TOWARD-THE-AD (Aad) MODELS

The basic concept in all of the Aad models is that consumers' attitudes about commercials sometimes influence their attitudes toward brands and their intentions to purchase. Those who accept the concept of the Reasonable Consumer find objectionable the idea that people's feelings about ads could influence their attitudes toward brands. And, of course, unless one accepts the assumption that a brand's attributes include its advertising, Aad models are inconsistent with the multi-attribute models. Most Aad models also include the concept of involvement. For example, it is often assumed in these models that, whenever the consumer operates with low-involvement processing, the cognitive processing necessary for thoughtful brand evaluation disappears, and the consumer takes heuristic shortcuts such as liking the brand if its ad is liked.

The Aad models were introduced by Mitchell and Olson (1981) and Shimp (1981). Shimp suggested that liked ads create positive feelings or affect, and this affect is then transferred to the brand. Affect transference is often conceptualized as a classical conditioning process, although a simple "association by contiguity" explanation is more parsimonious. MacKenzie, Lutz, and Belch (1986) introduced the possibility that attitude toward the ad may affect brand attitude directly or via brand cognitions, or that attitude toward the ad may affect purchase intention without being mediated either by brand cognitions or by brand attitudes. In general, there seems to be little question that Aad influences consumer responses to brands, but the path(s) by which this occurs remain controversial.

CONDITIONING MODELS OF COMMERCIAL PROCESSING

Consumer researchers generally refer to "classical conditioning" of responses to commercials, but because there is little evidence that humans can be classically conditioned (Allen & Madden, 1985; McSweeney & Bierley, 1984), the present discussion will focus on the more general concept of conditioning, meaning the automatic connecting of stimulus and response elements as a function of their proximity in time or space. For example, the presence of a beautiful woman next to a bottle of perfume may lead to the associating of responses to the woman with the brand name of the perfume. This would mean that, on reoccurrence of the brand name, the individual might experience the same positive feelings as were experienced when the woman was present. These positive feelings might in turn influence verbally indexed attitudes toward the brand, and thereby influence the likelihood that it will be purchased. As can be seen, the conditioning model is virtually complete in its rejection of conscious, rational operations in consumers.

One of the earliest presentations of data in support of such a conditioning process was Rossiter and Percy's (1980) demonstration that an ad with high visual emphasis on a beer produced greater positive brand attitudes toward the beer. Mitchell (1983) showed that a brand connected with a picture for which there was strong positive affect also showed more positive brand attitudes. Gorn (1982) showed that people were more likely to select the color of ballpoint pen that they had seen advertised with likable than with unlikable music. Most recently, Shimp and his colleagues (Stuart, Shimp, & Engle, 1987) showed that the direction and magnitude of attitude changes toward brands were consistent with predictions from classical conditioning experiments. These manipulations included the influence of number of pairings, latent inhibition due to subject preexposure to the conditioned stimulus, and the fact that forward conditioning of attitudes was superior to backward conditioning.

EMOTION-BASED MODELS OF COMMERCIAL PROCESSING

Seven years ago, Plummer and Holman (1981) suggested that understanding how viewers' emotions were affected by advertising was a critical issue. In the ensuing years, advertising researchers have embarked on various approaches to modeling how emotion plays a role in the processing of advertising. As in any new pursuit, definition of terms and assumptions about basic mechanisms have been diverse. Although psychologists studying emotion have tended to define the concept in terms of multiple aspects (including subjective experience, cognitive processes of appraisal and labeling of the subjective experience, and psychophysiological responses), most advertising researchers have relied upon appraisal processes alone. Indeed, one of the most frequent approaches has involved attempts to identify all the words that people use to describe their emotional responses to advertising (Aaker, Stayman, & Vezina, 1987; Allen, Machleit, & Marine, 1987; Batra, 1984; Holbrook & Batra, 1987; Holbrook & Westwood, 1989).

Some of these approaches start from psychological models of emotion and then ask which emotions are relevant for discriminating responses to advertising. For example, Holbrook and Westwood (1989) hypothesized that Plutchik's (1980) taxonomy of eight emotions (acceptance, disgust, fear, anger, joy, sadness, anticipation, and surprise) would exhaustively characterize advertising responses. Other approaches have collected emotional terms from a review of the psychological literature and then tried to determine which ones were applicable to advertising responses. An example would be Holbrook and Batra's (1987) list of 22 emotions (surprise, sadness, disgust, anger, shame, anxiety, affection, activation, confusion, attention, competence, helplessness, surgency, skepticism, pride, serenity, tension, desire, faith, gratitude, purity, and involvement). Some approaches have been selective rather than exhaustive. Aaker, Stayman, and Hagerty (1986) concentrated on warmth. Friestad and Thorson (1985) concentrated on positive, negative, neutral, and poignant feelings. More recently, Thorson (1986) expanded the list to include the emotions that seemed to account for the greatest variance in responses to advertising (disgust-anxiety, calm-peaceful, warm, poignant, drive-surgency and neutral).

In yet another approach, Stephens and Russo (1987) simply identified for individual commercials the emotions that the creators of the commercials had intended for them to elicit.

Although the attempts to identify emotional labels are most useful in describing consumer responses, there also exist several models of how emotion operates as people watch commercials. Most of the models are cognitive. For example, Batra and Ray (1986a) suggest that affective responses should be added to other cognitive response variables when analyzing what consumers say about commercials. They demonstrated that affective responses categorized as SEVA (surgency, elation, vigor, activation), deactivation, social affection, and neutral would account for attitudes toward commercials and brands even after the effects of other cognitive response variables (support and counterarguments, execution discounting and bolstering) were first removed. One of the most popular conceptions of the role of emotion is that it operates indirectly on brand attitudes via attitude toward the commercial (Edell & Burke, 1987; Gardner et al., 1985; MacKenzie, Lutz, & Belch, 1986).

A competing theoretical idea about the role of emotion is that it becomes associated via conditioning with other elements in the commercial, including memory for the whole commercial and attitude toward the brand. Srull (1983) suggested that, when consumers are asked to evaluate brands as they process ads, moods induced by the ads affect brand attitudes via mood state associations. Friestad and Thorson (1985) suggested that emotion experienced during television commercials becomes associated (via conditioning principles) with all aspects of the memory for the commercial and the brand.

It is important to note that models of how emotion operates in the processing of advertising are often integrated with other aspects of consumer processing, including involvement (Batra & Ray, 1986b), attitude toward the ad (Edell & Burke, 1987), and cognitive responding (Batra & Ray, 1986a).

ATTENTIONAL MODELS OF COMMERCIAL PROCESSING

A final area of theory about how commercials affect viewers concerns the impact of attentional demands. The approaches here are diverse. Certain areas of attitude theory suggest that distraction from the processing of commercials will reduce the accessing of relevant background information and thereby reduce counterarguing (Petty & Cacioppo, 1979). One test of the distraction hypothesis is to compress commercials so that they are presented at speeds 20% to 60% faster than normal. Moore, Hausknecht, and Thamodaran (1987) showed that brand attitudes for products in radio commercials with strong arguments were unaffected by compression, but brand attitude for commercials with weak arguments became increasingly positive as exposure rate increased. They concluded that distraction of attention alters the cues that consumers use to form brand attitudes, and hence it changes attentional processing.

In another approach, limited capacity attention theory is used to explain the effects on reaction time to a secondary task of greater audio and video complexity in commercials and presence of the audio and video channels of commercials (Thorson, Reeves, & Schleuder, 1985), whether the scenes in commercials are presented in correct or scrambled orders (Thorson, Reeves, & Schleuder, 1987), and whether commercials are presented at normal or compressed speeds (Schleuder, Thorson, & Reeves, 1988). These researchers suggest that changes in response time to a tone, light, or tactile stimulus presented while consumers are watching television can be used to understand what stimuli in television commercials place additional demands on attentional processing. Further, they hypothesize (Thorson, Reeves, & Schleuder, 1987) that commercials are processed at a sensory level, where the modality of the secondary task, the degree of compression of the commercials, and momentary changes in audio and video complexity produce differentially slowed reaction times. Commercials are also processed at a meaning level, where global changes in audio and video complexity (e.g., more idea units per unit time or more edits and scene changes) and scene disordering differentially slow reaction times.

In a last example of approaches to theorizing about how attention affects the processing of commercials, Rothschild and his colleagues have used the alpha frequency of the EEG pattern (brain waves) to index locations in commercials where added attentional demands are present. These studies have shown that commercials in which there is added attention paid (i.e., which show suppression of the alpha frequency) are better recalled and recognized (Rothschild et al., 1986). The studies have also shown (Rothschild et al., 1988) that easily identifiable variables in commercials (words on the audio track, superimposed words on the visual track, package appearance, person movement, edits, scene changes, dissolves, and zooms and pans) are associated with hemi-spheric differences in the EEG patterns consistent with hypotheses about attention to verbal and visual variables. The authors conclude that EEG can be used to index attention and hence to predict at a micro (within-commercial) level where learning of commercial content will be enhanced and where it will suffer.

CONCLUDING COMMENTS

For the patient reader who has slogged through most pages of this review, some important issues about television commercials as mass media messages will already be apparent. Many of the gaps and areas for future research will also be apparent. However, for the reader who turned here directly from the first page of the review, some conclusions and generalizations should be highlighted.

Probably the most important point of this review is that describing commercials so that they can be sampled in such a way as to allow people's responses to them to generalize to responses to all the commercials in the whole world (or at least lots of others) is neither an easy task nor one that anyone has accomplished. Of the endless ways that commercials could be described or categorized, many obvious methods or systems have been attempted. It seems likely that, as the qualitative or cultural approaches become more common, these will lead to new and exciting ways to describe commercials (e.g., Williamson, 1978). Undoubtedly, many alternatives remain for further discovery and artic-ulation. One hopes that a review like the present one will at least provide a condensed dictionary of dimensions along which television messages, particularly of the persuasive type, may vary.

Another point of this review is that the inherent complexity of commercial structure, and uncertainty about how best to capture that complexity, have led to the development of many models of how commercials affect the information processing of their viewers. Al-though many of these models borrow concepts from each other (as when, for example, the ELM suggests that conditioning is the dominant processing mechanism under low-involvement circumstances), many of the models simply ignore processes centrally hypothesized by other models (as when, for example, the involvement models fail even to mention attentional processes). Only the hierarchy models appear to include all reasonable stages of processing, but they are simply too complex at this point to test empirically and, therefore, serve more a heuristic than a research-guidance role.

Early in the chapter, it was suggested that the study of commercials and their impact might serve as an analogue for the study of other kinds of mass media messages, including news stories, television and radio programs and films of various genres, the presidential debates, and so on. Often the focus in studying these other kinds of media messages is on learning or comprehension and not persuasion. When, however, the concern is with attitude impact, then presumably the same models that are being used to understand commercials may well be relevant. The study of commercials also may serve as an analogue to the study of other messages, in that the task of devising a taxonomy of these other messages is a necessary one. For example, although genre often guides selection of television programs, certainly there is great diversity within situation comedies, mysteries, and adventure action programs, to mention only a few. Indeed, it may be that fast-moving programs or programs about women determine viewing processes and that genre differences are not particularly important.

Finally, the reader should again be reminded of the implicit metaphysical assumptions made here. The consumer information processing (CIP) approach has obviously informed the discussion. CIP, however, is only one of many research orientations that one might adopt toward the television commercial. The research reported here is clearly administrative, that is, it endeavors to answer questions of interest to those who create and use commercials for their own purposes. Thus limited in its scope, this review is only a drop in the bucket of characterizations and theories about commercial structure and impact. An exciting prospect is the day when nonadministrative and administrative research channels can flow together, each enriching the other with its concepts and findings. For now, one is best left knowing that the literature reported here does exist, that it can be useful, considering carefully its limitations.

REFERENCES

Aaker, D. A., & Bruzzone, D. E. (1981). Viewer perceptions of prime-time television advertising. *Journal of Advertising Research, 21*, 15-23.

Aaker, D. A., & Norris, D. (1981). *Characteristics of television commercials perceived as informative* (Working paper). Berkeley: University of California.

Aaker, D. A., Stayman, D. M., & Hagerty, M. R. (1986). Warmth in advertising: Measurement, impact and sequence effects. *Journal of Consumer Research, 12,* 365-381.

Aaker, D. A., Stayman, D. M., & Vezina, R. (1987). *Identifying feelings elicited by advertising.* Manuscript, University of California at Berkeley, School of Business.

Alba, J. W., & Hutchinson, J. W. (1987). Dimensions of consumer expertise. *Journal of Consumer Research, 13,* 411-454.

Allen, C. T., Machleit, K. A., & Marine, S. S. (1987, October). *On assessing the emotionality of advertising via Izard's Differential Emotions Scale.* Paper presented at the Association for Consumer Research, Boston.

Allen, C. T., & Madden, T. J. (1985). A closer look at classical conditioning. *Journal of Consumer Research, 12,* 301-315.

Alwitt, L. F. (1985). EEG activity reflects the content of commercials. In L. F. Alwitt & A. A. Mitchell (Eds.), *Psychological processes and advertising effects* (pp. 201-220). Hillsdale, NJ: Lawrence Erlbaum.

Anderson, D. R. (1987, October). *Analysis of lengths of TV viewing sessions.* Paper presented at the Association for Consumer Research, Boston.

Atkin, C., & Block, M. (1983). Effectiveness of celebrity endorsers. *Journal of Advertising Research, 23,* 57-61.

Batra, R. (1984). Affective advertising: Role, processes, and measurement. In R. A. Peterson, W. D. Hoyer, & W. R. Wilson (Eds.), *The role of affect in consumer behavior: Emerging theories and applications* (pp. 53-85). Lexington, MA: D. C. Heath.

Batra, R., & Holbrook, M. B. (1987). Development of a set of scales to measure affective responses to advertising. *Journal of Consumer Research, 14,* 404-420.

Batra, R., & Ray, M. L. (1985). How advertising works at contact. In L. Alwitt & A. A. Mitchell (Eds.), *Psychological processes and advertising effects* (pp. 13-44). Hillsdale, NJ: Lawrence Erlbaum.

Batra, R., & Ray, M. L. (1986a). Affective responses mediating acceptance of advertising. *Journal of Consumer Research, 13,* 234-249.

Batra, R., & Ray, M. L. (1986b). Situational effects of advertising repetition: The moderating influence of motivation, ability and opportunity to respond. *Journal of Consumer Research, 12,* 432-445.

Belch, G. E. (1985). The effects of message modality on one- and two-sided advertising messages. *Advances in Consumer Research* (Association for Consumer Research), *12,* 21-26.

Bell, D. (1976). *The cultural contradictions of capitalism.* New York: Basic Books.

Book, A., & Carey, N. (1970). *The television commercial.* Chicago: Crain.

Boorstin, D. J. (1962). *The image.* New York: Atheneum.

Brock, T. C. (1967). Communication discrepancy and intent to persuade as determinants of counterargument production. *Journal of Experimental Social Psychology, 3,* 269-309.

Burnkrant, R. E., & Sawyer, A. G. (1983). Effects of involvement and message content on information processing intensity. In R. J. Harris (Ed.), *Information processing research in advertising* (pp. 43-64). Hillsdale, NJ: Lawrence Erlbaum.

Carefoot, J. L. (1982). Copy testing with scanners. *Journal of Advertising Research, 22,* 25-27.

Choi, Y., & Thorson, E. (1983). Memory for factual, emotional, and balanced ads under two instructional sets. In A. D. Fletcher (Ed.), *Proceedings of the American Academy of Advertising* (pp. 160-164). Knoxville: University of Tennessee.

Commager, H. S. (1950). *The American mind.* New Haven, CT: Yale University Press.

Cost of TV spot pegged at $145,600. (1989, March 6). *Advertising Age,* p. 68.

Cushing, P., & Douglas-Tate, M. (1985). The effect of people/product relationships on advertising processing. In L. Alwitt & A. A. Mitchell (Eds.), *Psychological processes and advertising effects* (pp. 241-260). Hillsdale, NJ: Lawrence Erlbaum.

DDB Needham Lifestyles Study. (1987). [Available from DDB Needham Worldwide, 303 East Wacker Drive, Chicago].

Deighton, J. (1984). The interaction of advertising and evidence. *Journal of Consumer Research, 11,* 763-770.

Edell, J. A., & Burke, M. C. (1987). The power of feelings in understanding advertising effects. *Journal of Consumer Research, 14,* 421-433.

Faber, R. J., & Storey, M. C. (1984). Recall of information from political advertising. *Journal of Advertising, 13,* 39-44.

Feasley, F. (1984). Television commercials: The "unpopular art." *Journal of Advertising, 13,* 4-10.

Fishbein, M., & Ajzen, I. (1975). *Belief, attitude, intention and behavior: An introduction to theory and research.* Reading, MA: Addison-Wesley.

Friestad, M., & Thorson, E. (1985). *Effects of four types of emotion-eliciting TV messages on memory and judgment.* Madison: University of Wisconsin, Journalism and Mass Communication.

Friestad, M., & Thorson, E. (1987, August). *Encoding and retrieval instructions and the impact of emotional commercials.* Paper presented at the American Psychological Association, New York.

Galbraith, J. K. (1967). *The new industrial state.* Boston: Houghton Mifflin.

Gardner, M. P. (1985). Does attitude toward the ad affect brand attitude under a brand evaluation set? *Journal of Marketing Research, 22,* 192-198.

Gardner, M., Mitchell, A., & Russo, J. E. (1985). Low involvement strategies for processing advertisements. *Journal of Advertising, 14,* 4-12.

Gorn, G. J. (1982). The effects of music in advertising on choice behavior: A classical conditioning approach. *Journal of Marketing, 46,* 94-101.

Gorn, G. J., & Weinberg, C. B. (1983). Comparative advertising: Some positive results. In R. P. Bagozzi & A. M. Tybout (Eds.), *Advances in consumer research* (Vol. 10, pp. 377-380). Ann Arbor, MI: Association for Consumer Research.

Greenwald, A. G. (1968). Cognitive learning, cognitive response to persuasion, and attitude change. In A. G. Greenwald, T. C. Brock, & T. C. Ostrom (Eds.), *Psychological foundations of attitudes* (pp. 148-170). New York: Academic Press.

Greenwald, A. G., & Leavitt, C. (1984). Audience involvement in advertising: Four levels. *Journal of Consumer Research, 11,* 581-592.

Haley R. I., Richardson, J., & Baldwin, B. M. (1985). The effects of nonverbal communications in television advertising. *Journal of Advertising Research, 24,* 11-18.

Haller, T. B. (1972). Predicting recall of TV commercials. *Journal of Advertising Research, 12,* 43-46.

Haugtvedt, C., Petty R. E., Cacioppo, J. T., & Steidley, T. (1987, October). *Personality and ad effectiveness: Exploring the utility of need for cognition.* Paper presented at the Association for Consumer Research, Boston.

Hefzallah, I. M., & Maloney, W. P. (1979). Are there only six kinds of TV commercials? *Journal of Advertising Research, 19,* 57-64.

Hill, R. P. (1987). The impact of interpersonal anxiety on consumer information processing. *Psychology and Marketing, 4,* 93-106.

Hilliard, R. (1976). *Writing for TV and radio.* New York: Hastings House.

Holbrook, M. B., & Batra, R. (1987). Assessing the role of emotions as mediators of consumer responses to advertising. *Journal of Consumer Research, 14,* 404-420.

Holbrook, M. B., & Westwood, R. A. (1989). The role of emotion in advertising revisited: Testing a typology of emotional responses. In P. Cafferata & A. Tybout (Eds.), *Cognitive and affective responses to advertising* (pp. 353-372). Lexington, MA: Lexington.

Horn, M., & Atkin, M. (1987, October). *The changing commercial environment.* Paper presented at the Association for Consumer Research, Boston.

Houston, M., & Rothschild, M. (1977). *A paradigm for research on consumer involvement* (Working paper 11-7-46). Madison: University of Wisconsin, School of Business.

Jackson, S., & Jacobs, S. (1983). Generalizing about messages: Suggestions for design and analysis of experiments. *Human Communication Research, 9,* 169-191.

Kapferer, J., & Laurent, G. (1986). Consumer involvement profiles: A new practical approach to consumer involvement. *Journal of Advertising Research, 25,* 48-56.

Kehret-Ward, T. (1987, October). *Transformational analysis of goal-relevant object schema.* Paper presented at the Association for Consumer Research, Boston.

Kintsch, W., & van Dijk, T. A. (1978). Toward a model of text comprehension and production. *Psychological Review, 85,* 363-394.

Kisielsus, J., & Sternthal, B. (1986). Examining the vividness controversy: An availability valence interpretation. *Journal of Consumer Research, 12,* 418-431.

Krugman, H. E. (1965). The impact of television advertising; Learning without involvement. *Public Opinion Quarterly, 29,* 349-356.

Lang, A. (1987). *Heartrate as a measure of attention to television.* Unpublished doctoral dissertation, University of Wisconsin-Madison, School of Journalism and Mass Communication.

Lastovicka, J. L. (1983). Convergent and discriminant validity of television commercial rating scales. *Journal of Advertising, 12,* 14-23.

Laurent, G., & Kapferer, J. N. (1988). Measuring consumer involvement profiles. *Journal of Marketing Research, 21,* 41-53.

Lavidge, R. J., & Steiner, G. A. (1961). A model for predictive measurement of advertising effectiveness. *Journal of Marketing, 25,* 59-62.

Leavitt, C. (1968). Response structure: A determinant of recall. *Journal of Advertising Research, 8,* 3-6.

Leavitt, C. (1970). A multidimensional set of rating scales for television commercials. *Journal of Applied Psychology, 54,* 427-429.

Leavitt, C., Wadell, C., & Wells, W. (1970). Improving day-after recall techniques. *Journal of Advertising Research, 10,* 13-17.

Levitt, T. (1970). The morality (?) of advertising. *Harvard Business Review, 48* 84-92.

MacKenzie, S. B., & Lutz, R. J. (1982). *Monitoring advertising effectiveness: A structural equation analysis of the mediating role of attitude toward the ad.* Unpublished manuscript, University of California, Los Angeles.

MacKenzie, S. B., Lutz, R. J., & Belch, G. E. (1986). The role of attitude toward the ad as a mediation of advertising effectiveness: A test of competing explanations. *Journal of Marketing Research, 23,* 130-143.

McConville, M. N., & Leavitt, C. (1968). Predicting product related recall from verbal response. *Proceedings, American Psychological Association Annual Convention* (pp. 677-678). Washington, DC: American Psychological Association.

McEwen, W. J., & Leavitt, C. (1976). A way to describe TV commercials. *Journal of Advertising Research, 16,* 35-39.

McGuire, W. J. (1969). An information-processing model of advertising effectiveness. In H. L. Davis & A. J. Silk (Eds.), *Behavioral and management sciences in marketing.* New York: Ronald.

McSweeney, F. K., & Bierley, C. (1984). Recent developments in classical conditioning. *Journal of Consumer Research, 11,* 619-631.

Mitchell, A. A. (1983). The effects of visual and emotional advertising: An information-processing approach. In L. Percy & A. G. Woodside (Eds.), *Advertising and consumer psychology* (pp. 197-218). Lexington, MA: Lexington.

Mitchell, A. A., & Olson, J. C. (1981). Are product attribute beliefs the only mediator of advertising effects on brand attitudes? *Journal of Marketing Research, 18,* 318-332.

Moore, D. L., Hausknecht, D., & Thamodaran, K. (1987). Time compression, response opportunity, and persuasion. *Journal of Consumer Research, 13,* 85-99.

Nelson, R. P. (1973). *The design of advertising.* Dubuque, IA: William C Brown.

Nouwen, H. (1980, July). Silence, the portable cell. *Sojourners,* p. 22.

Nowak, G., & Thorson, E. (1986, August). *The effects of involvement, message appeal, and viewing conditions on memory and evaluation of TV commercials.* Paper presented at the Association for Education in Journalism and Mass Communication, Norman, OK.

Pechmann, C., & Stewart, D. W. (1989). The multidimensionality of persuasive communications: Theoretical and empirical foundations. In P. Cafferata & A. Tybout (Eds.), *Cognitive and affective responses to advertising* (pp. 31-66). Lexington, MA: Lexington.

Percy, L., & Rossiter, J. R. (1980). *Advertising strategy.* New York: Praeger.

Petty, R. E., & Cacioppo, J. T. (1979). Issue involvement can increase or decrease persuasion by enhancing message-relevant cognitive responses. *Journal of Personality and Social Psychology, 37,* 1915-1926.

Petty, R. E., Cacioppo, J. T., & Kasmer, J. A. (1987). The role of affect in the elaboration likelihood model of persuasion. In L. Donohew, H. Sypher, & E. T. Higgins (Eds.), *Communication, social cognition, and affect* (pp. 177-143). Hillsdale, NJ: Lawrence Erlbaum.

Petty, R. E., Cacioppo, J. T., & Schumann, D. (1983). Central and peripheral routes to advertising effectiveness: The moderating role of involvement. *Journal of Consumer Research, 10,* 135-146.

Petty, R. E., Kasmer, J., Haugtvedt, C., & Cacioppo, J. T. (1987). Source and message factors in persuasion: A reply to Stiff's critique of the elaboration likelihood model. *Communication Monographs, 54,* 233-249.

Petty, R. E., Ostrom, T., & Brock, T. C. (Eds.). (1981). *Cognitive responses in persuasion.* Hillsdale, NJ: Lawrence Erlbaum.

Plummer, J. T., & Holman, R. (1981). *Communicating to the heart and/or mind.* Paper presented at the American Psychological Association Annual Convention, Los Angeles.

Plutchik, R. (1980). *Emotion: A psychoevolutionary synthesis.* New York: Harper & Row.

Pollay, R. W. (1986). The distorted mirror: Reflections on the unintended consequences of advertising. *Journal of Marketing, 51,* 18-36.

Potter, D. M. (1954). *People of plenty.* Chicago: University of Chicago Press.

Preston, I. (1982). The Association Model of the advertising communication process. *Journal of Advertising, 11,* 3-15.

Preston, I., & Thorson, E. (1984). The expanded Association Model: Keeping the hierarchy concept alive. *Journal of Advertising Research, 24,* 59-66.

Puto, C. P. (1986). Transformational advertising: Just another name for emotional advertising or a new approach? In W. D. Hoyer (Ed.), *Proceedings of the Division of Consumer Psychology* (pp. 4-6). Washington, DC: American Psychological Association.

Puto, C. P., & Wells, W. D. (1984). Informational and transformational advertising: The differential effects of time. In T. C. Kinnear (Ed.), *Advances in consumer research* (Vol. 11, pp. 638-643). Ann Arbor, MI: Association for Consumer Research.

Ray, M. (1973). Marketing communication and the hierarchy-of-effects. In P. Clarke (Ed.), *New models for mass communication research* (pp. 147-176). Beverly Hills, CA: Sage.

Reeves, B., Thorson, E., Rothschild, M., McDonald, D., Goldstein, R., & Hirsch, J. (1985). Attention to television: Intrastimulus effects of movement and scene changes on alpha variation over time. *International Journal of Neuroscience, 27,* 241-255.

Reid, L. N., Lane, W. R., Wenthe, L. S., & Smith, O. W. (1985). Creative strategies in highly creative domestic and international television advertising. *International Journal of Advertising, 4,* 11-18.

Rossiter, J. R. (1981). Predicting Starch scores. *Journal of Advertising Research, 21,* 63-68.

Rossiter, J. R., & Percy, L. (1980). Attitude change through visual imagery in advertising. *Journal of Advertising, 9,* 10-16.

Rothschild, M. L., Hyon, Y., Reeves, B., Thorson, E., & Goldstein, R. (1988). Hemispherically lateralized EEG as a response to television commercials. *Journal of Consumer Research, 15*(2), 185-198.

Rothschild, M. L., Thorson, E., Reeves, B., Hirsch, J. E., & Goldstein, R. (1986). EEG activity and the processing of television commercials. *Communication Research, 13,* 182-220.

Salmon, C. (1986). Perspectives on involvement in consumer and communication research. In B. Dervin & M. J. Voight (Eds.), *Progress in communication sciences* (Vol. 7, pp. 243-268). Norwood, NJ: Ablex.

Schleuder, J., Thorson, E., & Reeves, B. (1988, May). *Effects of time compression and complexity on attention to television commercials.* Paper presented at the International Communication Association Annual Meeting, New Orleans.

Schlinger, M. J. (1979). A profile of responses to commercials. *Journal of Advertising Research, 19,* 37-46.

Schlinger, M. J., Alwitt, L. F., McCarthy, K. E., & Green, L. (1983). Effects of time compression on attitudes and information processing. *Journal of Marketing, 47,* 79-85.

Schumann, D. W. (1986). *Exploring the program/commercial relationship: How does attitude toward the program affect attitude toward the advertised products?*. Unpublished doctoral dissertation, University of Missouri, Department of Psychology.

Schumann, D. W., & Thorson, E. (1987). *The influence of viewing context on commercial effectiveness: A selection-processing model*. Manuscript, University of Tennessee, Department of Marketing, Logistics and Transportation.

Sherif, M., & Cantril, H. (1947). *The psychology of ego-involvement*. New York: John Wiley.

Sherif, M., & Hovland, C. (1961). *Social judgment: Assimilation and contrast effects in communication and attitude change*. New Haven, CT: Yale University Press.

Shimp, T. A. (1981). Attitude toward the ad as a mediator of consumer brand choice. *Journal of Advertising, 10,* 9-15.

Smith, R. E., & Swinyard, W. R. (1982). Information response models: An integrated approach. *Journal of Marketing, 46,* 81-93.

Smith, R. E., & Swinyard, W. R. (1983). Attitude-behavior consistency: The impact of product trial versus advertising. *Journal of Marketing Research, 20,* 257-267.

Srull, T. K. (1983). Affect and memory: The impact of affective reactions in advertising on the representation of product information in memory. In R. P. Bagozzi & A. M. Tybout (Eds.), *Advances in consumer research* (Vol. 10, pp. 520-525). Ann Arbor, MI: Association for Consumer Research.

Stephens, D. L., & Russo, J. E. (1987). *Predicting post-advertising attitudes* (Working paper). College Park: University of Maryland, College of Business.

Stewart, D. W., & Furse, D. H. (1985). Analysis of the impact of executional factors on advertising performance. *Journal of Advertising Research, 24,* 23-26.

Stewart, D. W., & Furse, D. H. (1986). *Effective television advertising*. Lexington, MA: Lexington.

Stiff, J. B. (1986). Cognitive processing of persuasive message cues: A meta-analytic review of the effects of supporting information on attitudes. *Communication Monographs, 53,* 75-89.

Stout, P. A., & Leckenby, J. D. (1986). Measuring emotional response to advertising. *Journal of Advertising, 15,* 35-42.

Stout, P. A., & Leckenby, J. D. (1988). Let the music play: Music as a nonverbal element in television commercials. In S. Hecker & D. W. Stewart (Eds.), *Nonverbal communication in advertising* (pp. 207-224). Lexington, MA: Lexington.

Stuart, E., Shimp, T., & Engle, R. (1987). Classical conditioning of consumer attitudes: Four experiments in an advertising context. *Journal of Consumer Research, 14*(3), 334-349.

Thorson, E. (1983). Propositional determinants of memory for television commercials. In J. Leigh & C. R. Martin (Eds.), *Current issues and research in advertising* (pp. 139-156). Ann Arbor: University of Michigan, Graduate School of Business Administration.

Thorson, E. (1986). *Characterizing commercials that produce viewer emotion* (Technical report). Madison: University of Wisconsin, School of Journalism.

Thorson, E., & Friestad, M. (1986). The effects of emotion on episodic memory for TV commercials. In P. Cafferata & A. Tybout (Eds.), *Advertising and consumer psychology*. Lexington, MA: Lexington.

Thorson, E., Heide, M. P., & Page, T. (1987, October). *Prediction of viewer response profiles from executional aspects of commercials*. Paper presented at the Association for Consumer Research, Boston.

Thorson, E., & Leavitt, C. (1986, August). *Probabilistic functionalism and the search for a taxonomy of commercials.* Paper presented at the American Psychological Association, Washington, DC.

Thorson, E., Reeves, B., & Lometti G. (1984, May). *Effects of animation in children's toy commercials.* Paper presented at the International Communication Association, San Francisco.

Thorson, E., Reeves, B., & Schlueder, J. (1985). Message complexity and attention to television. *Communication Research, 12*(4), 427-454.

Thorson, E., Reeves, B., & Schlueder, J. (1987). Local and global complexity and attention to television. In M. M. McLaughlin (Ed.), *Communication yearbook* (Vol. 10). Beverly Hills, CA: Sage.

Thorson, E., & Rothschild, M. L. (1983). Using a text comprehension analysis to compare recall and recognition of TV commercials. In L. Percy & A. G. Woodside (Eds.), *Advertising and consumer psychology.* Lexington, MA: Lexington.

Thorson, E., & Snyder, R. (1984). Viewer recall of television commercials: Prediction from the propositional structure of commercial scripts. *Journal of Marketing Research, 21,* 127-136.

Thorson, E., & Wells, W. D. (1987). How message order affects responses. In *Research quality: Back to basics* (pp. 71-80). New York: Advertising Research Foundation.

Thorson, E., & Zhao, X. (1987). *Memory for TV commercials as a function of onsets and offsets in watching.* Manuscript, University of Wisconsin-Madison, Journalism and Mass Communication.

Thorson, E., Zhao, X., & Friestad, M. (1987, October). *Attention to program context in a natural viewing environment: Effects on memory and attitudes toward commercials.* Paper presented at the Association for Consumer Research, Boston.

Webb, P. H., & Ray, M. L. (1979). Effects of TV clutter. *Journal of Advertising Research, 19,* 7-12.

Wells, W. (1987, October). *Lectures and dramas.* Paper presented at the Association for Consumer Research, Boston.

Wells, W. D., Leavitt, C., & McConville, M. (1971). A reaction profile for TV commercials. *Journal of Advertising Research, 11,* 11-18.

Williamson, J. (1978). *Decoding advertisements: Ideology and meaning in advertising.* London: Marion Boyars.

Wright, P. (1973). The cognitive processes mediating acceptance of advertising. *Journal of Marketing Research, 10,* 53-62.

Zaichowsky, J. L. (1985). Measuring the involvement construct. *Journal of Consumer Research, 12,* 341-352.

Zaichowsky, J. L. (1987). The emotional aspect of product involvement. In M. Wallendorf & P. F. Anderson (Eds.), *Advances in consumer research* (Vol. 14, pp. 32-35). Ann Arbor, MI: Association for Consumer Research.

Chapter 9

MESSAGE FEATURES AND ENTERTAINMENT EFFECTS

Jennings Bryant

IN 1960, DAVID BERLO (p. 12) boldly anchored his treatise on communication theory with the often-quoted statement that "we communicate to influence—to affect with intent." From the perspective of message sources, that thesis arguably may have been true. From the standpoint of message *receivers*, however, especially the consumers of modern mass media messages, Berlo's claim fails to capture either the locus of communication behavior or its intent. Perhaps Neil Postman's more recent but equally bold indictment of Americans as hedonistic gobblers of entertainment messages provides a more accurate image of modern message receivers, for Postman shifts the emphasis from persuasive to entertainment messages and from implicitly passive to reflexively active receivers when he argues that we are *amusing ourselves to death* (1985).

Whether examined from the perspectives of interpersonal or mass communication, it would appear that we have become avid seekers of entertainment. And those sources—individual or institutional—that provide us with entertainment messages that satisfy our desire for gaiety, diversion, and the lighter side of life are valued highly. Many of us select our friends, at least in part, because they have a good sense of humor (e.g., Byrne, 1971). Students confess that in choosing their classes they frequently first determine whether a teacher is likely to be amusing and entertaining as well as effective (e.g., Bryant & Zillmann, 1988; Downs, Javidi, & Nussbaum, 1988). Massive audience defections from newscasts occur when competing stations choose to air entertaining programs—even syndicated "antiques"—in the traditional news hour (e.g., Bogart, 1980). Children's selection of informational and educational programs depends, at least partially, on whether the programming contains entertainment embellishments (Wakshlag, 1985). Advertisers increasingly seem to be adding entertainment to their persuasive messages; in fact, it has been noted that some advertisers may be shifting goals from making their persuasive messages entertaining to making their entertaining messages persuasive (Hajdu, 1988). Yes, seen from a receiver's perspective, or from the perspective of sources who must woo receivers in an overly complex message environment, the message of choice is likely either to be embellished with entertainment features or to be "pure" entertainment.

Unfortunately, for a variety of reasons, communication research traditionally has examined only the peripheral and incidental, rather than the primary and intended effects of entertainment messages, especially of mass entertainment. Using the language of sociological functionalism (e.g., Merton, 1967), *latent* entertainment message effects have been scrutinized extensively whereas *manifest* ones have been all but ignored. For example, the antisocial effects of consuming media violence have received far greater scholarly attention (Linz & Donnerstein, this volume) than have the effects of media violence on viewer enjoyment, yet the producers and directors who have treated us to so much gratuitous as well as dramatically instrumental violence have done so not because they wanted receivers to commit acts of aggression but because they wanted to maintain our attention on the big or small screen and to produce a riveting dramatic experience that would entertain. Until recently, these manifest effects of entertainment messages have been given extremely short shrift. As Bryant and Zillmann (1986, p. xvi) note: "Although many scholars have examined the side-effects of entertainment . . . few have examined its intended, primary effect: entertainment."

From the standpoint of a comprehensive analysis of message effects, this oversight has been unfortunate, because recent theoretical research into entertainment has given us valuable insights into the complex nature of the process of interrelationships between sources and receivers. It has also focused considerable attention directly on message effects. Following a brief description of the epistemological purview of entertainment research traditions as they relate to the study of message effects, a review of some of the more revealing entertainment message-effects research will be provided, focusing first on the variety of ways entertainment responses have been assessed, then on the myriad message features that seem to produce or mitigate entertainment effects.

MESSAGE EFFECTS IN
ENTERTAINMENT RESEARCH TRADITIONS

At least four "traditions" have emerged to study the structure, functions, uses, and effects on enjoyment of consuming the routine, ritualized media messages that so dominate entertainment today. These relatively distinct traditions have given very different degrees of emphasis to message effects, ranging from practically ignoring the place of messages in entertainment to giving message effects a central focus in the entertainment analysis.

On one end of the message-effects continuum has been *"uses and gratifications"* research (e.g., Blumler & Katz, 1974; Rosengren, Wenner, & Palmgreen, 1985), an area of significant activity and influence for more than a decade. A primary goal of this domain of inquiry is to understand media audience members' perceived needs and conscious motives for using media messages. Much of the research from this social scientific perspective has examined consumption of television and other electronic media, and the focus of the inquiry has been on the audience member—the selector and receiver of entertaining messages—rather than on elements of the messages that are selected. The primary technique employed has been the structured interview, and questionnaires have been the primary research instrument. Although in recent years some attention has been paid to message elements and effects (e.g., Rubin, 1986), the preponderance of research in this area has been conducted as if the nature of messages were a trivial element in the process of attaining gratification. For better or for worse, the popularity of uses and gratifications research would seem to be one of the primary reasons for the recent deemphasis of message-effects analysis in mass communication research.

A second set of perspectives for investigating entertainment has been stimulated by research from various disciplines affiliated primarily with the humanities. Using traditional rhetorical analysis, innovative textual and message systems analysis, and numerous other critical techniques and skills, scholars in this tradition have considered the structure, themes, symbols, and apparent meanings of media messages.

The focus in this tradition has been on message analysis rather than on any aspect of message effects or measured entertainment impact. In fact, in *critical analysis* camps, more emphasis typically has been given to examining programs that critics have perceived as innovative or of exceptionally high quality (e.g., *St. Elsewhere, Slap Maxwell*) than to assaying the appeal or entertainment impact of more formulaic programs that may have been equally or even more popular. Fortunately, some progress has been made recently in the latter regard as well (e.g., Gitlin, 1987).

The media industries themselves have directly or indirectly supported the third entertainment research tradition: *applied audience research*. Within this amalgamous category can be found divergent degrees of attention to message-effects analysis. For example, the huge electronic media "ratings" industry (e.g., Nielsen, Arbitron) has utilized several types of measurement techniques to provide advertisers and programmers with information on the size and composition of the audience reached by a given television or radio program, magazine, or newspaper (e.g., Beville, 1988; Wober, 1988). In the United States, most of these assessments have been limited to providing an index of exposure to various messages rather than a measure of the messages' entertainment value to various audiences. In fact, several services that have attempted to assess dimensions of the quality of the viewing experience have failed financially. Television Audience Assessment, Inc., was a highly visible recent example (Beville, 1988). Government or publicly supported audience assessment services in other countries have measured entertainment value and impact more directly (e.g., Gunter, 1985, 1987; Wober, 1988; see Morley, 1980, 1986) and have contributed more substantially to our knowledge of the effects of message features on enjoyment.

In the United States, that sphere of applied audience research that has been concerned most directly with shaping message features to achieve desired audience entertainment responses is the formative research and evaluation industry, a so-called service branch of the entertainment industry. Many films, television programs, commercials, and advertisements are extensively pretested—prior to accruing the expenses typically occurred in final production, postproduction, and distribution—to determine whether they achieve the desired impact (e.g., Johnstone & Ettema, 1986; Mielke, 1983). In these instances, "impact" typically is defined so as to include some dimension of entertainment value. If the message system does not "measure up" to accepted criteria, typically it is revised. At first glance such evaluative research would seem to add considerably to our knowledge of message effects in the entertainment context. Unfortunately, two factors operate to limit such potential utility. First, most such research results are treated as proprietary. Some heavy users of formative research will make their results available to scholars (e.g., Children's Television Workshop); however, the vast majority of media message producers and distributors who use formative evaluation take great care to guard the security, and thereby the economic value, of their findings. Second, historically, much formative evaluation has been conducted with small (and sometimes purposively nonnormative) samples that do not satisfy the assumptions of most inferential statistical tests utilized within the academic community. These limitations of access and generalizability render the results of formative evaluation research far less useful than they otherwise could be in clarifying the impact of various features of entertaining messages.

The most recent entry into the traditions analyzing entertainment messages comes from the behavioral and cognitive sciences and is frequently referred to as *entertainment theory*. The first general reviews of this blend of psychological and communication approaches to the study of entertainment have been published very recently (e.g., Zillmann & Bryant, 1986), although reviews of empirical and theoretical research into particular types of entertainment messages are nearly two decades old (e.g., Goldstein & McGhee, 1972). The principle tools employed have been laboratory or field experiments. Early examples of this research tested, among other things, proposals derived from survey research on motives for consuming entertainment, theoretical propositions derived from emotion and motivation theory generally, and some of the speculative claims of many of the foremost thinkers of Western society (e.g., Plato, Aristotle, Freud, Hazlett, Hobbes, McDougall). Investigations have focused on a variety of elements in entertainment messages that affect enjoyment and on various factors in the appeal of different message genres (e.g., comedy, horror). It is this most recent entry into the entertainment research traditions that provides the greatest emphasis on message features and entertainment effects, so this approach will provide the bulk of the material for our examination of message effects in entertainment.

THE DIVERSITY OF ENTERTAINMENT RESPONSES

"Entertainment" clearly is a multidimensional phenomenon. When examined at the conceptual level: "The term 'entertainment' includes the concepts of diversion, escape, companionship, and play, to name only a few" (Fischer & Melnik, 1979, p. xiii). Even when considered less abstractly, more behaviorally, in terms of the ways we respond to entertaining media messages, the issue remains complex. We *root, root, root* for the home team. We *sigh* with the unrequited lovers on soap operas. We *shriek* with terror at the ghoul on the horror show, *squeal* and *swoon* over the latest rock idol, *laugh* at comedy, *cry* at melodrama, *shiver* and *shudder* at suspense. All this and much, much more is done in the name of entertainment. Moreover, any one of these rough categories of entertainment responses readily can be subdivided into more refined units for measurement and analysis. To cite just one of many examples: Notables representing perspectives as divergent as those of Charles Darwin (1872) and Arthur Koestler (1964) have formulated extensive typologies of laughter, ranging from "a simple low-level bodily expression of cheerfulness at one end and paroxysms of violent laughter at the other" (Pollio, Mers, & Lucchesi, 1972, p. 213). Needless to say, such complexity has led to divergent schemes of coding and to assessing dependent variables in vastly divergent ways (e.g., LaFrance, 1983).

DIVERSITY IN ASSESSING ENTERTAINMENT RESPONSES

Without entering fully into the domain of methodological analysis and criticism, it may be instructive to examine rather generally the levels and types of direct and indirect assessments typically utilized to measure entertainment impact. Not only will this enable us to see how far from traditional knowledge-generating and persuasion-based conceptions of message effects we have moved, it will also facilitate understanding of our future discussion by providing shorthand labels for those diverse dependent measures to be considered.

Exposure. As previously indicated, the American media industries' predominant index of viewer, reader, or listener acceptance of an entertainment message has been that of *exposure* (Beville, 1988; Webster & Wakshlag, 1985). Whether measured in ticket sales at box offices, subscription lists, circulation figures, or any one of several types of audience ratings, exposure provides a gross index of how many consumers saw, read, or heard a particular entertainment message. In the commercially oriented American mass media environment, the true purpose of exposure indices is to enable advertisers to determine which entertainment "vehicle" they should use to deliver their ulterior messages to the largest possible number of the right kinds of potential consumers at the lowest possible cost. Because in this system entertainment value per se is secondary to the entertaining message's potential to deliver an audience for advertisements or commercials, advertisers rarely have seen fit to support more extensive analyses of audiences' enjoyment of the entertaining messages they have chosen to consume. Exposure is an extremely imprecise index of entertainment, far too imprecise to provide useful data regarding the effects of particular message variables, but it has long dominated American mass entertainment and promises to continue to do so in the immediate future.

Selective exposure. Whereas exposure serves as the preferred industry index, *selective exposure* is the closely related construct of choice of most entertainment theorists. At its most general level, selective exposure is defined as *"behavior that is deliberately performed to attain and sustain perceptual control of particular stimulus events"* (Zillmann & Bryant, 1985b, p. 2). Selective exposure to media messages, typically to television programs, has been assessed in laboratory studies (e.g., Bryant & Zillmann, 1984) as well as in field experiments (e.g., Schleicher, 1981). The typical procedure has included manipulating antecedent conditions (i.e., subjects have been placed in good versus bad moods, in conditions of boredom versus stress, and so on), then unobtrusively assessing what specific entertaining messages subjects choose to consume. Typically the messages have been created or selected according to desired differentiations in stimulus characteristics. Selective exposure has been assessed via the frequency of selection of particular programs and the duration of exposure. Occasionally subjects' interpretations of their own motivations for selection have been ascertained following assessment; more frequently they have not.

Selective exposure studies offer a dramatic departure from the traditional media-effects paradigm. In selective exposure experiments, the dependent measure of choice is "the effect *on* message selection for consumption. Not the effect *of* the consumption of selected messages; nor, as in conventional media-effects research, the effects *of* the consumption of messages that, for the most part, were selected by a party other than the consumer" (Zillmann & Bryant, 1985b, p. 6). In time, selective exposure theory is likely to modify as well as complement media-effects research, given that the social and psychological impacts of entertaining media messages on consumers who self-select massive quantities of a particular type of programming toward which they have pronounced affinities is apt to yield very different message effects than those studies in which subjects are forced to watch programming in which they have little interest and that they would seldom if ever select on their own. The fusion of selective exposure and message-effects research should be a major step toward verisimilitude in mass communication theory.

Attention. During the past several years scholars have assessed a number of message reception and perception processes that are commonly perceived to be corollaries of entertainment responses (e.g., Reeves, Thorson, & Schleuder, 1986). Perhaps the most frequently studied is *attention,* which has been investigated as a predictor of entertainment responses (e.g., Bryant, Zillmann, & Brown, 1983) as well as a dependent measure of considerable interest in its own right (e.g., Anderson & Collins, 1988; Anderson & Lorch, 1983). Most commonly assessed is visual attention to television, for, as Anderson and Collins (1988, p. 15) report, "If television is an influential medium of communication and entertainment, it is so partly by its power to gain and maintain attention."

Most of the entertainment research that has employed attention as a dependent variable has been laboratory-based and has employed child subjects. Various operationalizations of attention have been used: "In television research, inferences about attention are made based on recognition or recall, from secondary tasks administered concurrently with TV viewing, from electrophysiological recordings, from self-ratings, and most commonly, from visual orientation toward the TV screen, or 'looking'" (Anderson & Collins, 1988, p. 15). Considerable effort has been expended in addressing the question of whether attention is a function of specific features of a television message. More precisely, the question has been asked: How much is attention a message effect? Although never strictly deterministic, early studies in this area emphasized the number and diversity of media message properties (e.g., pace, color, pixilation) that controlled visual attention to television (e.g., Anderson & Levin, 1976; Huston et al., 1981); whereas later studies have tended to emphasize the interaction between receiver variables and message properties in accounting for attention to television as well as for enjoyment of its contents (e.g., Anderson & Collins, 1988).

Arousal. Behavioral scientists frequently have relied upon the notion of *arousal* in explaining the appeal of entertainment fare (e.g., Berlyne, 1971; Christ, 1985; Zillmann, 1982). If arousal is conceptualized as *"a unitary force that energizes or intensifies behavior that receives direction by independent means"* (Zillmann, 1982, p. 53), it is necessary for cognitive components to be incorporated into the explanatory models to provide "independent means" to account for the hedonic valence produced by message properties. Perhaps the most comprehensive of such explanatory models is excitation-transfer theory (Zillmann, 1971, 1983b), which has been called upon to explain the appeal of violence, pornography, music, suspense, and sports, among other types of entertainment.

Because of the requirement of relatively delicate instrumentation, most studies assessing arousal are conducted in research laboratories. Cortical arousal typically is assessed in alpha wave blocking as recorded in electroencephalograms (e.g., Reeves et al., 1986). In contrast, autonomic arousal has been measured in diverse ways, including systolic and diastolic blood pressure, heart rate, vasoconstriction, and skin conductance (Zillmann, 1982).

In most entertainment research in which arousal has been assessed, specific media message content has been found to be a significant source of arousal, presenting a strong prima facie argument for significant media message effects in entertainment. As Zillmann (1982, p. 57) noted, "There can be no doubt that exposure to television can be highly arousing . . . and that this arousal can foster affective reactions of considerable intensity." However, receiver factors have not been ignored either, and they have been found to be significant as well; for example, "Television's capacity to generate notable increments in autonomic arousal thus favors the relatively unaroused person" (Zillmann, 1982, p. 57).

Affective displays. As has been indicated, consumption of entertainment fare frequently results in obtrusive affective displays, ranging from cheers to boos, from laughter to crying. Quite frequently, such overt behavioral displays have been assessed, either simultaneously and "live" or from videotapes of facial reactions to watching media fare. Sometimes the judgments of observed behaviors have been relatively obtrusive and subjective (e.g., Lull, 1980); more typically, they have been as unobtrusive and nonreactive as possible, with the interpreters utilizing assessment procedures that were as objective and scientifically replicable as feasible (e.g., Zillmann & Bryant, 1980). Implicit in the use of such behavioral measures is the assumption that differentiation in message factors will produce discernibly different affective reactions. Such has frequently been found (Zillmann & Bryant, 1986).

Reported and rated enjoyment. Under the assumption that viewers, listeners, and readers of entertainment fare are able to assess at least somewhat accurately their own affective responses and will report such with some veracity, numerous investigations have relied on self-reports of enjoyment. Some responses have been open-ended; others have used ordinal scaling, especially with children (e.g., "yucky, OK, pretty good, neat"; Zillmann, Hay, & Bryant, 1975); but most have used interval-level scales, either polar (e.g., ranging from "no enjoyment" to "extreme enjoyment") or bipolar (e.g., ranging from "hated it" to "loved it"). By and large, such scaling efforts have proven to be rather reliable and have achieved high correlations with more unobtrusive and directly observable behavioral measures. Moreover, evaluation of entertainment ratings for the same programs viewed in different cultures (United States versus United Kingdom) have shown a rather high correlation, further substantiating the reliability of ratings of appeal and enjoyment (Wober, 1988).

Gratifications sought and obtained. The uses and gratifications tradition has tended to move the furthest from analyzing direct expressions of enjoyment, assessing instead the reasons respondents give for consuming entertainment fare, typically measured relatively abstractly through sets of numerous scales of a variety of types. As is common with assessments of subjectively interpreted experiences generally, results have been diverse and have ranged dramatically in terms of reliability (e.g., Rosengren et al., 1985). Nonetheless, from an immense number of studies has emerged a rather consistent set of factors expressing *gratifications sought and obtained* by consumers of entertaining messages. Frequently included among the entertainment-related factors for media consumption are habit, arousal, companionship, relaxation, escape, and passing time (e.g., Rubin, 1986). An extremely useful addition to entertainment research would be a set of investigations merging the uses and gratifications tradition with behavioral entertainment research. Among the potentially beneficial goals would be a clarification of the relationship between entertainment and gratification.

MESSAGE FEATURES AS FACTORS IN AUDIENCE APPEAL

The effects of message features on audience appeal would seem to be of great importance and value to the media entertainment industries; therefore, prior to examining basic research in the area of entertainment theory, the applied perspective of the entertainment industries will first be considered.

THE ENTERTAINMENT INDUSTRIES' IMPLICIT THEORIES

Although seldom articulated, at least not publicly, the media entertainment industries seem to operate with several implicit notions of the role of message features in producing audience entertainment responses. The degree of attention paid to message features at different levels of the industry hierarchy varies greatly. Although each medium has peculiarities, the case of television will be used to exemplify this diversity.

Television message distributors and exhibitors typically consider their message systems in terms of discrete programs that fit into particular genres (e.g., action-adventure, situation comedy). Programs within a genre share many message features and formats, and their writers share common goals for producing specific audience entertainment responses (e.g., suspense, mirth). Most industry representatives refer to the scheduling and exhibition of these message system units as "programming" (e.g., Eastman, Head, & Klein, 1985). Programming at the network level (e.g., ABC, CBS, NBC, PBS) tends to be strategic rather than tactical and takes a marketing perspective. On the whole, at this level less emphasis is given to message features per se than to audience preferences for programs or even genres as determined via exposure patterns as measured by audience ratings. (Networks do have divisions charged with developing programs, and they are directly concerned with message formats and features, of course; but such units are a very small part of network operations.) Time after time, networks spokespersons respond to criticisms of programming content with some variant of this: "We only provide what the viewers want, whatever that is!"

(e.g., Diamond & Mahony, 1988); and from their dominant operating perspective, that would appear to be true. As a concrete indication that this perspective extends to the context of the academic study of mass entertainment, a recent textbook chapter, "Prime-Time Network Programming" (Lewine, Eastman, & Adams, 1985), whose senior author, Robert Lewine, has served as vice-president of programming at all three commercial networks, did not once discuss the role of message features in contributing to audience appeals. Instead, the chapter focused on elements like television seasons, audience flow, line-ups, program life span, program ratings, and placement, along with scheduling exotica like lead-ins, hammocking, tent-poling, stunting, and churn. Research has indicated that such factors do contribute to exposure (e.g., Webster, 1985; Webster & Wakshlag, 1983), but it is highly unlikely that these elements are as important in creating and sustaining audience enjoyment as specific message attributes. Apparently the skills needed by a network programmer are perceived to be accurate instincts and the ability to discern popular tastes, not sensitivity to nuances in message design that may produce entertainment responses (Turner, 1987). If programming philosophies at this level included theories of entertainment that feature systematic considerations of the importance of message elements, they are proprietary. Rather, the dominant operational philosophies at this level result in practices such as extensive audience testing (including pretesting) and unbridled imitation of programs that attain high ratings, generally retaining established formats and sticking with talent with high performer Qs (i.e., familiarity and appeal; e.g., Beville, 1988).

Non-prime-time network programming, network-affiliated station programming, independent station programming, and cable system programming seem to exemplify the same strategic rather than tactical, marketing-oriented, bottom line intensive programming philosophy (Eastman et al., 1985). It is only when program creation and production are considered that message features are given substantial attention.

Many, if not most, writers, producers, and directors of entertainment television programs seem to believe that their carefully crafted messages produce all sorts of direct effects, especially when what is being assessed is enjoyment or prosocial behavior. (Strangely, when antisocial effects are considered, alleged message potency seems to diminish rapidly.) Although our focus is on message factors that produce entertainment responses, it is nonetheless noteworthy how often creative teams point with pride to the obtrusive prosocial effects their message has. For example, the creators and producers of the typically "fluffy" *Happy Days* frequently have noted that, when Fonzie received a library card, record numbers of young viewers became eager, first-time library patrons. Similarly, Norman Lear has taken credit for raising consciousness and altering behavior positively:

> I do know that when we do a show on *Good Times* about black men dying of hypertension, that within the next two weeks more black men in the country than ever before go into clinics for checkups. I know that when we do a show in which Edith [Bunker of *All in the Family*] comes home with a lump in her breast and talks about having found it herself, and the value of certain tests, that women all over the country . . . go in for the same tests. (Wilde, 1976, p. 202)

Amazingly, when Norman Lear and many of his creative kin try to explain how they go about constructing television or filmic messages that evoke massive *entertainment* responses, they become much less cogent and loquacious. For example, in attempting to explain how he creates humor, Norman Lear notes: "I've got a mechanism in my belly. My belly says this is funny; my belly says this is in good taste, and this is in bad taste" (Wilde, 1976, p. 203). Mel Brooks does no better in responding to the question of why comedy is so difficult to analyze: "I think because it's like vapor. . . . It's difficult even to describe it. I can't get words around the feeling" (Wilde, 1976, p. 51). Of course, not all entertainment writers and producers are so obtuse about the construction of their craft. Alfred Hitchcock, for instance, has been extremely precise and lucid regarding the sorts of message-manipulation strategies required to produce maximal suspense (e.g., Truffaut, 1967). Film critics tend to agree that Hitchcock, more than most *auteurs*, demonstrated such competence with filmic message construction that his famous suspense sequences exerted uniform and extensive control over his audiences. The following anecdote illustrates the powerful, direct message effects often ascribed to Hitchcock films and the sensitivity to audience reactions attributed to the master of suspense:

> The Hitchcock thrillers are constructed so carefully, graphically and imaginatively that they speak an international language. Several years ago, an associate tested this by calling theater managers in Toronto, Paris

and Honolulu where *The Birds,* one of the most imaginatively terrifying pictures ever made, was playing. He asked for the audience reactions at random times during the film, then checked to see if the master could indeed describe those reactions at given moments. Hitchcock assumed his most panda-like pose and pinpointed with complete accuracy every laugh and every shudder in *The Birds.*

"Remarkable," said his astounded friend.

"Nonsense," drawled the imperturbable King Alfred. "If I hadn't known how the audience was going to react, I daresay I would not have risked all that time and money by making the film in the first place." (Steward-Gordon, 1973)

Such attributions of audience control through entertainment message manipulation help to explain why Hitchcock is referred to as "the most famous *behaviorist* filmmaker of all times"—because the audience is perceived as "surrendering almost completely to the filmmaker" and engaging in "behavior which is near-global, primitive, and surrendering" (Norden, 1980, p. 74, emphasis added).

Suspense is not the only area in which writers and producers tend to believe in the importance of precision in message construction as well as in strong message effects. Another genre about which such claims are very frequently made is comedy. As an index of the credence given to the importance of message precision in this area, comedy writers sometimes are referred to as "humorous-verbiage technicians" (e.g., Wilde, 1976, p. 2). A statement by Goodman Ace is representative of this dedication to message crafting as the key to creating mirth: "'The basic rule is that it [a joke] should be phrased correctly. A word out of place will spoil the whole joke.' After lots of years, he says, 'You learn to put the right word in the right place so that the rhythm is there, and the joke makes sense'" (Wilde, 1976, pp. 4-5). The perceived communication competence of the best comedians and the alleged powerful impact of their messages is attested to by Wilde: "Their influence on society is immeasurable. They are the word-picture painters, grammar innovators, word coiners, phrase makers, colloquial-expression designers of our times" (Wilde, 1976, p. 6).

Although considerable diversity exists among writers, producers, and directors in their claims for pronounced message effects from their craft, it is clear that many of the most successful strongly believe that the right ingredients mixed with precision and delivered with sensitivity will create their most highly desired message effect: entertainment.

MESSAGE RESEARCH IN
ENTERTAINMENT THEORY

During the past 15 years, numerous empirical investigations into mass entertainment theory have been conducted. Many of these studies have systematically examined the impact specific message features have on listeners', readers', and viewers' entertainment experiences. In some of these investigations, message variables have been the only factors involved. More typically, a combination of message feature variables and audience variables—which have been hypothesized to alter reactions to message content or to the uses of the messages—have been utilized. Zillmann and Bryant (1986, p. 311) note in summary fashion that both types of variables have yielded significant effects on enjoyment: "Entertaining messages are capable of gratifying respondents because of unique intrinsic properties, along with the respondents' idiosyncratic appraisals of these properties." Representative studies dealing with a sampling of message properties that have been found to enhance or otherwise mediate entertainment responses will be reviewed, beginning with those studies featuring investigations of message effects relatively independent of receiver or context factors.

MESSAGE EFFECTS EXAMINED IN RELATIVE
ISOLATION FROM RECEIVER FACTORS

The medium is the message. Perhaps the most appropriate place to begin an examination of research that focuses primarily on message effects in entertainment is with the relatively global notion that the entertainment media are inherently attractive. In a comprehensive statement of this position, Singer (1980) argues:

> From a cognitive standpoint, the television medium has an especially powerful appeal. As noted earlier, the human brain appears organized to respond to movement in the environment, perhaps as a survival of adaptive evolutionary self-defense or hunting tendencies. We find the moving picture very difficult to ignore, and in the presence of the television set we cannot resist our eyes wandering in its direction. The most insipid game show or stereotyped-cowboy movie can still draw the attention of almost anybody who is somewhere near a television set. The constant movement and pattern of change that characterize the screen produces a continuous series of orienting reflexes in us, and it is hard to habituate to

the set (the way we can to other sounds or sights) because of the great variations in degree of movement and in the appearance and reappearance of various characters.

Unfortunately, such claims for general message system effects in entertainment have not been subjected to adequate testing at the molar level (see Watt & Welch, 1983). To date, probably the closest approximation of such comes from research on the effects of the "formal features" of television on viewer attention and appeal. "Formal features are defined as characteristic attributes of the medium which can be described without reference to particular content" (Anderson & Collins, 1988, p. 17). Using methodology derived partially from media industry formative evaluation procedures, Anderson and Levin (1976; Levin & Anderson, 1976) examined the potential of specific attributes of a *Sesame Street* program to attract young children's visual attention to the television screen. Of the 44 program elements examined, many of which were form variables relatively independent of semantic requirements, 31 attributes were found to be determinants of visual attention to the screen. The children were found to be "more attentive in the presence of women, children, eye contact, puppets, peculiar voices, animation, movement, lively music, rhyming, repetition and alliteration, and auditory change." In contrast, they tended "to watch less in the presence of adult men, animals, inactivity, and still drawings" (Anderson & Levin, 1976, p. 811). Many of these early findings have been supported (and greatly extended) by other investigations, especially by those of the CRITC group (e.g., Calvert, Huston, Watkins, & Wright, 1982; Campbell, Wright, & Huston, 1987; Huston & Wright, 1983). "Results of research on formal features have been surprisingly robust, with each research group generally replicating the other's findings" (Anderson & Collins, 1988, p. 17).

In a more molecular investigation, which brought the concern with formal features more directly into an entertainment perspective, Bryant and Zillmann (1981) sampled audiovisual special effects from children's television programs, pretested their attention-getting potential and hedonic valence, and matched them with humorous stimuli on the criteria of interest. The matched humorous versus nonhumorous (special effects) stimuli, differentiated according to attention-getting potential (low, high) and hedonic valence (neutral, pleasant), were then systematically interspersed into educational television programs employing a factorial design. Children's acquisition of information from and enjoyment of the embellished educational segments were assessed in recall tests and via rated enjoyment. For younger children (5- and 6-year-olds), no appreciable differences were found on learning, although the programs having more pleasant stimuli were rated as more enjoyable, regardless of whether the insertions were humorous or nonhumorous. For older (7- and 8-year-old) children, more pleasant embellishments, whether humorous or not, yielded substantially greater information acquisition and higher rated enjoyment than the less pleasant ones. For children then, significant message effects on enjoyment were clearly in evidence, even from semantically meaningless message embellishments. The form of the message system does seem to make a difference in children's enjoyment of television programming.

The appeal of violence. Another area of entertainment theory research in which several investigations have been conducted almost exclusively in terms of message effects is in assessing the appeal of violence. Diener and DeFour (1978) selected 62 episodes from prime-time network broadcasts and coded the amount of violence occurring within each. Individual episode violence scores were correlated with an index of exposure for the programs—National Nielsen ratings. A very low and nonsignificant relationship was found. In a related experiment reported in the same article, a version of an adventure program was viewed by subjects either unedited or with the violence edited out. The uncut version was liked (measured in rated enjoyment) somewhat more than the edited version, but the effect was not found to be statistically significant.

A related investigation into the appeal of sports violence did yield significant message effects for violence on entertainment. Bryant, Comisky, and Zillmann (1981) selected and pretested plays from professional football telecasts that varied in their degree of roughness or violence (low, intermediate, high) yet were equated on other stimulus dimensions. Viewers rated their enjoyment of each play. The enjoyment of football plays was found to increase with the degree of roughness or violence; however, this relationship was reliable for male viewers only. The findings were interpreted as suggesting that, "at least for male viewers, a high degree of aggressiveness is a critical ingredient of the enjoyment of watching sports contests" (Bryant et al., 1981, p. 256). Again, message effects on enjoyment were in evidence.

Message effects in the enjoyment of suspense. The complex rationales that constitute theories of the enjoyment of suspenseful entertainment fare have been detailed elsewhere (e.g., Zillmann, 1980; Zillmann & Bryant, 1986) and are beyond the scope of the present chapter. However, for the present purposes it may be instructive to note that suspense and enjoyment have been successfully produced via message manipulations. In the first empirical investigation into the enjoyment of suspense, Zillmann, Hay, and Bryant (1975) manipulated the level of suspense (low, intermediate, high) and the resolution of suspense (resolved, unresolved) in a specially created children's television adventure story. The differentiation in level of suspense was accomplished through altering descriptions of the antagonists and via subtle changes in the story line as well as by customizing the story visuals accordingly. The variation in outcome uncertainty was achieved by changing the ending of the story. Arousal, rated enjoyment, and judged affective displays of pleasure were found to increase with increments in suspense. Differences in enjoyment as a function of the resolution occurred only under high levels of suspense.

Other suspense investigations also have relied exclusively on message variables for the creation of empathic distress. For example, Bryant (1978) created a suspenseful radio drama using the stock plot of a Western hero in peril. Five different levels of suspense were produced by manipulating various message elements. The source of the resolution of suspense was also varied via message manipulations—the hero either escaped through his own actions or through the intervention of the cavalry. Once again, enjoyment was a function of the level of suspense. Moreover, compared to the resolution of suspense by an outside agent, rated and judged enjoyment of the story were greater when the hero-protagonist resolved the dilemma by his own wit and gall.

These studies, along with several other investigations into the enjoyment of suspense, indicate that message variables do make a critical difference. In an area such as suspense, where enjoyment relies heavily on rather pronounced excitatory elements, it seems that receiver idiosyncrasies are less important than in other areas of entertainment (e.g., humor) where cognitive subtleties are more crucial to enjoyment.

The paucity of "pure" message-effects research in entertainment theory. From an epistemological perspective, the fact that "pure" message effects have been observed in entertainment theory research is perhaps less significant than the fact that the vast preponderance of research conducted in this domain has not relied exclusively on the most simplistic sorts of message-effects perspectives. In fact, the studies previously discussed are substantially more than one-half of the entertainment theory research that has relied exclusively on the premise that the form or the content of the message alone has the capacity to produce relatively consistent entertainment effects. Far more common are studies that incorporate evaluations of mediating receiver factors, whether organismic characteristics, perceptual distinctions, or user interpretations and actions—in addition to message factors, of course—in determining essential elements of the entertainment experience. It is to such investigations that we now turn.

MESSAGE EFFECTS EXAMINED IN
CONJUNCTION WITH RECEIVER FACTORS

A substantial number of receiver variables have been employed in conjunction with stimulus or message variables in entertainment research. Some receiver variables have been manipulated; others have been measured. Included among the latter have been (see Hsia, 1988) organismic factors (e.g., age, gender, stage of the menstrual cycle), demographic variables (e.g., political party affiliation, race), personality variables (e.g., sensation seeking, Machiavellianism, dominance/submissiveness), as well as a variety of complex construct variables adapted from social, cognitive, and physiological psychology (e.g., disposition, equity, moral judgment, sympathetic activation). The reasons for employing receiver variables in conjunction with message factors have been almost as diverse as the variables themselves. Some have been employed primarily to increase measurement precision (e.g., La Fave, Haddad, & Marshall, 1974); others to allow theoretical interpretation of maturation factors (e.g., Zillmann & Bryant, 1975). But the majority seem to have been utilized because the theoretical propositions under investigation demanded considerations of the interplay of message properties and receiver attributes (e.g., Zillmann & Bryant, 1974) or of message features and reception processes (e.g., Zillmann & Bryant, 1980). A comprehensive literature review is beyond the scope of this chapter; therefore, only a modest sampling of studies that indicate the interplay of message and receiver variables in the entertainment process will be examined.

Combinations of message factors with receiver variables. Possibly the first empirical investigation in what has become the entertainment theory tradition was conducted by Wolff, Smith, and Murray (1934). It combined receiver variables—ethnicity and gender—with message manipulations—in this case, the humorous disparagement of Jews versus non-Jews and of men versus women. It was found that jokes disparaging Jews were appreciated more by non-Jews than by Jews; similarly, men appreciated jokes ridiculing women more than did women, while women found jokes ridiculing men funnier than did men. Similar findings have been reported in later years (e.g., La Fave, 1977), leading most recently to the following disposition theoretic formulation, which clearly incorporates message and receiver characteristics in its basic propositions: "Mirth, then, is said to vary proportionally with the negativeness of the affective disposition toward the disparaged party and with the positiveness of the affective disposition toward the disparaging party, and jointly so" (Zillmann, 1983a, p. 92).

Combinations of message factors with receiver perceptions. A closely related set of investigations has examined the interplay between message variables and receiver perceptions of various sorts as they influence the entertainment experience. In many if not most instances, the receiver perceptions involved have been produced by manipulations in message variables, but the resultant differentiations in perceptions have been assessed, and the theoretical interpretations have been based more on altered perceptions than on the message manipulations per se. A case in point is an investigation into enjoyment of the "human drama of athletic competition" (ABC *Wide World of Sports*). Bryant, Brown, Comisky, and Zillmann (1982) utilized systematic variations in the commentary of a televised tennis match to create viewer perceptions that the featured players were either hated enemies, devoted friends, or had unspecified feelings toward each other. Viewers' perceptions of the players and play were altered by the commentary as desired. Moreover, "the findings demonstrate that watching a televised sports contest in which the opponents are perceived as hated foes, rather than as good friends or as neutral opponents, creates the greatest enjoyment for spectators" (Bryant et al., 1982, p. 117). In numerous other investigations, viewers', listeners', or readers' perceptions have been found to be a more critical mediator of enjoyment than content differences per se (see Gunter, 1985).

Combinations of message factors with reception processes. A smaller number of studies has examined the interplay of message variables with reception processes. The investigation to be examined as an exemplar case included receiver disposition as a factor, so it also illustrates a more complex case of the previous category of investigations. Zillmann and Bryant (1980) conducted a study in which subjects were treated rudely or in a normal manner by a female investigator, establishing a negative versus a neutral affective disposition toward her. Subjects then witnessed the investigator in one of three conditions, with the experimental message system containing a manipulation in "jokework" as well as misfortune experienced by the experimenter: (a) she experienced a misfortune that was associated with innocuous humor cues; (b) she experienced the same misfortune, but the humor cues were not present; or (c) the same humor cues were present, but no misfortune was experienced. Enjoyment was assessed in unobtrusively recorded facial expressions, which were later examined for indications of mirth. A misattribution theory of tendentious humor was developed, based on Freudian explanations of humor processes, to account for the findings that, under conditions of neutral disposition, mirth in response to the misfortune plus the humor cues was the sum of the mirth reactions to the component parts in isolation; whereas under conditions of negative affective dispositions, mirth in response to the combination of misfortune and humor cues greatly exceeded the sum of the responses to the components. The presence of humor cues was posited to serve the function of freeing inhibitions and thereby liberating mirth.

Emphasis on receiver variables. In relatively rare instances, message variables have been neither manipulated nor measured in entertainment theory research. On such occasions, the role of messages has not been deemed to be unimportant; rather particular message features have been held constant to determine the interplay of key receiver variables. For example, Bryant (1979) assessed subjects' sensation seeking, creating two conditions representing levels of this variable (low, high). Subjects later viewed a suspenseful portion of an action-adventure television program and rated their enjoyment of the program at two points in the action (climax, resolution). Sympathetic excitation was also assessed at these key points. Low-sensation seekers' level of excitation in response to the suspenseful climax was significantly higher than that of high-sensation seekers. Low-sensation seekers also reported experiencing more distress at the climax, and they enjoyed the resolution of the suspense more than did high-sensation seekers. In this instance, even though the key message features (i.e., climax, resolution) were held constant, they provided the stimulus differentiation required for the assessment of enjoyment and for the theoretical interpretation of the findings.

The centrality of messages in entertainment theory. Although the four strategies of inquiry in entertainment theory just described and illustrated vary in terms of the degree of emphasis given to message variables in entertainment research, there is no denying the importance of key message attributes, features, and formulas in each investigation. In most traditional entertainment research, the role of messages has been central and vital to the propositions under investigation as well as to the entertainment theory under construction.

CONTEXT EFFECTS IN ENTERTAINMENT THEORY

Although the present focus is on messages, it would be derelict not to consider briefly the importance of context in the entertainment experience. Both social and cultural contexts have been found to mediate the enjoyment of entertainment.

Much of the consumption of entertaining messages occurs in *social* contexts. The area of entertainment theory that has received the greatest attention in this regard is the facilitative influence of the laughter of others on one's own entertainment responses. Whether examined in interpersonal contexts (e.g., Chapman, 1973) or as "canned" laughter that accompanies many comedies on television (e.g., Cupchik & Leventhal, 1974), the laughter of others generally does seem to make things funnier to most people.

A more complex type of social context effect on entertainment has been investigated by Zillmann, Weaver, Mundorf, and Aust (1986), who showed male and female undergraduates a horror movie in the company of same-age, opposite-gender peer companions. The companions were of high versus low initial appeal and expressed either mastery, distress, or affective indifference in response to the horror movie. Measures of affective reactions to the movie indicated that men enjoyed the movie most in the presence of a distressed woman and least in the company of a mastering woman. Women, in contrast, enjoyed the movie most in the company of a mastering man and least in the company of a distressed man. The findings were interpreted as consistent with gender-role socialization. Obviously, message effects on enjoyment were mediated by the interpersonal and social context of the viewing.

The *cultural* contexts of entertainment also have an impact on enjoyment. Even from a cursory evaluation of popular culture, it is obvious that our primary sources of merriment change from one generation to the next. One has only to compare the disinterested responses of today's youthful audience watching *Easy Rider* to the intense emotional reactions of a comparable audience of the 1960s to the same movie to realize that culture affects affective reactions.

A more objective indication of the fact that message factors that create optimal conditions for enjoyment change over time is available from the comparison of two pretests of the same entertainment stimuli, conducted nearly a decade apart. In a study conducted in 1977, Comisky and Bryant (1982) created and pretested several different characterizations and portrayals of a film protagonist in order to determine the most appropriate "hero" for a population of college students. The subjects showed a strongly positive disposition toward a larger-than-life, altruistic, freedom fighter who struggled to rescue others at his own peril. They were less positive toward the protagonist when he was presented as a rather ordinary, good man, lacking in unusual valor. A version depicting the protagonist as a selfish, antisocial recluse created an even less positive disposition. Eight years later (Bryant & Brown, 1985), another pretest of precisely the same stimulus materials was conducted on a similar population. This time the formerly extremely well-liked, larger-than-life protagonist was liked less than those in either of the other two versions. The preferred "hero" in the more recent test was that of the ordinary, man-next-door characterization. Although the message units had remained the same over time, the cultural context had obviously changed and, with it, the audiences' taste in heroes.

Other shifts in entertainment responses over time have been found in attempts to replicate enjoyment of messages featuring provocation and retaliation. In 1973, college students reported the highest level of enjoyment in response to a series of jokes featuring retaliatory equity (Zillmann & Bryant, 1974). In 1982, an attempted replication, employing the same stimulus materials with a similar population, indicated a more pronounced liking for different versions of the same jokes—those featuring mild overretaliation (Bryant & Brown, 1982). It would appear that certain receiver perceptions, perhaps those related to notions of "right" and justice, are readily subject to shifts in cultural values. These altered perceptions, in turn, effect humor appreciation.

These demonstrated context effects should serve as a reminder that meanings really are in people; messages just provide the symbol system through which meaning is negotiated. This is a lesson to which creators and producers of entertainment messages must remain constantly mind-ful, especially in an age in which transnational and international traffic in entertainment has become an everyday affair. They offer a lesson to entertainment theorists as well. If entertainment theory is to accommo-date these subtle actions of receivers on message systems, it will have to consider more systematically elements of intercultural and interna-tional communication, and longitudinal analyses will have to become more frequent.

THE EMERGING SOVEREIGN CONSUMER IN ENTERTAINMENT THEORY

When the prototypical denizen of the Information Age is considered, the description that emerges almost always includes elements of mes-sage abundance and choice (e.g., Salvaggio & Bryant, 1989). When normative entertainment consumption is examined, the prototypical characterization would appear to be accurate. The average person in search of an evening's entertainment today can select from nearly 150 prime-time television programs, from hundreds of songs available on the radio, from prerecorded videocassettes by the thousands readily available from the home library or at the corner video store, from hundreds of popular magazines from newsstands, from thousands of popular books available at the local library, from scores of albums (or audiocassettes or CDs), from at least a handful of movies available at local multiscreen cinemas, and from an ever increasing barrage of specialty games and entertainment software. The selection process is rendered manageable by a plethora of entertainment programming guides. And the actual act of selection is made almost effortless by programmable hardware activated and directed by ubiquitous remote controls. Indeed, for most of us, the Information Age may more aptly be called the Entertainment Age, and its archetype really is the "sover-eign consumer." No wonder we seem to be amusing ourselves to death (Postman, 1985).

To study the sovereign entertainment consumer with some degree of verisimilitude, scholars have had to adjust their research paradigms and protocols. Several shifts have occurred of late, the most important of which may be the focus on selectivity in the consumption of entertain-ment fare.

SELECTIVE EXPOSURE TO ENTERTAINMENT

Emerging theories of selective exposure to entertaining messages have continued to maintain a focus on message properties, in addition to incorporating active audience selection processes and principles. In fact, perhaps the most comprehensive detailing of the central propositions of modern selective exposure theory is called "A Theory of Affect-Dependent *Stimulus* Arrangement" (Zillmann & Bryant, 1985a, p. 158, emphasis added). The fourth proposition of this theory focuses on the selection of entertainment fare: "To the extent that the control of stimulation is limited to environmental stimuli, individuals are inclined to arrange and rearrange their environment so as to best accomplish the stipulated ends" (p. 158). The "stipulated ends" are the termination of aversive stimulation and the perpetuation and intensification of pleasurable experiential states. "In the theory of affect-dependent stimulus arrangements, it has been assumed that certain stimulus types have particular effects, and that they have these effects with consistency" (p. 163). In other words, although this theory focuses on the selective behavior of individuals, and it alleges that individuals have the ability to select messages that, when consumed, will provide them with optimal psychological benefits, the argument that particular messages have special potential to serve these entertainment functions is retained. For example, Zillmann and Bryant (1985a, p. 164) claim: "There can be no doubt about the fact that messages, both informative and entertaining ones, can differ greatly in their capacity to arouse respondents." Other stimulus characteristics that serve "excitatory homeostasis, the maximization of positive affect, and the minimization of aversion" (p. 186) have been considered as well. These include the cognitive intervention potential of entertaining messages, their hedonic valence, their arousal potential, and mood-stimulus affinity. Moreover, the end to the search for message elements that systematically influence selective exposure is nowhere in sight.

Although numerous tests of selective exposure hypotheses have been conducted, a single investigation will be detailed to illustrate the nature of the research on interactions of message *users* with message properties in the process of selecting entertainment fare to achieve desired affective states. (The relatively passive term *receiver* somehow does not seem appropriate for selective exposure perspectives.) The focus of an investigation by Bryant and Zillmann (1984) was the determination of whether people actually spontaneously select entertainment television programming that is beneficial to them in whatever experiential state they are in. In order to test this, subjects were placed in states of boredom versus stress and then allowed to watch television. They could select from six programs, three of which it had been determined via pretesting were exciting, while the other three were relaxing. Selective exposure was unobtrusively measured in terms of time of exposure to each program. The data revealed that exciting programs were selected by bored subjects significantly more than stressed subjects and that relaxing programs were selected by stressed subjects significantly more than by bored subjects. Effects of selection and exposure on excitation were also assessed. It was found that almost all subjects had chosen material that helped them to escape effectively from undesirable excitatory states. A few bored subjects elected to watch relaxing fare and remained in a state of subnormal excitation. Subsequent inquiry revealed psychologically valid reasons for staying ultrarelaxed. For example, one subject wanted to go to bed soon and thought that remaining as relaxed as possible would aid in getting to sleep. The prevailing conclusion is that people can and frequently do make intelligent choices in selecting programs whose message attributes will serve their needs. Fortunately, the sovereign consumer typically seems to choose messages with the potential to produce beneficial results.

THE PLACE OF MESSAGE VARIABLES IN FUTURE ENTERTAINMENT THEORY AND RESEARCH

In concluding their discussion of the state of the art in contemporary selective exposure theory, Zillmann and Bryant (1985a, p. 187) note:

> The model disregards, however, many cognitive processes that presumably accompany and possibly influence selective behavior. The integration of these processes into models with greater predictive accuracy is obviously desirable. Also, many stimulus properties that influence choice behavior may have gone entirely unnoticed. They need to be uncovered and their effects eventually integrated into the models, too.

In terms of the integration of cognitive processes, progress has already been made. Although technically beyond the scope of a discussion of messages, it should be noted that Bargh (1988) has carefully considered the extent of automatic influences and the place of goal-directed processing in altering affective states in both mass and interpersonal communication. In delineating areas of conscious versus unconscious decision making, Bargh indicates future research domains in which cognitively oriented approaches, such as uses and gratifications research, may be particularly useful; areas in which more behavioral assessments would seem to be more appropriate are suggested as well.

Further challenges have been issued also. In articulating a theory of mood management through entertainment that posits specific message-effects patterns from selecting and consuming entertainment fare, Zillmann (1988, p. 168) recommends the incorporation of telic factors into selection models: "For the more accurate prediction of entertainment choices as mood management it will have to be determined exactly what consumption experience individuals *expect* from particular pieces of entertainment, because it is these individuals' perception of things to come that makes them seek out or avoid exposure to the pieces in question" (emphasis added).

In each of these hints of the future agenda of entertainment theory research, the centrality of messages and the perceived importance of the focus on message effects remains. If one considers the everyday efforts of the industrial base of mass entertainment, this seems particularly appropriate. A tremendous amount of time, effort, and money is poured into the production of successful public entertainment fare. Much of this industry effort is focused directly on effective entertainment message design and production. To ignore such message emphases in our entertainment theories would be cavalier indeed.

Such message centrality is in no way a denial of the notion that "meanings are in people, not in messages." Rather it is a recognition of the fact that mass entertainment is a search for common symbols that touch us all and permit us to rekindle our exuberant spirit and our joy. Such is mass entertainment.

REFERENCES

Anderson, D. R., & Collins, P. A. (1988). *The impact on children's education: Television's influence on cognitive development.* Washington, DC: U.S. Department of Education.

Anderson, D. R., & Levin, S. (1976). Young children's attention to *Sesame Street*. *Child Development, 47,* 806-811.

Anderson, D. R., & Lorch, E. P. (1983). Looking at television: Action or reaction? In J. Bryant & D. R. Anderson (Eds.), *Children's understanding of television: Research on attention and comprehension* (pp. 1-33). New York: Academic Press.

Anderson, J. A., & Avery, R. K. (1988). The concept of effects: Recognizing our personal judgments. *Journal of Broadcasting & Electronic Media, 32*, 359-366.

Bargh, J. A. (1988). Automatic information processing: Implications for communication and affect. In L. Donohew, H. E. Sypher, & E. T. Higgins (Eds.), *Communication, social cognition, and affect* (pp. 9-32). Hillsdale, NJ: Lawrence Erlbaum.

Berlo, D. K. (1960). *The process of communication*. New York: Holt, Rinehart & Winston.

Berlyne, D. E. (1971). *Aesthetics and psychobiology*. Englewood Cliffs, NJ: Prentice-Hall.

Beville, H. M., Jr. (1988). *Audience ratings: Ratio, television, and cable* (rev. ed.). Hillsdale, NJ: Lawrence Erlbaum.

Blumler, J. G., & Katz, E. (Eds.). (1974). *The uses of mass communications: Current perspectives on gratifications research*. Beverly Hills, CA: Sage.

Bogart, L. (1980). Television news as entertainment. In P. H. Tannenbaum (Ed.), *The entertainment functions of television* (pp. 209-249). Hillsdale, NJ: Lawrence Erlbaum.

Bryant, J. (1978). [The effect of different levels of suspense and of the source of the resolution of suspense on the appreciation of dramatic presentations]. Unpublished data.

Bryant, J. (1979, November). *The effect of sensation seeking on the enjoyment of the climax and the resolution of suspenseful drama*. Paper presented at the annual convention of the Speech Communication Association, Chicago.

Bryant, J., & Brown, D. (1982). [Retaliatory equity as a factor in humor appreciation: An attempted replication]. Unpublished data.

Bryant, J., & Brown, D. (1985, April). *Clarifying the suspense dilemma*. Paper presented at the annual convention of the Broadcast Education Association, Las Vegas, NV.

Bryant, J., Brown, D., Comisky, P. W., & Zillmann, D. (1982). Sports and spectators: Commentary and appreciation. *Journal of Communication, 32*(1), 109-119.

Bryant, J., Comisky, P., & Zillmann, D. (1981). The appeal of rough-and-tumble play in televised professional football. *Communication Quarterly, 29*, 256-262.

Bryant, J., & Zillmann, D. (1981). [Humor and audiovisual fireworks in educational television: Effects on learning and enjoyment]. Unpublished data.

Bryant, J., & Zillmann, D. (1984). Using television to alleviate boredom and stress: Selective exposure as a function of induced excitational states. *Journal of Broadcasting, 28*, 1-20.

Bryant, J., & Zillmann, D. (Eds.). (1986). *Perspectives on media effects*. Hillsdale, NJ: Lawrence Erlbaum.

Bryant, J., & Zillmann, D. (1988). Using humor to promote learning in the classroom. *Journal of Children in Contemporary Society, 20*, 49-78.

Bryant, J., Zillmann, D., & Brown, D. (1983). Entertainment features in children's educational television: Effects on attention and information acquisition. In J. Bryant & D. R. Anderson (Eds.), *Children's understanding of television: Research on attention and comprehension* (pp. 221-240). New York: Academic Press.

Byrne, D. (1971). *The attraction paradigm*. New York: Academic Press.

Calvert, S., Huston, A., Watkins, B., & Wright, J. (1982). The effects of selective attention to television forms on children's comprehension of content. *Child Development, 53*, 601-610.

Campbell, T., Wright, A., & Huston, A. (1987). Form cues and content difficulty as determinants of children's cognitive processing of televised educational messages. *Journal of Experimental Child Psychology, 43*, 311-327.

Chapman, A. J. (1973). Social facilitation of laughter in children. *Journal of Experimental Social Psychology, 9*, 528-541.

Christ, W. G. (1985). The construct of arousal in communication research. *Human Communication Research, 11*, 575-592.

Comisky, P., & Bryant, J. (1982). Factors involved in generating suspense. *Human Communication Research, 9*, 49-58.

Cupchik, G. C., & Leventhal, H. (1974). Consistency between expressive behavior and the evaluation of humorous stimuli: The role of sex and self observation. *Journal of Personality and Social Psychology, 30*, 429-442.

Darwin, C. R. (1872). *The expression of the emotions in man and animals*. London: Murray.

Diamond, E., & Mahony, A. (1988, August 27). Once it was "Harvest of Shame"—Now we get "Scared Sexless." *TV Guide*, pp. 4-7, 10-11.

Diener, E., & DeFour, D. (1978). Does television violence enhance program popularity? *Journal of Personality and Social Psychology, 36*, 333-341.

Downs, V. C., Javidi, M. M., & Nussbaum, J. F. (1988). An analysis of teachers' verbal communication within the college classroom: Use of humor, self-disclosure, and narratives. *Communication Education, 37*, 127-141.

Eastman, S. T., Head, S. W., & Klein, L. (Eds.). (1985). *Broadcast/cable programming: Strategies and practices* (2nd ed.). Belmont, CA: Wadsworth.

Fischer, H.-D., & Melnik, S. R. (Eds.). (1979). *Entertainment: A cross-cultural examination*. New York: Hastings House.

Gitlin, T. (Ed.). (1987). *Watching television*. New York: Pantheon.

Goldstein, J. H., & McGhee, P. E. (Eds.). (1972). *The psychology of humor*. New York: Academic Press.

Gunter, B. (1985). *Dimensions of television violence*. Hants, United Kingdom: Gower.

Gunter, B. (1987). *Poor reception: Misunderstanding and forgetting broadcast news*. Hillsdale, NJ: Lawrence Erlbaum.

Hajdu, D. (1988, July 30). Why the *Cheers* gang switched to Stroh's beer. *TV Guide*, pp. 29-31.

Hsia, H. J. (1988). *Mass communications research methods: A step-by-step approach*. Hillsdale, NJ: Lawrence Erlbaum.

Huston, A. C., & Wright, J. C. (1983). Children's processing of television: The informative functions of formal features. In J. Bryant & D. R. Anderson (Eds.), *Children's understanding of television: Research on attention and comprehension* (pp. 35-68). New York: Academic Press.

Huston, A., Wright, J., Wartella, E., Rice, M., Watkins, B., Campbell, T., & Potts, R. (1981). Communicating more than content: Formal features of children's television programs. *Journal of Communication, 31*, 32-48.

Johnstone, J., & Ettema, J. S. (1986). Using television to best advantage: Research for prosocial television. In J. Bryant & D. Zillmann (Eds.), *Perspectives on media effects* (pp. 143-164). Hillsdale, NJ: Lawrence Erlbaum.

Koestler, A. (1964). *The act of creation*. London: Hutchinson.

La Fave, L. (1977). Ethnic humour: From paradoxes towards principles. In A. J. Chapman & H. C. Foot (Eds.), *It's a funny thing, humour* (pp. 237-260). Oxford: Pergamon.

La Fave, L., Haddad, J., & Marshall, N. (1974). Humor judgments as a function of identification classes. *Sociology and Social Research, 58*, 184-194.

LaFrance, M. (1983). Felt versus feigned funniness: Issues in coding smiling and laugh-ing. In P. E. McGhee & J. H. Goldstein (Eds.), *Handbook of humor research: Basic issues* (pp. 1-12). New York: Springer-Verlag.

Levin, S., & Anderson, D. (1976). The development of attention. *Journal of Communi-cation, 26*(2), 126-135.

Lewine, R. F., Eastman, S. T., & Adams, W. J. (1985). Prime-time network television programming. In S. T. Eastman, S. W. Head, & L. Klein (Eds.), *Broadcast/cable programming: Strategies and practices* (2nd ed., pp. 119-145). Belmont, CA: Wadsworth.

Lull, J. (1980). The social uses of television. *Human Communication Research, 6,* 197-209.

Merton, R. K. (1967). *On theoretical sociology: Five essays, old and new.* New York: Free Press.

Mielke, K. W. (1983). Formative research on appeal and comprehension in 3-2-1 CON-TACT. In J. Bryant & D. R. Anderson (Eds.), *Children's understanding of television: Research on attention and comprehension* (pp. 241-263). New York: Academic Press.

Morley, D. (1980). *The nationwide audience.* London: British Film Institute.

Morley, D. (1986). *Family television: Cultural power and domestic leisure.* London: Comedia.

Norden, M. F. (1980). Toward a theory of audience response to suspenseful films. *Journal of the University Film Association, 32,* 71-77.

Pollio, H. R., Mers, R., & Lucchesi, W. (1972). Humor, laughter, and smiling: Some preliminary observations of funny behaviors. In J. H. Goldstein & P. E. McGhee (Eds.), *The psychology of humor* (pp. 211-239). New York: Academic Press.

Postman, N. (1985). *Amusing ourselves to death: Public discourse in the Age of Show Business.* New York: Penguin.

Reeves, B., Thorson, E., & Schleuder, J. (1986). Attention to television: Psychological theories and chronometric measures. In J. Bryant & D. Zillmann (Eds.), *Perspectives on media effects* (pp. 251-279). Hillsdale, NJ: Lawrence Erlbaum.

Rosengren, K. E., Wenner, L. A., & Palmgreen, P. (Eds.). (1985). *Media gratifications research.* Beverly Hills, CA: Sage.

Rubin, A. M. (1986). Uses, gratifications, and media effects research. In J. Bryant & D. Zillmann (Eds.), *Perspectives on media effects* (pp. 281-301). Hillsdale, NJ: Lawrence Erlbaum.

Salvaggio, J. S., & Bryant, J. (Eds.). (1989). *Media use in the Information Age: Emerging patterns of adoption and consumer use.* Hillsdale, NJ: Lawrence Erlbaum.

Schleicher, M. P. (1981). *The use of humor in facilitating voluntary selective exposure to televised educational programs.* Unpublished doctoral dissertation, University of Massachusetts, Amherst.

Singer, J. L. (1980). The power and limitations of television: A cognitive-affective analysis. In P. H. Tannenbaum (Ed.), *The entertainment functions of television* (pp. 31-65). Hillsdale, NJ: Lawrence Erlbaum.

Steward-Gordon, J. (1973, May). Alfred Hitchcock, master of menace. *Readers Digest,* pp. 173-178.

Truffaut, F. (1967). *Hitchcock.* New York: Simon & Schuster.

Turner, R. (1987, April 25). So these are the perpetrators! Meet the men who decide what you'll see. *TV Guide,* pp. 8-10.

Wakshlag, J. (1985). Selective exposure to educational television. In D. Zillmann & J. Bryant (Eds.), *Selective exposure to communication*. Hillsdale, NJ: Lawrence Erlbaum.

Watt, J. H., Jr., & Welch, A. J. (1983). Effects of static and dynamic complexity on children's attention and recall of televised instruction. In J. Bryant & D. R. Anderson (Eds.), *Children's understanding of television: Research on attention and comprehension* (pp. 69-102). New York: Academic Press.

Webster, J. G. (1985). Program audience duplication: A study of television inheritance effects. *Journal of Broadcasting & Electronic Media, 29*, 121-133.

Webster, J. G., & Wakshlag, J. J. (1983). A theory of television program choice. *Communication Research, 10*, 430-446.

Webster, J. G., & Wakshlag, J. (1985). Measuring exposure to television. In D. Zillmann & J. Bryant (Eds.), *Selective exposure to communication* (pp. 35-62). Hillsdale, NJ: Lawrence Erlbaum.

Wilde, L. (1976). *How the great comedy writers create laughter*. Chicago: Nelson-Hall.

Wober, J. M. (1988). *The use and abuse of television: A social psychological analysis of the changing screen*. Hillsdale, NJ: Lawrence Erlbaum.

Wolff, H. A., Smith, C. E., & Murray, H. A. (1934). The psychology of humor: I. A study of responses to race-disparagement jokes. *Journal of Abnormal and Social Psychology, 28*, 341-365.

Zillmann, D. (1971). Excitation transfer in communication-mediated aggressive behavior. *Journal of Experimental Social Psychology, 7*, 419-434.

Zillmann, D. (1980). Anatomy of suspense. In P. H. Tannenbaum (Ed.), *The entertainment functions of television* (pp. 133-163). Hillsdale, NJ: Lawrence Erlbaum.

Zillmann, D. (1982). Television viewing and arousal. In D. Pearl, L. Bouthilet, & J. Lazar (Eds.), *Television and behavior: Ten years of scientific progress and implications for the Eighties: Vol. II. Technical reports* (pp. 53-67). Rockville, MD: National Institutes of Mental Health.

Zillmann, D. (1983a). Disparagement humor. In P. E. McGhee & J. H. Goldstein (Eds.), *Handbook of humor research: Basic issues* (pp. 85-107). New York: Springer-Verlag.

Zillmann, D. (1983b). Transfer of excitation in emotional behavior. In J. T. Cacioppo & R. E. Petty (Eds.), *Social psychophysiology: A sourcebook* (pp. 215-240). New York: Guilford.

Zillmann, D. (1988). Mood management: Using entertainment to full advantage. In L. Donohew, H. E. Sypher, & E. T. Higgins (Eds.), *Communication, social cognition, and affect* (pp. 147-171). Hillsdale, NJ: Lawrence Erlbaum.

Zillmann, D., & Bryant, J. (1974). Retaliatory equity as a factor in humor appreciation. *Journal of Experimental Social Psychology, 10*, 480-488.

Zillmann, D., & Bryant, J. (1975). Viewer's moral sanction of retribution in the appreciation of dramatic presentations. *Journal of Experimental Social Psychology, 11*, 572-582.

Zillmann, D., & Bryant, J. (1980). Misattribution theory of tendentious humor. *Journal of Experimental Social Psychology, 16*, 146-160.

Zillmann, D., & Bryant, J. (1985a). Affect, mood, and emotion as determinants of selective exposure. In D. Zillmann & J. Bryant (Eds.), *Selective exposure to communication* (pp. 157-190). Hillsdale, NJ: Lawrence Erlbaum.

Zillmann, D., & Bryant, J. (1985b). Selective-exposure phenomena. In D. Zillmann & J. Bryant (Eds.), *Selective exposure to communication* (pp. 1-10). Hillsdale, NJ: Lawrence Erlbaum.

Zillmann, D., & Bryant, J. (1986). Exploring the entertainment experience. In J. Bryant & D. Zillmann (Eds.), *Perspectives on media effects* (pp. 303-324). Hillsdale, NJ: Lawrence Erlbaum.

Zillmann, D., Hay, T. A., & Bryant, J. (1975). The effect of suspense and its resolution on the appreciation of dramatic presentations. *Journal of Research in Personality, 9*, 307-323.

Zillmann, D., Weaver, J. B., Mundorf, N., & Aust, C. F. (1986). Effects of an opposite-gender companion's affect to horror on distress, delight, and attraction. *Journal of Personality and Social Psychology, 51*, 586-594.

Chapter 10

THE EFFECTS OF VIOLENT
MESSAGES IN THE MASS MEDIA

Daniel G. Linz and Edward Donnerstein

THEORIZING AND EMPIRICAL RESEARCH about the effects of violent mass media on aggressive attitudes and behavior have shifted away from an emphasis on "one-sided" conditioning and learning principles toward more "reciprocal" analyses. These more recent theoretical analyses have also benefited from work within the burgeoning field of cognitive psychology. One of the more sophisticated of these reciprocal cognitive models (Huesmann, 1986) attempts to explain how a heavy diet of television violence sets into motion a sequence of cognitive processes that results not only in viewers being more aggressive but also in their developing increased interest in seeing more television violence. The first goal of this chapter is to review work on violent message content and audience response as it has developed from an early emphasis on simple psychological principles to account for the effects of violent messages *on* individuals to more complex models accounting for the interaction *between* individuals and the mass media.

The second goal of the chapter is to raise two general questions about violent mass media that have come to interest us in recent years and that have been somewhat neglected up to this point. The first is the role emotional factors play in mediating reactions to violent mass media. The second involves the effects of fellow viewers' reactions to violent

AUTHORS' NOTE: Preparation of this chapter and the various studies conducted by the authors and cited herein were supported by National Institute of Mental Health Grant no. MH40894.

media as a mediating variable. In addressing these questions, we will briefly summarize a series of studies in which we try to account for the effects of exposure to sexualized violence against women through emotional desensitization processes. We will also describe more recent work on the effects of fellow audience member responses on reactions to sexually violent mass media.

LEARNING THEORIES AND MASS MEDIA VIOLENCE

Two theoretical approaches dominated early investigations of the impact of mass media violence. Both of these approaches were fashioned around basic principles in classical conditioning and instrumental learning. These early conceptions of the effects of violent mass media on behavior were often guided by a kind of one-sided determinism— violent mass media (the environmental factor)—was theorized to shape and control behavior through rather automatic processes. One of the first theoretical accounts of mass media violence effects relied on the principles of classical conditioning—whereby certain stimuli come to elicit aggressive behavior impulsively or involuntarily.

Classical conditioning. Berkowitz (1973) noted that other psychologists (e.g., Staats & Staats, 1958) had demonstrated that respondents could be trained to have negative or positive attitudes toward certain names by pairing these names with pleasant or unpleasant words. Berkowitz reasoned that verbal and other symbolic stimuli could produce aggressive responses because of their conditioned emotional value. Certain stimuli will elicit impulsive aggressive responses from people who are set to respond in an aggressive manner as a result of the pairing of previously neutral stimuli with aggressive events.

A series of investigations demonstrated that certain aggressive "cues" often elicited aggressive behavior. Following the procedures developed by Staats and Staats, for example, Berkowitz and Knurek (1969) trained men to have negative attitudes toward one of two names. The men were later made angry and asked to take part in another experiment involving a discussion with two fellow students (actually confederates of the experimenters), one of whom had the critical name. The confederates (blind to which subjects had been conditioned) rated each man for his level of hostility during the discussion. The results indicated that those men who had learned to associate negative attitudes toward a particular name were rated as more hostile toward the confederate with that name. Other research indicated that association with cues of violence in a media portrayal that resemble those encountered later, such as the victim in the portrayal with the same name or similar characteristics as someone toward whom the viewer holds animosity, will lead to higher levels of aggression (Berkowitz & Geen, 1967). Still other work (Berkowitz & LaPage, 1967) indicated that the mere presence of objects that have come to signify aggression in our society, such as weapons, will facilitate increases in aggressive behavior. Later, laboratory studies that examined male aggression against a female following media exposure showed that physical aggression against a female by a male was greatest when the media victim was portrayed as similar to a likely real-life target (e.g., Donnerstein, 1980; Donnerstein & Hallam, 1978).

Social learning theory. Social learning theory (Bandura, 1971, 1973) held that aggressive modes of response are acquired either through direct experience or indirectly through the observation of aggressive models. Unlike the Berkowitz approach, which emphasized that many violent media effects are not produced voluntarily, social learning theory as advanced by Bandura emphasized instrumental learning. Through the observation of aggressive models the observer comes to learn which behaviors are "appropriate"—that is, which behaviors will later be rewarded and which will be punished. Implicit in this approach is the assumption that most human behavior is voluntarily directed toward attaining some anticipated reward.

Many laboratory studies have demonstrated that children acquire novel aggressive behaviors on the basis of examples set by models. Typically these studies have involved exposing children to an aggressive model who is either rewarded or punished for aggressive behavior. After watching a model who is positively reinforced for aggression, the children observers are more likely to behave in a similar manner (Bandura, 1965; Bandura, Ross, & Ross, 1963). Studies such as these suggested that viewing a model's aggressive behavior could inhibit or disinhibit aggressive behavior. In the parlance of instrumental learning embraced by theorists at the time: A model's actions could come to serve as informative cues or *discriminative stimuli* signaling probable consequences for observers, prompting them to behave in similar ways if rewarded and inhibiting them if punished. This relatively straightforward approach to mass media effects gained wide acceptance among social psychologists. Most research in the ensuing years has centered on those variables that facilitate the acquisition of aggressive responses through observational learning. Another factor important for predicting when a model will be imitated is the viewer's identification with the actor or actress. Research has supported the notion that children (and adults) are most likely to imitate a model they perceive as having valued characteristics (Huesmann et al., 1978; Singer & Singer, 1980; Turner & Fenn, 1978). It is interesting that research on the effects of media violence on children has revealed that both males and females are likely to identify with male rather than female models (Bandura et al., 1963; Huesmann et al., 1978).

The original formulations revised. In the last decade, researchers have taken issue with the idea that either classical conditioning or social learning theory gives a full account of the effects of exposure to violent mass media (Berkowitz, 1984). The learning theory perspective holds that media influences are due largely to permission-giving or disinhibitory processes. Accordingly, people in the audience are assumed to be predisposed to engage in some antisocial behavior but are reluctant to do so until they are told that the behavior would be profitable. While this notion of disinhibition may apply in some cases, it cannot account for a substantial portion of aggression-enhancing influences. The generality of the effect also seems troubling to a traditional instrumental learning theory interpretation, which, as noted above, holds that a model's actions could come to serve as discriminative stimuli signaling probable consequences for observers. This would imply that the viewer's behavior physically resembles the depicted action. Most of the experiments in the area employ aggression measures that are physically quite different from the depiction.

Berkowitz (1984) points out that, if observational learning refers to the lasting acquisition of novel behavior or new knowledge, many media influences cannot be attributed to such learning. Some media effects are transient and are subject to a "time decay." Phillips and Hensley (1984), for example, examined the effects of publicized accounts of the punishment of violent behavior. They examined the patterns of over 140,000 U.S. homicides before and after media publicity about prizefights, murder acquittals, life sentences, death sentences, and executions. The authors found that the number of white murder victims significantly decreased several days after some highly publicized punishment took place. But these effects were relatively short-lived. They were able to show that most deterrent effects take place within a four-day period following the event. Similar delays might also occur for other forms of television violence.

Because of these shortcomings Berkowitz (1984) and his colleagues (Berkowitz & Rogers, 1986) have proposed that, far from being firmly learned patterns of response, many media effects are immediate, transitory, and relatively short-lived. But these researchers have rejected classical conditioning as the appropriate model for explaining these effects. Instead, they have offered an explanation influenced by theorizing in cognitive psychology (Neisser, 1967). Basically, the explanation is as follows: When people witness an aggressive event through the mass media, ideas are activated that for a short period of time tend to evoke other related thoughts. These thoughts then come to influence subsequent social evaluations or interactions. So now the fact that the mere presence of an aggressive cue (e.g., slides of weapons) may increase the willingness to punish an available target (e.g., Leyens & Parke, 1975) is attributed to the activation of semantically related thoughts rather than involuntarily conditioned responses.

Two cognitive processes drawn from two bodies of theory in cognitive psychology are presumed to operate here. The first involves a cognitive theory about associative pathways in the brain (e.g., Anderson & Bower, 1973). This theory holds that elements of thought, feeling, and prior memories can be thought of as "nodes" in a network of pathways in the brain. The strength of these associative pathways is determined by a variety of factors, the most important being *semantic relatedness*. The second process involves the notion of "spreading activation" (Collins & Loftus, 1975)—the theory that when a thought is brought into awareness, or "activated," this activation radiates from its particular node along the associative pathways to other nodes. The result is that after an idea is activated there is a greater likelihood that it and associated thought elements will come to mind again. This process of thought activation has been termed a "priming effect." Berkowitz suggests that aggressive ideas brought on by viewing violence in the mass media can prime other semantically related thoughts, increasing the probability that they will come to mind. Once these additional thoughts have come to mind, they influence aggressive responding in a variety of ways.

Many studies provide direct evidence for the notion that the activation of aggressive ideas through exposure to violence in the mass media primes other aggression-related thoughts, which in turn may have important social consequences. In a study by Carver, Ganellan, Froming, and Chambers (1983), for example, participants who were presented with a brief film depicting a hostile interaction between a businessman and his secretary evaluated an ambiguous stimulus person as more hostile. In another experiment (Berkowitz, Parke, & West; cited in Berkowitz, 1973, pp. 125-126), children were asked to read either comic books featuring war scenes or a neutral comic book. Children who read the war comics were more likely to choose words with aggressive connotations to complete sentences later presented by the experimenters than subjects who had read the neutral comics. Other studies have shown that people who have witnessed certain types of violent encounters through the mass media (e.g., depictions of sexual violence) are more likely to favor violence in interpersonal situations (Malamuth & Check, 1981).

There is also evidence to suggest that being primed with aggressive thoughts often leads to aggressive acts. Carver et al. (1983) showed that men who were induced to have aggressive thoughts by means of a sentence completion task delivered the most intense electric shocks to other men. Other studies (e.g., Worchel, 1972) have shown similar results.

Cognitive variables (thoughts) are assumed to intervene to increase the chances that people viewing violence will be assaultive themselves. One of the most important of these is the "meaning of the aggressive message" imparted by the viewer. Unless the scenes depicted are considered aggressive by viewers, aggression-related thoughts will not be activated. For example, Berkowitz and Alioto (1973) hypothesized that contact sports are most likely to stimulate aggressive behaviors in observers when the observers believe the players are trying to hurt one another. Male subjects were angered and then exposed to a film of either a prizefight or a football game. Before viewing either of the events the subjects were led to believe that the contest was either aggressive in nature (the opponents were trying to injure each other) or nonaggressive (the contestants were professionals unemotionally engaged in their business). When given a chance to shock the person who had angered them earlier, the males who had seen the supposedly aggressive encounter behaved more punitively. Once an aggressive meaning has been imparted to an event, the probability that other aggressive thoughts will be primed increases. Men who were asked to think of themselves as the winner of a fight rather than the referee and were asked to think "hit" each time the victor landed a blow were more aggressive to a fellow student who had tormented them earlier (Turner & Berkowitz, 1972). According to Berkowitz, the "hit" ideas could have served as aggression retrieval cues, especially for those subjects who thought of themselves as the fight victor. When subjects said the word *hit* and at the same time imagined themselves punching their opponents, memories of past experiences with fighting may have been primed.

The reformulation offered by Berkowitz is appealing because it provides a way of unifying several tangents of mass media violence research by invoking one relatively simple explanation. As we have noted, several authors (e.g., Dorr, 1981; Tannenbaum & Gaer, 1965) have suggested that the observer's identification with media characters influences the extent to which the observer will mimic the aggressive behavior. The reformulation by Berkowitz suggests that viewers who identify with the actors they see are vividly imagining themselves as these characters and are thinking of themselves as carrying out the depicted actions. Such identification with the aggressor in a movie should activate high-imagery-aggressive thoughts and the subsequent priming of this kind of idea might influence subsequent behavior. A study by Turner and Layton (1976) in which subjects were asked to learn lists of words that were either high or low in imagery value and either aggressive or neutral in meaning supports the idea that priming subjects with high-imagery-aggressive thoughts will result in more violent behavior. Subjects were most punitive if they had previously encountered the high-imagery-aggressive words.

Early research on behavioral modeling and instrumental learning, also cited above, (Bandura, 1971) has demonstrated that the audience's willingness to attack someone is greatly influenced by the observed aggressor's outcomes. It is as if viewers draw a lesson from what they see: What happens on the screen might also happen to them if they engage in the same behavior. Berkowitz's reformulation would hold that, when observers witness the consequences of the aggressor's actions, other occasions in which there was the same type of outcome are recalled. With this kind of outcome now vividly in mind, as the availability heuristic (Tversky & Kahneman, 1973) suggests, the viewers might overestimate the frequency and probability of the same type of consequence. Thus observing desirable consequences for a given behavior may increase viewers' willingness to perform that kind of behavior themselves.

UNDERSTANDING THE INTERACTION BETWEEN THE INDIVIDUAL AND VIOLENT MASS MEDIA

So far, the theories of media violence effects we have discussed all share one common problem—they are primarily one-sided. Media effects are presumed to arise from the environment—either cues in the environment that evoke fairly automatic short-lived reactions (i.e., Berkowitz, 1973) or from information the viewer obtains about rewards and punishments that shapes aggressive behavior (i.e., Bandura, 1973). Even the more recent theorizing and empirical research we have described (Berkowitz, 1984) account for mass media effects in a rather one-sided way. Viewers' thoughts are primed by events in the mass media that cause a short-lived increase in the tendency to view other events in an aggressive light. There is no attempt to account for recipient expectation, active audience construal of messages, or the continued interaction of the viewer with the mass media. The focus has mainly been on experiments in which the participants see only one or a few aggressive depictions, which are best viewed as accounts of the immediate impact of exposure to violence on cognition and behavior.

This leaves at least two very important questions unaddressed: First, what are the consequences of exposure to mass media violence for future violent media use? Once the individual has been exposed to mass media violence, is he or she altered in a way so that future goals and plans incorporate violence viewing? A second and perhaps more narrowly focused question concerns the emotional consequences of repeated viewing of mass media violence. Does repeated exposure to violence cause viewers to become desensitized or less emotionally reactive to the consequences of "real-life" violence? We will attempt to answer the first question by describing two models that emphasize the reciprocal nature of the viewer and the media event: theorizing and empirical research undertaken by Bandura in a reformulation of social learning theory and a developmental theory of mass media violence effects proposed by Huesmann et al. (1986). The second question is addressed in work on the effects of repeated exposure to violence and desensitization.

Social cognitive theory. In an attempt to explain lengthier and more varied sequences of behavior than the single acts that presumably result from violence accounted for by earlier analyses, several theorists now say that the effects of mass media violence are best explained by assuming at least a bidirectional process. Bandura (1988), in an extensive elaboration of social learning theory, offers a set of broad principles that might be thought of as a general model of human psychosocial functioning. While it is not specifically a theory of mass media effects (rather, it is an attempt at an exhaustive summary of cognitive factors affecting human social behavior), Bandura's social cognitive theory, as it is now termed, tries to take into account the interaction of violent messages with recipient cognitions, goals, and plans. The foundation of this model is a notion Bandura calls the "triadic reciprocal causation" between behavior, cognitions, and the external environment. In this theory behavior, cognitions and other personal factors, as well as environmental events, all operate as interacting determinants that influence each other bidirectionally (Bandura, 1988).

Bandura accords a central role to four psychosocial processes: (a) symbolizing capacity, (b) self-regulatory capability, (c) self-reflective capability, and (d) vicarious learning processes. The role of symbolizing capacity is fairly straightforward—symbolizing provides us with the tools for understanding, creating, and regulating our environment. Through the use of symbols, people process and transform transient experiences into cognitive models. These models are used to guide future thought and action. Social cognitive theory devotes much attention to the *social* origins of thought and symbolizing and to the mechanisms through which these social factors exert their influence. Unfortunately, space does not permit us to elaborate further on this aspect of the theory. It is sufficient here to note that the first assumption of the theory is that people have the capacity to transform their experiences into abstract cognitive models to guide future behavior.

The theory also asumes that people are "self-reactors" with the capacity for self-direction. Self-standards are used to set goals and people seek satisfaction in the fulfillment of these goals. Discrepancies between behavior and personal standards generate self-reactive influences that serve as motivators and guides for action. At its most basic level, effective cognitive functioning, according to Bandura, also involves comparisons of our own thoughts with some kind of social standard. This self-reflection allows us to distinguish accurate and faulty thinking. The mass media, particularly television, may play a primary role in cognitive functioning by allowing the viewer to verify thoughts through a *vicarious* mode. Observing other people's transactions with the environment and the effects they produce serves as a way of checking the "correctness" of one's own thinking. Vicarious thought verification is not simply a *supplement* to direct or enactive experience. Symbolic modeling, according to Bandura, greatly expands the range of verification experiences that cannot otherwise be attained by personal action. These metacognitive activities sometimes foster veridical thought, but they can produce faulty thought patterns as well. Verification of thought by comparison with distorted televised versions of social reality for example, can foster shared misconceptions (Gerbner, 1972).

Indeed, virtually all learning resulting from direct experience can occur vicariously by observing people's behavior and its consequences for them. A great deal of information about human values and behavior is gained from models portrayed through the pictorial or symbolic world of the mass media. People then act on these images of reality. The more people's images of reality depend upon the media's symbolic environment, the greater the media's social impact.

According to Bandura, several mechanisms govern symbolic modeling. The first and most obvious are attentional processes—these determine what is selectively observed and what information is extracted from modeled events. The second involves retention of information through active rehearsal processes. In order to retain information it must be transformed or restructured in the form of social rules. The third subfunction is the behavioral production process through which symbolic conceptions are translated into appropriate courses of action. Here, Bandura speculates that we engage in a conception matching process. Essentially, a pattern of behavior is enacted and then compared against a conceptual model. The behavior is then modified on the basis of this comparison. The fourth process is a motivational one. Here Bandura distinguishes between acquisition and performance. People are not assumed to perform everything they learn. Performance of observationally learned behavior is influenced by three major types of rewards—direct, vicarious, and self-produced.

This expanded version of social learning theory moves us considerably from the idea that modeling is simply a process of "monkey see, monkey do." Instead, it takes account of more "abstract" processes whereby "rules" are learned that can be applied to new situations or that can be used for innovative behavior across situations. There are several steps involved in learning about abstract rules for social behavior. First the viewer must extract the relevant features from social exemplars. Next, this new information must be integrated into composite rules. Finally, the rules are then used to produce new instances of behavior. The challenge for mass media researchers studying the effects of violence is to specify exactly what features of the media event are attended to, and how these are cultivated into new competencies.

We already know that modeling influences can strengthen or weaken inhibitions on behavior that has been previously learned. These effects are determined primarily by information that is conveyed about the probable consequences of modeled action. These include observers' judgments of their ability to accomplish the modeled behavior, their perception of the modeled actions as producing favored or aversive consequences, and inferences that similar or dissimilar consequences would result if they themselves were to engage in analogous activities. The disinhibitory effects of modeling are most clearly shown in studies involving exposure to aggressive sexual behavior (Malamuth & Donnerstein, 1984). But, again, the process is not simply one of the viewer merely mimicking the model's behavior. Instead, the enactment of violent behavior is regulated by two types of sanctions—social sanctions and internalized self-sanctions. Televised aggression is often shown in ways that may weaken restraints over aggressive conduct (Goranson, 1970; Halloran & Croll, 1972; Larsen, 1968). In televised representations, physical and verbal aggression is often shown as a solution to interpersonal conflicts. Aggression is portrayed as socially acceptable, relatively successful; and it is socially sanctioned by "superheroes" triumphing over evil by violent means.

A reciprocal effects developmental model. Huesmann (1986) draws upon ideas in social cognitive theory to explain the effects of televised violence, especially the notion that learning the appropriate course of action in a situation involves the retention of behavioral rules or "scripts" through active rehearsal. In this model, as in social cognitive modeling, social strategies that are learned through watching violent television are tried in the immediate environment and if reinforced are retained and used again. The most important contribution of the social developmental model proposed by Huesmann (1986), however, is the explication of personal and *interpersonal* factors as intervening variables that link violence viewing and aggression.

Past empirical research has established five variables as particularly important in maintaining the television-viewing/aggression relationship (see Huesmann & Malamuth, 1986). These are the child's (a) intellectual achievement, (b) social popularity, (c) identification with the television characters, (d) belief in the realism of the violence shown on television, and (e) amount of fantasizing about aggression. According to Huesmann, a heavy diet of television violence sets into motion a sequence of processes, based on these personal and interpersonal factors, that result not only in the viewers being more aggressive but also in their developing increased interest in seeing more television violence.

Research suggests that children who have poorer academic skills behave more aggressively. They also watch television with greater regularity, watch more violent programs, and believe violent programs are accurate portrayals of life (Huesmann & Eron, 1986). Huesmann speculates that aggressiveness interferes with the social interactions between the viewer and his or her teachers and peers that are needed in order to develop academic potential. Slow intellectual achievement may be related to heightened television violence viewing for two reasons. First, heightened television viewing in general may interfere with intellectual achievement (Lefkowitz, Eron, Walder, & Huesmann, 1977). It may also be that children who cannot obtain gratification from success in school turn to television shows to obtain vicariously the successes they cannot otherwise obtain. Aggressive children may also be substantially less popular with their peers (Huesmann & Eron, 1986). Longitudinal analyses suggest, however, that the relationship between unpopularity and aggression is bidirectional. Not only do more aggressive children become less popular, but less popular children seem to become more aggressive. In addition, less popular children view more television and, therefore, see more violence on television.

Identification with television characters may also be important. Children who perceive themselves as like television characters are more likely to be influenced by the aggressive scripts they observe (Huesmann, Lagerspetz, & Eron, 1984). This may be particularly true for boys. At the same time, more aggressive children tend to identify with aggressive characters, and those who identify more with television characters behave more aggressively.

For an aggressive behavior script to be encoded in memory and maintained, it must be salient to a child. Huesmann speculates that realistic depictions are relatively salient depictions. If a violent action is perceived as totally unrealistic, it is unlikely to receive very much attention. Early investigations of televised violence have emphasized this variable as a determinant of imitative effects (e.g., Feshbach, 1972). Later investigations by Huesmann and his colleagues have confirmed that the relation between violence viewing and aggression is heightened for children who believe that the violence is representative of real life (Huesmann et al., 1984).

Finally, the maintenance of aggressive scripts might be accomplished through the rehearsal of these scripts in the child's mind. Research has shown that children's self-reports of violent fantasies are positively correlated with both aggression and greater television viewing (Huesmann & Eron, 1986).

Considered together, the interrelations of each of these variables suggest a reciprocal process in which violence viewing and aggressive behavior perpetuate each other. This process is illustrated in Figure 10.1. It may be described as follows: Children who are heavy viewers of television violence will see characters solving interpersonal problems by behaving aggressively. To the extent that these children identify with the aggressive characters they observe, and believe that the aggression is realistic, they will fantasize about and encode in memory the aggressive solutions they observe. If aggressive behaviors are emitted in the appropriate situations, the aggressive behaviors will be reinforced with desirable outcomes. But if aggressive behavior becomes habitual, it will interfere with social and academic success. The more aggressive child will become less popular at school with peers and especially with teachers. These academic and social failures may lead to aggression, but, just as important, they may also lead to more regular television viewing. It is hypothesized that children might obtain satisfactions that they are denied in their social lives from television and might be better able to justify their own aggressive behavior after seeing more aggression in the media. The cycle of aggression, academic and social failure, violence viewing, and fantasizing mutually facilitating each other then continues.

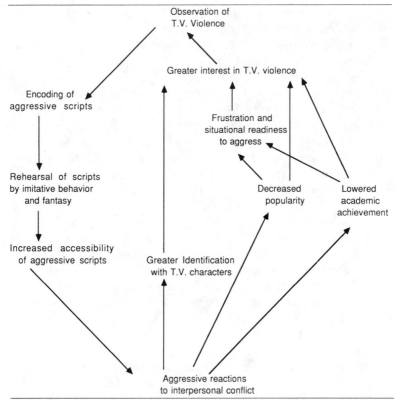

Figure 10.1 Huesmann's Reciprocal Model of Long-Term Effects of Mass Media Violence

SOURCE: Adapted from Huesmann (1986).

Desensitization to mass media violence. The models advanced by Bandura (1986) and Huesmann (1986) deal nearly exclusively with *cognitive* processes that may operate with long-term exposure to media violence. In both of these models heavy emphasis is placed on cognitive scripts and abstract rules for social behavior that may be imparted to the viewer through continued use of violent mass media. Somewhat neglected in these approaches is the role of emotions. Generally, research on affective reactions to violent messages has been concerned with the possibility that continued exposure to violence in the mass media will undermine feelings of concern, empathy, or sympathy viewers might have toward victims of actual violence. Most of the previous work on desensitization to media violence has involved exposure to rather mild forms of television violence for relatively short periods of time (e.g., Cline, Croft, & Courrier, 1973; Thomas, 1982; Thomas, Horton, Lippencott, & Drabman, 1977). More recently, Linz, Donnerstein, and Penrod (1984) measured the reactions of college-age men to films portraying violence against women, often in a sexual context, viewed across a five-day period. Comparisons of first- and last-day reactions to the films showed that, with repeated exposure, initial levels of self-reported anxiety decreased substantially. Furthermore, subjects' perceptions of the films also changed from the first day to the last day. Material that was previously judged to be violent and degrading to women was seen as significantly less so by the end of the exposure period. Subjects also indicated they were less depressed and enjoyed the material more with repeated exposure. Most important, these effects generalized to a victim of sexual assault presented in a videotaped reenactment of a rape trial. Subjects who were exposed to the sexually violent films rated the victim as less severely injured compared to a no-exposure control group. In another study, (Linz, Donnerstein, & Penrod, 1988) subjects were also less sympathetic to the rape victim portrayed in the trial and less able to empathize with rape victims in general, compared to no-exposure control subjects and subjects exposed to other types of films. Longer film exposure was necessary to affect the violence-viewing subjects' general empathic response.

Linz et al. (1988) suggested that the viewers were becoming comfortable with anxiety-provoking situations much as they would if they were undergoing exposure therapy. Further, it was suggested that self-awareness of reductions in anxiety and emotional arousal may be instrumental in the formation of other perceptions and attitudes about the violence portrayed in the films, which are then carried over to other contexts.

A substantial amount of literature now exists on the behavioral treatment of pathological fears demonstrating that simply exposing a patient to the situations or objects he or she is frightened of will significantly diminish the anxiety or negative affect that was once evoked by the objects or situations (Foa & Kozak, 1986; Ullman & Krasner, 1969). It has recently been proposed that exposure therapy is effective because it first evokes a fear memory (Lang, 1977, 1979). Once evoked, this memory is then available for some form of cognitive

modification. Certain self-awareness processes have also been suggested as a contributing factor to the effectiveness of exposure therapy
(Wilkins, 1971). Foa and Kozak (1986) have speculated that a patient's
perception of his or her own habituation in the presence of a feared
stimulus plays an important role in helping the patient habituate to that
stimulus. Self-awareness of reduced anxiety may provide the patient
with information that short-term physiological habituation has occurred
and leads to dissociation of response elements from stimulus elements
of the fear structure. The new information might also facilitate changes
in negative valence associated with the feared stimulus. Patients may
also begin to evaluate the "badness" of the feared stimuli in a less
exaggerated manner.

Similar processes may operate when subjects are repeatedly exposed
to graphic media violence. Once viewers are emotionally "comfortable"
with the violent content of the films, they may also evaluate the film
more favorably in other domains. Material originally believed to be
offensive or degrading to the victims of violence may be evaluated as
less so with continued exposure. A reduction in the level of anxiety may
also blunt viewers' awareness of the frequency and intensity of violence
in the films. Reductions in anxiety may serve to decrease sensitivity to
emotional cues associated with each violent episode and thereby reduce
viewers' perceptions of the amount of violence in the films. Consequently, by the end of an extensive exposure period, viewers may
perceive aggressive films as less violent than they had initially. These
altered perceptual and affective reactions may then be carried over into
judgments made about victims of violence in other more realistic
settings.

This model proposed to account for the carryover effects generally
supported by correlational data, but only weakly (Linz et al., 1988). We
reasoned that subjects would use their self-perceived levels of anxiety
and negative affect to define and evaluate violence and degradation. We
argued that, as subjects became calm in the presence of violence,
material that was originally perceived to be violent and degrading
would seem less so. The results revealed a positive correlation between
self-reported levels of negative affect or arousal (i.e., tenseness, nausea,
nervousness, looking away, and so on) and perceptions of how much
violence the movies contained and how degrading the movies were to
women. Perceptions of violence in the films were, in turn, significantly,

but not overwhelmingly correlated with sympathy for the victim subsequently presented in the rape trial.

Future investigations should be undertaken to determine the extent to which the desensitization effects generalize to victims in other contexts. Averill, Malmstrom, Koriat, and Lazarus (1972) have found that, while habituation to an accident scene viewed in isolation carried over to an identical scene embedded in a complete movie, there was little habituation to other similar but nonidentical scenes in the same movie. In contrast, Thomas et al. (1977) report that children who watched a violent police drama appeared subsequently to be desensitized to a dissimilar violent episode as evidenced by their failure to intervene in a fight between other children. Adults who watched the same drama also showed desensitization to dissimilar films involving actual police brutality. Would the same effects found in Linz et al. (1988) be observed if subjects had been presented with a male victim of violence in the dependent measure task rather than a female victim?

Other factors influencing aggressive behavior. While theorizing about the relationship between exposure to violent mass media and aggressive behavior has become more sophisticated, there has been at the same time an accumulation of research findings over the years that while not necessarily integrated into any particular theory have led researchers to realize that mass media effects are nearly always "interactive" effects, in a statistical sense. In other words, it has become increasingly apparent to social scientists that the best way to describe the effects of exposure to violent media is to say that "for some people, some of the time" exposure to violence will result in aggressive behavior. As Berkowitz (1986) observes, very few persons actually attack anyone after they watch others fight. There are simply too many environmental and personal factors that operate to restrain the individual from actually engaging in aggressive behavior. While there may be "main effects" of observed violence for the average viewer most of the time, these are in the form of aggressive ideas that might come to mind for a brief period, harsh judgments that might be made of others, or hostile words that might be uttered to some offending party soon after exposure. The likelihood of actual violence among most viewers is probably very low. On the other hand, if conditions are right, exposure to media violence may lead to aggressive behavior. Aggressive behavior following a violent media depiction will most often be mediated by an interaction between exposure to the depiction and a mixture of characteristics of the individual viewer and characteristics of the environment.

Many of the personal and environmental characteristics that may strengthen or weaken media violence effects have been summarized by others (e.g., Berkowitz, 1986) and we will mention only a few of the most important of these here. For example, whether or not a person will choose to expose him- or herself to media violence in the first place might be dependent on several factors: prior histories of personal aggressiveness (Liebert, Sprafkin, & Davidson, 1982) or apprehension about crime and violence that may be alleviated by exposure to crime shows in which "good guys" win out (Wakshlag, Vial, & Tamborini, 1983; Zillmann, 1980). Audience factors such as approval or disapproval of media violence by fellow observers also appear to play a role in whether or not aggressive reactions are displayed or restrained (Dunand, Berkowitz, & Leyens, 1984; Grusec, 1973; Hicks, 1968). The simple availability of a victim after seeing violence as well as more subtle victim characteristics such as similarity between available targets after exposure and victims portrayed in the media event may influence subsequent aggressiveness (Berkowitz & Geen, 1967; Donnerstein, 1984; Geen & Berkowitz, 1966).

Additional factors related to the individual viewer's disposition while viewing violence and the interpretation of the media event are also important. For example, there is a consensus among aggression researchers that people who are angry at the time of their exposure to media violence are especially likely to respond aggressively. Other studies have demonstrated that the degree to which viewers believe the media depictions to be realistic influences subsequent aggression. In general, subjects who view what they believe is realistic violence behave more aggressively (Berkowitz & Alioto, 1973; Feshbach, 1972; Geen, 1975). Finally, even simple attentional factors such as whether the viewer attends primarily to the violence depicted in the story or instead focuses on myriad other scenes and stimuli present in most media depictions will determine if an individual will behave aggressively after exposure.

Other reviews (e.g., Geen & Thomas, 1986) have pointed to demographic characteristics, such as age and sex, that may affect aggressive responding after exposure to media violence. Investigators have noted, for example, that older children are more likely to comprehend violent TV shows in terms of the aggressor's motivations rather than in terms of raw outcomes (Collins, Sobol, & Westby, 1981). This is important, according to the authors, because young children who are less able to make subtle distinctions seem to respond in "all or none" fashion to violence, becoming increasingly aggressive no matter what the content of the violence depiction. On the other hand, older viewers, such as college-age subjects, may be especially reactive to certain types of portrayals (e.g., revenge scenarios) and not particularly aggressive after viewing others. Sex differences in reactiveness to aggression—males more likely to show increased aggression after exposure to a violent film (e.g., Cantor, Zillmann, & Einsiedel, 1978)—are also apparent (although these differences may be diminishing due to changes in the pattern of socialization for girls in our society).

SEXUAL VIOLENCE IN THE MASS MEDIA AND INTERPERSONAL PROCESSES

The developmental theory proposed by Huesmann (1986) tries to take into account the effects of mass media violence on interpersonal behavior and how certain interpersonal factors (specifically failures with peers and teachers at school) might then compel the viewer to seek out more violent media. This theory is especially interesting as it places emphasis on a few of the social interaction variables that may be thought of as both a cause and a consequence of mass media violence. What other questions might an integrative theory of interpersonal processes and violent mass media effects address? Because we have been particularly interested in the effects of pornography and sexual violence (e.g., Donnerstein, Linz, & Penrod, 1987), especially those depictions that juxtapose violence against women with sexual scenes ("slasher films"), we will limit our discussion to the effects of these materials.

An indirect effects model. Malamuth and Briere (1986) have proposed an "indirect effects" model in which they consider a variety of individual, interpersonal, and societal variables that may be causally related to sexual violence. According to these authors, cultural factors such as the mass media may influence sexually aggressive behavior but they do so only indirectly through changes in attitudes, perceptions, and beliefs about sexual aggression, sexual arousal to aggression, and other motivations and personality characteristics. In complex combinations, these intermediate variables may lead to antisocial behaviors including aggression. Like Huesmann (1986) and Bandura (1988), Malamuth and Briere (1986) devote special attention to potential media influences on thought patterns that are stored in memory as "rules" for guiding behavior. These rules may form part of a larger cognitive structure that includes beliefs about what behaviors are appropriately desirable or acceptable in male-female relations. These belief systems may be thought of as "schemas" (Fiske & Taylor, 1984) or "scripts" for behavior (e.g., Abelson, 1981; Gagnon & Simon, 1973). Regardless of the label, the important assumption, as with Huesmann (1986) and Bandura (1988), is that the information is stored in the form of abstract rules for behavior rather than as a collection of specific experiences.

Experimental laboratory research has linked certain messages common in the mass media about violence against women to changes in thought patterns. Several studies (Malamuth & Check, 1980; Malamuth, Haber, & Feshbach, 1980) in which males were exposed to rape with a "positive" consequence for the victim (e.g., she became sexually aroused), rape with negative consequences, or mutually consenting sex have revealed that those exposed to positive rape portrayals perceived a second rape depiction as less negative than those first exposed to other messages. Another investigation (Malamuth & Check, 1985) indicated that men exposed to positive rape portrayals believed a higher percentage of women would derive pleasure from being sexually assaulted. Another experimental study conducted outside the laboratory yielded similar effects for attitudes about interpersonal violence and sexual assault (Malamuth & Check, 1981).

Thought patterns supportive of aggression against women, in combination with other variables, may be related to aggression in naturalistic settings. Malamuth (1986) measured 155 men on three sets of variables: motivational factors for sexual aggression (sexual arousal to aggression, hostility toward woman, dominance as a motive for sex), disinhibition factors including attitudes condoning sexual aggression and antisocial personality characteristics, and an "opportunity" variable level of sexual experience. These rape predictors were then correlated with self-reports of sexual aggression. Considered individually, each of the variables was only moderately related to sexual aggression. Interactive combinations of these variables, on the other hand, allowed for far more accurate prediction. Men who had relatively high scores on all of these variables were also highly aggressive in their sexual interactions with women.

Audience-mass media interactions. The model proposed by Malamuth and the desensitization model by Linz et al. described earlier are attempts to explain how perceptions of appropriate or desirable interpersonal behavior are engendered or modified through exposure to sexually violent mass media. This is the first and most important level of inquiry into the effects of sexually violent mass media on interpersonal behavior. We would suggest, however, that a more fully integrated theory of violent mass media and interpersonal behavior would need to guide empirical investigations into at least three additional areas. These would include interpersonal influences on the *use* of sexually violent mass media, interpersonal influences on perceptions of and attitudes toward the content of violent mass media itself, and interpersonal interactions during the sexually violent mass media event itself that may determine future interpersonal behavior.

Interpersonal influences on the *use* of certain forms of mass media have been studied by many researchers (see Gumpert & Cathcart, 1979). Dominick (1974), for example, contrasted radio use by children with few interpersonal relationships to use by those children with many relationships. He found that children with low peer group membership listened more to the radio and did so more for information than for entertainment than children with many peer relations. Similar investigations should be undertaken to determine if preferences for certain forms of mass media violence can be predicted from a variety of interpersonal variables—peer group interactions among them. Little is known about the effects of interpersonal factors on sexually violent material.

There is research to suggest that teenagers obtain a substantial amount of information about sexual relations through the mass media. Survey research indicates that the major source of sex information for youths is the peer group (Haffner & Kelly, 1987), but that this source of information has been declining over the years. The gap in sex education has been filled by the media rather than by parents (Roberts, 1982). Research on the frequency of exposure to sexually violent mass media indicates that a sizable portion of the undergraduate male population has access to these messages. Demare, Briere, and Lips (1987) in a survey of 222 Canadian undergraduate men found that 36% were exposed at least once to sexually violent pornography, and 13% reported having viewed such materials more than twice in the past year. Other research (e.g., Check, 1985) indicates that up to a third of youths between the ages of 12 to 17 report viewing sexually explicit films at least once a month. A recent survey conducted in Great Britain with a representative sample of children and adults indicates that 45% of children report having seen at least one videocassette that would be legally classified as obscene on the basis of the nature of the violence it portrays. The authors of this study echo our own concerns when they state: "The first knowledge of sexual life acquired by these children may come from viewing films in which sexual conduct is inextricably entwined with violence, hatred, coercion and the humiliation of women in particular" (Roth, 1985, p. 3).

New media technologies such as cable television and video recorders have undoubtedly lead to much wider dissemination of sexually violent materials in the last few years. However, no scientific studies documenting this greater availability exist. Similarly, no empirical investigations of the interpersonal factors that promote interest in sexual violence among children and youth have been undertaken. As a starting point it may prove fruitful to examine some of the same variables found to predict radio use among teens. It may be the case, for example, that adolescents with relatively unstable peer group relations or infrequent peer contact rely much more heavily on the mass media for information about what constitutes "appropriate" sexual behavior.

Investigations into the impact of interpersonal influences on the *perception* of mass media content and attitudes about the sexually violent mass media event itself might also be fruitful. Here the reactions of fellow audience members might be of particular interest. It has been demonstrated that the mere presence of a cospectator can alter perceptions of a message (Balance, Coughlin, & Bringmann, 1972). To date, several studies have considered the effects of commentaries presented by a co-observer during a violent film as one way of altering the impact of film exposure. Hicks (1968) found that positive and negative commentaries presented by an adult during a violent film produced corresponding disinhibition and inhibition effects when that adult remained with the 5- to 9-year-old subjects during a postexposure test of imitative performance. Other research has shown that older children were affected by the adults' comments even in the adults' absence (Grusec, 1973). There was greater imitation when comments were positive than when they were negative, and they were significantly faster in summoning help when the content of a violent film was evaluated neutrally (Horton & Santogrossi, 1978). In a study by Drabman and Thomas (1977), 5-year-old boys observed a short aggressive or a prosocial film either alone or in the company of a classmate. The audience variable had no noticeable effect upon the prosocial behaviors of the subjects, but it had a significant effect upon aggressive reactions. Dunand, Berkowitz, and Lyens (1984) have found similar results with older subjects. Male university students demonstrated greater aggressive behavior after having watched a violent film with an active confederate (one who reacted positively by gestures and voice to the content of a film) than for those in the company of a passive one. Zillmann, Weaver, Mundorf, and Aust (1986) found that men exposed to violence in the presence of an apparently frightened female companion, as compared to a nonexpressive female companion, enjoyed the movie most in the presence of the distressed woman and least in the company of a woman who appeared to be callous to the violence. Women, in contrast, enjoyed the movie most in the company of a callous man and least in the company of a distressed man.

More recently we have examined the effects of a cospectator's presence on a variety of judgments about sexually violent displays (Niemczycki, Linz, & Donnerstein, 1988). In the first study, we were interested in whether or not viewing sexual violence in the presence of an opposite-gender companion would alter affective responses to the violence, change viewer perceptions of the amount of sexual violence in the material, and affect viewer judgments of how degrading the films were to women.

Four groups of men were enlisted to view a condensed version of a popular R-rated film that contained scenes of sexual coercion. The woman in the film is portrayed as initially resistant but later is sexually aroused by violence. The men watched the film in the presence of a female viewing companion whom they believed was a fellow subject in the experiment. In one group the female companion indicated verbal and nonverbal approval of the film, including the sexually violent episodes. In another group she expressed verbal and nonverbal disapproval of the film. In a third, neutral condition she remained silent and passive. A fourth and fifth group of men either watched the film alone or did not view a film.

The results indicated that there were no differences between the groups of men in their perceptions of the amount of sex and violence in the film. There were, however, differences in the way they felt about the films. The men enjoyed the film most in the presence of a female companion who expressed positive reactions to the film and enjoyed it least with a female companion who expressed negative reactions to the film. It is interesting that the men enjoyed the film less in the neutral condition in which the woman was present but silent than in either the positive or the control condition. The men in the negative and neutral conditions also found the films more embarrassing and upsetting, and found the films more degrading to women than either the positive reaction or the no-companion control subjects.

In a second study we replicated the design of the original study and added three additional conditions involving male confederates as viewing companions. In these conditions male companions were either present and silent or indicated verbal and nonverbal approval or disapproval during the film. The results for viewing with the female companion were nearly identical to the first study. Men liked the film best when the woman approved and they felt uncomfortable when she either made a disapproving comment or was merely present as a silent viewing partner. The reactions of the male viewing companions, whether negative or positive, made little difference to the men in their evaluations of the film. These results suggest that there may be important differences in a viewers' reactions to mass media sexual violence depending not only on the perception of the media event itself but also on how the male viewer incorporates the reactions (or assumed reactions) of those around him. In particular this study points to the difference in importance of expressions of female versus male support of sexual violence as a mediator of responses to sexual violence.

Personal interviews with preadolescents who watch "slasher films" on a regular basis suggest that these films are often viewed on videocassette in the home and are typically viewed in the presence of peers. We would speculate that viewing these films in groups not only hastens the process of desensitization to the sexual violence in the films but also facilitates certain interpersonal goals important to the viewer outside of the viewing situation itself. Zillmann et al. (1986) suggest that viewing slasher films affords youngsters the opportunity to prove their fearlessness or courage, both to themselves and to their peers. These authors note that in contemporary society male adolescents and preadolescents are expected to exhibit a calm demeanor in the presence of danger, whereas this expectation does not apply to female adolescents. They argue that female adolescents are encouraged to freely express distress, fear, and panic—analogous to the women of earlier times who depended on and presumably appreciated the protection provided by men. Through excitatory habituation (see Grings & Dawson, 1978) or desensitization processes that result from the frequent consumption of horror movies, the male adolescent can rapidly grow callous enough not to be disturbed by most of the mayhem he sees on the screen. This can then be demonstrated to his peers through outward expressions of boredom or even amusement in the face of the violence. These demonstrations may facilitate two compatible interpersonal goals. Outward expressions of desensitization to sexual violence may provide a means by which male peers acknowledge his fearlessness, and his female peers might find comfort in such a display of coping, as it might evoke traditional and comfortable ideas about the male's capacity for protectiveness. According to Zillmann et al. (1986) if men are eager to show off their fearlessness, and women appreciate the comfort implicit in this show of mastery by a male companion, it follows that males should grow fond of females who express distress because this gives them the opportunity to comfort and "get closer." Women who show callousness or desensitization, on the other hand, prove their independence and deny this opportunity. The situation reverses for women's attraction to male companions. Women should come to like those men who prove fearless and provide comfort, and they should be least accepting of men who wince in the face of terror. The authors exposed male and female college students to a slasher film in the presence of a same-age opposite-gender companion. The companion expressed desensitization and callousness, showed no reaction, or showed distress. Measures were obtained of the companion's physical attractiveness, the companion's desirability as a working partner, and the subject's tendency to agree with an apparently erroneous statement. The investigators found that displays of callousness significantly enhanced the physical appeal of the low-appeal male companion. This companion also benefited from the display of mastery in that more positive traits were ascribed to him. On the female side, in contrast it was the highly attractive companion who showed a gain in positive traits. The display of sensitivity in the face of the violence reduced the desirability of both male and female companions as working mates. In working together, female subjects showed a clear tendency to acquiesce to assertions by their companions who had shown callousness.

The findings of this study indicate that affective reactions to violence and to companions with whom violence is consumed appear to follow established gender-specific rules for conduct. The mass media event becomes a vehicle by which audience members express themselves and can facilitate certain interpersonal goals. In this way reactions to sexually violent mass media events are being used by the viewers in a highly active way to facilitate future social relations.

SUMMARY AND CONCLUSIONS

The evolution of theory and research on the effects of violence in the mass media has taken us from simple learning models to more elaborate reciprocal cognitive models that attempt to account for the effects of the mass media not only on a person's aggressive behavior but also on increased interest in seeing more mass media violence, which, in turn, may lead to even greater levels of violence. These more contemporary approaches have moved us from the study of the effects of violent messages *on* individuals to the elaboration of complex models to account for the interaction *between* individuals and the mass media.

Our discussion in the last section would suggest that one especially interesting task for investigators in the area of mass media violence would be to augment these reciprocal cognitive models with a consideration of *audience* reactions to the violence itself, as well as the viewers assessment of others' reactions. Such an "interactive approach" takes us beyond even the more elaborate cognitive models proposed to date by considering violent media viewing as a social event that is used by participants to further interpersonal goals.

REFERENCES

Abelson, R. P. (1981). The psychological status of the script concept. *American Psychologist, 36,* 715-729.

Anderson, J., & Bower, G. (1973). *Human associative memory.* Washington, DC: Winston.

Averill, J. R., Malmstrom, E. J., Koriat, A., & Lazarus, R. S. (1972). Habituation to complex emotional stimuli. *Journal of Abnormal Psychology, 80,* 20-28.

Balance, W. D., Coughlin, D., & Bringmann, W. G. (1972). Examination of social context effects upon affective responses to "hot" and "cool" communications media. *Psychology Reports, 31* 793-794.

Bandura, A. (1965). Vicarious processes: A case of no trial learning. In L. Berkowitz (Ed.), *Advances in experimental psychology* (Vol. 2, pp. 1-55). New York: Academic Press.

Bandura, A. (1971). *Social learning theory.* New York: General Learning Press.

Bandura, A. (1973). *Aggression: A social learning analysis.* Englewood Cliffs, NJ: Prentice-Hall.

Bandura, A. (1988). Social cognitive theory of mass communication. In J. Groebel & P. Winterhoff (Eds.), *Empirische Medienpsychologie* (pp. 44-77). Munchen: Psychologie Verlags Union.

Bandura, A., Ross, D., & Ross, S. A. (1963). Imitation of film-mediated aggressive models. *Journal of Abnormal and Social Psychology, 66*, 3-11.

Belson, W. A. (1978). *Television violence and the adolescent boy.* Farnborough: Teakfield.

Bem, D. (1967). Self perception: An alternative interpretation of cognitive dissonance phenomena. *Psychological Review, 74*, 183-220.

Berkowitz, L. (1973). Words and symbols as stimuli to aggressive responses. In J. Knutson (Ed.), *Control of aggression: Implications from basic research* (pp. 113-143). Chicago: Aldine-Atherton.

Berkowitz, L. (1974). Some determinants of impulsive aggression: Role of mediated associations with reinforcements for aggression. *Psychological Review, 81*, 165-176.

Berkowitz, L. (1984). Some effects of thoughts on anti- and prosocial influences of media events: A cognitive-neoassociation analysis. *Psychological Bulletin, 95*, 410-427.

Berkowitz, L. (1986). Situational influences on reactions to observed violence. *Journal of Social Issues, 42*, 93-106.

Berkowitz, L., & Alioto, J. (1973). The meaning of an observed event as a determinant of its aggressive consequences. *Journal of Personality and Social Psychology, 28*, 206-217.

Berkowitz, L., & Geen, R. G. (1967). Stimulus qualities of the target of aggression: A further study. *Journal of Personality and Social Psychology, 5*, 364-368.

Berkowitz, L., & Knurek, D. A. (1969). Label-mediated hostility generalization. *Journal of Personality and Social Psychology, 13*, 200-206.

Berkowitz, L., & LaPage, A. (1967). Weapons as aggression-eliciting stimuli. *Journal of Personality and Social Psychology, 7*, 202-207.

Berkowitz, L., & Rogers, K. H. (1986). A priming effect analysis of media influences. In D. Zillmann (Ed.), *Advances in media effects research.* Hillsdale, NJ: Lawrence Erlbaum.

Cantor, J. R., Zillmann, D., & Einsiedel, E. F. (1978). Female responses to provocation after exposure to aggressive and erotic films. *Communication Research, 5*, 395-412.

Carver, C., Ganellen, R., Froming, W., & Chambers, W. (1983). Modeling: An analysis in terms of category accessibility. *Journal of Experimental Social Psychology, 19*, 403-421.

Chaplin, E. W., & Levine, B. A. (1980). The effects of total exposure duration and interrupted versus continuous exposure in flooding. *Behavior Therapy, 12*, 360-368.

Check, J. V. P. (1985). Hostility toward women: Some theoretical considerations. In G. W. Russell (Ed.), *Violence in intimate relationships.* Jamaica, NY: Spectrum.

Cline, V. B., Croft, R. G., & Courrier, S. (1973). Desensitization of children to television violence. *Journal of Personality and Social Psychology, 27*, 360-365.

Collins, A., & Loftus, E. (1975). A spreading-activation theory of semantic memory. *Psychological Review, 82*, 407-428.

Collins, W. A., Sobol, B. L., & Westby, S. (1981). Effects of adult commentary on children's comprehension and inferences about a televised aggressive portrayal. *Child Development, 52*, 158-172.

Demare, D., Briere, J., & Lips, H. M. (1987). Violent pornography and self-reported likelihood of sexual aggression. *Journal of Research in Personality, 22,* 140-153.

Dominick, J. R. (1974). Children's viewing of crime shows and attitudes on law enforcement. *Journalism Quarterly, 51,* 5-12.

Donnerstein, E. (1980). Aggressive-erotica and violence against women. *Journal of Personality and Social Psychology, 39,* 269-277.

Donnerstein, E. (1984). Pornography: Its effect on violence against women. In N. Malamuth & E. Donnerstein (Eds.), *Pornography and sexual aggression* (pp. 53-81). New York: Academic Press.

Donnerstein, E., & Berkowitz, L. (1983). *Effects of film content and victim association on aggressive behavior and attitudes.* Unpublished manuscript, University of Wisconsin-Madison.

Donnerstein, E., & Hallam, J. (1978). Facilitating effects of erotica on aggression against women. *Journal of Personality and Social Psychology, 36,* 1270-1277.

Donnerstein, E., Linz, D., & Penrod, S. (1987). *The question of pornography: Research findings and policy implications.* New York: Free Press.

Dorr, A. (1981). Television and affective development and functioning: Maybe this decade. *Journal of Broadcasting, 25,* 335-345.

Drabman, R. S., & Thomas, M. H. (1977). Does watching violence on television cause apathy? *Pediatrics, 57,* 329-331.

Dunand, M., Berkowitz, L., & Leyens, J. P. (1984). Audience effects when viewing aggressive movies. *British Journal of Social Psychology, 23,* 69-76.

Feshbach, S. (1972). Reality and fantasy in filmed violence. In J. Murray, E. Rubinstein, & G. Comstock (Eds.), *Television and social behavior* (Vol. 2, pp. 318-345). Washington, DC: Department of Health, Education and Welfare.

Fiske, S. T., & Taylor, S. E. (1984). *Social cognition.* Reading, MA: Addison-Wesley.

Foa, E. B., & Chambless, D. L. (1978). Habituation of subjective anxiety during flooding in imagery. *Behavior Research and Therapy, 16,* 391-399.

Foa, E. B., & Kozak, M. J. (1986). Emotional processing of fear: Exposure to corrective information. *Psychological Bulletin, 99*(1), 20-35.

Gagnon, J. H., & Simon, W. (1973). *Sexual conduct: The social sources of human sexuality.* Chicago: Aldine.

Geen, R. (1975). The meaning of observed violence: Real versus fictional violence and effects of aggression and emotional arousal. *Journal of Research in Personality, 9,* 270-281.

Geen, R. G., & Berkowitz, L. (1966). Film violence and the cue properties of available targets. *Journal of Personality and Social Psychology, 3,* 525-530.

Geen, R. G., & Thomas, S. L. (1986). The immediate effects of media violence on behavior. *Journal of Social Issues, 42*(3).

Gerbner, G. (1972). Violence in television drama: Trends and symbolic functions. In G. A. Comstock & E. S. Rubinstein (Eds.), *Television and social behavior: Vol. 1. Media content and control.* Washington, DC: Government Printing Office.

Goranson, R. E. (1970). Media violence and aggressive behavior: A review of experimental research. In L. Berkowitz (Ed.), *Advances in experimental social psychology* (Vol. 5, pp. 2-31). New York: Academic Press.

Grings, W. W., & Dawson, M. E. (1978). *Emotions and bodily responses: A psychophysiological approach.* New York: Academic Press.

Grusec, J. (1973). Effects of co-observer evaluations on imitation: A developmental study. *Developmental Psychology, 8,* 141.

Gumpert, G., & Cathcart, R. (Eds.). (1979). *Intermedia: Interpersonal communication in a media world.* New York: Oxford University Press.

Haffner, D. W., & Kelly, M. (1987). Adolescent sexuality in the media. In *Transitions: Focus on youth and family.* Washington, DC: Center for Populations Options.

Halloran, J. D., & Croll, P. (1972). Television programs in Great Britain: Content and control. In G. A. Comstock & E. A. Rubinstein (Eds.), *Television and social behavior* (Vol. 1, pp. 415-492). Washington, DC: Government Printing Office.

Hicks, D. (1968). Effects of co-observer's sanctions and adult presence on imitative aggression. *Child Development, 38,* 303-308.

Horton, R. W., & Santogrossi, D. A. (1978). Mitigating the impact of televised violence through concurrent adult commentary. In *Resources in education.* (ERIC Document Reproduction Service No. ED 177 412)

Huesmann, L. R. (1986). Psychological processes promoting the relation between exposure to media violence and aggressive behavior by the viewer. *Journal of Social Issues, 42*(3), 125-140.

Huesmann, L. R., & Eron, L. D. (Eds.). (1986). *Television and the aggressive child: A cross-national comparison.* Hillsdale, NJ: Lawrence Erlbaum.

Huesmann, L. R., Eron, L. D., & Yamel, P. (1986). Intellectual functioning and aggression. *Journal of Personality and Social Psychology, 50,* 232-244.

Huesmann, L. R., Fischer, P. F., Eron, L. D., Mermelstein, R., Kaplan-Shain, E., & Morikawa, S. (1978, September). *Children's sex-role preference, sex of television model, and imitation of aggressive behaviors.* Paper presented at the meeting of the International Society for Research on Aggression, Washington, DC.

Huesmann, L. R., Lagerspetz, K., & Eron, L. D. (1984). Intervening variables in the TV violence-aggression relation: Evidence from two countries. *Developmental Psychology, 20,* 746-775.

Huesmann, L. R., & Malamuth, N. (1986). Media violence and antisocial behavior: An Overview. *Journal of Social Issues, 42,* 1-6.

Kazdin, A. E., & Wilcoxin, L. A. (1976). Systematic desensitization and nonspecific treatment effects: A methodological evaluation. *Psychological Bulletin, 83,* 729-758.

Landman, J., & Manis, M. (1983). Social cognition: Some historical and theoretical perspectives. In L. Berkowitz (Ed.), *Advances in experimental social psychology* (Vol. 16, pp. 49-123). San Francisco: Academic Press.

Lang, P. J. (1977). Imagery in therapy: An information processing analysis of fear. *Behavior Therapy, 8,* 862-886.

Lang, P. J. (1979). A bio-informational theory of emotional imagery. *Psychophysiology, 16,* 495-512.

Larsen, O. N. (1968). *Violence and mass media.* New York: Harper & Row.

Lefkowitz, M. M., Eron, L. D., Walder, L. O., & Huesmann, L. R. (1977). *Growing up to be violent: A longitudinal study of the development of aggression.* New York: Pergamon.

Leyens, L. P., & Parke, R. (1975). Aggressive slides can induce a weapons effect. *European Journal of Social Psychology, 5,* 229-236.

Liebert, R. M., Sprafkin, J. N., & Davidson, E. S. (1982). *The early window: Effects of television on children and youth.* New York: Pergamon.

Linz, D., Donnerstein, E., & Penrod, S. (1984). The effects of multiple exposures to filmed violence against women. *Journal of Communication, 34,* 130-147.

Linz, D., Donnerstein, E., & Penrod, S. (1988). The effects of long-term exposure to violent and sexually degrading depictions of women. *Journal of Personality and Social Psychology, 55*(5), 758-768.

Malamuth, N. M. (1986). Predictors of naturalistic sexual aggression. *Journal of Personality and Social Psychology, 50*, 953-962.

Malamuth, N. M., & Briere, J. (1986). Sexual violence in the media: Indirect effects on aggression against women. *Journal of Social Issues, 42*, 75-92.

Malamuth, N. M., & Check, J. V. P. (1980). Penile tumescence and perceptual responses to rape as a function of victim's perceived reactions. *Journal of Applied Social Psychology, 10*, 528-547.

Malamuth, N., & Check, J. V. P. (1981). The effects of mass media exposure on acceptance of violence against women: A field experiment. *Journal of Research in Personality, 15*, 436-446.

Malamuth, N., & Check, J. V. P. (1985). The effects of aggressive pornography on beliefs in rape myths: Individual differences. *Journal of Research in Personality, 19*, 299-320.

Malamuth, N., & Donnerstein, E. (Eds.). (1984). *Pornography and sexual aggression.* New York: Academic Press.

Malamuth, N., Haber, S., & Feshbach, S. (1980). Testing hypotheses regarding rape: Exposure to sexual violence, sex differences, and the normality of rape. *Journal of Research in Personality, 14*, 121-137.

Neisser, U. (1967). *Cognitive psychology.* New York: Appleton-Century-Crofts.

Niemczycki, J., Linz, D., & Donnerstein, E. (1988). *The effects of fellow audience member reactions on evaluations of sexually violent media.* Unpublished manuscript, University of California, Santa Barbara.

Paul, G. L., & Bernstein, D. A. (1973). *Anxiety and clinical problems: Systematic desensitization and related techniques.* Morristown, NY: General Learning Press.

Phillips, D. P., & Hensley, J. E. (1984). When violence is rewarded or punished: The impact of mass media stories on homicide. *Journal of Communication, 34*(3), 101 ff.

Rabinovitch, M. S., Markham, J. W., & Talbot, A. D. (1972). Children's violence perception as a function of television violence. In G. A. Comstock & E. A. Rubinstein (Eds.), *Television and social behavior* (Vol. 5., pp. 231-252). Washington, DC: Government Printing Office.

Roberts, E. J. (1982). Television and sexual learning in children. In D. Pearl, L. Bouthilet, & J. Lazar (Eds.), *Television and behavior: Ten years of scientific research and implications for the eighties* (Vol. 2, pp. 209-223). Washington, DC: Government Printing Office.

Roth, M. (1985). Introduction: The socio-psychological phenomenon of violence. In G. Barlow and A. Hill (Eds.), *Video violence and children.* New York: St. Martins.

Singer, J. L., & Singer, D. G. (1980). *Television, imagination and aggression: A study of preschoolers' play.* Hillsdale, NJ: Lawrence Erlbaum.

Staats, A. W., & Staats, C. (1958). Attitudes established by classical conditioning. *Journal of Abnormal and Social Psychology, 57*, 37-40.

Tannenbaum, P., & Gaer, E. P. (1965). Mood changes as a function of stress of protagonist and degree of identification in film-viewing situation. *Journal of Personality and Social Psychology, 2*, 612-616.

Thomas, M. H. (1982). Physiological arousal, exposure to a relatively lengthy aggressive film, and aggressive behavior. *Journal of Research in Personality, 16*, 72-81.

Thomas, M. H., Horton, R. W., Lippencott, E. C., & Drabman, R. S. (1977). Desensitization to portrayals of real-life aggression as a function of exposure to television violence. *Journal of Personality and Social Psychology, 35,* 450-458.

Turner, C., & Berkowitz, L. (1972). Identification with film aggressor (covert role taking) and reactions to film violence. *Journal of Personality and Social Psychology, 21,* 256-264.

Turner, C., & Fenn, M. R. (1978). *Effects of white noise and memory cues on verbal aggression.* Paper presented at the meeting of the International Society for Research on Aggression.

Turner, C., & Layton, J. (1976). Verbal imagery and connotation as memory induced mediators of aggressive behavior. *Journal of Personality and Social Psychology, 33,* 755-763.

Tversky, A., & Kahneman, D. (1973). Availability: A heuristic for judging frequency and probability. *Cognitive Psychology, 5,* 207-232.

Ullman, R. E., & Krasner, L. V. (1969). *Case studies in behavior modification.* New York: Holt, Rinehart & Winston.

Valins, S., & Ray, A. A. (1967). Effects of cognitive desensitization on avoidance behavior. *Journal of Personality and Social Psychology, 7,* 345-350.

Wakshlag, J., Vial, V., & Tamborini, R. (1983). Selecting crime drama and apprehension about crime. *Human Communication Research, 10,* 227-242.

Wilkins, W. (1971). Desensitization: Social and cognitive factors underlying the effectiveness of Wolpe's procedure. *Psychological Bulletin, 76,* 311-317.

Worchel, S. (1972). The effects of films on the importance of behavioral freedom. *Journal of Personality, 40,* 417-435.

Zillmann, D. (1980). Anatomy of suspense. In P. H. Tannenbaum (Ed.), *The entertainment functions of television* (pp. 133-163). Hillsdale, NJ: Lawrence Erlbaum.

Zillmann, D., Weaver, J. B., Mundorf, N., & Aust, C. F. (1986). Effects of an opposite-gender companion's affect to horror on distress, delight, and attraction. *Journal of Personality and Social Psychology, 51,* 586-594.

Chapter 11

MESSAGE EFFECTS
Retrospect and Prospect

James J. Bradac, Robert Hopper, and
John M. Wiemann

IN THE PRECEDING CHAPTERS a number of issues have been raised directly or indirectly and these have important implications for the study of message effects. In this concluding chapter we will highlight, summarize, and discuss these issues, and where possible we will suggest specific implications for the advancement of knowledge in this area. As Bowers suggests in this volume's first chapter, progress in the study of messages can be inferred from the quantitative facts: Studies of "message variables" have proliferated in the last 20 years. Qualitative progress is apparent also, and this has been indexed throughout this volume. The issues to be discussed here address the qualitative progression of our knowledge, both in the past and in the future. They can be labeled: *conceptualizing messages, explaining effects, the social cognitive turn, the linguistic turn, message comparability, evaluator role, contextual versus acontextual approaches, single versus repeated exposure,* and *monological versus dialogical situations.*

CONCEPTUALIZING MESSAGES

Researchers and theorists in the message-effects paradigm have not been very analytical about the meaning of *message* in their various endeavors (see Bradac, 1986; Hopper, 1988). Accordingly, our focus on "messages" specifically as the object of communication study is not always helpful in circumscribing our domain of inquiry. Investigators

frequently proceed as though they and the consumers of their investigations share a precise notion of *message,* but this apparent precision
collapses under scrutiny. Those definitions of *communication* that can
be isolated (Bowers & Bradac, 1984) have typically been operationa-
lized in a common sense fashion reflecting Western orientations to
specific sorts of events: a film or a television program (for examples,
see Linz & Donnerstein, this volume; Bryant, this volume), a brief
persuasive speech (Burgoon, this volume), a 15-second commercial
spot (Thorson, this volume), or a script for a hypothetical employment
interview (Giles, Wilson, & Conway, 1981). There is nothing inherently
wrong with this common sense approach, which views *message* as a
primitive term, but at some point we will have to go beyond the cultural
constraints imposed by this mode of operation. Also, as our explanations become more subtle and interesting, we will have to distinguish
the effects of messages from those of other theoretical entities (e.g.,
culturally based beliefs; Aiu, 1988; Wiemann, Chen, & Giles, 1986).

But if we attempt to go beyond commonsense uses of convenience
to the presumption that we know what the necessary and sufficient
conditions are for some motion/action to be considered "message," we
risk reaping a whirlwind of Type 1 error. What, for example, is "message" (and to what degree) in an employment interview context? Here
is a list of possibilities: a transcript of the greetings of the parties, the
list of open-ended questions used by the interviewer, the firmness of
the interviewee's handshake, the way the interviewee is dressed, the
length of the interview, some tremor of fingertips by the applicant
perhaps showing nervousness, a consent form signed by the interviewer, and the color of the walls in the interview room. Now any of
the items on this list could withstand message-centered analysis, but
should these items partake equally in membership in the class "message"? What criteria, naive or technical, may we bring to bear on the
concept "message," such that we might evaluate the degree to which
inquiries focus on messages and hence fall within the domain(s) of
communication studies? This becomes a concern given a proliferation
of studies of communication effects that apparently have no or little
message focus. To give one instance, reconsider briefly the classic
Hovland and associates' studies on speaker credibility and persuasion
(Hovland, Janis, & Kelley, 1953). A number of these studies varied
nothing at all in the persuasive speech except attributions of the
speaker. By contrast, inquiries by Schegloff (1979) on opening words

of telephone conversations study only verbal and nonverbal materials—perhaps in ways that slight the role of individual communicators. Our point in raising this issue is not to praise certain studies or blame others, but rather to ask how we could make any defense of the precise domain of communication studies if pressed to do so. (Perhaps this inquiry will teach us the unwisdom of such defense; since Aristotle it has been widely argued that communication study can have no proper subject matter.)

Apart from considerations of defense, there are three criteria (and no doubt several others) worth thinking about when attempting to distinguish messages from other objects. The first might be labeled "symbolicity." Some behaviors are perceived as arbitrarily signifying something while others are perceived as having natural connections to their referent. The essence of symbolicity is the arbitrary pairing of the signifier and the signified in a sign (Saussure, 1915/1959). In Cronkhite's (1986, p. 234) words, "There is a recognized continuum of symbolicity or arbitrariness ranging from symptoms, which are completely non-arbitrary, through rituals, which are somewhat arbitrary semblances of symptoms or their referents, to symbols that are totally arbitrary." One could argue that, to the degree that a sign is perceived to be highly arbitrary, it is most likely to be taken as an attempt to convey meaning by the sign's perceiver (see von Cranach & Vine, 1973). And in some sense the attempt to convey meaning is at the heart of message sending.

Another interesting and useful criterion is "coherence," both internal and external. Some behaviors are perceived as forming a unit or a set, as fitting together in some plausible fashion (internal coherence); a story must have an opening and a closing (Berger, this volume). Some behavioral units or sets are perceived as connecting with other behavioral units or sets; an answer typically follows a question (Sanders, this volume). There are constitutive rules, schemas, mental models, or plans that dictate or allow for connectedness (Berger, this volume; Cappella & Street, this volume; Johnson-Laird, 1985; Planalp, 1985; Sanders & Martin, 1975). Most persons in everyday life distinguish coherent from incoherent behaviors, perhaps assigning message value primarily to the former (but others, e.g., psychiatrists, find message value in the incoherent). It has been suggested that persons in everyday life indeed do make judgments of the coherence of communicative behavior (Kellermann & Lim, this volume; Kellermann & Sleight, 1989). Regardless of the role of coherence in everyday or naive thinking, it should be noted that coherence figures prominently in technical theorizing about messages (Bowers, Elliott, & Desmond, 1977; Grice, 1975; Hopper, 1988; Sanders, 1986).

The third (and final) criterion to be discussed in this section might be labeled "intentionality or purposiveness." Some behaviors are perceived as being directed to an audience in order to produce a response that will enable the emitter of the behavior to achieve a goal—strategic or persuasive communication is the paradigm case here. On the other hand, some behaviors are perceived as being accidental, nondirectional, thoughtless, and so on. There is good reason to believe that participants in communication events distinguish between behaviors that are perceived to be high or low in purposiveness; this is the realm of "attributed intentionality" (Bowers, this volume; Bowers & Bradac, 1984). Some scholars suggest a strong distinction between intentional and unintentional messages; for instance, Motley and Camden (1988, p. 16) argue that "intentional and unintentional message transmissions may be sufficiently different fundamentally to require their conceptual separation in the study of communication" (see also Buck, 1988). But what sort of separation? For example, a Freudian would perhaps emphasize the role of repression and unconscious patterning in unintentional messages— and make studies of such patterns (e.g., parapraxis) a cornerstone of their communication theory (see, for instance, Motley, Camden, & Baars, 1979). Saussure (1959), by contrast, simply deletes unconscious considerations from the scope of semiotic studies.

Thus a given behavior may be perceived as symbolic, coherent, and intentional, while another may be perceived as nonarbitrary, incoherent, and unintentional. These distinctions may prove useful in attempts to distinguish messages from other objects or, more particularly, to distinguish one type of message from another. Regarding the latter point, perhaps we can be slightly more succinct in our research if we can hold some basic distinctions between kinds of messages by offering *taxonomies* of message types. Thorson's observations in this volume regarding the need for a taxonomy of advertisement types can be extended to any and all domains of messages. A message taxonomy may be motivated by a general, technical theory specifying criterial attributes on the one hand or by a subjective model reflecting criteria used by naive communicators in everyday life (on this theme, see also Giles & Hewstone, 1982). The two types of taxonomies may be similar in some ways while differing in others, as is the case with technical versus naive taxonomies of behaviors displaying "intelligence" (Sternberg, Conway, Ketron, & Bernstein, 1981).

The issue of privileging either naive or technical taxonomies is a thorny one. Technical taxonomies may be based upon rigorous observation and the coding of empirically verifiable communicative behaviors; hence these may be viewed by some as having a kind of scientific accuracy. On the other hand, participants' less specific folk taxonomies are the categories that are actually used in interaction. Of course, these naive taxonomies can be viewed as objects of scientific study in their own right. The situation is analogous to the choice of studying language from either an "etic" or an "emic" perspective. At this point it would probably be a mistake to rely exclusively or even more heavily upon one perspective than the other. We note in passing that this issue is complicated by various methodological issues, such as reliance upon self-report data versus reliance upon audio and video recordings of messages. We also note that approaches that entail "objective" analysis of symbolic materials by experts with special theories, and approaches that depend upon "subjective" construals of untutored respondents, can work in concert. For example, fictional and nonfictional discourse can be inspected by the researcher/theorist in order to isolate putative message-type exemplars (Hopper, 1988) and subsequently these exemplars can be evaluated along a similarity-dissimilarity dimension by naive respondents. Respondent evaluations can be subjected to multidimensional scaling in order to gain information about the distinction between exemplars that are criterial for respondents, and respondent-generated distinctions can be compared to those of the researcher/theorist (Hopper & Bell, 1984).

EXPLAINING EFFECTS:
THE SOCIAL COGNITIVE TURN

In the fourth chapter of this volume, Berger observes that "communication researchers have devoted considerable energy to studying the relationships between various nonverbal and paralinguistic cues emitted by sources and a variety of social and personal judgments listeners make based on these cues, while completely ignoring how the content of what is being said is being understood or misunderstood." The implication is that to some extent the effects of message variables on social evaluation are mediated by comprehension: If we perceive that we do not understand a speaker, we may lower evaluations of communicator competence if the context is one where understanding is expected; on the other hand, if we expect to have difficulty comprehending discourse and we perceive that we do not understand, evaluations of communicator competence may not be lowered (see Kellermann & Lim, this volume; Kellermann & Sleight, in press). Perceived comprehension by message recipients is one effect of messages that may help to *explain* other effects, such as social evaluation or attitude formation.

Along the same line, a number of researchers have investigated the consequences of "powerful" and "powerless" speech styles (O'Barr, 1982). "Powerful" language is held to be comparatively terse, fluent, and direct, while "powerless" language is relatively mitigated and disfluent. Warfel (1984) suggests that we use a more neutral term like *generic* rather than *powerful,* because to date the research operationalizations of the "powerful" style have entailed the noninclusion in a message of particular language features, such as hedges, qualifiers, and tag questions. Apart from the issue of terminology, researchers have argued that persons using "powerful" language are evaluated more positively on the dimensions of competence and attractiveness than are persons using "powerless" language (Bradac & Mulac, 1984; Erickson, Johnson, Lind, & O'Barr, 1978) but it is not at all clear *why* this is so. In this case message comprehension is probably not a mediating variable; rather, it has been suggested that it may be the case (a) that "powerful" language is perceived to be an indicator of a powerful person (there is supporting evidence here; Bradac & Mulac, 1984) and that in our society message recipients have a positive regard for persons who have power over others, or (b) that "powerful" language is perceived to indicate high *self*-control and that in our society message recipients value this personality attribute (Bradac, Wiemann, & Schaefer, in press; Goffman, 1967). Message recipients' perceptions of communicator self-control versus control over others constitute competing explanations of the positive effects of "powerful" language on social evaluation. As in the case of perceived message comprehension, perceived control (over self or other) is a cognitive variable that may be useful in explaining particular effects.

The preceding paragraphs suggest two related themes that are unmistakable in the chapters constituting this volume and in recent message-effects literature: There is a search for *explanations* of consistently obtained message effects and the explanations that have been offered have a *social cognitive* bias. For example, Petty and Cacioppo (1986) have suggested that arguments in a message will be scrutinized by message recipients when these persons perceive the personal relevance of the message to be high, as when they believe they will have to debate the arguments subsequently in a public situation. On the other hand, where personal relevance is low, arguments may not be evaluated closely; instead message recipients will attend to nonsubstantive attributes of the situation, such as communicator attractiveness. Thus, where personal relevance is high, a message containing weak arguments should not produce attitude changes in the direction advocated by the communicator, while a message containing strong arguments should—the message will be subjected to "central processing." Where personal relevance is low, an attractive communicator should be more persuasive than an unattractive one regardless of argument strength because the message will be processed "peripherally."

One of the most widely invoked explanatory structures in the realm of message effects is speech accommodation theory (Giles, 1973; Giles, Mulac, Bradac, & Johnson, 1987). The essential idea here is that one speaker may converge to the message style of another, such as by using the same dialect, or he or she may diverge, such as by switching from using the same dialect to using a different one. In initial interaction contexts, where speaker intent is ambiguous or unknown, convergence will be evaluated favorably while divergence will be evaluated unfavorably. The favorable evaluation attaching to convergence will occur because the convergent act will be viewed as an attempt on the part of the message sender to appear similar to the message recipient—an overture that will be viewed as polite, friendly, and so on. Divergence will be viewed as an attempt to appear dissimilar. A message recipient's attribution of high choice on the part of the message sender can intensify the favorable and unfavorable evaluations attached to convergence and divergence, respectively; attribution of low choice, as when the message sender is viewed as being the pawn of situational norms, can attenuate positive and negative evaluations.

Another social cognitive theory that has been used to explain message effects is uncertainty reduction theory (Berger & Bradac, 1982; Berger & Calabrese, 1975). Like speech accommodation theory, uncertainty reduction theory has as much to say about message antecedents as it does about message consequences. If a message sender's uncertainty about his or her interlocutor is high, he or she will seek information from the other (typically by asking questions or passively observing), will exhibit a low level of intimacy, and will strongly reciprocate the other's behavior. The message sender's nonintimate reciprocal information seeking will in turn affect the uncertainty level of the message recipient. Specifically, if the message recipient expects this type of communicative behavior from the message sender, it will reduce the recipient's uncertainty level. Generally, substantive and stylistic message features that are expected will reduce message recipient uncertainty, while unexpected message features will increase uncertainty. Message features that violate expectations and thereby increase uncertainty can be evaluated positively or negatively depending upon whether the violating features constitute pleasant or unpleasant surprises (Burgoon & Miller, 1985) and whether the violator is seen as rewarding or not (Burgoon & Hale, 1988).

In addition to speech accommodation theory and uncertainty reduction theory, other social cognitive theories have influenced thinking in particular domains, such as in the effects of violent mass media content as discussed in Chapter 10 by Linz and Donnerstein. Recall these authors' discussion of Berkowitz's cognitive-neoassociation theory, Bandura's social cognitive theory of mass communication, and Huesmann's reciprocal model of the long-term effects of mass media violence.

The search for richer and more interesting explanations of message effects will continue, and almost certainly these explanations will continue to have a social cognitive flavor in the foreseeable future. There is ample room for the inclusion of new concepts drawn from research traditions that have had little impact upon the message-effects tradition thus far. For example, following Sanders's suggestion (Chapter 7), message-effects researchers and theorists may want to investigate how initial messages constrain subsequent ones, how these constraints are understood by interactants or consumers of mass media messages, and how these understandings of constraints interact with message form and substance to affect the evaluative reactions of message recipients. An immersion into the literature of conversation analysis (CA) may be called for here (Hopper, 1988; Hopper, Koch, & Mandelbaum, 1986). Or, to give another example of possibilities for future extension, it will probably prove useful to examine the notion that certain kinds of evaluative judgments are unique to the processing of symbolic artifacts; for example, under some circumstances message recipients may render "coherence judgments" and these may in turn affect judgments of communicator competence and attractiveness (Kellermann & Lim, this volume; Kellermann & Sleight, 1989). Here too the CA literature may prove helpful. These examples point to the next section of this chapter.

THE LINGUISTIC TURN

Many scholars agree that much of contemporary scholarship has undergone a "linguistic turn" (Rorty, 1967), although message-effects research has barely been affected by this revolutionary move. In the linguistic turn, issues that were formerly discussed as problems of metaphysics, epistemology, psychology, or research method are increasingly being studied as issues relating to details in the use of speech and language. In its simplest characterization, the linguistic turn may be thought of as a change toward studying any phenomenon "X" by studying the word X and related words (Rorty, 1967, p. 4).

To understand human experience or thinking, study language. But what is language? As twentieth-century thought unfolds, thinkers turn away from treating language as some abstract conceptual structure and toward treating conversation as spoken practical activity (Austin, 1962; Wittgenstein, 1953). The initial focus upon "language" has evolved into foci upon "pragmatics" of speech action and finally into studies of "conversation." From these perspectives, description of the details of language use is the first priority, and, until these details are understood, scholars taking the linguistic turn will criticize the social cognitive position as premature, facile, and ungrounded.

Issues of language-in-use are being forcefully addressed in the school of "conversation analysis." (For exemplars of this approach, see Mandelbaum, 1987; Moerman, 1987; Sacks, Schegloff, & Jefferson, 1974; and the essays in Atkinson & Heritage, 1984. For discussion of conversation analysis as a research method—here are the definitive contrasts with social cognitive approaches—see Hopper, Koch, & Mandelbaum, 1986; Sacks, 1984; West & Zimmerman, 1982.) Conversation analysts offer inroads toward succinct description of messages, but they offer no direct road to the study of message effects. Nevertheless, work in this tradition has implications for message-effects researchers. For example, one might examine how conversations about newscasts can mediate the informational or persuasive effects of this type of message.

In the present volume the influence of the linguistic turn is most evident in Sanders's chapter. Sanders's suggestions, paired with the recent history of language pragmatics and conversation analysis, show that forays into message structure—in person, on the phone, and in television talk shows or drama—may eventually change the face of effects research by shedding new light on message characteristics. One twinkle in this direction may appear in a study by Hopper and Drummond (1988) comparing the closings of telephone calls in interpersonal communication with those on radio call-in programs. This provides data about the effect of "mediation" on language form; but there remains a gap between this kind of work and studies of audience effects.

In brief, research taking the linguistic turn offers more of a critique of current message-effects research than constructive evidence regarding how messages affect comprehension or attitudes toward sources. These studies point out the complex structuration of messages and the danger of premature inferences about communication effects made in ignorance of this complexity. Perhaps the next book that is written on the topic of message effects will contain a larger number of articles that reflect the linguistic turn. Such a book will contain material that blurs the boundaries between pragmatics and effects research, an outcome that would be consistent with the goals articulated by Bowers in the first chapter of this volume.

MESSAGE COMPARABILITY

In our research on message effects we make claims like the following: The use of high-power language in a message is directly related to evaluations of source competence and attractiveness (Erickson et al., 1978); high-intensity language facilitates attitude change when it is used by a highly credible source (Burgoon, Jones, & Stewart, 1975); use of a nonstandard accent by potential employees may increase the likelihood of employers assigning them to low-status positions (de la Zerda & Hopper, 1979); high lexical diversity is directly related to judgments of communicator status and solidarity (Bradac & Wisegarver, 1984); and so forth. To some extent such claims are based on the results of multiple studies, that is, they represent replicated findings. It is also the case that attempts at replication have failed to support other potential generalizations (Jackson & Jacobs, 1983). Both successful and unsuccessful attempts to replicate claims of the form described above have a common problem: Any message variable instantiated in research necessarily exists at a certain level or degree of strength, and this has rarely been indicated by researchers. So, typically, consumers of research reports and potential replicators of reported research do not know just how highly intense a high-intensity speech is, or just how powerful a "powerful" statement is, or just how violent a violent film is, or just how lexically diverse a high-diversity message is. Thus, potentially, one researcher's "high-intensity" message may be equivalent in the ratio of intense to nonintense words to another's "moderate-intensity" message, although both researchers may use the label "high-intensity" to describe their experimental manipulation (Bradac, Bowers, & Courtright, 1979). Where this kind of imprecision exists, failure to replicate outcomes is almost guaranteed, and where replicated findings are reported we can have no sense of the parameters of a particular effect. In the terminology used by Mulac and Kunkel (this volume), this is potentially a problem of both construct validity and external validity.

There are two ways around this problem. First, researchers can specify precisely the level of the variable(s) used in their research by indicating the ratio of instantiations of the variable in a message to noninstantiations. For example, what is the ratio of high-intensity words to all words used in a speech? In other cases, other sorts of ratios are appropriate; for example, in examining the effects of lexical diversity, one can calculate a mean-segmental type-token ratio for each message used by breaking each message into, say, 50- or 25-word segments, obtaining the ratio of different words to total words for each segment, and then obtaining the average ratio by adding the ratios for each segment and dividing by the total number of segments. Thus the effects of messages exhibiting MSTTRs of .82 can be compared with the effects of messages exhibiting MSTTRs of .72. There is some evidence that an MSTTR of .82 is an average level for college students' spontaneous utterances in an interview situation (Bradac, Konsky, & Elliott, 1976), so this might be labeled "moderate" diversity, and .72, which is two standard deviations below the mean, might be labeled "low" diversity. Here "moderate" and "low" (and "high") have a precise meaning that can be carried across replications. Also, this sort of ratio can be used within a single study to explore style shifting; researchers can specify degree or magnitude of shift very precisely (Bradac, Mulac, & House, 1988). It should also be noted that this sort of quantification can call researchers' attention to the possibility that their manipulations are extremely strong—for example, three standard deviations higher or lower than average—and, therefore, unusual or atypical. An effect that can be obtained only with an extreme manipulation may be of little interest or at least of limited generalizabilty (Bell, Zahn, & Hopper, 1984).

An alternative approach involves subjective scaling, for example, through the use of magnitude estimation techniques. Here researchers can equate levels of message variables within or across studies by using messages that are perceived to reside at the same point along a magnitude curve by a group or groups of respondents. Just as objective increases in luminosity can be scaled with reference to subjective estimates of brightness (typically yielding a cube root power function), so can objective message features be subjectively scaled. For example, degree of accentedness in spoken messages has proven amenable to magnitude estimation techniques (Brennan, Ryan, & Dawson, 1975). It seems likely that other message variables—such as "powerful" versus "powerless" styles, violent versus nonviolent scenes, and high versus low lexical diversity—can be successfully subjectively scaled also. In some cases it might be useful to combine subjective magnitude estimations with the objective ratio calculations indicated above.

EVALUATOR ROLE

As suggested above, one of the major classes of message effects examined involves evaluative judgments of communicators and their messages (Zahn & Hopper, 1985). Thus in a particular study researchers may examine the effects of one or more message variables on evaluations of a communicator's intellectual abilities (Brown, Giles, & Thackerar, 1985), employment suitability (Hopper, 1977), social attractiveness (Bradac & Wisegarver, 1984), or communicative competence (Wiemann, 1977). In virtually all of the research, evaluators have been persons who have listened to, viewed, or read one or more versions of a message. They have not been interactants; thus they have not been in any sense responsible for the object of evaluation—another person's message (Street, 1985). They have only rarely been the audience for whom the message was intended. Rather, they have been "disinterested third parties" asked to render a judgment about one communicator's effectiveness in a given speaker-audience or interactant-interactant event. To be sure, there are important situations in which a disinterested third party is asked to render a communication-relevant judgment, such as in marital counseling sessions or interview training classes. But there are many other situations in real life in which evaluators participate in the message exchange or, as in the case of mass media consumption, are highly interested parties who are actively involved with the message. As participants or involved consumers, they may evaluate message features differently than when they are in the role of disinterested third parties. For example, a very rapid speech rate may seem to indicate high speaker competence (Brown, 1980) when one does *not* have to really grasp the details of a message or to formulate a response to the communicator (Brown et al., 1985; Street, 1985). Thus some of our generalizations about message effects may be limited to third-party respondents, although this is typically not acknowledged in the literature (see Cappella & Street, this volume).

The implication is that we should increasingly compare the evaluative consequences of messages responded to by participants on the one hand and by observers on the other (Street, Mulac, & Wiemann, 1988). And by extension it may be interesting and useful to examine self-evaluations (Spitzberg & Cupach, 1984); that is, there are situations in which we produce messages that we later evaluate (as when we revised the prose that constitutes this chapter). Are there systematic differences among self-evaluations, evaluations made by observers, and evaluations made by participants? There appear to be (Street et al., 1988). The literature on self-monitoring (Snyder, 1979) and rhetorical sensitivity (Hart, Carlson, & Eadie, 1980) may prove useful here. A further extension of the idea of widening the range of evaluative roles included in message research is to compare the judgments of technical experts with those of naive respondents. Typically, studies of the evaluative consequences of messages have used naive respondents exclusively. This is a definite limitation, because in some contexts the evaluations of technical experts and naive respondents are systematically and even radically different (Bradac, Martin, Elliott, & Tardy, 1980).

CONTEXTUAL VERSUS ACONTEXTUAL APPROACHES

Before 1970, much of the research on message effects virtually ignored the role of context. In many studies respondents received no information about the context in which a message was delivered. In some cases "unreal" messages were used, such as passages from *Alice in Wonderland* (Buck, 1968), in order to sever connections with imagined real-world contexts. In other cases the context of communication was briefly described to respondents but was constant in all conditions; that is, context was not included as a variable in the design of experiments. This message-without-context approach was a product of perspectives that were influential in the 1950s and 1960s, namely, the Chomskian focus upon abstract (disembodied) grammatical rules on one hand and, ironically, the behaviorist emphasis on simple S-R connections on the other (where message is S and attitude change is R).

Increasingly in the 1970s and now in the 1980s, steady progress can be seen in the incorporation of context as a variable in message studies. In a review of research on language variables, Giles and Wiemann (1987) developed a rough typology for describing this work as progressing from treating language as *reflecting* context, to *building* upon context, to the most recent move of treating language as *determining* context. The first of these approaches (language reflects context) takes the position that language use is prescribed and proscribed largely by the situation in which it is spoken, including normative demands and characteristics of speaker and audience. The second approach (language builds upon context) assumes that language derives much of its meaning from the context in which it is used. From these two perspectives contextual features can be viewed as variables that can intensify, attenuate, or even reverse the effects of particular message variables (Bradac et al., 1979).

For example, it appears that respondents' beliefs about a communicator's level of status prior to message reception are related additively to status-linked message features, such as standard versus nonstandard accent, in the production of postmessage judgments of the communicator's status (Ryan & Bulik, 1982): The highest postmessage status ratings are given to high initial status-standard accent and the lowest to low initial status-nonstandard accent, with the combinations high initial status-nonstandard accent and low-initial status-standard accent falling between these extremes. Other message-context relationships of an additive form have been noted also—for example, the relationship between lexical diversity and perceived situational formality (Bradac, Konsky, & Davies, 1976), between speaker gender and gender-linked language (Mulac, Incontro, & James, 1985), and between perceived situational formality and speech rate (Street, Brady, & Putman, 1983). To give a different example, language intensity and communicator gender appear to interact in the production of effects such that high-intensity male and low-intensity female combinations produce relatively high levels of attitude change compared to the combinations low-intensity male and high-intensity female (Burgoon, Jones, & Stewart, 1975). Still another example involves the general variable "context of message reception." This refers to the conditions under which a message is processed by message recipients. Consumers of mass media entertainment who are highly aroused prior to exposure may prefer less arousing programs than consumers who experience low arousal prior to exposure (Bryant, this volume; Bryant & Zillman, 1984). A male viewing a film depicting violence against women may evaluate the film differently when a female is present than when the coviewer is a male (Linz & Donnerstein, this volume).

Some theorists have argued recently that messages create contexts (Giles & Hewstone, 1982), the third approach identified by Giles and Wiemann (1987). The implication is that contexts are not merely given to communicators before the fact but rather evolve as messages are exchanged or consumed. It has been suggested, in fact, that an utterance *is* the context for utterances that follow (e.g., Bavelas, 1983; Schegloff & Sacks, 1973). Strategic message choices can be used to manipulate the environment and consequently influence one's interlocutor (see Sanders, this volume). In this view the creation of communication context is a primary message effect, which might well mediate other effects, such as comprehension or social evaluation.

Relationships between message variables and contextual variables are potentially complex and are greatly in need of specification. Almost certainly it will be some time before any general, systematic claims can be made about the message-variable/context relationship. Researchers should routinely include context as a variable in the design of experiments. And descriptive, naturalistic studies should be conducted increasingly in order to discover which contextual features seem likely to affect the interpretation and evaluation of messages (Hopper & Stucky, 1986). At this point the issue is not so much whether context should be included or not in message-variable research but which contextual variable should be scrutinized given the message variable of interest?

One attribute that seems potentially important for a variety of message features is perceived communicator intention. That is, what do message recipients believe about the intentions of a given communicator and how do beliefs about intention affect message outcomes such as comprehension and evaluations of communicator competence? For example, as suggested above a number of studies have shown that "powerful" language produces a relatively positive judgment of communicator competence. But if respondents believe that the communicator intended to appear powerless because he or she believed that the appearance of powerlessness would increase chances of achieving a desired goal, will they still judge "powerful" language as more competent than language that is "powerless" (Bradac & Mulac, 1984; Wiemann & Bradac, in press)? As important as the contextual variable "perceived intention" appears to be, it has been included in only a few studies of message effects (e.g., Brown et al., 1985).

SINGLE VERSUS REPEATED EXPOSURE

The vast majority—probably 99%—of the message-effects studies reported in the literature have exposed respondents to a single message upon one occasion prior to measuring their attitudes or impressions. Thus whatever generalizations we can offer are largely limited to initial-exposure situations. Such situations are important, as when we are exposed to a political candidate's first televised speech, but there are many more situations where we are exposed to a particular communicator or to a particular message upon many occasions. For example, the very notion of a political campaign indicates that multiple messages will be delivered across time. And, of course, the effects of campaigns have been studied intensively (indeed the next volume in this series will survey much of this research), but in most cases campaign studies have taken a macro perspective and, therefore, have not focused upon the details of message substance and form. Or we are sometimes exposed to the same advertisement over and over again. The obvious question is this: Are the effects produced by an initial message comparable to the effects produced by a message heard for the twentieth time? The answer is almost certainly: no. So the more meaningful question becomes: Just how do the effects differ?

There are a number of possibilities here. An initial message may establish a frame of reference that is used to judge subsequent messages; in such a case, assimilation or contrast effects may occur (Bradac, Davies, & Courtright, 1977; Sherif, Sherif, & Nebergall, 1965). Or the nth message in a series may be evaluated more favorably than the first one due to "mere exposure" or related processes (Zajonc, 1968). Or respondents' reactions may diminish in intensity or become less favorable with repeated exposure due to the basic psychological process of habituation to stimuli. Regarding the latter possibility, some research indicates that heavy consumers of violent films may become desensitized to violence as a result of repeated exposure to message content (Linz & Donnerstein, this volume; Linz, Donnerstein, & Penrod, 1984). The effects of repeated exposure to advertisements on favorableness judgments has been studied closely (Burgoon, this volume; Thorson, this volume), and there is some evidence that evaluations become more positive with repeated exposure up to a point after which favorableness judgments reach a plateau or diminish. This outcome may reflect both the "mere exposure" and the habituation processes described above. But there is a great deal of room for research that examines how details of message form and content interact with repeated exposure in the production of evaluative reactions to advertisements (and other types of messages). Given the ubiquity of multiple message exposure and the rarity of significant one-shot communication events, we should drastically increase the extent to which we incorporate repeated exposure as a variable in our studies of message effects.

MONOLOGICAL VERSUS DIALOGICAL SITUATIONS

Somewhat related to the previous issue is our tendency to study the effects of one communicator delivering a single message (typically a speech or an essay) instead of studying the effects of two or more communicators delivering multiple messages upon a given occasion. Overwhelmingly, we have studied monologues instead of dialogues in our empirical research. This is another limitation parallel to the limitations described previously, because monological effects may not be generalizable to dialogical contexts. For example, the use of English in a message may produce neutral ratings of sociability in a monological context, but in dialogue where an initial speaker has spoken French (say, in Quebec), the same English message may be perceived as comparatively unfriendly (Genessee & Bourhis, 1982).

There are some currents in the large sea of message-effects research that are pushing us in the direction of dialogical studies and will probably continue to do so in the future. For one thing, there is increasing recognition of the importance of interactive communication contexts (Cappella & Street, this volume; Street & Cappella, 1985), and coupled with this is the realization that much of the past research has ignored these contexts. Inter- and intraspeaker message sequences are now being examined by groups of researchers who in the past were disinclined to go beyond isolated discourse units, such as linguists (Clark & Carlson, 1982), and special groups of researchers have emerged who take as their special task examination of the details of these sequences (Hopper et al., 1986; Sanders, this volume). There are also theoretical developments that point us in the direction of dialogue; for example, as suggested above speech accommodation theory is having an increasing impact in this area (Giles et al., 1987), as are related theories such as discrepancy arousal (Cappella & Greene, 1982) and expectancy (Burgoon, this volume; Burgoon & Hale, 1988). A hypothesis derivable from speech accommodation theory is that if a message recipient perceives a message source as having a benign or altruistic intention and if the source switches from a high-diversity style to a low-diversity style in order to converge to the style of the message recipient, the source should be evaluated favorably by the message recipient (and by disinterested third parties as well). To test this sort of hypothesis, researchers must examine dialogical situations; monological messages are not relevant in this case.

Finally, although perhaps obvious, it may be worth pointing out that the study of message effects in dialogical contexts pertains as certainly to mass media events as it does to communication events that are not mediated, that is, which are face-to-face. For example, network television coverage of the Democratic and Republican conventions in the summer of 1988 featured frequent discussions between two anchorpersons regarding convention events. Large sections of local newscasts involve banter between coanchorpersons. Situation comedies and to some extent even action programs include as a primary feature interactions between characters. Parallel examples could be given for various types of radio programs and even for some aspects of newspapers and magazines.

CONCLUSION

In this chapter several issues have been raised that both reflect past progress in the study of message effects and point to future possibilities for research and theory construction. Some general implications are these:

(1) We should become increasingly mindful of the meaning of *message* in our work on message effects. It is the distinct impression of the authors of this chapter that investigators in the message-effects paradigm have tended overwhelmingly to examine a few types of messages, such as persuasive speeches, while ignoring a large variety of other types, such as newscasts, marital arguments, and routine conversations. The important and likely possibility is that message type interacts with substantive and stylistic message features, including nonverbal behaviors, in the production of effects; such an interaction would qualify previously obtained results. In the words of Hopper and Stucky (1986, p. 1): "We must find better ways to be factual and empirical about the stuff of messaging. We must concentrate upon messages themselves, not simply the antecedents and consequences of messages."

(2) We should broaden our social cognitive focus in attempting to explain replicable message effects. Examination of naive understandings of communication context and message sequencing may prove especially revealing. It will probably prove useful increasingly to test a priori social cognitive models of message effects; in some areas, such as message evaluation research, a priori model testing studies have been few and far between.

(3) Becoming more precise about the ways in which message variables are instantiated may facilitate attempts at replication. In many cases this will mean quantifying variables in some way against either theoretical-objective or respondent-subjective criteria. Such quantification may take us beyond the use of slippery natural-language terms such as "high" or "low" (intensity, diversity, fear, violence, humor, or whatever).

(4) We should go beyond the single-shot monological paradigm case in message-effects research. This will entail investigating the effects of particular message variables as a function of exposure to multiple instances in a wide variety of interactive contexts. We should also increasingly use in our studies respondents who are actively involved in message processing and exchange, going beyond the heavy reliance upon uninvolved third parties, which is an earmark of past practice.

We believe that attention to the above injunctions and to Bowers's seven admonitions in the first chapter of this volume will conduce to future qualitative progress in the message-effects paradigm.

REFERENCES

Aiu, P. (1988). *Chinese beliefs about talk: Pursuing a cross-cultural model.* Unpublished master's thesis, University of California, Santa Barbara.

Atkinson, J., & Heritage, J. (Eds.). (1984). *Structures of social action.* Cambridge: Cambridge University Press

Austin, J. L. (1962). *How to do things with words.* Cambridge, MA: Harvard University Press.

Bavelas, J. (1983). Situations that lead to disqualification. *Human Communication Research, 9,* 130-145.

Bell, R. A., Zahn, C. J., & Hopper, R. (1984). Disclaiming: A test of two competing views. *Communication Quarterly, 32,* 28-40.

Berger, C. R., & Bradac, J. J. (1982). *Language and social knowledge: Uncertainty in interpersonal relations.* London: Edward Arnold.

Berger, C. R., & Calabrese, R. J. (1975). Some explorations in initial interaction and beyond: Toward a developmental theory of interpersonal communication. *Human Communication Research, 1,* 99-112.

Bowers, J. W., & Bradac, J. J. (1984). Contemporary problems in human communication theory. In C. C. Arnold & J. W. Bowers (Eds.), *Handbook of rhetorical and communication theory* (pp. 871-893). Newton, MA: Allyn & Bacon.

Bowers, J. W., Elliott, N. D., & Desmond, R. J. (1977). Exploiting pragmatic rules: Devious messages. *Human Communication Research, 5,* 235-242.

Bradac, J. J. (1986). Threats to generalization in the use of elicited, purloined, and contrived messages in human communication research. *Communication Quarterly, 34,* 55-65.

Bradac, J. J., Bowers, J. W., & Courtright, J. A. (1979). Three language variables in communication research: Intensity, immediacy, and diversity. *Human Communication Research, 5,* 257-269.

Bradac, J. J., Davies, R. A., & Courtright, J. A. (1977). The role of prior message context in evaluative judgments of high- and low-diversity messages. *Language and Speech, 20,* 295-307.

Bradac, J. J., Konsky, C. W., & Davies, R. A. (1976). Two studies of the effects of lexical diversity upon judgments of communicator attributes and message effectiveness. *Communication Monographs, 43*, 70-79.

Bradac, J. J., Konsky, C. W., & Elliott, N. D. (1976). Verbal behavior of interviewees: The effects of several situational variables on verbal productivity, disfluency, and lexical diversity. *Journal of Communication Disorders, 9*, 211-225.

Bradac, J. J., Martin, L. W., Elliott, N. D., & Tardy, C. H. (1980). On the neglected side of linguistic science: Multivariate studies of sentence judgment. *Linguistics, 18*, 967-995.

Bradac, J. J., & Mulac, A. (1984). A molecular view of powerful and powerless speech styles: Attributional consequences of specific language features and communicator intentions. *Communication Monographs, 51*, 307-319.

Bradac, J. J., Mulac, A., & House, A. (1988). Lexical diversity level and magnitude of convergent versus divergent style shifting: Perceptual and evaluative consequences. *Language & Communication, 8*, 213-228.

Bradac, J. J., Wiemann, J. M., & Schaefer, K. (in press). The language of interpersonal control. In J. M. Wiemann & J. A. Daly (Eds.), *Communicating strategically*. Hillsdale, NJ: Lawrence Erlbaum.

Bradac, J. J., & Wisegarver, R. (1984). Ascribed status, lexical diversity, and accent: Determinants of perceived status, solidarity, and control of speech style. *Journal of Language and Social Psychology, 3*, 239-255.

Brennan, E. M., Ryan, E. B., & Dawson, W. E. (1975). Scaling of apparent accentedness by magnitude estimation and sensory modality matching. *Journal of Psycholinguistic Research, 4*, 27-36.

Brown, B. L. (1980). Effects of speech rate on personality attributions and competency evaluations. In H. Giles, W. P. Robinson, & P. Smith (Eds.), *Language: Social psychological perspectives* (pp. 294-300). Oxford: Pergamon.

Brown, B. L., Giles, H., & Thackerar, J. N. (1985). Speaker evaluations as a function of speech rate, accent, and context. *Language & Communication, 5*, 207-220.

Bryant, J., & Zillman, D. (1984). Using television to alleviate boredom and stress: Selective exposure as a function of induced excitational states. *Journal of Broadcasting, 28*, 1-20.

Buck, J. (1968). The effects of Negro and White dialectal variations upon attitudes of college students. *Speech Monographs, 35*, 181-186.

Buck, R. (1988). Emotional education and mass media: A new view of the global village. In R. P. Hawkins, J. M. Wiemann, & S. Pingree (Eds.), *Advancing communication science: Merging mass and interpersonal processes* (pp. 44-76). Newbury Park, CA: Sage.

Burgoon, J. K., & Hale, J. L. (1988). Nonverbal expectancy violations: Model elaboration and application to immediacy behaviors. *Communication Monographs, 55*, 58-79.

Burgoon, M., Jones, S. B., & Stewart, D. (1975). Toward a message-centered theory of persuasion: Three empirical investigations of language intensity. *Human Communication Research, 1*, 240-256.

Burgoon, M., & Miller, G. R. (1985). An expectancy interpretation of language and persuasion. In H. Giles & R. N. St. Clair (Eds.), *Recent advances in language, communication, and social psychology* (pp. 199-229). London: Lawrence Erlbaum.

Cappella, J. N., & Greene, J. O. (1982). A discrepancy-arousal explanation of mutual influence in expressive behavior for adult-adult and infant-adult interaction. *Communication Monographs, 49,* 89-114.

Clark, H. H., & Carlson, T. B. (1982). Hearers and speech acts. *Language, 58,* 332-373.

Cronkhite, G. (1986). On the focus, scope, and coherence of the study of human symbolic activity. *Quarterly Journal of Speech, 72,* 231-246.

de la Zerda, N., & Hopper, R. (1979). Employment interviewers' reactions to Mexican American speech. *Communication Monographs, 46,* 126-134.

Erickson, B., Johnson, B. C., Lind, E. A., & O'Barr, W. (1978). Speech style and impression formation in a court setting: The effects of "powerful" and "powerless" speech. *Journal of Experimental Social Psychology, 14,* 266-279.

Genessee, F., & Bourhis, R. Y. (1982). The social psychological significance of code switching in cross-cultural communication. *Journal of Language and Social Psychology, 1,* 1-27.

Giles, H. (1973). Accent mobility: A model and some data. *Anthropological Linguistics, 15,* 87-105.

Giles, H., & Hewstone, M. (1982). Cognitive structures, speech, and social situations: Two integrative models. *Language Sciences, 4,* 187-219.

Giles, H., Mulac, A., Bradac, J. J., & Johnson, P. (1987). Speech accommodation theory: The first decade and beyond. In M. McLaughlin (Ed.), *Communication yearbook* (Vol. 10, pp. 13-48). Newbury Park, CA: Sage.

Giles, H., & Wiemann, J. M. (1987). Language, social comparison, and power. In C. R. Berger & S. H. Chaffee (Eds.), *Handbook of communication science* (pp. 350-384). Newbury Park, CA: Sage.

Giles, H., Wilson, P., & Conway, T. (1981). Accent and lexical diversity as determinants of impression formation and employment selection. *Language Sciences, 3,* 92-103.

Goffman, E. (1967). *Interaction ritual.* New York: Anchor.

Grice, H. P. (1975). Logic and conversation. In P. Cole & J. L. Morgan (Eds.), *Syntax and semantics: Vol. 3. Speech acts* (pp. 41-58). New York: Academic Press.

Hart, R., Carlson, R. E., & Eadie, W. F. (1980). Attitudes toward communication and the assessment of rhetorical sensitivity. *Communication Monographs, 47,* 1-22.

Hopper, R. (1977). Language attitudes in the job interview. *Communication Monographs, 44,* 346-351.

Hopper, R. (1988). Speech, for instance: The exemplar in studies of conversation. *Journal of Language and Social Psychology, 7,* 47-63.

Hopper, R., & Bell, R. (1984). Broadening the deception construct. *Quarterly Journal of Speech, 67,* 288-302.

Hopper, R., & Drummond, K. G. (1988). Language and media: A micro-analytic view. *Critical Studies in Mass Communication, 5,* 163-166.

Hopper, R., Koch, S., & Mandelbaum, J. (1986). Conversation analysis methods. In D. G. Ellis & W. Donahue (Eds.), *Contemporary issues in language and discourse processes* (pp. 169-186). London: Lawrence Erlbaum.

Hopper, R., & Stucky, N. (1986, December). *"Message" research in the future.* Paper presented at the meeting of the Speech Communication Association, Chicago.

Hopper, R., & Williams, F. (1973). Speech characteristics and employabilty. *Speech Monographs, 40,* 296-302.

Hovland, C. I., Janis, I. L., & Kelley, H. H. (1953). *Communication and persuasion.* New Haven, CT: Yale University Press.

Jackson, S., & Jacobs, S. (1983). Generalizing about messages: Suggestions for design and analysis of experiments. *Human Communication Research, 9,* 169-191.

Johnson-Laird, P. N. (1983). *Mental models.* Cambridge, MA: Harvard University Press.

Kellermann, K., & Sleight, C. (1989). Coherence: A meaningful adhesive of discourse. In J. Anderson (Ed.), *Communication yearbook* (Vol. 13, pp. 95-129). Newbury Park, CA: Sage.

Linz, D. E., Donnerstein, E., & Penrod, S. (1984). The effects of multiple exposures to filmed violence against women. *Journal of Communication, 34,* 130-147.

Mandelbaum, J. (1987). Couples sharing stories. *Communication Quarterly, 35,* 144-171.

Moerman, M. (1987). *Talking cultures.* Cambridge: University of Cambridge Press.

Motley, M., & Camden, C. T. (1988). Facial expression of emotion: A comparison of posed expressions versus spontaneous expressions in an interpersonal communication setting. *Western Journal of Speech Communication, 52,* 1-22.

Motley, M., Camden, C. T., & Baars, B. J. (1979). Personality and situational influences upon verbal slips: A laboratory test of Freudian and pre-articulatory editing hypotheses. *Human Communication Research, 5,* 195-202.

Mulac, A., Incontro, C. R., & James, M. R. (1985). A comparison of the gender-linked language effect and sex-role stereotypes. *Journal of Personality and Social Psychology, 49,* 1099-1110.

O'Barr, W. M. (1982). *Linguistic evidence: Language, power, and strategy in the courtroom.* New York: Academic Press.

Petty, R. E., & Cacioppo, J. T. (1986). *Communication and persuasion: Central and peripheral routes to attitude change.* New York: Springer-Verlag.

Planalp, S. (1985). Relational schemata: A test of alternative forms of relational knowledge as guides to communication. *Human Communication Research, 12,* 3-29.

Rorty, R. (Ed.). (1967). *The linguistic turn: Recent essays on philosophical method.* Chicago: University of Chicago Press.

Ryan, E. B., & Bulik, C. M. (1982). Evaluations of middle class speakers of Standard American and German-accented English. *Journal of Language and Social Psychology, 1,* 51-62.

Sacks, (1984). Notes on methodology. In J. M. Atkinson & J. Heritage (Eds.), *Structures of social action* (pp. 21-27). Cambridge: Cambridge University Press.

Sacks, H., Schegloff, E. A., & Jefferson, G. (1974). A simplest systematics for the organization of turn-taking for conversation. *Language, 50,* 696-735.

Sanders, R. E. (1986). *Cognitive foundations of calculated speech.* Albany: SUNY Press.

Sanders, R. E., & Martin, L. W. (1975). Grammatical rules and explanations of behavior. *Inquiry, 18,* 65-82.

Saussure, F., de (1959). *Course in general linguistics* (W. Baskin, Trans.). New York: McGraw-Hill. (Original work published 1915)

Schegloff, E. (1979). Identification and recognition in telephone conversation openings. In G. Psathas (Ed.), *Everyday language: Studies in ethnomethodology.* New York: Irvington.

Schegloff, E., & Sacks, H. (1973). Opening up closings. *Semiotica, 30,* 289-327.

Sherif, C. W., Sherif, M., & Nebergall, R. E. (1965). *Attitude and attitude change: The social judgment-involvement approach.* Philadelphia: W. B. Saunders.

Snyder, M. (1979). Self-monitoring processes. In L. Berkowitz (Ed.), *Advances in experimental social psychology* (Vol. 12, pp. 86-131). New York: Academic Press.

Spitzberg, B., & Cupach, W. (1984). *Interpersonal communication competence*. Beverly Hills, CA: Sage.

Sternberg, R. J., Conway, B. E., Ketron, J. L., & Bernstein, M. (1981). People's conceptions of intelligence. *Journal of Personality and Social Psychology, 41*, 37-55.

Street, R. L., Jr. (1985). Participant-observer differences in speech evaluation. *Journal of Language and Social Psychology, 4*, 125-130.

Street, R. L., Jr., Brady, R. M., & Putman, W. B. (1983). The influence of speech rate stereotypes and rate similarity on listeners' evaluations of speakers. *Journal of Language and Social Psychology, 2*, 37-56.

Street, R. L., Jr., & Cappella, J. N. (Eds.). (1985). *Sequence and pattern in communicative behaviour*. London: Edward Arnold.

Street, R. L., Jr., Mulac, A., & Wiemann, J. M. (1988). Speech evaluation differences as a function of perspective (participant versus observer) and presentational medium. *Human Communication Research, 14*, 333-363.

von Cranach, M., & Vine, I. (1973). Introduction. In M. von Cranach & I. Vine (Eds.), *Social communication and movement* (pp. 1-25). London: Academic Press.

Warfel, K. (1984). Gender schemes and perceptions of speech style. *Communication Monographs, 51*, 253-267.

West, C., & Zimmerman, D. H. (1982). Conversation analysis. In K. R. Scherer & P. Ekman (Eds.), *Handbook of methods in nonverbal research* (pp. 506-541). Cambridge: Cambridge University Press.

Wiemann, J. M. (1977). Explication and test of a model of communicative competence. *Human Communication Research, 4*, 143-157.

Wiemann, J. M., & Bradac, J. J. (in press). Meta-theoretical issues in the study of communicative competence: Structural and functional approaches. In B. Dervin & M. Voight (Eds.), *Progress in communication sciences* (Vol. 9). Norwood, NJ: Ablex.

Wiemann, J. M., Chen, V., & Giles, H. (1986, November). *Beliefs about talk and silence in a cultural context*. Paper presented at the annual meeting of the Speech Communication Association, Chicago.

Wittgenstein, L. (1953). *Philosophical investigations* (G. Anscombe, Trans.). London: Macmillan.

Zahn, C. J., & Hopper, R. (1985). Measuring language attitudes: The Speech Evaluation Instrument. *Journal of Language and Social Psychology, 4*, 113-123.

Zajonc, R. (1968). Attitudinal effects of mere exposure. *Journal of Personality and Social Psychology* (Monograph Supp.), *9*, 1-27.

ABOUT THE CONTRIBUTORS

CHARLES R. BERGER (Ph.D., Michigan State University) is Professor of Communication Studies at Northwestern University. His research interests include the role of uncertainty reduction and cognitive plans in interpersonal communication. He has coedited two volumes, *Social Cognition and Communication* (with M. E. Roloff) and *Handbook of Communication Science* (with S. Chaffee), and he has coauthored a book, *Language and Social Knowledge* (with J. J. Bradac). He has also served as editor of *Human Communication Research.*

JOHN WAITE BOWERS (Ph.D., University of Iowa, 1962) is Professor and Chair of the Department of Communication at the University of Colorado, Boulder. He is coeditor (with Carroll C. Arnold) of the *Handbook of Rhetorical and Communication Theory*, former editor (1978-1980) of *Communication Monographs*, and former president (1984) of the Speech Communication Association. He was the first recipient of that association's Robert J. Kibler Memorial Award.

JAMES J. BRADAC (Ph.D., Northwestern University) is Professor of Communication Studies at the University of California, Santa Barbara. His research focuses upon the role of language variables in person perception and social evaluation. He coauthored *Language and Social Knowledge* (with C. R. Berger). He is currently editor of *Human Communication Research.*

JENNINGS BRYANT (Ph.D., Indiana University, 1974) is Professor of Communication and holder of the Reagan Chair of Broadcasting in the Department of Broadcast and Film Communication at the University of Alabama. His research interests are in mass communication processes, effects, and theories.

MICHAEL BURGOON (Ph.D., Michigan State University, 1970) is Professor and Head of Communication and Professor of Family and Community Medicine at the University of Arizona, Tucson. He has published extensively on persuasion, public opinion, and the social effects of the mass media. He is a Fellow of the International Communication Association.

JOSEPH N. CAPPELLA (Ph.D., Michigan State University, 1974) is Professor and Chair in the Department of Communication Arts, University of Wisconsin-Madison. His research interests focus on interaction patterns in adult and infant populations, mathematical and statistical methods for representing these patterns, and the cognitive and emotional bases for interaction.

EDWARD DONNERSTEIN is Professor and Chair of the Communication Studies Program at the University of California, Santa Barbara.

A social psychologist, he taught at the University of Wisconsin prior to his position at the University of California. His major research interest is in mass media violence and he has published widely in this area. His most recent books include *The Question of Pornography: Research Findings and Policy Implications* (with Daniel Linz and Steven Penrod) and *Pornography and Sexual Aggression* (with Neil Malamuth).

ROBERT HOPPER (Ph.D., University of Wisconsin-Madison) is Charles Sapp Professor in the Department of Speech Communication at the University of Texas, Austin. His research interests include the role of speech and language in interpersonal evaluations and decision making. Currently he is focusing upon the analysis of conversation in various contexts. His work has been published in the major journals in communication and allied disciplines, and he is author or coauthor of several books including *Human Message Systems* and *Children's Speech* (with R. Naremore). In 1987 he was plenary speaker at the Third International Conference on Social Psychology and Language in Bristol, England.

KATHY KELLERMANN is on the faculty at Michigan State University. Her research program centers on the relationship between thought and talk with specific interest in the role knowledge structures play in the production and interpretation of conversational behavior. She is on the editorial board of *Communication Monographs* and *Human Communication Research* and has published in both of these journals as well as in numerous edited books.

DALE KUNKEL (Ph.D., Annenberg School of Communications, University of Southern California, 1984) is Assistant Professor of Telecommunication at Indiana University, Bloomington. He previously served as a Congressional Science Fellow for the U.S. House of Representatives Subcommittee on Telecommunications. His interests center on the social effects of mass media with particular emphasis on children and television policy issues.

TAE-SEOP LIM is Assistant Professor at the University of Colorado. His research program centers on interaction analysis with a specific focus on conversational and linguistic behavior.

DANIEL G. LINZ is Assistant Professor of Communication at the University of California, Santa Barbara. He is also a research associate in the UCLA Center for the Study of Women. His research over the past several years has focused on the effects on males of exposure to various forms of media violence against women and the effects of pretrial publicity on jury decision making. His research interests include the legal policy implications of research on the mass media for legal decision making.

ANTHONY MULAC (Ph.D., University of Michigan, 1969) is Professor of Communication Studies at the University of California, Santa Barbara. He has published widely in the area of social group language differences and language effects. Currently his research focuses on interpersonal communication: gender-linked verbal and nonverbal differences, partner influences on gender differences, and their effects on observer judgments.

ROBERT E. SANDERS (Ph.D., University of Iowa) is Associate Professor and Chair of the Department of Communication at the State University of New York, Albany. His research has centered on problems of coherence and relevance in message exchanges and on interpretation of discourse (including nonverbal displays). He is author of *Cognitive Foundations of Calculated Speech*. He is currently editor of the journal, *Research on Language and Social Interaction*.

RICHARD L. STREET, Jr. (Ph.D., University of Texas, 1980) is Associate Professor in the Department of Speech Communication, Texas A & M University. His research interests include the study of communicative processes and outcomes in various contexts such as physician-patient encounters, interviews, and adult-child interactions.

ESTHER THORSON is Associate Professor in the School of Journalism and Mass Communication at the University of Wisconsin-Madison. Her research focus has been advertising. Publications in marketing and communication journals include analyses of the language of advertising, the use of physiological responses to index advertising effects, the role of emotion and product involvement in processing advertising, the impact of program context on the effectiveness of advertising, and studies of naturalistic television viewing behavior. *Advertising Age: The Principles of Advertising*, a textbook of readings and analysis of recent news stories in *Ad Age*, has just been published by National Textbook.

JOHN M. WIEMANN (Ph.D., Purdue University) is Professor of Communication Studies at the University of California, Santa Barbara. He has coedited two previous volumes in the Sage Annual Reviews of Communication Research series, *Nonverbal Interaction* (with R. Harrison) and *Advancing Communication Science: Merging Mass and Interpersonal Processes* (with R. P. Hawkins and S. Pingree), and he is coediting *Communicating Strategically* (with J. A. Daly). His research interests include communicative competence, cross-cultural influences upon beliefs about talk, nonverbal communication, and conversation. He has been a W. K. Kellogg Foundation National Fellow and a Fullbright-Hays Senior Research Scholar at the University of Bristol.